TIKOPIA RITUAL AND BELIEF

D1108764

TIKOPIA RITUAL AND BELIEF

RAYMOND FIRTH

F.B.A.

Professor of Anthropology in the
University of London

BEACON PRESS, BOSTON

CONTENTS

ILLUSTRATIONS

Between pages 96-7

INTRODUCTION

The set of essays in this book constitutes Volume II of my studies on Tikopia religion and associated topics. (Volume I is represented by *The Work of the Gods in Tikopia*, London School of Economics Monographs on Social Anthropology, Nos. 1 and 2, 1940, second edition, 1967; *Rank and Religion in Tikopia*, a work long in draft, and the publication of which will now follow soon, I hope, is intended to be Volume III.)

All but one of the essays have been published before. (Chapter 14, on spirit mediumship, is new and has beeen written especially for this volume.)

To give the reader a general idea of the background to the rites and beliefs described, I have given as Chapter I, under the head of an 'Outline of Tikopia Culture', my original report on research in Tikopia prepared immediately after my return from my first expedition in 1928–9. Then follow chapters on ritual procedures in three characteristic fields—childbirth and adolescence; status display; and organized friendship—which cut across lineage structure. The first two of these essays take up the problem of the representativeness of ritual, which I think is of importance and has often been overlooked. The essays on rumour, dreams and suicide illustrate action and belief in various fields where irrational motivations of individuals are expressed in a commingled personal and social idiom. The studies of rumour and of suicide have, I think, some originality as contributions to areas little worked by anthropologists. The studies of *mana*, 'magic' and totemism, too, were designed to put forward various rather unorthodox views.

These essays are not simply a study in 'primitive' practice and ideology. Traditionally Tikopia ritual and belief were very complex, and the increasing contact of the Tikopia with the outer world, including proselytizing Christianity, gave rise to some fresh complexities. Most of the essays include data collected not only in 1928–9 but also in 1952 on my second expedition and refer to various aspects of social change. The last three essays in particular, with the final commentary from 1966, illustrate some of the intricate adjustments Tikopia have made, especially in their beliefs, to the new challenging situations.

The essays in this volume deal with a variety of Tikopia ideas and practices. But they all have in common the same component of interest with concerns beyond the technology, economics and social relations of everyday affairs. Ceremonies for children or ceremonies of bond friendship involve practices carried out with formality and attention to more than technical detail. This indicates that these practices have a general referent, and signify a type of social relationship exceeding that of the immediate occasion. The interpretation of dreams, ideas of 'magic' or assertions about the possession of *mana*, assume the operation of forces and the existence of entities outside the ordinary technical sphere. Most of the situations described display a commingling of components, so that formalization of behaviour is linked with a belief in the presence or operation of spirit powers or other extra-human forces.

Tikopia traditional belief postulated an elaborate spirit world peopled by ghosts of the recently dead, spirits of ancestors and a great range of other types of spirits, including many who have never been men. These were believed to be able to affect the lives of men in many ways, from encounters with spirits in dreams to action by spirits on the fertility of crops and catches of fish. Many of these spirit figures were built into the structure of the Tikopia religious system by associating them with lineages and lineage leaders, especially in the standard rite of the kava, which involved invocation of the spirits and libations and offerings to them. In *The Work of the Gods in Tikopia* and elsewhere I have described aspects of this religious system. But there were many Tikopia performances and ideas which were either apart from the major religious system or were linked only peripherally with it. For the most part the essays in this book deal with such phenomena. The field of ritual and belief was very rich in the traditional state of Tikopia society, and there were very few operations in daily life which did not involve some aspects of a ritual character.

The notions of ritual and its close analogue ceremonial have been much debated in social anthropology. My own view is that the most convenient way to look at ritual is to consider it as a formal set of procedures of a symbolic kind, involving a code for social communication, and believed to possess a special efficacy in affecting technical and social conditions of the performers or other participants. The formality of these procedures lies in the fact that they are directed not simply to the solution of an immediate technical problem by the most economical means, but are regarded as having in themselves a certain validity irrespective of their technical concomitants. Because of their general validity, apart from the individual situation, they tend to be given a repetitive routinized character which in itself is regarded as strengthening their significance. This significance is basically symbolic in that the physical behaviour of the participants 'stands for' relations of another kind, as between man and an aspect of Nature or man and putative spirits. Many rituals are performed to maintain an existing situation from degeneration; others to change the situation, if only to restore it to an original state of well-being. Ceremonial (ceremony) I regard as a species of ritual in which, however, the emphasis is more upon symbolic acknowledgement and demonstration of a social situation than upon the efficacy of the procedures in modifying that situation. Whereas other ritual procedures are believed to have a validity of their own, ceremonial procedures, while formal in character, are not believed in themselves to sustain the situation or effect a change in it. In these terms the 'ceremonies' for children and the privilege 'ceremonials' of Chapters 2 and 3 would be classed as rituals; the formal procedures of bond friendship described in Chapter 4, however, would be classed as ceremonies. (Compare also the statements on p. 73 of Chapter 2.)

A few minor changes have been made to the text of articles for this publication. Much of the Tikopia text in the original articles has been omitted as being of interest primarily to linguistic specialists. In Chapters 3 and 6, for convenience, two articles have been merged in each case. Most of the plates have been replaced.

For permission to publish these essays I am indebted to Professor A. P. Elkin, the editor of *Oceania* (for Chapters 1, 2, 3, and 11); to Messrs Hutchinson, publishers of *Custom is King, Essays Presented to R. R. Marett on his 70th Birthday* (for Chapter 4); to the editor of *Psychiätry* (for Chapter 5); to the editor of *The Journal of Abnormal and Social Psychology* (for Chapter 6); to the editor of *Man* (for Chapter 6); to Professor E. E. Evans-Pritchard and Kegan Paul, Trench, Trubner & Co, Ltd, editor and publishers of *Essays Presented to C. G. Seligman* (for Chapter 7); to the editor of the *Journal of the Polynesian Society* (for Chapter 8); to Dr Hilde Thurnwald, the editor of *Sociologus* (for Chapter 9); to Dr J. D. Freeman, Professor W. R. Geddes and Thomas Avery & Sons Ltd (for Chapter 10); to the editor of *Mankind* (*Official Journal of the Anthropological Societies of Australia*) (for Chapter 12); to the editor of *Ethnologica* (for Chapter 13); and to the Cambridge University Press (for Chapter 15).

I wish here to acknowledge my debt to the Australian National Research Council, who financed my first expedition to Tikopia in 1928–9 and to the Australian National University, who financed the second expedition, in 1952. I am greatly indebted also to James Spillius, who accompanied me to Tikopia in 1952, and who remained on the island for a year after I left. Contributions from his material appear in several chapters. The participation of Mr Spillius was facilitated by the Carnegie Corporation of New York and the Australian National University.

In the summer of 1966 I was able to visit Tikopia again and observe the effects of radical economic and social change upon ritual and belief. For this renewed opportunity of systematic investigation I am greatly indebted to grants from the Hayter Fund of the University of London and from the Wenner-Gren Foundation for Anthropological Research.

I was also helped greatly by the hospitality and other facilities generously given me by officials of the Western Pacific High Commission and British Solomon Islands Protectorate, especially Mr T. Russell, Mr J. Tedder, and Mr D. G. Cochrane; and by Mr J. Walton, managing-director of Levers Pacific Plantations Pty. I am grateful also for the stimulating companionship of my colleague Dr Torben Monberg, who at some inconvenience to his own plans took time away from his study of Bellona to share the long voyage to Tikopia and the alternation of monotony and drama which seems characteristic of research there. In preparing my visit to Tikopia I benefited considerably from discussions with Mr Ishmael Tuki, the first Tikopia to take a University course in England, and with Dr and Mrs Eric Larsen, who had conducted anthropological research in 1964–5 both on Tikopia and at Nukufero, a Tikopia colony in the Russell islands.

For preparation of material for the original articles and final commentary I am grateful for the help afforded me by grants at various times from the Behavioral Sciences Division of the Ford Foundation, the Research Committee of the London School of Economics and the Wenner-Gren Foundation for Anthropological Research. As a Fellow in 1959 of the Center for Advanced Study in the Behavioral Sciences, at Palo Alto, I benefited from many facilities and the advice of numerous colleagues.

London, 1966.   RAYMOND FIRTH

CHAPTER 1

OUTLINE OF TIKOPIA
CULTURE

(1930)

In 1928 I set out under the auspices of the Australian National Research Council to study the social anthropology of the people of Tikopia, and to obtain information on the problem of the relation of Polynesian to Melanesian cultures. The only study of Tikopia made hitherto was that of the Rev W. J. Durrad, a member of the Melanesian Mission, who spent two months there in the course of his work in 1910. The results of these observations, necessarily of a somewhat incomplete character, were published by the late Dr Rivers in 1914, in his *History of Melanesian Society*.

The island is small and isolated, being an extinct volcanic crater lying 120 miles south-east from Vanikoro, the nearest white habitation; the only communication is by means of the Melanesian Mission steam yacht *Southern Cross*, which calls once or twice a year. It was on this vessel that I reached Tikopia in July 1928, and was visited by her again in October of the same year, bringing a supply of stores. In July 1929 she called again, when I left the island. I wish to acknowledge here the kindness of the Mission in allowing me to travel on the *Southern Cross*, and the hospitality of the Right Reverend Bishop John Steward, now retired, and the Right Reverend Bishop Molyneux, Bishop of Melanesia, as well as that of Captain H. Burgess, his officers and the members of the Mission staff who facilitated my work in every way possible.

To establish friendly contact with the natives proved a simple matter, and the acquiring of their language presented no exceptional difficulty, my previous knowledge of Maori, imperfect as it was, being of the greatest assistance, since the grammatical structure of the two languages is in many respects identical. I was also helped by the Vocabulary compiled by Mr Durrad and edited by Archdeacon H. W. Williams (later Bishop of Waiapu), to both of whom I am also indebted for personal interest in other ways. To assist the ordinary camp routine I took with me from Tulagi as personal servant a boy from Luaniua (Lord Howe Island), secured through the kindness of Mr J. C. Barley, Deputy Commissioner of the British Solomon Islands Protectorate, and found that the similarity of the language and culture of his own island to that of Tikopia rendered him much more suitable than a Melanesian would have been.

All food and specimens acquired from the natives were obtained either by gift-exchange or barter, the use of money being entirely unknown. Adzes and axes, chisels and other tools are greatly esteemed; knives, calico and beads are also of distinct value, while pipes, tobacco and fish-hooks are useful as ordinary small currency. The comparative lack of coconuts, trochus shell and bêche-de-mer offers no incentive to European traders to visit the island. Many articles were received by me in the form of gifts, but in such case a return present was immediately advisable.

The progress of my research was unimpeded for the first three months, by which time I had acquired considerable fluency in the native language. The use of English had been given up after the first month. Data on social organization and economic life were fairly easily acquired and this was facilitated by attendance at ceremonies connected with birth, sub-incision and a funeral, all of which took place soon after my arrival.

Enquiries in the sphere of religion, however, met with little response, and my attempts to gain further information provoked the antagonism of the chiefs, which persisted for several months. By following a steady policy of conciliation coupled with evidences of respect for their customs and beliefs, this attitude was gradually overcome, and I was later enabled to observe even their most important rites—a six-weeks' cycle of ceremonies in connection with houses, canoes, yam cultivation and dances—as a participant, and to obtain from the chiefs the sets of formulae used on these occasions. I was also given their general *kava*, i.e. the names of their ancestors and deities and the invocations addressed to them. In the last five months of my stay I was thus able to collect data giving a very full account of the most esoteric aspects of Tikopia culture.

As regards demography, a census of the people was taken, recording the name, village, dwelling-house and family of each person, as also his or her approximate age and kinship status in the group. The population at that date was 1,288, and from consideration of genealogies and the record of recent births and deaths it appears to be stable, or slightly increasing—at all events it is in a vigorous, healthy state. This can be clearly attributed to the persistence of the old forms of culture. A diary in which I recorded from day to day the main events occurring in the community shows the fullness and interest of life to the Tikopia. The apathy and depression so characteristic of a number of other Polynesian peoples at the present time, and correlated with the loss or deprivation of their former culture have as yet found no grip upon these islanders.

16

In the field of material culture attention was concentrated more on the economic than on the technological side of industry. More than 500 specimens of Tikopia workmanship, however, were collected, as well as a considerable number of objects from the various Melanesian islands visited *en route*.

In its general nature the mode of life of the Tikopia is very rich and vivid; the people are cheerful and animated, lead an active, busy existence, and while they spend much time in the preparation of their food, devote also a great deal of attention to ceremonial and religious affairs.

ECONOMIC CONDITIONS[1]

Food is plentiful on the island and in great variety, taro and bread-fruit being the staples of diet, but supplemented by bananas, yams, and coconuts as well as by sago, chestnuts, canarium almonds and various fruits of trees requiring no cultivation. Fish are caught in a great number of ways by hook and net, but the absence of any extensive reef system prevents any large, constant supply from being obtained. In a period of rough weather the people may taste no fish for several weeks at a time, and then live entirely on vegetable food. The pig is lacking, and other flesh food there is none, most of the birds, such as the pigeon, being regarded as uneatable by the majority of the population for religious reasons. Many of the people have never tasted meat of any kind. Manioc and certain varieties of yam and banana have been introduced by the native Mission teachers and voyagers from time to time, and have proved useful in time of famine. Tobacco, brought at an early date, probably by whalers, is now grown freely, and the natives of both sexes show a great craving for it. Pipes, in consequence, are eagerly demanded. Betel-nut of two varieties is chewed by all, and *kava* is prepared, but, being used for religious purposes, is rarely drunk. The elaborate *kava* ceremonial of social intercourse, so characteristic of the Polynesians of Tonga and Samoa, is entirely absent, being replaced by a ritual of offering libations to ancestors and other deities.

The island of Tikopia is not large, measuring at a liberal estimate only three miles by two, and the population, over 1,200, is obviously considerable. Nevertheless, the soil is very fertile, and there is no reason to fear any immediate serious shortage of food. Normally there is more than sufficient for the needs of the people, and in the periods between crops they resort, if necessary, to sago which has been cooked with *Cordyline* root for several days in a large communal oven. This yields a quantity sufficient to last each participant family for several weeks, and is excellent food.

[1] A fuller account is given in *Primitive Polynesian Economy*, London, 1939; 2nd ed., 1965.

17

By celibacy of the younger male members of the family, and other checks, the population is retained at a level consonant with the available food supply, and no distress is felt. Tentative suggestions to transport a section of the people to another island in order to cope with an imagined over-population are made without knowledge of the real state of affairs of the island, and any attempt to give effect to such proposals would in my opinion be disastrous to the people. Even if another island could be found free from malaria, filariasis, and other tropical diseases, which are not operative in Tikopia, the wrench to the social system and to the sentiments of the people by such a severance would react very strongly on their vitality. Moreover, as I have ascertained, the Tikopia themselves would be opposed to any such permanent migration.

Recruiting of native labour from the island would also be fraught with grave dangers to the population. The community from its isolated situation is a remarkably healthy one, and normally, except as the result of occasional epidemics contracted from visiting European vessels, none except weakly infants and old people die. Previous experience has shown that Tikopia, in common with the natives of Rennell Island, when removed from their home have little resistance to disease, and nostalgia being added to the depressing effect of a novel illness, this in many cases proves fatal. The survivors, even if they do not suffer permanent deterioration of physique from diseases such as malaria or tuberculosis, are likely to be the carriers of the seeds of such disease to their healthy relatives on the island, and so to promote that decimation and wastage of population which has been such a pathetic feature in the history of so many Polynesian groups.

From the more immediate economic point of view of the white employer this recruiting of labour would be ill-advised, as the amount of work obtained from these natives would probably, as on previous occasions, not cover the outlay involved in food and transport.[1]

The economic structure of Tikopia society centres in the chiefs. They are acknowledged to be the supreme owners of the land, and the commoners hold title from them. The whole island, right to the mountain top 1,200 feet above the sea, is divided into *tofi*, gardens or orchards in which coconuts, bananas, breadfruit and other trees grow thickly, intersected with patches of cultivation of yams or taro. Each of these *tofi* is owned immediately by a single family group, which has a number of such areas in various parts of the island. The members of each family group, usually comprising several households, take food by mutual arrangement, according to requirements, from this ground. A certain

---

[1] Radical changes in the situation of the Tikopia have occurred during the last generation, with the result that the opinions expressed in the last paragraphs no longer hold. (Cf. my *Social Change in Tikopia*, 1959.)

individuality of ownership is observed in connection with patches of taro and the like, which if planted by one brother or cousin will not be touched by another without express permission but, generally speaking, the foodstuffs in the *tofi*, especially as regards the more permanent sources, as coconuts, chestnuts, and bananas, are drawn upon freely by any member of the group, the equity of the arrangement being maintained by the contribution of that person to the common work of cultivation. Moreover, the close observation kept by every one of the group on the treatment of their joint property by their fellow-members makes for restraint in use.

The organization of economic life follows very closely the grouping afforded by the kinship system. Husband and wife with their children work in co-operation to bring in food for the household, tasks being apportioned according to capacity and customary usage. Men and women have each their own particular economic sphere, the division of labour being along fairly obvious lines. The men, for instance, do all the work with canoes, and so engage in line fishing, set large nets in the lake, and catch flying-fish by torchlight at night—a most spectacular proceeding. The women daily search the reef with hand-nets and scoop up all that comes their way, including small fry and crabs. The men build houses, make canoes, bowls, head-rests and other wooden objects, manufacture nets, including those for the use of their women-folk, and do most of the heavy work of breaking up the soil for gardening with digging sticks. The women plait mats for floor-covering and bedding, beat out the bark cloth strips and squares which are still worn as garments by all, and do most of the weeding of the cultivations and the tending of the taro crops, the planting of which is done indifferently by them or by their male relatives. Women, too, keep the water bottles of the household filled and attend to the daily ovens, though here they are generally assisted by the younger men of the family.

When assistance is needed in his own work a man calls in the help of his brother or his sons, while his wife's brother or his sister's husband will usually come to his aid with a contribution of raw produce if it is a question of preparing one of those ceremonial gifts of food which form such a feature of Tikopia society. Scarcely a day passes without baskets of food being carried from one village to another or across the island in payment of some obligation incurred in connection with the command of a chief, the visiting of a new baby, sub-incision, a boy's first torch-light fishing, a marriage, a death, a recovery from an illness or the like, and months may elapse before all the customary usages are fulfilled. Another prominent feature in the economic life is the exchange of property, in particular, rolls of *kafa* (sinnet), *menga* (pandanus leaf mats), and *mami* or *fakamaru* (bark cloth), which marks the performance of certain ceremonies. In connection with funeral rites, indeed, as many as eight different sets of gifts may have to be made, each, of course, involving a counter-gift; on these, as on so many other occasions, the principal people concerned are the mother's brothers of the chief actor, or on the other hand his sister's sons.

SOCIAL ORGANIZATION[1]

By reason of the small size of the Tikopia community all the inhabitants, with the exception of the younger children, are well known to one another, and are all connected by ties of kinship. These, however, are cut across by the associations formed by local grouping, which though not fully acknowledged in the formal religious and ceremonial life of the community, have, nevertheless, great weight in influencing the actions of the people.

The social unit which first meets observation is the village (*kainga*, *potu*) also termed the dwelling place (*noforanga*), a number of houses built in irregular formation at some spot of natural advantage. Of these villages there are about fifteen of varying size in the island, all on the low land and near the sea. Each house (*paito*) in the village is usually the home of an individual family, a man with his wife and children, though sometimes two married brothers, or a father and son with their respective families may share the same dwelling. When children grow up and marry, the sons often settle down near their father, building houses adjacent to his; the daughters, since marriage is patrilocal, are absorbed into other households and may go away to other villages. In such case they often re-visit their parents' home. In Tikopia near relatives call on one another very frequently. All the immediate members of a family sleep in the dwelling, there being no men's club house as in many parts of Melanesia. Some *tamaroa* (bachelors) have huts of their own if they so desire. The men normally sit and sleep towards one side of the house, termed *mata paito*, where the immediate ancestors and other members of the family have been buried, and which has a certain esoteric significance. The women and children live and sleep on the *tuaumu* side, where the fires are located, and the common doorways.

In ordinary economic affairs, as gardening, fishing or sago making, each village draws mainly on its own personnel, but relatives are frequently asked to visit each other to give assistance in work.

A division of great importance in the ordinary life of the native is that into the districts. The island is bisected roughly along the N-S line into two 'sides' (*fasi*), Faea and Ravenga by name, between the inhabitants of which is a very ancient rivalry. Between villages on the same side of the island there is very little opposition of interests, but it

[1] For full details see *We, The Tikopia: A Sociological Study of Kinship in Primitive Polynesia*. London, 1936; 2nd ed., 1959.

is quite otherwise with the two districts. Belittling of each other's achievements, slanderous talk, accusations of theft, jealous guarding of property, and in these days bitter resentment of any acquisition of European goods by its rival is the common attitude of one district towards the other. This is the more notable since the district division, which is purely residential arrangement, cuts clean across the clan division, and it is this latter which is the formally acknowledged system and the basis of all grouping for the major social and religious ceremonies. Moreover, the entry of the greater part of the present inhabitants of Faea into their district took place in relatively historic times, i.e. about eight generations ago, prior to which the ancestors of the people of both districts lived in Uta, a small area at the inner corner of the lake.

The fundamental kinship group in Tikopia is naturally the family of parents and children, sometimes termed *fanaunga*, who generally, as already mentioned, live in a hut by themselves. In the more formal aspects of social life the unit, that is the group of people which is responsible for things being carried out, and of which the natives commonly speak as a whole in discussing the course of affairs, is the *paito*. By this is meant a patrilineal group of persons closely related, descended from a male ancestor a few generations back. Normally, the *paito* comprises a group of brothers and first or second cousins in the male line with their children and grandchildren, and also the sisters, father's sisters and daughters of these people. The children of any of these females belong primarily not to their mother's but to their father's *paito*. It would seem, however, that a Tikopia may legitimately speak of his own mother's and mother's brothers' group also as 'his' *paito*, but such a usage apparently implies the recognition of the importance of this type of kinship bond rather than of any actual principle of matrilineal descent.

As a rule one man is the acknowledged head of the *paito*, i.e. he is the most direct descendant in the senior line from the common ancestor, and has most voice in control of the family lands and property. Great importance attaches in Tikopia to the eldest son, *te urumatua*, and he and his father mutually defer or 'listen' (*fakarongo*) to each other in family affairs.

If a family group continues generation after generation to be vigorous and prolific then a splitting-off may occur and a subsidiary *paito* is formed, with a separate name. It is still affiliated to its parent group, but regards itself as more or less autonomous in ordinary social affairs, as marriage, or funeral ceremonies. In religious rites the old status still obtains, since the head of the original group is the only person fully capable of performing the requisite ceremonies and representing the *paito* in its relation to its parent clan and remote ancestors. Native

21

terminology recognizes this affinity between two such related groups. They have different names and may function independently but on occasion they may take joint action, or a man of one may deputize for a man of the other; the explanation given then is simply that they are '*te paito sokotasi*', 'the one family'.

The relation between parent *paito* and its offshoots helps to explain the status of these primary groups in regard to the clan. This latter, termed *kainanga*, is essentially composed of a number of *paito*, including that of the chief, from which the clan takes its name, and certain of these *paito* trace descent from various ancestors along the chiefly line. Those *paito* which are not in the line of descent from chiefs are accounted for as members of the *kainanga* by the fact of inclusion after conquest, or adoption of an immigrant from another island, the progenitor of the *paito* marrying a female relative of the chief who was his protector, and thus founding a family group. Certain of the most important *paito* again trace their membership of the clan to mythic association of their original ancestor with a remote clan chief.

Of the clans there are four in the island, Kafika, Tafua, Taumako and Fangarere, ranking in that order for religious purposes. The term 'clan' is used as the most convenient designation for these divisions termed by the natives *kainanga*, though they do not conform in all respects to the more rigid definition of the term. They are unilateral groups, tracing descent through the father line, but are not exogamous. People usually marry out of their own *kainanga*, but many cases of inter-*kainanga* marriage occur and excite no comment. Some Tikopia postulate an exogamous rule, and declare that all inter-clan alliances are bad. This opinion is not generally held, and seems to be but a personal exaggeration of the sentiment against the marriage of near relatives. There is a very definite feeling among all the people against the union of first cousins of any variety, and that of second cousins also hardly finds enthusiastic approval. Statements that exogamy is the marriage rule appear to rest on this basis, since there is a likelihood of two people of the same clan being fairly close kin.

Descent and succession are patrilineal, as also is inheritance to a large degree. But as is natural, kinship is also recognized in the maternal line, and great importance attaches in Tikopia eyes to the *paito* from which a man's mother comes. '*Te paito ko ia ne afu mai i ei*', 'The family he sprang from it', is the conventional way of referring to this group, and it is regarded as being as much the origin (*tafito*) of a man as is his father's *paito*. Contact with the mother's kin is close in everyday life, especially with the *tuatina*, the mother's brothers, but the importance of these in native sociology is seen to the full only on ceremonial occasions. At the birth of a child it is one of the *tuatina* who performs the rite of the *afi*, reciting a formula while a flaming torch is held before the eyes of the new-born child, to render it skilful in all the pursuits of man or woman as the case may be. At the incision of a boy it is his *tuatina* who performs the actual operation, and who receives large quantities of mats, sinnet and other property. In all the less important rites of boyhood or girlhood the *tuatina* plays his part, either as assistant or as donor of piles of bark cloth to his *iramutu,* his sister's child. Sickness brings the *tuatina* again into the field. His duty and privilege it is to prop up the body of his *iramutu* with his own, and to ease the suffering if possible; even more important in native eyes is the *maro,* a pile of eight or ten pieces of bark cloth brought along on recovery, together with the *renga,* the turmeric with which he smears the neck, breast and shoulders of the patient. This usage represents an affirmation of the kinship bond with the mother's people, and more particularly involves the gods of the latter *paito* on the side of the woman's child. Death is the supreme occasion for the exercise of the functions of the mother's brother; he it is who buries his sister's child.

This relationship of *tuatina* to *iramutu* does not cease on the death of the former. His sons or nearest male relatives carry out the duties. The person concerned is the *tamu tapu* (literally 'sacred child') of their whole *paito,* the child of the woman from their group. A Tikopia can never be without *tuatina* while any men of his mother's *paito* are alive, and even were this *paito* to become extinct, some other *paito,* bearing in mind a distant tie of relationship, would undertake the obligation. The salient features of Tikopia kinship organization are the reception of name, titles and property from the father's line, and the reliance on people of the mother's group for assistance and instruction at times of individual crisis and the performance of customary rites.

Social life in Tikopia tends to pivot around the chiefs. Termed *ariki,* one rules each clan, and has in native theory absolute authority over the lives and property of his people. The *ariki* is elected or rather selected by any powerful party immediately after the death of his predecessor, while the customary wailing is beginning, and differences of opinion not infrequently occur as to who shall be chosen. Swift action is imperative on the part of any other chief who wishes his own nominee to have the position, for once the new chief is formally installed on the knees of his proposers, and hailed as *ariki,* no change is possible. Primogeniture is the rule, and it is only when the heir apparent, *te ariki fakasomo,* 'the growing chief', is still a lad, when the dead chief has no male issue, or when it is desired to revert to the main line of descent after the reign of some collateral kinsman, that any real dispute is likely to take place. On election the chief gives up his former house name and becomes 'Te Ariki Tafua', 'Te Ariki Kafika', etc. The latter-named chief, who is the supreme religious head of the island, *te ariki tu,* the standing chief, bears also the name of Ti Namo, as the premier chief of Anuta does that of Ti Anuta, honorific titles, comparable to that of Tui Tonga.

The power and influence of a chief are great. He is treated with respect in ordinary social intercourse, his opinion is received with deference, his wrath is feared. 'If a chief is angry with a man, where shall he go,' say the natives, 'has he a land to which he can retreat?' In extreme cases, where a man has committed some grave offence against the chief's dignity or against custom, the chief says, 'Go to your land the sea' ('*Poi ki tou fenua te moana*'). It is a sentence of death; the man launches his canoe and sets out on the face of the ocean to perish of thirst or be engulfed in a storm, or be devoured by man-eating sharks. Theoretically there is no escape. In practice, however, another chief may save the victim. He forbids him to leave and keeps him until the anger of the first chief has cooled. The man then takes presents of sinnet cord, mats, and a valuable bonito hook (*pa*) with bone or tortoiseshell barb, and wailing out his repentance in a formal dirge, crawls to the feet of the chief and makes his peace.

The function of safeguarding the people from the anger of their chiefs is also performed by the *maru*, who in addition are the executive officials of the chief and act in general to preserve law and order.[1] The number of *maru* may vary from time to time. All a chief's own brothers are *maru*, and others of his near paternal kinsmen. Their rank and prestige also differ greatly. The eldest son of a chief always has considerable influence by virtue of his position as future *ariki*, but here as in other cases personality counts for much. At the present time the *maru* of greatest power, exceeding in some ways that of the chiefs, is an old man, father's brother to the present Ariki Taumako and formerly of great personal courage and impressiveness. For many years his influence was exerted on the side of leniency, of curbing the violence of chiefs and their families, and this charge he has handed on to his son.

This sense of conscious responsibility for the people under one's charge is a very strongly marked feature of Tikopia society. All the chiefs have it in varying degree, and a special expression, *fau te fenua*, to 'encircle' or 'guard' the land, connotes this supreme function of watching over the interests of the community, restraining violence and marking down evil-doers.

The *maru*, whose duty this is in more direct sense, act in this manner as a check upon the authority of the chiefs. More subtly, however, they also sustain the dignity of the chiefs. For a sentence uttered by an *ariki* in a moment of anger and perhaps through insufficient cause, goes forward in normal style until the *maru* step in and prevent the victim

[1] See 'Authority and Public Opinion in Tikopia' in my *Essays on Social Organization and Values*, London School of Economics Monographs on Social Anthropology, No. 28, London, 1964, pp. 123–44.

from executing it. This is done with the utmost respect for the *ariki*, the man soon afterwards humbles himself and makes his peace, and the chiefly dignity is saved from having to admit a mistake, and revoke in a calmer moment an unjust or too harsh sentence.

Of different type from the *maru*, whose functions are purely in the realm of public order, and whose power rests on their relationship to chiefs and their individual personality, are the *pure* (*matapure* or *pure matua*), the 'Elders', who are the counsellors of the chief, and whose most important functions are in the sphere of religion.

RELIGION

The religious system of Tikopia is essentially of the one structure with the political and social system, and in fact provides force and sanction to the working of this latter. The most prominent place in the ritual is taken by the chiefs, supplemented by their respective *pure*. They recite the formulae to their ancestors and higher gods to give food, health and welfare to the land and its people. They perform ceremonies primarily for the benefit of their own *paito*, or in the case of the chiefs, of their own clan, but all, particularly the latter, give a more general tone to their invocations. Moreover, the partition of function whereby one chief and his deities control taro, another yams, another coconuts, another breadfruit, means that invocations are addressed on behalf of the community as a whole.

Tikopia religion centres in the *atua*, spiritual beings, of whom each *ariki* and each *pure* has a set of his own. These include the line of his family ancestors, *puna*, who have held office, from his immediate predecessor back to the originator of the group, and in addition a number of *atua lasi* (great deities) sometimes termed *tupua*, who have never lived as men. These *atua* are of varying rank or degree of importance, and are so distributed that each chief has one of the principal ones as his main deity. The highest *atua* of all in point of power is a deity of the culture-hero type, who lived in Tikopia as a man and chief of surpassing size and strength, instituted a number of customs and performed some remarkable feats. After this he was killed by a mortal man, and going, without doing violence to his slayer, to the abode of the great *atua*, induced them thereby to hand over to him their *mana*, their supernatural power, by means of which he attained supremacy among them. As this *atua* was chief and ancestor of the Kafika clan, the Ariki Kafika in consequence holds the primacy among the chiefs. Each of the latter, however, counts this god as being in his pantheon, having a separate *rau* or name for him. But the control of the other chiefs over this *atua* is inferior to that of the Ariki Kafika, whose bond of relationship with him is so much more intimate. This usage of *rau*, of names,

25

applies in other cases also, and enables several groups to have an interest in the same deity, though he is always primarily the *atua* of one of them. This interlocking system of gods obviously provides a very strong element in binding together the Tikopia community on its socio-religious side.

The extremely interesting cycle of ceremonies performed twice a year[1] in connection with sacred canoes and houses, the harvest and planting of the yam, and concluding with a laudatory dance to the gods of a most picturesque kind, is a perpetuation, to native ideas, of the work of this culture-hero. His name is so sacred that it is very rarely mentioned, and then only in low tones, and normally all reference to him is avoided. Knowledge of all *atua* of a group, especially their various names, is held to be the property of the chiefs and elders who exercise it, and unauthorized discussion is resented.

The most typical feature of Tikopia religious ritual is the *kava* ceremony. On the more important occasions a formula is recited along a plant of *kava* denuded of its leaves, and held up in one hand by the officiating *ariki* or *pure* who bends over it. Following this, offerings of food are set out for the gods concerned, while a bowl of *kava* is prepared. Cups of this are then carried to the *ariki*, who pours out libations to his deities with appropriate invocations dealing with canoes, fish, taro, breadfruit, recovery from disease, etc., according to the circumstances. The whole ritual is of a very formal nature, each act being very carefully defined in place and time, with minute observance of detail according to traditional usage. Only the chief or elder may recite the *kava* formulae; his relatives and clansmen are in attendance to assist in preparing food, and show to the *atua* a proper recognition of the importance of the occasion.

Association of the clans with certain animals or plants, which may be termed totemism, is a very minor feature of Tikopia religion, and has its basis in the belief that the various *atua* of the clan, for their own purposes, sometimes take shape in these birds, fish, crustacea, etc., or enter into them. Normally these creatures are regarded as being purely natural objects; it is only when they behave abnormally, as when a bird runs towards a person in the path instead of away from him, that the presence of an *atua* is deduced, and the thing regarded as really *tapu*. Certain of the more repulsive fish are always termed *atua*, and said to be *tapu*, but this is as much by reason of the aversion of the native from them as from any idea that they may at that particular moment be harbouring a supernatural being. Birds of certain species

[1] See my *Work of the Gods in Tikopia*, London School of Economics Monographs on Social Anthropology, Nos. 1 and 2, London, 1940; 2nd ed. 1967; also Raymond Firth & James Spillius, *A Study in Ritual Modification: The Work of the Gods in Tikopia in 1929 and 1952*, Royal Anthropological Institute Occasional Paper, No. 19, London, 1963.

are sometimes killed for thieving, though they are recognized as serving as embodiments (*fakatino*) for one's own or other clan *atua* on occasion.

Not only do the *atua* appear in the lower orders of Nature; they also 'jump into' men. Possession by ancestors and even by the higher deities is a characteristic feature of Tikopia religion, and each chief has his *taurātua*, his medium in whom his forebears, and more especially his principal *atua* appear and converse with him. These are the men whom Gaimard has described as 'high priests'. The *taurātua* function only at certain important religious ceremonies, or when the chief is desirous of receiving information on any serious issue. There are a host of minor mediums, *vaka atua*, 'vessels of the gods', who are possessed by deities of lesser importance, and by ancestors not long dead. These people are called in on occasions of sickness, loss at sea, storms or other critical times, pass into a light trance, and converse freely with the household in deep jerky tones, purporting to be the voice of the actual spirit. The phenomena are apparently those of auto-hypnosis, and the medium retains but an imperfect recollection of the conversation in which he has taken a leading part. The medium often receives food and betel-nut in return for his services, but there is little if any conscious fraud. It is worthy of note that many persons who have become mediums have displayed prior symptoms of a coma or mild periodic insanity.

A fairly intricate set of beliefs is concerned with death. For five days after burial the body lies in the ground, mourned by its relatives, who also engage in a heavy series of exchange of valuables. On the fifth day, piles of bark cloth are set out in the house near the grave, food is brought in baskets and offerings made; it is then that the ancestors of the dead person are believed to come down from their abode, take up, not the corpse, but its *ora*, its spiritual counterpart, and one shouldering the food, another the valuables—in essence alone, of course—and another bearing the dead man before him on his hands, move off in procession to Rangi, the spirit-world.

Here again the social structure persists, even in the after-life. There are different Rangi of the different clans, each presided over by its principal *atua*, and some other *atua* of importance have also Rangi of their own. Arrived there, the newcomer is taken to pay his respects to the *atua* of his family and clan, and it is for this purpose, as offerings, that the food and bark cloth accompany him. The new spirit, before taking up permanent abode, must be cleansed from the taint of mortality, and for this purpose goes to a *vai furu tangata*, a 'man cleansing pool', in which he is immersed and kept for five days. At the end of this period he is released; all traces of his mortality have been washed away. This is peculiarly the function of the *fuanga*, the *atua* of the family of a person's mother, i.e. the deity of his *tuatina*. Maternal kinship counts, even in the after-world. If the spirit is one of importance, as that of a chief, then his *fuanga* fits him out with his *vave*, by sticking a branch of some aromatic shrub at the back of his waist-cloth as an ornament. The *vave* denotes literally his speed, but is used in a more figurative sense to imply not only his power of movement, but also his power in a more general fashion. Deities to whom appeal is efficacious are those of much *vave*, of great speed. The supreme god, the culture-hero of whom mention has already been made, is thus characterized in particular. His path is the flash of the lightning in the heavens. Speed and power are regarded as being practically synonymous, giving an interesting socio-dynamic concept.

As in most Polynesian religions, there is a series of Rangi—*Heavens* they may well be called—one above the other. The number is commonly given as ten, but actually it differs from clan to clan. In these Rangi the *atua* live much as on earth. Ideas differ as to whether they cultivate food or steal it from the orchards of men, but opinion is unanimous on this one point—that the *atua* spend most of their time in dancing. It is also stated that the *atua* grow old and weak, and that then they are revivified and rejuvenated by plunging into the *vai furu tangata*, whence they emerge young and vigorous.

HISTORY OF THE CULTURE

To give a description of the origins of Tikopia culture is more simple if one follows the native accounts than if one attempts to arrive at an accurate historical estimate. For about two centuries back from the present time the data are fairly clear. but beyond this they become very imperfect and soon can be regarded only as myth.

According to the native story, the island was pulled up from the sea in true Polynesian style, and on it were found a man plaiting sinnet and a woman making a mat. This pair, who were really *atua*, were the progenitors first of the family of principal gods, and later, through them, of men, from whom the present Tikopia are descended. Running somewhat parallel with this narrative, and intersecting it at certain points, is the tale of the entry of the ancestors or ancestral gods of Kafika into the land, while a third set of stories, this time on a somewhat less mythical plane, describes the arrival of a canoe from Luaniua (Ontong Java) and the creation and peopling of the low land of Tikopia.

Coming down to more historic times, the island is said to have been then inhabited by three sets of people. The most numerous, Nga Faea, sprung from the Luaniuans, were occupying the present district of Faea, and Nga Ravenga who are said to have been white-skinned and autochthonous, occupied the other side of the island. Nga Ariki, 'The Chiefs', were the third party, and also claim *afu kere* 'soil descent'. Curiously, however, the clans of Taumako and Tafua and several of the principal families of Kafika are said to have become extinct for various reasons in the distant past, and to have been reconstituted in each case by some immigrant from another island. as Uvea, Tonga, or Valua. It is a point of honour nowadays to be able to claim an autochthonous line of ancestors, and it may be supposed that this story of a general replacement implies either an attempt to provide a fictitious antiquity for one's descent, or some common catastrophe which struck these families at a blow and well-nigh exterminated them, leading either to an actual substitution of stock, or to vagueness as to former names and events, disguised under this form of narrative. The whole subject presents some very tangled problems, which one cannot attempt to elucidate here without adducing the full evidence.[1]

After this, however, the course of events is fairly plain, and can be obtained in detail from the descendants of all parties concerned. Nga Ariki were at this time cooped up in Uta, a small district at the inner corner of the lake. Spurred on by shortage of food, the people of Taumako attacked one night those of Nga Ravenga and exterminated them, with the exception of one child, whose mother, the daughter of the Ariki Kafika, fled with her babe to her father for protection. This boy, a son of the slain chief of Nga Ravenga, afterwards was given a Tongan woman in marriage and thus became the progenitor of the present Fangarere clan. The people of Taumako then spread out and occupied the vacant district of Ravenga. A generation or so passed, and then the chief of Tafua, spurred on by this example, invaded Faea and dispossessed the inhabitants. The initiative in this was actually taken by the *pure* in Marinoa, a *paito* of Kafika, whose stony hillside orchard in Ravenga gave him no satisfaction. Urging on the Ariki Kafika of the day, *kava* was made and Nga Faea were 'magicked' out of their territory. Struck with fear they took to their canoes and men, women, and children, led by their chief, went out to sea. A few survivors, children of rank, were taken under the wing of the Kafika and Taumako chiefs, and are *paito pure*, counsellor families, at the present day. Subsequent re-allotment of cultivations modified the situation then created, but broadly speaking, nowadays, as the result of these thrusts on the part of the 'chiefs', Tafua occupy Faea and Taumako hold Ravenga, while Kafika, as befits the rank of their chief, have ground in both districts, and Fangarere, of Nga Ravenga ancestry, possess a limited number of orchards in Ravenga. The few families descended from the remnant of Nga Faea are scattered, and hold lands in fief from their respective chiefs. Since that time there has been no great movement of population in the island.

Native tradition states that the ancestors of the principal families came separately from various islands, Pukapuka, Luaniua, Tonga, Valua (in the Banks), Samoa, Rotuma, Uvea and Anuta. A critical

[1] For further details see my *History and Traditions of Tikopia*, 1961.

29

analysis of their legends and tradition would support this view of their mixed origin. Despite a Tongan invasion about eight generations ago, and other occasional contacts, the Tongan element in the population is said to be small, unlike that of neighbouring Anuta, which is held to be composed almost wholly of Tongans, with a sprinkling of people from Uvea. In this connection it is interesting to note that the language and culture of Anuta differ quite considerably from those of Tikopia. The comparative freedom of both these small islands from European contact and influence renders them of considerable importance in the study of Polynesian culture.

CHAPTER 2

CEREMONIES FOR CHILDREN[1]

(1956)

Ceremonies with a child as the central figure appear to have been common in ancient Polynesia, and still exist in many of the islands in spite of the disintegrative effects of contact with European culture. My reasons for presenting this material are partly ethnographic and partly sociological. Previous records on this subject from Tikopia are fragmentary, and from the rest of Polynesia are still very incomplete. Moreover, the analysis of the data has tended to dwell on the technological and magical aspects of the ceremonies, as against the social relationships of the persons involved.[2] In many cases the socialization and other processes involved in the latter seem more relevant to an understanding of why these ceremonies exist and how they operate. Again, consideration of the changes in Tikopia by 1952, as compared with 1929, throws further light on the social functions of the ceremonies.

Van Gennep, Radcliffe-Brown and later writers have shown that the ultimate basis of these ceremonies for children lies in the attempt of the society to celebrate the advent of a new human being to its ranks, and to surround with a social aura the transition of this individual from one social state to another. Yet here come problems. In Tikopia, every ceremony of birth or initiation does not find the whole society assembled round the child, but only a certain limited set of individuals. What determines who shall come and who shall stay away? From my earlier analysis[3] it is clear that in Tikopia the answer to this question lies in an understanding of the functions of the ceremony as an expression of kinship ties. Then, every ceremony involves some kind of display, presentation or exchange of goods; what determines the extent of this economic participation?

A further problem lies in the fact that in Tikopia not every child figures as the centre of the same set of ceremonies. Why should some go through the full series and others not? How does this relate to the notions of

---

[1] Reprinted from *Oceania*, Vol. XXVII, 1956, under the title of 'Ceremonies for Children and Social Frequency in Tikopia'.

[2] An exception to this is the valuable contribution of H. Ian Hogbin, 'Transition Rites at Ontong Java,' *Journal of the Polynesian Society*, Vol. XXXIX, 1930, pp. 94–112, 201–20.

[3] *We, The Tikopia*, 1936, pp. 466–7.

society welcoming every new member ceremonially and strengthening itself thereby? What is the social function of such ceremonies of inter-mitted frequency. Finally, if these ceremonies have the important social functions generally attributed to them, how is it that they have become so attenuated in the course of a generation? How can the society have let go institutions of such alleged value to it?

The answers to such problems need more detailed analysis than has often been given to them.

DESIRE FOR CHILDREN

If a ceremony to celebrate a new member of a society is to have any meaning, the new member must be assumed to be normally welcome. It is a pertinent question, then, to inquire how far children in Tikopia are welcome. In general, the Tikopia do desire children. From the sentimental point of view children serve the Tikopia as objects of affection: they are repositories of family traditions and heirs of family lands and property; they serve a utilitarian purpose in doing some of the work of the household, and later in caring for their parents or other kin in old age. The institution of the 'adhering child', a custom prac-tically analogous to adoption, though without legal transfer, provides childless adults with the economic services and company of children. But the incorporation of the child in its second home is incomplete, and it is recognized that as a substitute for real offspring this is not entirely satisfactory.[1] On this point a pathetic statement was made to me by Pa Nukuomanu, who had no children of his own. 'It is good to have a true child', he said. 'A child who is "different" goes (to carry out commands) but grumbles "Where is their child? I am completely dead with the doing of their work".' Barrenness is regarded as a matter for regret, not of shame, and it is thought that either husband or wife may be responsible. Usually, supernatural interference with the woman is regarded as the cause.

The desire for children, however, is restricted by certain social canons and economic needs. Two kinds of children not wanted are those which are the product of unions not legitimized or not expected to be legitimized by the marriage ceremony, and those which threaten the food supplies of a family in which already there are a number of offspring. Here abortion or infanticide at birth have been traditional mechanisms of elimination. In the case of a child so put out of the way, the ordinary ceremonies at birth and death are not performed. It is treated as a social accident, and ignored as far as possible. This would seem to prove that the normal ceremonies are performed not simply to celebrate the birth

---

[1] A detailed discussion of these points is given in *We, The Tikopia*, pp. 159–69, 180–6, 203–6, 485–9.

of the child but to signalize the reception of the child by society. (Though secrecy is observed about the birth of a child to an unmarried girl, this is from shame at her unmarried state. No stigma is traditionally incurred by the act of infanticide itself.)

I have already recorded material on these practices in 1928–9.[1] As regards abortion, the observations then made were found to be valid also in 1952–3. Although the practice was reprobated by the Mission teachers, it was known to occur, and although no quantitative estimate could be made it appeared to be fairly common among unmarried girls. Once a certain confidence had been established it was found that cases were talked of freely. For example, one of my friends told me of a girl in Nukutungasau house who had *tafi na manava* (literally rubbed down her belly), that is, who had used manipulation and stones to terminate her pregnancy. She was unmarried and had had relations with her father's brother's son, an association improper in Tikopia eyes (*tau kave maori ne sara*). The attitude of my friend towards this was not censorious but rather sympathetic. He said, 'The women of this land have aching wombs.'

On occasion, however, either the girl is unsuccessful in her attempt or reluctant to make it, and the child is born. It does appear that even nowadays, despite the moral views of the Mission and perhaps some inkling of Government disapproval, the possibility of infanticide exists. Certainly I was told in 1952 of cases in which, since my former visit, children had been saved by the intervention of some kinsman or kinswoman who rescued them and brought them up. Moreover, I was told of another quite recent case of the same kind. Again, it is not always clear whether a pregnancy has been terminated by abortion or whether the child has been removed after birth. In one case, a well-known man was the father of a child by an unmarried woman, herself illegitimate. Previously he had 'done wrong' with one of his female cousins; it was said that one child was stillborn from this relation and a second was *tamate*, put to death. This expression may mean infanticide or it may mean a late abortion.

On the other hand, a child born out of wedlock may be allowed to live either because of compassion of one of the kinsfolk who rescues it or from respect for the moral law introduced by the Mission. In 1952–3 there were several young children in Tikopia described as *tama i te ara*, 'children from the path'. Though they were more in number than in 1928–9, illegitimacy cannot be said to be frequent. Typical of one such case was the rescue of the daughter of a woman, of Nikiua lineage, by her kinsman, Pa Marakei. I saw the child, a little girl of about two, and she had been adopted as 'an adhering child' by this man. He said, 'The woman was pregnant but was not married—a child from the path.

[1] We, the Tikopia, pp. 414, 527–30.

33

It was taken up by me and made to live by me, to become my daughter.'

A reflection of the general desire for children and of the economic role they are expected to fill in the household is seen by the common interpretation of certain occupational dreams as tokens of conception.[1] If a woman dreams that she goes fishing with a scoop net, the conventional female implement, or fills water bottles at a spring and brings them home, a customary female task, it is held that she will conceive and bear a girl child. If she dreams of sea fishing, a male pursuit, then her child will be a boy. If her husband or any other member of the family dreams along similar lines the interpretation will follow this pattern. There seems to be a very probable element of wish-fulfilment here.

An interesting question would be whether unmarried girls who are pregnant, or pregnant wives who do not want children, have similar dreams. I have no material on this. But one might hazard as an hypothesis for testing that the physiological changes might force the psychological issue. The dream patterns seem hardly sufficiently standardized for them to be socially demanded even in such cases.

The sequence of ceremonies connected with a normal birth may now be described (as of 1929). For ease in following the account I give first a synopsis of them in order, with their Tikopia names.

CEREMONIES BEFORE BIRTH
(Kin specified in each case in relation to child)

Furifuri o te memea	...	'Turning of the child'—by mother's female relative.
Furunga kere	... ...	'Cleansing of the caul'—by mother's relatives.
Fakafanaunga	... ...	'Causing to bear'—by mother's male relative.

CEREMONIES AFTER BIRTH

Fakamenga	... ...	'Putting to sleep'—display and exchange of mats.
Asinga	... ...	Application of turmeric by mother's consanguineal female kin to father's consanguineal female kin.
Ama fanaunga	... ...	Similar to *asinga*.
Kava makariri	... ...	'Cold kava'—food from father's to mother's kin.
Fanaunga ...	... ...	'The giving birth'—oven of father's group divided into:
(a) *Popora o te siki*	...	'Basket of the catching'—to midwife.
(b) *Popora te afi*	...	'Basket of the Fire'—to mother's brother; not reciprocated.
(c) *Fanaunga* ...	...	'The giving birth'—to mother's consanguineal kin; reciprocated by *tutungauru*.
(d) Food given to *fare masikitanga* – father's sisters.		

[1] An analysis is given in Chapter 7.

Ta Afi	'The Fire'—by mother's brother; associated with:	
(a) *Tutungauru* ...	Food from mother's brother to child.	
(b) *Rau koroa*	Food and bark-cloth from mother's kin to child; reciprocated by *fakaotingauso*.	
Fakaotea	'The nooning'—invitation of the child by mother's brother.	
Fakatavanga	'The seeking'—bringing the child home.	
Fakaotingauso	'The finishing of the umbilicus'—gift from father's consanguineal kin to mother's consanguineal female kin.	

PREGNANCY

Among the Tikopia, pregnancy often precedes marriage—though hardly so regularly as to be called a marriage pattern. But as illegitimacy of a child is a matter of social disapproval, when a girl becomes pregnant she usually tries to induce her lover to marry her out of hand; pregnancy thus often provides the occasion for the wedding ceremony.

The attitude of the Tikopia towards the state of pregnancy is the same as that of many other primitive peoples. In the case of a married pair it is regarded as a normal physiological phenomenon entirely removed from any need for embarrassment, shame or concealment. Even children are quite *au fait* with the phenomenon and with them, as with their elders, it is a subject of ordinary comment. Down by the spring one evening there were two little boys, the younger of whom had that pot-bellied look which infants in Tikopia are apt to get through too much starchy food. The other looked at him and said: 'What an enormous belly—like someone who is about to give birth!' This was a serious observation on his friend's silhouette.

The term to describe a woman who is pregnant is *ku nofo ma na manava*; the basic translation is 'she has dwelt with her belly' a rather curious ascription of duality to the phenomenon. The expectant mother goes about her work in the ordinary way, eats no special food, wears no special dress or ornament, and receives no privileged treatment by others. Taboos of pregnancy do not appear to exist either for husband or wife; and the closest approximation to a taboo comes in the belief that the pregnancy of a woman tends to rob her husband of efficacy or success in his everyday pursuits. If he goes fishing, then his catch will not be good; if he digs food, then the crop will not be great, nor the individual tubers large. He has not a 'food hand'. A Tikopia will attribute this to the *tapu* associated with pregnancy, but this *tapu* is manifested only by such lack of success and by no positive regulations. It is really a diminution of *mana*. What it does show, however, is the linkage of the husband with the woman and her unborn child—a socio-psychological prototype of a prenatal couvade.

When a married woman is in an advanced state of pregnancy two performances may take place. The one is regarded as physiological treatment. The mother or some other elderly female relative of the woman goes and massages her abdomen. The object of the manipulation, according to the Tikopia, is to change the foetus over from one side of the womb to the other in order to separate it from the after-birth. It is held that if this is not done the results may be bad; the placenta will block the outlet for the child and make birth difficult. 'She goes to turn the child in the concavity of the belly of its mother to take the placenta and lay it aside.' The act is described as 'the turning of the child' (*te furifuri o te memea*). Its purport is not to invert the child for presentation. This latter is believed to be effected by magic.

The other is a more formal performance and takes place only for the first pregnancy, the *mataki manava*. The woman goes to the house of her parents, where turmeric is put on her head and the upper part of her body. As the pigment is rubbed on a formula is recited, such as the following[1]:

> Your earth will be cleansed away
> Continue to dwell, listen,
> And then descend.

This is addressed to the unborn child. It is held that there is a film in the womb which if not cleansed away will cover the face of the child when it is born. The film is described by the word *kere*, the basic equivalent of which is 'earth', but which is also used in a wider reference (which might be termed linguistically as a marginal equivalent) for all kinds of sedimentary deposits. In this case it is clearly the caul which is meant. The ceremony is known as the *furunga kere*, the 'cleaning of the caul'. Another term for it is *ara pou* or, as given by some informants, *aro pou*.[2] The term *ara pou* is used for the first-born child itself. Later pregnancies are termed *tutu a tama*, 'the succession of children', and for them no ceremonies of this kind are performed. The reason for the differentiation is not explicit in Tikopia formulations. Pa Teva said 'We do not know what was the basis for the rejection of this ceremony' (in the later pregnancies). Nor can they explain why children other than first-born should not be thought to emerge with the caul.

The real point seems to lie in the economic and social accompaniments of the rite. It is essentially an act of interest in the woman and

---

[1] Tikopia texts of this and succeeding formulae have been given in the original article.

[2] Neither term translates easily: literally, *ara* means a path, and *aro* means to paddle; *pou* means a post. There is perhaps a general notion of the first-born being a support (post) to the family, but to the Tikopia the expression is 'just a name' for the ceremony.

her prospective offspring on the part of the family from which she came. After the smearing on of the turmeric her kin present food and valuables to her husband's group. Mats, bark-cloth blankets and girdles are given, and are reciprocated by the husband's kin next day. It will be seen later how this is merely one of the great series of exchanges that, centring on the child, take place between the two kin groups. These kin groups, while expressible in terms of lineage components, are not simply representative of the two patrilineages of child's mother and child's father. Other kin contribute from, e.g., the child's mother's mother's patrilineage, and child's father's mother's patrilineage. For a child of high rank further kin also may take part. Sometimes the woman's kin take the initiative and visit her in her mother's house. One effect of having an initial pregnancy rite in this way is that it marks the conversion of the woman to her new state of a child-bearer. This interpretation rests of course on the assumption that child-bearing is an act of positive significance to the society or at least to some group in it. More important still, the involvement of a man's kin in the birth of a child means that a prior relationship of a socially acknowledged kind must have been set up between the man and the mother of the child. Hence this ceremony is part of the system which ensures that marriage normally shall precede the birth of the child, and thus acts as a spur to legitimization. This perhaps explains in part the lack of interest in the performance of it for later children.

The omission of this ceremony for a first-born child does indeed result in its being born with a caul, according to the Tikopia. They gave as an instance the case of Nau Avakofe junior, who gave birth before the turmeric was applied, and the face of the child was covered with a film. The reason for not complying with custom was that the house of Porima, the woman's kin, had cut their bark-cloth trees but had not yet beaten the material. They thought that the woman would not give birth for some time, and then found that they were too late. So they performed the ceremony on the day of the birth of the child, at the same time as other ritual—much to the amusement of the village.

The *kere* (caul) on the face of the child is not known accurately by the Tikopia to be a membrane. 'Is it perhaps the interior of the belly of its mother?' they ask.[1] Incidentally, a married couple are supposed to cease intercourse some nights before the birth of the child. Otherwise, it is said, the child will be covered with slime, which (I was told in

---

[1] The Tikopia do not hold the view which appears to have been common in European countries, that to be born with a caul is lucky. Part of this luck of caul-birth, it appears, is protection from drowning. One might think that the Tikopia, set in the midst of the ocean wastes, might have found such a belief useful. But they have another avenue of protection, in their pagan gods and ancestors, who occasionally bear men up at sea and bring them to shore. Anyway, the Tikopia swim like seals, and can presumably afford to leave caul-protection to landlubbers.

1929) is licked off by the tongues of the women assisting at the birth—to the accompaniment of a severe scolding administered to the erring parents. In 1953, Spillius was similarly told by married men that the child would be born 'dirty'; it was also held that the unborn child might be damaged by the thrusting of the penis in copulation.

This discussion deals only with the normal course of birth. Though miscarriage in Tikopia appears to be fairly frequent, there is no regular treatment tried against it, nor ceremony practised to ward it off. However, it is regarded as due to malignant spirits. If a pregnant woman feels that she may have a miscarriage, she may get a spirit medium, a ritual elder or a chief to perform a protecting rite over her. But examination of this belongs to a discussion of sickness and the art of healing, to be treated elsewhere.

From practical experience the Tikopia are cognizant of the approximate length of time of gestation, and of the various stages in the development of the foetus. But several things may affect their clarity of statement. One is their measure of time by unnamed lunar months, which tends to introduce some uncertainty into their calculations. A second is the difficulty of being precise in abstract formulation. It appeared that much the same amount of indefiniteness about length of pregnancy existed in 1952 as in 1928–9, and that increased contact with Europeans had not given precision. For instance, when Pa Ngarumea was discussing with Spillius, he expressed surprise at finding the normal pregnancy period of European women given as nine months. He said that for Tikopia women it was ten months. The difference was due presumably to a calculation in lunar terms. When I asked Pa Nukumata what is the full term of pregnancy in Tikopia he said five months. When, startled, I asked for more details, he explained, 'When the child's second moon stands (in the sky) it has moved; in its third it has moved heartily; in its fourth it has picked up at the belly of its mother; in its fifth it has turned over and sought a path for itself to be born. The child which is overdue reaches its sixth (moon), but the child which is quick comes down at once.' Other people said, 'It depends upon the woman—one takes nine months, one takes eight, another takes ten—it is untrue to say six months.' But they agreed that a seven months child may occur in Tikopia, though they said most did not live. From such statements it is clear that various periods of pregnancy can be given—there is no *formula* of general knowledge. Yet apparent guesses wide of the mark are near to the truth if a different starting-point for the count be taken because of some difference in observation or interest. It does seem to be common for young women in Tikopia not to realize that they are pregnant until they are three months gone. (In making a comparison one should of course not over-estimate the sophistication of the great mass of European women in this respect.) If, for example, the babe is felt to move about the sixteenth or seventeenth week—as in Pa Nukumata's calculation—then this would make the due term about nine months in all.

It might be thought that one reason for uncertainty in the statements quoted about pregnancy may be because they were made by men. But this is probably not so. In Tikopia such things are discussed in mixed company, and men are closely concerned in affairs of gestation and birth.

The Tikopia expect the arrival of the child at a fairly definite day and discuss cases which are overdue. A woman who remains pregnant for some time after the expected date is said to be *kea*: 'she stays lazy'. I remember in 1928 the Ariki Taumako bursting out on one occasion in reference to the sister of Pa Nukurenga: *'When* is she going to give birth?'

PARTURITION

The act of bearing a child is termed *fanau*. It is significant to note that this word means 'to give birth' and not 'to be born'. Thus the Tikopia say *'fafine ne fanau nanafi'*—'a woman gave birth yesterday', not 'a child was born yesterday', as we normally should. The term *fanaunga* conveniently translated as 'family of children' means 'them to whom birth has been given', stress being laid on the act of delivery of the mother rather than on that of the emergence of the children.

It is held by the Tikopia that boys and girls tend to be born at different times of the moon. The *po tangata* are the nights when males are born, the *po fafine* those of females. The former comprise the early nights of the moon on the one hand and those of the third quarter on the other; the latter comprise those nights when the moon stands above in the sky and also those when the period of darkness is long. I doubt if any empirical evidence would support this statement. Pa Fenuatara pointed out to me that his last child, a male, was born in the early phase of the moon. 'But,' he added, 'some boys are born in the *po fafine*; some girls in the *po tangata*.'

Another curious piece of Tikopia lore is the idea that in olden times the ordinary physiology of birth was unknown, and that children were extracted by means of a cæsarean operation. Legends of this type occur in other Polynesian communities.[1]

The following is the Tikopia tale as given in 1928 by Seremata (Pa Maneve):

'In former times in this land when a woman was pregnant they

[1] For example, Maori (Best, *Maori as He Was*, Wellington, 1924, p. 52); Rarotonga (Gill, *Myths and Songs from the South Pacific*, London, 1876, p. 266); Marquesas (des Vergnes, *Revue Maritime et Coloniale*, Vol. LII, p. 726); Niue (S. P. Smith, *J.P.S.*, Vol. XII, Wellington, 1903, p. 102); Tuamotu (Caillot, *Mythes, Légendes et Traditions des Polynésiens*, Paris, 1914, pp. 58, 149).

waited a span of nights till the birth-time and then her abdomen was slit, slit in two, and the child forced out. Then the woman, its mother, was buried. They did not know of the way of giving birth to children.

'Then came a man from the west and lived in Tikopia in Nuaraki. He married and his wife became pregnant. Then came the family of the woman to cut open her belly; but the man objected and said they should leave her to dwell. The parents of the women thereupon said to him that she would die. Said the man, "No, she will not die." Then the parents of the woman called out to him: "By what way shall she give birth?" Then the man called back that she would give birth from her vulva. They gave vent to an exclamation of surprise (*vevei rei*). So they dwelt and left the matter in the hands of the man. They waited and waited and the woman gave birth. Her parents were astounded. They called to the husband: "Well, there now, well, there now! A woman gives birth from her vulva!" So when they had seen this they allowed the women of Tikopia to wait. They did not slit their abdomens.'

In answer to the question as to how the infant cut from its mother was fed it was said that it was handed over to another woman to feed. 'But,' it was added, 'there was no milk; it was not good.'

'This is a tale of olden times,' said Seremata, 'it is not a myth (*tara tupua*) from the gods, it is a story (*taranga*) of men.'

Although this story is regarded as being a description of the actual state of knowledge of the early population of the land there is no further evidence to show that it is integrated at all into the present institutions of the people. It appears to be part of the original stock of ancient Polynesian folk-lore preserved probably for its quaintness, its contrast to the present obstetrical methods of the people, and the opportunity it gives for speculative and somewhat salacious comment. It may be noted that, according to the Tikopia, the knowledge of correct birth procedure is not one of the items made known by a deity or culture hero, as many others are said to have been; but the benefactor was simply a nameless foreigner. (This tale does not appear to be of general currency in Tikopia. It is worth noting that neither my research assistant nor I had it made known to us in 1952–3. It is true that we made no inquiry about it, but in our various talks about pregnancy and birth it was never mentioned.)

When the time is drawing near for the child to be born a small ceremony is usually performed to facilitate the matter. This ceremony is different from the others previously mentioned in that it takes place when labour has begun or is expected shortly to begin. It may be described as an immediate birth rite in contrast to the other eventual birth rites. Members of the bilateral kin group (*kano a paito*) of the woman assemble, especially including her own mother and classificatory relatives of the same grade, and her own father and his close kin. They come together for the *fakafanau*, 'the causing to give birth'. One of her senior male relatives, an elder or a chief, comes to her, takes oil, and pouring it into his hand gently applies it to her belly with a stroking movement. This is the ritual act which serves as the vehicle for the operation of the power of the family ancestors and gods. The elder recites a formula. This is the one given me in 1928 by Pa Rangifuri (then heir to the Ariki Tafua) for such occasions:

> 'Male ancestor,
> Stand firm to make strong
> And give power to my hand.
> Be turned the face of the little child
> Down below.
> Erect the twice-breaking wave
> And send it down below.
> You come down on to your property
> Which has been spread out
> By your house of father's sisters and your house of grandparents
> That they may nurse you.'

The first part of this invocation appeals for *manu* to a particular ancestor or deity whom the family regard as likely to be interested. Then he is asked to present the child in the normal position to make birth easy, and to expedite labour by bringing on the flooding. This is referred to here as 'the twice-breaking wave'; other formulae refer to a larger succession of waves. The appeal is then directed to the child who is commanded to fulfil expectations without delay. The 'property' signifies on the one hand the actual cloth held to receive the child, and on the other the gifts spread out on his behalf in the house.

Another formula, this time from Pa Tavi, one of the ritual elders of the Ariki Kafika, is as follows:

> 'Make a flooded path for you to come down
> On to your property
> And your mats
> Which have been set there by your house of father's sisters
> That you may sleep on them.
> Erect an eight-times-breaking wave
> *Kokono konokono*.'

In this formula, as in the other, there is the triple reference to the facilitation of the act of birth by flooding; to the property prepared because of the birth; and to the kinship status of assistants. That is, we have the mechanics, the economics and the social linkage all given specific mention. The word *kono* could be loosely described as a term of imitative magic, since it is the conventional reproduction of the groans

41

made by woman in labour. The introduction of it here is to assist in bringing on that phenomenon. In this formula the intervention of spiritual beings, though not specifically invoked, is implied. The whole purport of it is to induce speedy and therefore easy delivery.

The recital of such a formula is not obligatory. The chief or elder comes usually only in cases of difficult parturition. In the ordinary way a set form of words of the second type is uttered by the father or husband of the woman or by one of her attendants while she is gripped at the back by people who have come to assist. The higher the rank of the woman, or the more difficult the birth, the more likely it is that resort will be had to a chief and therefore through him to the gods. There is no special formula for cases of difficult birth.

The situation in 1952–3 would appear to have been much the same as in 1928–9, save that with the advance of Christianity in the interim the role of mission teachers in providing prayers to assist in cases of difficult birth had increased as against pagan appeals by ritual elders and others. Such appeals had by no means died out.

The duration of labour appears to vary very considerably. Some women have a speedy delivery, others are one or two nights in labour. Some treat the matter very lightly. On feeling the pangs, they go down to the salt water, give birth to the child, and bring it up washed. The child does not sink when born in this fashion. 'It swims like a fish,' it is said, floating with head out of water. In May 1952 Nau Toa gave birth one afternoon to a girl child, a very tiny one, in her house. I saw her towards sunset out in the reef waters cleansing herself—washing away the *fi toto*, as a child said. After she had washed she came up the beach alone, moving slowly but with no help. She stood outside her house for a few minutes squeezing water from her garments, looking exhausted but giving a weak smile.[1]

Neither in 1928–9 nor in 1952 did I witness the actual birth of a

[1] In view of the popular idea that the women of primitive communities find birth a simple matter, it may be noted that this is by no means always the case. I have no relevant data from Tikopia, but cite views given me from elsewhere in the Solomons in 1929. According to Sister Berry of the Methodist Mission at Roviana, the Melanesian women there on whom a careful series of measurements was made were smaller in the pelvis and reproductive organs than European women. This, however, did not have the expected result of increasing the difficulty of labour, since the children born were approximately a pound lighter on the average than European children. They weighed 6·5 pounds at birth as against 7·5 pounds on the average. Of a series of 30 native children the birth-weight ranged from 4·5 to 8·5 pounds. Difficult parturition was, however, by no means uncommon in this district. Asphyxiation of the child due to haemorrhage of the mother was a constant danger. The native midwives did not apparently know how to cope with this; the ordinary remedies of plucking the child by the legs and shaking it, or pulling out the abdomen were not employed. Mrs Warren of the Melanesian Mission at Marovovo told me also that difficult parturition was common on the northern end of Guadalcanal. She admitted that her impression of the high proportion of such cases might not be entirely accurate, since she was usually called to assist only when normal delivery did not take place, but the number of such cases was considerable

child in Tikopia. Those which occurred in families of my close acquaintance were at times when I was occupied on other work. So also with Spillius. With other families there seemed no objection, but the people did not think we were greatly interested, and in fact we made no great effort to attend—mainly owing to the time factor. On several occasions, however, we attended the subsequent ceremonies soon afterwards. Here is a description by Pa Rangifuri in 1929 of the technique of accouchment:

'Delivery takes place in the ordinary dwelling place. The brothers of the woman sit at the rear and press with their feet on the buttocks of their sister, supporting her back. The woman wears no clothing, she has thrown it to one side, squatting on the floor. She leans back while her brothers push against her with their feet and press their hands against her shoulders. Her legs are open and she clasps her knees with her hands. Pushing her fundament forward, she strains with laboured grunts. In front of her sits a woman with a piece of soft bark-cloth, waiting to receive the child. If she is not prepared then the child may be born on to the floor mat, the head may come down and the neck twist. The husband will call out to the woman to have the piece of cloth ready. It is expected that the child will emerge head foremost because of the formula recited to the ancestors to turn the child down. The woman sits to watch for the time when the head of the child will appear. When it appears from its mother, from her vulva, she takes the piece of bark-cloth and catches the infant to support it. Hence she is called "the woman of the catching" (*te fafine o te siki*). The woman cries for the eight-times-breaking wave to come, that the little child may be brought down below, that it may descend to the path of men. The woman also calls out the formula. When the infant hears the formula recited to him he kicks with his feet against his mother and shoots down; he appears from his mother. When his head has appeared the mother has not ceased her groaning. And so it proceeds till he has completely emerged and there comes down the blood and the water.'

An extraordinary thing to many Polynesian students will be the presence of the brothers at this intimate occasion in their sister's life. It demonstrates how in Tikopia the element of restraint in the relations between brother and sister, particularly in the sphere of sex, operates in such a way as not to hinder the rendering of real assistance at critical times. In Tonga, Samoa, or Ontong Java the presence of brothers at such a time would be out of the question, though it is allowed among the Maori.

The midwife, as one may term the 'catcher' of the baby, is not specially chosen either for her kin relation or for her technical skill, though naturally an experienced woman is selected. There are no professional midwives in Tikopia. In cases of difficult birth, if ordinary physical means fail, the aid of the supernatural forces is invoked. A chief or an elder, or a spirit medium (*vaka atua*) is summoned.

As part of a general disquisition on sex relations Pa Tekaumata, a well-known spirit medium, gave the following information on the procedure at birth:

'As the child is born, women assemble and spread out the legs of the woman, drawing them back, while men come and press on her back. But the mother (*nana maori*) of the woman grasps the rear of her vulva below. It is termed the joining of her vulva down at her rectal orifice. She grips it and squeezes it together that it may not part, while the child is appearing outside. Then when the child has fallen down below they go and pull down the placenta, pull and pull it down until it falls. The cord is cut, and turmeric is fetched by her mother, who sits and anoints with it the lips of the woman's vulva. When this is done, hot water is prepared and the woman is pressed to drink that she may recover, that the seat of malignant activity there in the belly of the woman, the blood, may be driven down, that she may be well—and the *toko ara*. She struggles and struggles with the *toka ara*, and sweats.

'Then it is that my own people invite me and I go, the deity enters into me, I lay hands on her belly and it is conquered. It is no longer painful. But if we work and work and work over her without avail, then she is a woman who will go because of her belly, dying in childbirth.'

I did not ascertain precisely what the *toka ara* is, but presume it refers to a case of retained placenta and represents a portion of the afterbirth; the only form of manipulation of it known to the Tikopia is pulling on the umbilical cord.

After the child is born the umbilicus is smoothed out by the woman, tied and cut. In the case of a first-born son the cord is cut with a sliver of bamboo (*parakofe*) on a club. The idea of this is to give him skill: 'It is done to make him strong, to make him adept in the use of timber.' In the case of later children and, I think, also of females, the cord is severed with no special observances. It was tied in a simple knot in cases which I observed. The umbilical cord is termed *vava* or *uso*, a variant of the latter being *iso*.

The placenta is called *te fenua*, a homophone with the word for 'land'. It is also spoken of as 'the husk of the child', or 'the dwelling-place of the child'. It is realized that retention of it causes death, but I was assured in 1928–9 by the Tikopia that there had been no cases of this in recent years and we heard of none in 1952–3. The reason given is that the massage practised on the expectant mother some time before makes the afterbirth fall into a position easy for subsequent expulsion. This is the 'turning of the child' already mentioned. The afterbirth of male children is buried at once outside the eave on the non-sacred (*tuamu*) side of the house. That of female children is left until the morning—assuming that the birth takes place at night. Then it is observed that certain objects are present in the afterbirth; sometimes there are two, sometimes three, or even four; they are described as being sometimes pale, but more often black, and they move and crawl within the placenta. These are removed and buried separately. They are described as *uruuru atua*, manifestations of a supernatural being, and are said to be that of Feke, the Octopus Deity. If they were buried with the afterbirth they would affect the health of the child. It would either die or become insane. This precaution applies only to girl children because Feke the *atua* is noted for his lubricity. (The theme of heterosexual intercourse with supernatural beings resulting in the illness of mortals runs through many Tikopia customs.) The afterbirth of all children is buried in the path or in some well-trodden place, which must not be exposed to the sun. If the child is heard to hiccough then someone goes out and treads down the place where the afterbirth is buried: 'If the infant hiccoughs a person goes to stamp down the earth and make it firm, that the belly of the child may be firm.'

To these ideas, which, irrational to us, appear to the Tikopia to have received empirical verification, may be added another. After the child is born it is fed with *vatia*, sago-cream pudding, in coconut cups. One of these is finished every couple of days. They are not then burned in the fire but are hung up to the roof. They are left there until the child is big, long after the umbilical cord has fallen, though before the babe is able to turn over. Then they are burned. If this is done before, it is held that the child will make gurgling noises in its sleep (*me konokono*) as if it wished to excrete all the time.

The birth of the child is an event of interest to the relatives and to the inhabitants of the village or district where it takes place. Conversation about it forms one of the topics of the morning's gossip when people meet on the beach and in the paths before the day's work begins. Here is a sample of the laconic style of conversation overheard when Nau Taitai bore a child in Rofaea:

'Who has given birth?'
'Nau Taitai.'
'When?'
'Last night.'
'What?'
'A female.'

Most of the immediate relatives were present at the birth. But Nau Raroakau, the mother of Pa Taitai, was not there. The first question she asked was: *E lasi?* 'It is a big one?' The father usually displays interest and pride in the birth of his child, the latter particularly in the case of the first infant or two. He does not have much time to reflect on these sentiments, however, since he has to busy himself at once with the collection and preparation of quantities of food entailed by the customary obligations.[1]

POST-NATAL CEREMONIES

The advent of a first child means the creation of new kinship groups—the conversion of the woman's brothers into uncles (*tuatina*), her sisters into 'a house of mothers', and those of the man into 'a house of aunts'. The ceremonial demarcation and alliance which already exists between the husband's family and that of the wife is strengthened by reference to the child. An extensive series of presentations and exchange may now begin.

The first ceremonial procedure is termed the *fakamenga* or *fakameranga*, 'the putting to sleep' of infant and mother. This is performed for the eldest male child and the eldest female child only. The people of the *fare nana*, that is 'the mother's house', assemble with mats and bark-cloth. The families of both father and mother of the woman are represented in this group. For instance, when in 1929 Nau Fenuafara was brought to bed, people from Tereata and from Paiu attended (*v.* Genealogy, Fig. 1). The sisters or equivalent female kin of the father of the child come as the *fare masikitanga*, also with mats or bark-cloth. The function of the first group is to put the mother ceremonially to sleep; that of the second to do the same for the babe.

When Nau Taitai bore her second child I accompanied the *fare masikitanga*. The people entered the house in the early morning after the birth. The mother, smeared with turmeric on arms, back of the neck and shoulders, all over the head, the ears and the cheeks, was sitting up, her back against a house-post. The lower part of her body was covered with a mat, the upper part was bare. The child was held in the arms of another woman, resting on a piece of bark-cloth and not swaddled in any way. The women of the *fakamenga* started from their homes in parties of two or three carrying their mats under their arms, entered the house, and sat around the sides while their gifts were spread in the centre. At the upper end of the house opposite the door were gathered the *fare nana*, beside the mother, while at the lower end, near the infant, sat the *fare masikitanga*. There were less than a score of people present: 'We are not many because the land is busy at a funeral,' it was explained.

The actual ceremony was brief. The articles brought were spread out

---

[1] Twins (*masanga*) are sometimes born, and are not regarded with any special emotion. Several pairs were alive when I was in Tikopia in 1928–9 and again in 1952–3. Contrary to the opinion of W. H. R. Rivers (*History of Melanesian Society*, Vol. I, 1914, p. 313) mixed twins are known and treated in the normal way. But Spillius records that twins are regarded as being by nature unequal in strength, and that the weaker is thought likely to die young. The spirit of the dead twin may then be dangerous to the live twin. (See Raymond Firth. 'Twins, Birds and Vegetables', *Man*, N.S., Vol. I, pp. 1–17, 1966.)

carefully, mats at the bottom and bark-cloth blankets at the top. They are termed a *raura o fare kave*. The child, whose head was red with turmeric—as a sign of special status—was taken and gently laid on the pile, and then the upper couple of blankets were softly folded over the top of it. The infant was handled with the greatest delicacy. As one girl laid it down another watched and gently lifted the little hand which had got underneath its body. Another pile was spread beside the mother, and at the same time as her child, she lay down and a blanket was drawn over her head. She had not spoken a word.

Both mother and child rest there for a little while and are then taken out. Later, after the oven has been opened, the mats and cloth are folded. They may then be exchanged between the women of the two parties or not, according to choice. If a woman desires to take back her contribution it is quite in order, either because she does not wish to part with it at all or because she cannot find a suitable equivalent. Usually a number of exchanges do take place.

The formal 'putting to sleep' of mother and new-born babe is done in essentially the same manner as with the initiates after the ceremony of super-incision.[1] Whatever be the origin of this custom it has the function of bringing the central figure of the ceremony into actual bodily contact with the valued property displayed and exchanged on his or her behalf. No transference of magical virtue or of personality is alleged to take place; the importance of the procedure, which is taken very seriously, lies in the overt secular sphere of social relations. It is perhaps significant, however, that the occasions where persons are 'put to sleep' are those where they have just passed through a rather trying ordeal. This suggests that some concept of restoration of bodily energy is implied in making them lie down on the pile of bedding, but this aspect of the matter is given a very casual agreement by the natives. In any case the length of time the subject remains there is often not sufficient to be of much benefit to him as treatment for shock.

During the *fakamenga* food is prepared at the homes of both parties. The first item to emerge is a basket carried from the house of the father of the child to that of its principal mother's brother. If the woman is the daughter of a chief then the kava is made when the food arrives at the house. A fresh stem of the kava plant accompanies the gift and the gods are invoked in the usual way. If the woman is of common stock then there is no kava, and portions of the food are simply pinched off by the head of the house and thrown as offerings to the ancestors. In either case the ceremony has the effect of enlisting the supernatural forces of the woman's own family on behalf of the welfare of her child. In the case of a child of Sa Rangimatere in 1929 the Ariki Taumako was called in to throw offerings of food. The woman came from the lineage of

[1] See *We, The Tikopia*, pp. 449–51.

47

KINSHIP GROUPING ON THE BIRTH OF A CHILD—MAIN PARTICIPANTS CLASSIFIED

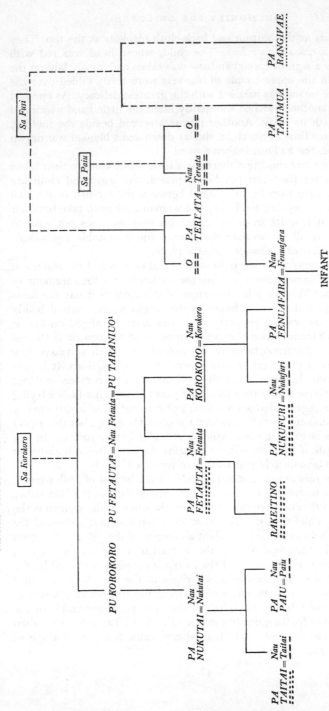

Key: —————— *paito te memea* (patrilineal representatives).
      – – – – – *fare masikitanga* (F.Sis. category).
      · · · · · · *tuatina* (M.B. category).
      = = = = = *fare nana* (mother's female kin).
      :::::::::: *a soko* (cooks).

Fig. 1

Rimanu, which had a temple sometimes used by the chief. He did not actually make the kava on this occasion because the woman was not of his own family, but the ritual link made him pay the compliment of attendance. This food, consisting of a bowl of pudding and a basket of vegetables, comes from the early morning oven, and is known as the *kava makariri*, though it is not cold food, as the name seems to imply. It is reciprocated in the evening. It was stated that this basket is prepared only in the case of a first-born child, but I did not verify this. It is really a preliminary gift, a kind of acknowledgement or announcement of the birth. As the morning draws on a large oven is prepared at the father's house. When it is opened in the late afternoon the contents are divided into four portions. One provides the *popora o te siki*, the basket given to the midwife for her services in 'catching' the babe; another is the *popora te afi* (see below); a third is given to the *fare nana* or may be carried to the *tuatina*. In either case it goes to the family of the woman who has borne the child, and is regarded as the reciprocal gift for the *tutungauru* (see later). This portion is called the *fanaunga*, 'the giving birth', a name which is also applied to the oven as a whole. The fourth portion of food is divided among the *fare masikitanga*, to recompense them for coming, and out of it also are fed any other assistants of no special status.

Mention has been made of Nau Taitai and her child being bedaubed with the crimson turmeric pigment. This is done by the women of the household where the birth takes place—in this case in that of the woman's father—and is a mark of attention, one might almost say of honour. Turmeric is used on many occasions in Tikopia to single out individuals who are at the moment of especial social interest and importance. Following on the *fakamenga* ceremony comes the *asinga*, which consists in the application by one of the *fare nana* of turmeric to the senior woman of the *fare masikitanga*. Another application to a different member of this group is of precisely the same kind, the two ceremonies being differentiated in hardly more than name. The latter is called *te ama fanaunga*. On the occasion of the accouchement of Nau Taitai it was performed by Nau Rangivete upon Nau Fenuato. About the *asinga* there was some debate. The *fare nana* said that the turmeric should be rubbed on the sister of Pa Taitai, but her mother objected. 'Let it not be put on the daughter,' she said, and selected the eldest daughter of Pa Pangisi instead. This was largely by way of paying a compliment to the social status of the leading mission teacher. The girl at first objected strenuously to being the recipient of this somewhat embarrassing honour, but at length submitted. Again Nau Rangivete acted as operator, being the sister of Nau Taitai. As soon as the bedaubing commenced the girl lowered her head and began to wail a dirge, as is the custom. In this case it was a dirge of the grandfather, most appropriate under the circumstances as being of a neutral order, having no direct reference to the relative kin status of any persons present. The object of these two ceremonial acts is said by the Tikopia to be the maintenance of the health of the child—it must be remembered that turmeric is associated with the Atua i Kafika, and its use is pleasing to him. 'The *ama fanaunga* is made that the babe may sleep well,' it is said; 'the *asinga* has the same basis, the child. They have one basis.' The differentiation between these two ceremonies is a product of multi-plication of effort, not of any deep functional separation. But one very obvious sociological function is the overt offering of tokens of respect by close mother's kin of the infant to close father's kin. Moreover, both parties are female and the ceremony is a formal demonstration of good relations between them. It can be regarded in part as an appre-ciation by the mother's female kin of the actions of the father's female kin in recognizing obligations towards mother and babe, and their legitimacy. In this sociological sense, the babe indeed has cause to 'sleep soundly'.

Accompanying the smearing on of turmeric is a present made by the *fare nana* to the true father's sister of the child. This consists of a mat bound up with a pile of bark-cloth, and members of the donor group combine to make it up. There is no return gift for this except the food from the oven. Sometimes there is one bundle, known as the *asinga*, sometimes two, the second of which corresponds to the *ama fanaunga*.

About the same time another minor event takes place. The 'woman of the *siki*' who has held the child at birth takes the leaves of an aromatic plant, anoints them with oil, and crushing them up rubs her hands well with them. This is a symbolic procedure done to 'clean' her hands—the word *fano* used here is the same as for ordinary cleansing, though the process is used only in ritual.

The 'woman of the *siki*' does not merely perform the technical role of midwife; she is also the representative of the spiritual powers respon-sible for the formation of the child. The Female Deity, goddess of women and all that pertains to them, is conceived as sitting by, invisible, watching the hands of the woman as they are spread to take the emerging babe. The bark-cloth sheet afterwards given to the woman in recom-pense for her services is also an acknowledgement to the Female Deity for her interest in the child. From the moment of its conception till its emergence into the world of men the child is under spiritual as well as mortal surveillance and care.

RECITAL OF THE FIRE FORMULA

Up to this point the ceremonial has been largely a woman's affair. Now it is the turn of the men. As the evening draws near some of the immediate mother's brothers of the infant make their appearance. They have come to perform the *afi*, the ritual of the fire. One of them brings a torch of plaited dry coconut leaf, of the type used for fishing at night, and a banana leaf also. The men seat themselves on *mata paito*, facing towards the centre of the house, and their principal takes the babe in his arms. An assistant lights the torch and holds it up so that the light falls on the face of the child. Then the man who is nursing it begins to recite a formula, addressed to the babe. The phrases are uttered quickly, but carefully, and with rather more conversational inflexion than is normally the case in set recitation. From time to time various other men interject a phrase, either to prompt the main speaker when he falters, or to mention something he may have overlooked. This privilege of interruption, rare in public recitals, gives the audience a voice in the proceedings, satisfies their interest in the child, and, to a smaller degree, allows them to manifest their sense of self-importance. And, what is unusual in Tikopia ritual, even a woman may have her say.

Awkwardness and nervousness in wielding the torch and reciting the formula before the crowd are often shown. It was for this reason apparently that at one ceremony I witnessed a young mother's brother (*tuatina*) started to laugh. He was immediately reproved by another: 'You're a nice sort of *tuatina* to laugh while the fire is being held'— was the burden of the rebuke.

Here is a fairly close rendering of what was said over the female child of Nau Taitai, recorded before the ceremony and checked during it.

> 'Light be your eyes from the fire which is set up
> For the doings of women
> To be adept in the weeding of taro
> And the making of fine mats
> And the plaiting of floor-coverings
> And the handling of the scoop-net
> That the fish wherever it goes
> May be caught by you
> And when you have brought in your hand-net
> Run hither and kindle the oven
> May you be adept in bark-cloth beating
> The preparation of the *masi*
> The planting of turmeric
> All the work of females to be grasped.'

The recital concluded, the torch is extinguished on the banana leaf, the child is handed back to the woman, and the company proceeds to the apportionment of food for a meal.

The purport of the recital is clear. The natives term it a *tarotaro*, that is a set form of words the utterance of which in the proper conditions exerts an influence on the object.[1] In this case it is held that the attention of the child, focused by the light of the flaming torch, is subjected to the force of the formula, and that it will thereby be induced to carry out its proper economic pursuits in later life with skill and care.

For a male child a corresponding set of tasks is mentioned:

'Light be your eyes from the fire which is set up
That you may grasp the doings of men
The deep-sea fishing of the ocean
The netting of the flying-fish
The fish which flies no matter where, to be caught
The paying out of the shark-hook, the angling for *kurakura*
The *kuani* netting, the diving for sea-snails, the deep-sea fishing, the bonito-
    trolling
May you be adept in cultivation
The planting of yams, the plucking of coconuts, and their planting
The planting of banana
The extraction of turmeric
The dubbing out of canoes
May you be adept in the building of canoes.'

Other phrases may be added to taste by anyone who thinks of them, as

'The garfish wherever he flies
May he be caught, be enclosed in your net.'

The custom is to run through all the phrases connected with the sea (*taranga o te moana*) first, and then to turn to those of the land (*taranga i nga uta*), but this is not a material point. In this as in other ritual affairs there is much variation in the skill of performers. A man who prides himself on his knowledge will run through the formula cleanly and neatly, keeping the order correct, whereas another will stumble through it, bungling the phrases, and having to be helped out every now and again when he gets stuck for an expression.

It is for this reason, largely, that so many departures are found from the rule that it is one of the principal *tuatina* who should recite the formula. Unless this man is of some seniority and experience he is likely to be shy at such a public appearance, and will either recite a very short form of words, or will depute his task to a more responsible person. For Nau Taitai's child, for instance, it was the maternal grandfather, Pa Nukutai, who did the job; for the child of Nau Fenuafara it was the paternal grandfather, Pa Korokoro. In this latter case the babe was held by Pa Fetauta, and the torch by Pa Rangivae, the representative of the *tuatina*, who had left the formula to Pa Korokoro since he was an elder accustomed to such things.

[1] See Chapter 9.

The *afi* is a picturesque ceremony. The ring of men and women seated in the darkness around the edges of the house, the chief actors in the centre, with the flickering light of the blazing torch shining on their bare brown bodies, on the paler skin of the tiny child lying peacefully on its bark-cloth in the arms of one of them, the touch of colour of the dark green banana leaf held by the torch-bearer, and of the crimson turmeric on the child's head—all combine to make a vivid impression, the effect of which is heightened by the serious measured rhythm and inflexion of the voice of the reciter, as with eyes bent on the child he urges upon it in colourful, expressive tones its future course of action. In the background is the still figure of the mother, also red with turmeric, sitting with legs straight out before her.

Pa Korokoro proceeded as follows. He began:

> 'Pa Fetauta! Assist me at the Fire of Pa Tafua which is being set up
> Unfold welfare here.'

Thus he appealed to his principal deity, and uttered the phrases of abasement, which mention the eating of excrement, and again asked for welfare. Then he announced the *afi* to Pa Saukirima (who was not present), and then announced it in his own name, as he did for Pa Fetauta. These customary acknowledgements over, he then embarked upon a long recital, of which the approximate form is given below. I obtained the text of what he was going to say from him before the ceremony, and checked it as he recited; the correspondence was fairly close, but there were many variations in order, some in wording, and a fair amount of repetition. This variation is of course quite legitimate. The formula is not regarded as a set of unalterable phrases, but as a recital of a prescribed general type, within which the taste or imagination of the reciter is allowed free play. In other words, it is a *free formula*. The main object is to cover the entire series of occupations in which the babe will later take part; it is left to the reciter to decide whether he will do this by general phrases or will mention each in detail. In this case the child was a girl. Pa Korokoro, being an elder of parts, naturally wanted to display his command of phraseology, and to make the recital as complete as possible. He received prompting and interjections from the man holding the torch, the real *tuatina*, but also from the holder of the babe, and from spectators. Then at the end of his formula he asked if there were any further phrases to supply. He was assured that he had covered the lot.

Here is his formula:

> 'Thy fire Pa Tafua has been announced to thee
> Unfold welfare
> That the child may sleep well.

Thy fire Pa Saukirima O!
Recite hither for welfare for her
To sleep well.
My own fire Pa Korokoro
Light be your eyes
Unfold welfare for her
Perfume a thing for her to eat
That the child may sleep well.
From its recitation that has been performed
Clear be its eyes for the work.
Wake up you for the taro
To be industrious in the clearing of the taro
To be healthy for your work.
Wake you up to go and clear for taro
The taro which stands overgrown
To be cleared on the moment and finished
Wake you up and the seedlings that I filled tie up completely to be carried on
    your back
Hasten you and when your parents are hungry go to the woods to gather food
    for your parents to come and cook it in the oven to be done quickly for your
    parents who hunger to be filled.
To go and get food
To go to the water
To carry a water-bottle
For your parents to drink.
Be fit in your water-carrying
Stride off, stride back
We who are thirsty
Now have become filled.
Climb up there to the mountain standing there
That you may be fit simply to get food.
Cut the leaves of giant taro which stands, to lever it out and proceed hither.
Light the oven
Cook it till it is done
Go and fetch the food-kits of your parents to put it in
Then we are filled.
Go and fetch the water-bottle
Then we have drunk
Then we are filled.
Indeed you are industrious.
Stand at the oven-border to uncover the oven at once to fill the food baskets
Go and give them to your parents
Fill the baskets of the relatives
Clear be your eyes for the fishing
The fish goes to a distance but bar it to dash hither to rest in your net
We have eaten of your netting
The fish that goes to a distance be turned by you to enter the net
When your parents are hungry, go and catch fish

Take your torch, go and take your net to go and fish.
Go and parcel up; parcel up a package for your parents and give them to eat
Parcel up a package for us relatives to carry
Parcel up a package for your brothers
Parcel up a package for your sisters
There they have eaten completely
There have eaten completely the relatives, and I have eaten of the package
Go and roast, there it is cooked
Give to eat, there I am filled
And distribute then to the relatives
There they have eaten completely
Go and give to your grand-parents; go and give to your fathers; go give a
     package to your mother; go and give a package to your brothers.
Then if there is one left, go and give a package to your brother
There we have eaten of your food-procuring.'

Pa Korokoro also made known to me the text of his 'Fire' formula to
be recited over a male child. Here it is, in translation:

'Recite to me Pa Tafua for welfare for him.
Now the announcement of the Fire is finished,
My own Fire.
Light be your eyes
That the club which descends
May be parried
That the adze which descends
May be parried
That the arrow which is shot at you
May be parried.
Light be your eyes for your net
That a flying-fish skimming above
May be caught.
The fish wherever he goes
When your line is let down may his gullet be drawn
To come and bite at the hook
That he may be hauled up
When a king-fish comes may his eyes be light for your hook
Wherever a fish goes
May he be turned to come
Lower down your line
That a *para* may bite at it
Let down and lower away your line
That a *kata* may bite at it
And be hauled up.
Then bring it hither for your parents
You go and net by torch-light to bring hither that we may eat.
Lower away your line from the reef there
That the *kurakura* may bite

Let down your hook
That the fish may observe it
And be hauled up
You bring hither (the result of) your seamanship
That we may eat of it.
Light be your eyes for your work
Stand there that seedlings may be planted immediately
And finished
Climb up to the mountain which stands there
And when you have arrived let seedlings be planted at once
Be energetic only for your work
Make your burden
And return again
To go and cultivate
Seedlings which I bundle up there, let them be planted immediately and
    finished.
Wake up for your parents are hungry
Make your shoulder-load to bring it here for your parents
Wake up and go to the woods to work
Light be your eyes for your work
Hasten off and stride back here
We are hungry.
Jump on your enormous stool
To go and grate coconut to make a pudding for us
We are hungry
But there we have become filled
Let the pudding be pounded immediately by you.
I desire food
Make it quickly
Is your oven rapid?
Go and pound quickly
Wrap up some pudding for us to eat
And don't go and do it leisurely
Hurry and make it quickly
Stride away, stride hither
I who am rushing off want food
Prepare it quickly that I may be filled
Let your eyes be light
For a *kurakura* to come and bite of your hook
That a *marau* may come and bite of your hook
That a *totonu* may come and bite of your hook
May a *natara* bite at your line
Let him bite quickly
May a *tokape* bite
In the doings of men
May the fish observe your hook
Light be your line
The doings of men have been enumerated to you

And may you grow up a sea-expert.
The doings of men now are complete in you
Turn your canoe along the reef there
Light be your eyes for the sea-snail
Create an orchard for yourself from the reef.'

It is acknowledged that the babe is too young to understand the exhortation of the Fire addressed to it—the one concerned in this case was actually asleep—but it is held vaguely to influence the child's future conduct, though it is not quite known how. Pa Korokoro said that the Female Deity is present and listens to the speech. But here again he could not say precisely how this affected the situation of the child. It may be noted though that the Female Deity is regarded as being responsible for the moulding of the child in its mother's womb, so that her presence at this ceremony is probably an extension of her creative activity. The formula is, however, of a definitely compulsive order and can be classed as 'magical'. The manner of the address, the imperative character of the phraseology, and the explanatory statements of the people all bear this out. The promotion of welfare in general and particularly of the economic ability of the child is held to be secured to some degree by the recital, in spite of the absence of clear comprehension on the child's part.

What appears to be an anomaly from this point of view is that the recital is delivered only over the first-born male and female children. Yet it is freely acknowledged 'Great is the industry of the last born'. The Tikopia have no direct explanation of why the omission of the formula in such cases produces no ill effects. They stress, however, the point that the ceremony is 'an honouring of the child' (*pereperenga o te memea*), or 'its recitation' (*ona muna*), that is, an address of welcome by the family of the mother's brothers. From this point of view when asked why the ceremony is not performed for junior children, the Tikopia say: 'It has been performed already.' There are several possible functions of this. One seems to be that the ceremony has an inclusive value for the offspring of the woman; performed over the eldest of each sex, it is valid for the whole of the succeeding family. Another is that once offspring of both sexes have been produced the economic needs of the household have been arranged for, and also the continuity of the family line. Moreover, as noted earlier, the importance attached to the ceremony helps to some extent to strengthen the sanctions of marriage.

As in other cases where there are no true brothers of the woman, some other male relatives of appropriate status assume the duties. When Nau Nitini gave birth to a girl the *afi* ceremony was performed by Pa Matatae and Pa Rangifatua. The former went because his paternal grandfather's sister had married into the family of Nukutaungaru, from which Nau Tongatapu, mother of Nau Nitini, came. Pa Rangifatua went because he represented the house of Raromanongi, another branch of the great house of Sao to which the father of Nau Nitini belonged. (The more general implications of this situation are examined later.)

The obligations of *tuatina* do not end with the formula. They spend part of their day in preparing food, and when they come to perform the ceremony they bring with them two baskets. One is called the *tutungauru*; this is food alone. The other is called the *rau koroa*; it is a secondary basket topped by a bark-cloth of the *fakamaru* type. These gifts are presented to the house of the father of the child. The bark-cloth is hung up on a shelf in the house where it stays from three to five days—until the umbilical cord has dropped. It is then taken down and spread out on the floor of the house. 'It is not certain to whom it is spread out; it is said that it is spread to ancestors of the child,' was a statement made by Pae Sao and other good informants. The *rau koroa* is then reciprocated to the house of the mother's brothers together with another bark-cloth. This is termed *te fakaotingauso*, 'the ending of the navel', or *te monongauso*, 'the blocking of the navel'. It has already been mentioned that the *tutungauru* is reciprocated by a portion of food from the oven of the *fanaunga*. In addition a small basket of food is given to the particular *tuatina* who comes to perform the ceremony, and this is not repaid. It is called *te popora te afi* or *te lingilingi o te afi*, both of which are descriptive of the occasion. A *lingilingi* technically speaking is a little mat plaited from coconut leaf, and holding a large plateful of food. Here, however, as is frequent, the term is a deprecatory one used for a much larger basket.

A considerable variety of food is traditionally assembled for such an occasion, At the birth of Nau Taitai's child in 1929, the food taken by her husband's people to Rofaea included green coconuts, breadfruit *masi*, taro pudding, bananas, and taro tubers. A cousin, a brother-in-law, and a neighbour of Pa Taitai all lent him a hand and the total number of workers including women was about a dozen. On this occasion the coconut oil for anointing the women (see above) was taken to Rofaea by Pa Taitai himself. The reason was that the oil of his wife's relatives had gone bad, having been spoilt by evil spirits. As always there is informal co-operation between sections of the people who formally have separate economic obligations. On the other hand there is often petty disagreement between people who are in ceremonial unity — expressed in sharp sayings, picking up of each other's words, and finding fault with each other's way of doing things.

This account of Tikopia post-natal ceremonies has had reference primarily to the situation in 1928–9. In 1952–3 these ceremonies had been much abbreviated, and reduced in essentials to two. One was the *fakamenga* of mother and babe, the laying in mats and bark-cloth, with its accompaniment of the *asinga*, the smearing on of turmeric on one of the father's female kin. (I saw one of these ceremonies in April 1952.) The other was the *kava makiriri*, the basket of food from father's household to household of child's mother's brother, with the corresponding reciprocation. Neither I nor my assistant saw or heard any mention of the *afi*, which must now be rarely if ever performed. And the elaborations of the *fanaunga* had been abandoned. As Pa Motuata said to me, 'When a woman gives birth the *fanaunga* has been given up; the *kava makariri* alone is made—once.'

SOCIAL DEBUT OF THE BABE

About a month after the birth of an eldest boy or girl it is carried to the house of its principal mother's brother, with whom it stays a week or ten days. This begins the *fakaperenga* of the babe, its 'honouring'. The usual exchanges of food take place. First the invitation to the child is implemented by a basket which is carried over to the house of the parents by a messenger of the *tuatina*. This is termed the *fakaoatea*, 'the nooning', though there is no particular connection with midday. The next day a corresponding basket is prepared in the house of the parents and is taken together with the child to the house of the mother's brother. After some days the child's people prepare another basket which is termed *te fakatavanga* and is carried to the house of the mother's brother. On the following day a reciprocal basket is prepared by this man and with it the child is brought back to the house of its parents. If the mother's brother objects to parting with the infant then later further food is prepared by the parent's household, and armed with this they 'seek' their child again. (*Fakatava* is equivalent to the ordinary term *sakiri*, meaning 'to seek'.) The terms *fakaoatea* and *fakatavanga* are generic,[1] being used in connection with marriage, funeral and other ritual. Broadly speaking, they represent the material aspect of invitation and response to a visit.

Shortly after the child returns home it is invited to go and stay with another household, and the same series of food exchanges takes place. Sometimes members of the *kano a paito* of the woman begin first, sometimes those of a man. There is no rule in this. With the babe go its mother and father and sometimes a brother or sister. These visits may go on for months until the child is able to crawl or even walk, and all the close relatives have had it as a guest. Very heavy economic obligations are thus imposed upon its father and immediate paternal kin.[2]

[1] *We, The Tikopia*, 1936, p. 563.
[2] W. H. R. Rivers is incorrect in implying that such visits are made only to the house of the father of the woman. One need not take seriously his suggestion that they indicate an ancient condition of mother-right (*History of Melanesian Society*, 1914, Vol. II, pp. 239–40).

The host need not be of the *kano a paito* of the child, he may be only a friend of the father. A man acts as host to the child of a relative or of a friend entirely on his own initiative. It is regarded as an honour paid to parents and child. But there is a further element involved by the fact that when one household has carried off the eldest child from another it is remembered and the reciprocal service is performed in due time. For example many years ago—perhaps about 1914—Pa Siamano carried off Pureseiroa, the eldest son of Pae Sao. When I was in Tikopia in 1929 a son was born after a long succession of girls to Pa Siamano, and so Pae Sao sent out a return invitation. On this occasion he had two sets of guests since he also invited the child of Pa Nukufuti, his wife's brother, and for a few days he was kept extremely busy making food. If the reciprocal invitation were not issued resentment might be harboured; as a rule, however, the complexity of economic relations with the same people in other directions is sufficient to induce compliance with custom. The Tikopia economic system must be regarded as an integral structure in which conformity to every item is dependent upon the existence of the other items. If each is viewed as an isolated transaction it is impossible to understand the elements of social compulsion involved. Yet breaches in this integral structure do occur and some of their implications are examined in the summary.

Such ceremonies help to draw attention to the child and to secure its position in the social structure by setting in motion around it the organizational machinery of kinship.

Some time after the birth, when the umbilical cord has dropped, the women of the *fare nana* go to the house of the child and there partake of food with the *fare masikitanga*. Food and one piece of bark-cloth are given them to take home. This is *te fakaotingauso*. It is the last of the ceremonies properly belonging to birth.

The care of the young child has been described in some detail in my earlier work. Here I am concerned with the more definite phases of its development.

No ceremony at all is associated with weaning, nor is there any specific term for this process. The Tikopia say simply 'the child has parted from the breast of its mother', using terms for separation or parting as of the strands of a rope. It is said that the child is weaned when it begins to crawl—a period earlier than in many native communities. As far as my observations go this is correct.

The husband resumes intercourse with his wife soon after the child is born, but it is held that the mother should not become pregnant again until her child is walking or crawling at least. If she becomes pregnant too soon then it is said the first child will be afflicted with diarrhœa: 'Its fundament is pressed down, it excretes in a stream.' If it seen that a child does not stand up and walk at the proper time but simply crawls, then it is known that the woman is again pregnant. Here again we have an irrational defence of a rational precaution.

This absence of taboo on intercourse between a woman who has given birth to a child and her husband is not very usual in Polynesia. In Ontong Java a woman who has given birth to her first child is traditionally secluded in her house for six months; during this time her husband returns to his father's house and may not visit his wife until the period of seclusion is ended. A ceremony precedes the resumption of their normal married life and only in the case of the serious illness of the woman is the stringency of the taboo ameliorated to allow her husband to see her.[1]

There is no ceremonial connected with the giving of personal names in Tikopia. A name is bestowed on a child soon after birth but may be changed at any time according to the whim of its parents. The father usually takes the initiative in naming but suggestions are often made by other members of the family, such as the father's sister. But any relative is free to put forward a name.

NOTABLE EVENTS OF INFANCY

The ritual performed around a child can be an extremely complex affair. Not only does it mark a stage in the child's social progress; it may be associated with the rank and prestige of the father and of necessity also with his economic resources. It is only by taking these factors into consideration that one can understand the intricate system of food-making and exchange which operates on such occasions, and the subtleties of the distinctions which the Tikopia draw between types of feast or presentation which to us seem identical in all but name. It would not be correct to regard the child merely as an excuse for parental ostentation; there is the explicit statement of the participants that the object is to honour the infant. Nevertheless, an opportunity is provided for a man to assert his wealth and social position thereby. There is also a religious element in some of these ceremonies, and here too ramification is manifold. The ritual is held to promote the welfare of the child; by reaction it also affects that of the community as a whole.

The ceremonies now to be described are performed only for first-born children and even then infrequently. The controlling factor here is the great amount of food necessary to carry them out in traditional style. To hold such a ceremony with meagre provision would be to invite ridicule. None of these ceremonies occurred during my stay in Tikopia in 1928–9 or 1952, so that the account here presented is at second-hand. It shows, however, how the basic themes are part of a general Tikopia pattern of ceremonial.

[1] H. Ian Hogbin, op. cit., p. 111.

The Pea[1]

For a female child the most important ceremony of this kind is the *pea*. To have been the subject of it is a definite title to rank. 'It is a custom for a child of the land, for a child of chiefs.' If a girl boasts of her social position or behaves as a person of importance she can be reduced to shame by the question: 'You, your feast was made at the *pea*?' Or people will say with a sneer: 'One hears that it is a child of rank, but has its feast been made at the *pea*?' The ceremony takes place before the child is of walking age, while it is still drinking milk from its mother; 'it feeds from the body of its mother, it is being suckled, it is still hung from her breast'.

The *pea* lasts for five days. The procedure is for one man, usually though not invariably a chief, to decide to make the ceremony for his daughter. He is known as the *tau anga*, 'the holder of the feast'. The term *anga* is used for the accumulation and distribution of any very large mass of food; I use the term feast to translate it. That of the *pea* is known as *te na*, or *te fakatakanga*. The base of the latter word is *taka*, 'a maiden', hence it may be described as 'the maiden's ceremony'. Other men who have first-born daughters of appropriate age join in by invitation or perhaps at their own suggestion, with the principal, and assist him in making the feast from the supplies of their own gardens and orchards and those of their relatives. These assistants are usually few. The feast is made only by people who have plenty of food, hence the phrases: *te anga o nga maroro*, 'the feast of the robust', or *te anga o nga mafi*, 'the feast of the industrious', applied to it.

Each day food is prepared. On the first day the major contributions are taken to the house of the principal man. The main oven (*umu lasi*) is made ready. When the food is cooked baskets are filled for each little girl who is taking part. One goes to the *pea*, another to the house of the principal mother's brother of each child. With the food goes the infant, decorated with trochus shell arm-rings, shell beads and other valuables. Sinnet cord and bark-cloth are sent too. At the house of the mother's brother the child is received with ceremony, its ornaments are removed and others are substituted, this stripping and re-clothing a person being a form of exchange much favoured by the Tikopia. The sinnet and other things are reciprocated by pieces of equal value and the basket of food is replaced by another. The child is then carried back with all these things to its father's house. This aspect of the ceremony is known as the *tama pa tonu*, 'the definitely acknowledged child'. It is a confirmation of a social and not of a religious order. 'The idea of doing it is to mark a child of rank.' The feast itself can be described as 'the food portion of the children'. It is said to be made for *manu* (efficacy).

The food of the feast is treated in special ways. In the morning, for

[1] Briefly referred to in my *Primitive Polynesian Economy*, 1939, p. 229.

62

instance, taro are grated into a large bowl which is covered over and carried to the scene. There it is distributed and carried off to make *masi*. Each day the large oven is prepared about midday and in the evening *roi* is made —special food made with sago flour and coconut cream and cooked through the night. This is put in the oven and taken out on the following morning. Then the kava ceremony takes place. The woman who in each generation is known by the title of Nau Ariki, that is the eldest daughter of the Ariki Kafika, presides. She is regarded as a chief for the occasion, 'The *pea* obeys her.' Hers is the kava that is made there and in accordance with custom the kava liquid is prepared in the bowl, but the stem of the plant is not present; that is, the ritual is not of the most intense character. Through the Female Chief the *pea* and its child participants are brought under the ægis of the Female Deity.

The heart of the *pea* from the social point of view is the dance. 'Te Pea' is the name of a piece of ground near the north end of the house Taramoa, and this is the only site for these ceremonies. The name is applied also to the dance. This takes place only during the day-time. It starts in the morning after the kava has been performed, goes on till midday, and then after a pause continues till night. During the pause the midday kava is performed. Each female child in whose honour the *pea* is made is smeared with turmeric and taken to the dance. For four days the women dance alone. No men take part; they are preparing food. The men eat at midday; the women in the evening. The dance of the *pea* is prohibited to married women; only girls and 'broken ears', that is widows, take part. The specific name for the dance of the *pea* is *Fakararo-koka* (this has no connection with the place Rarokoka in Uta).

The songs of the *Fakararokoka* are of a peculiar kind. They are short, with a strong marked rhythm, and more cryptic than dance songs usually are in Tikopia. These characteristics generally imply that a song is an ancient one.[1] The Ariki Kafika and his son gave me a dozen examples, which are given below in full, on account of their traditional character. In commenting on them the chief said: 'Dances of men? Dances of the gods, the origination of the maidens' ceremony. Sacred dances.'

On the evening of the fourth day of the *pea* the men go out and fish, drawing a seine net on the reef. This is termed *fifi vae*, 'laving their feet', or *Sa Runga*, after the spirits of the hills who descend to fish by night.[2] The next morning the women dance as usual.

But in the evening the men go and ornament themselves with aromatic flowers and foliage, and this time they dance, while it is the women

---

[1] For texts and translations, see later. Songs of the *tuaro* type in *Work of the Gods*, 1940, pp. 277–9, may be compared with them.

[2] The same fishing performance takes place as part of the rites of Somosomo in the *Work of the Gods* (1967, pp. 399–401). That of the *Pea* also has definite religious significance.

who are barred from participation. They have merely to sit and watch. The men dance in the style of the *tusoko*, going round in a circle. People of the various clans sit apart from each other, as at the sacred Work of the Gods in Uta; each clan has its own resting place. The dance is in fact a sacred ceremony.

The following morning—the sixth day—each man who has a daughter in the *pea* gets a group of young people to come and eat at his house. No kava is performed on this morning. The principal of the *pea* has allotted these groups as workers to each of his collaborators. All the young people, men and girls, go and *sanga*, that is they work in the cultivations breaking up the ground for planting, putting in taro sets, etc. They go first to the orchard of the principal of the feast and work there; this is termed the *sanga tapu*, and the oven for the occasion is known as the *aso sanga*, the 'day of cultivation'. Taro is planted for all those who have children taking part in the *pea*, and they are reimbursed to some extent for their economic outlay. The remainder of the food from the morning meal is carried to the woods, to the spot in each orchard where the cultivation is to be done, and eaten there. The work goes on all day. Meanwhile the ovens are prepared in each house of the *pea* group. As the working parties come in they each repair to the house of their host, for whom they have been labouring. He for his part has prepared baskets of food proportionate to the number of workers, and also a number of small baskets for immediate consumption. The people eat together, then each member of the party shoulders his basket and goes off to his home. This is the completion of the *pea* and its *sanga*.

According to Pa Tekaumata the conclusion of the *pea* was marked by the transference of the dance from Ravenga to Faea, to Matautu. After it had finished here the Female Chief went to the place where the stone known as *te fatu o a fakasoroanga* stood in the orchard of the Raroakau family in Rotoaia and made obeisance to it. This stone was the emblem of the Female Deity of Kafika. It was uprooted by mission converts and incorporated in the wall of the *fare sul*, the schoolhouse, at Putafe (now known as St Mary) when Christianity came to Faea. This act had a curious effect. Mosquitoes are the beasts of the Female Deity. They are called her *nonono* (the *nono* is a tiny midge-like fly, harmless, which swarms during the monsoon season), and she normally keeps them in quantity shut up in her basket in which every woman keeps her paraphernalia. But when her stone was thus rudely torn out and put to profane use she released these creatures in anger and so nowadays the mosquitoes swarm in clouds in Tikopia. So said my informant—a mission adherent.

A few general observations on the *pea* ceremonies will put them more in perspective. The fundamental elements involved are the honouring of first-born girls, the restriction of this mark of honour to the children of wealthy men, and the translation of wealth into social status. The recreational aspect is also important, and the initiation of the child into the dance. Then there is the religious element: the association of some songs with the Female Deity, the leading part played by her representative, the Female Chief of Kafika, the obeisance to her stone. The ceremony may be regarded then as an ostensible means of associating the daughters of men of rank with spiritual powers of an essentially feminine order, and in reality even more as a means whereby the more prominent men of the community can express their position by massing their resources in bulk and utilizing them to initiate co-operative work and exchange. The work, however, is not a serious item in the communal economy since the *pea* takes place so infrequently. Pae Sao remembered offhand having seen only five *pea*, including those of the sister of Pa Rarovi, a daughter of the former Ariki Kafika, a girl in Fenutapu, and the daughter of Pae Avakofe—all families of rank. This gives a rough average of one such ceremony every seven or eight years.

But not only did I not see any *pea*; in 1952 I heard no mention of *pea*, nor did Spillius, though he discussed with girls of rank the ceremonies they had passed through or expected to pass through. Considering the association of the *pea* with the Female Deity and other pagan concepts, it may now be regarded as virtually abandoned.

Fakararokoka Songs of the *Pea*

Tafito: Koutou fafine taka
    Fakarongorongo pe ai
    Te na e ngarue.

Kupu: Tere fekau ki Fongotaia
    Taia mai se kofe
    Ma sofe soi a nofine
    Sofe maru ko nofine
    Sofe maru ko nofine.

This song refers directly to the *pea*, which is unusual. In olden days bamboo was used as a knife to cut vegetable food such as the *soi*, which is a potato-like fruit growing from an aerial vine. It is used largely in times of food shortage. The word *maru*, 'soft', refers to the fact that the bamboo sliver cuts badly. *Fongotaia* is a cliff at the side of Tumauki, facing towards Faea. The song is:

'You, the maidens
Listen whose is the feast contribution
That is being prepared.

Swift messenger to Fongotaia
Fell me a bamboo
To cut the soi of the wife
Cuts softly does the wife
Cuts softly does the wife.'

Another example refers to the dance and to the splayed out branch of foliage which the dancer sticks in the back of his belt as an ornament.

Tafito: Foti kuvo pui moi Korofou   *Kupu: Isu kena, isu kena*
    Foti kovo pui moi Korofou   *Te manu ata takoto.*
    Fesopoki atu, fesopoki mai
    Fesopoki atu, fesopoki mai.

Korofau is a famous site for the gathering of aromatic foliage for dance ornaments. The second stanza is composed about the *akiaki*, the white tern of the lake which hovers fluttering above the canoe of the traveller. *Ata*, which describes the purity of its plumage, was said to be a term of respect here. There is no apparent connection between the stanzas of this song. The translation is:

'Break the *kava pi* from Korofau   Bright beak, bright beak
Break the *kava pi* from Korofau   The white bird lies sleeping.'
Leap that way, leap this way
Leap that way, leap this way.

Quite a number of these songs refer to ordinary domestic pursuits, simply describing them in rhythmic terms. For example:

Tafito: E amo kifea te kausaro   *Kupu: E oro tue moto tue.*
    Ne oro sokiri moto tue

The translation is:

        'Where is being borne the coconut-grating stool?
        They went to seek a grating edge.'

The *mata* (*moto* in cantonic form) is the serrated edge of the *tue*, the blade of coconut shell (nowadays of iron) which is lashed to the head of the stool as a grater. The second stanza of this song is merely the repetition of words in the first in a non-significant order. It was explained that the mention of the stool referred to the feast in progress, but this is probably merely a gloss.

Another song is composed on a very simple theme.

Tafito: E tui ou korokoro   *Kupu: Fenatu au ma mata ki oi*
    Rangarangaia i korokoro.   *F. tui ona korokoro.*

The translation is:

'Your beads are being strung   I went to look at her
Lift up your shell beads.   Stringing her shell beads.'

Another song of this style is:

Tafito: Te ika akau, te ika futi   'The fish of the reef
    Ka futi futi marie.   The fish haul in
                  Will haul, haul, gently.'

Kupu: Oie! Anuta E!
    Tu moi te vaka moi toi.

Oie! Anuta. E!
The canoe stands in from the sea.'

Of this song it was said: 'It is an ancient song, indeed: we do not know from whom.'
Another is:

Tafito: Nia o te Motuso
    Ke vakaia ke mata E!

Kupu: A motu o te tuo fenua
    Ke rāma e nga paroro.

Translation:
'What is there at Motusa
That people go round to see? E!

Islands in the rear of the land
With torchlight fishing for the *paroro*.'

Motusa is a rocky islet at the northern end of the island at Tufenua sometimes visited by sightseeing parties. The *paroro* is a reef animal, which formerly used to be collected and eaten at Tufenua.
Another song is:

Tafito: E fosa fosa te ufi e roroa
Kupu: Te ufi sorisori kese
    Te ufi sorisori kese.

'Is rooting, roots the yam deeply
The yam given away to others
The yam given away to others.'

There is no explanation of the precise significance of this song—it is said merely to be performed in honour of the yam as it grows its tubers. It may be noted, however, that the yam has sacred affiliations in Tikopia.
Another song concerns the Female Deity who is described as 'the second chief of Kafika', who lives in the heavens, and occupies herself with plaiting pandanus fibre mats, the skilled work of women. Her name, Sina, which is sacred in Tikopia, will be familiar to Polynesian scholars, as that of the moon-goddess. (In Tikopia Sina has no connection with the moon, which is inhabited by a female *atua* named Tangiau.)

Tafito: Ko Sina e nofo i te Rangi
    Ake atu ra i nga tai.

Kupu: Ka Sina ra
    Ka Sina ra
    Ka riaki mai tau raranga.

The translation is:

'Sina dwells in the heavens
She went up there from the shore

Sina there
Sina there
Will throw back the edge of her plaiting.'

Another female deity is mentioned in a different song. It is:

Tafito: Te Tepa ke tu moi
    Marirea ke tu moi

Kupu: Rangi ka sa
    Ka tokai mai.

Translation:

'Te Tepa may stand here   The Heavens will appear
Marirea may stand here   Will peer from their seat.'

Te Tepa has her dwelling in Suakava, in Namo, a traditional site of Tafua. The song was made to her by Nau Fiora, the principal Female Deity of Tafua, who like her is a man-eating *atua*. Marirea may be also the name of a deity, but was said by the Ariki Kafika to be untranslatable—'the speech of the gods alone, an expression which we do not know; there is no indication as to what it refers'. This is a difficulty common to all these *fakararokoka* songs, as to all the most sacred chants of Tikopia: their original frame of reference has dropped from memory, and one has to consider them simply as song units in the present-day ceremonies.

In the original of this song the word which I have given as 'peer' is *tokai*. The action which signifies is that of putting the hands to the ground as one sits cross-legged, and bending over as if to get up. It is thus that *atua* (gods) look down over the rim of the heavens to view the affairs of men—in this case with intent to devour them.

A song of apparently archaic type is the following:

> *Vanu ke vanu ke ao*
> *Vanu ke vanu ke ao*
> *Oia.*

This is quite untranslatable. 'It is not speech; it is a dance of the gods,' said the Ariki Kafika.

The theme of man-eating *atua* occurs in several of these songs. Here is another:

Tafito: Mimiti mai atua revao   *Kupu: Furi ne ta, furi i fora*
   Fakemataku atua revao.   *Nai maua nai kaina*
                                                               Nai maua nai kaina.

Translation:
'Chirrup hither, god of the woods   He has turned to flee, to flee to the
Making afraid, god of the woods.   lowlands
                                                              He is seized, he is eaten
                                                              He is seized, he is eaten.'

This is composed about the *atua revao*, of whom a multitude live in the orchards, making strange noises at times and interfering with mankind. Sometimes they purse their lips and make a chirping sound which draws the attention of men. The song describes the fate of one unhappy individual who listened, and fled too late.

The Fangainga

In addition to the *pea* there is another ceremony which sometimes takes place for an eldest female child. This is known as the *fangainga*, the 'feeding'. It is also a feast, and is associated with the first feeding of the child with fish. Food is planted by the father, and when the girl is two or three years old and the food is ready in the cultivations, it is gathered together. The feast is made on two successive days.

On the first day the food is brought in to the house of the parents, *roi* is made in the evening, and the following morning it is taken out of the oven and carried to the house of the child's mother's brother. Later in the day the major oven is prepared and the food carried there also, together with fish, sugar cane, and ripe bananas. At the house of the principal mother's brother the oven has been prepared also, and the cooked food is reciprocated, but no repayment is made for the bananas, the fish and the other adjuncts. The ripe banana, used elsewhere for certain highly ritual activities, as at Kafika and Somosomo,[1] is deemed an essential element. The following day other valuables are exchanged. The representatives of the mother's family come and carry off the child to their home, taking with her quantities of sinnet, paddles, beads, bonito hooks and shell neck ornaments. They then distribute these articles among themselves, each person claiming what he desires. And according to his choice so will his return present be. Whoever has taken a bonito hook will give back a bonito hook of like quality; who has taken a package of turmeric will return one of equivalent size. These things are taken in a mass to the house of the child's parents, and are there apportioned among the relatives in accordance with the initial contribution of each. Further details of this system of exchange are given in connection with initiation. It is said that the little girl is fed with fish for the first time at the house of the mother's brother; she has been debarred (*fakatapu*) from this food from birth in view of the ceremony.

The affairs described are as of 1928–9. There were no *fangainga* celebrations in 1952–3, nor did we hear mention of them. There is no particular religious reason why they should have been abandoned, but shortage of food barred any such ceremonies then.

The Taumaro

The ceremonies for a boy are not quite parallel to those for a girl, because male initiation is not restricted to the eldest in a family, and the importance of the event tends to eclipse that of any female celebration.[2] But there is one kind of ceremony which does correspond closely to those just described. This is the *taumaro*. The name means literally 'the donning of the waist-cloth', but this latter act is described by a

---

[1] *Work of the Gods*, 1967, pp. 246, 399.
[2] See *We, The Tikopia*, pp. 423, 427.

cognate expression, *taunga maro*, and takes place with very little formality.

The *taumaro* is made only for eldest sons, and like the *pea* originates with some man of rank. He announces that he is going to make a feast for his son, whereupon the heads of other families ask to join him and include their sons in the same occasion. The child is usually about two years old when this takes place, though there is considerable latitude. 'If it is made when the child has turned over merely, it is well; if it is made, however, when the child is big, it is well, when it has dwelt a long time.'

The *taumaro* has as its food basis not the ripe banana but ordinary raw food. Especially, a great amount of taro is accumulated. The kava is made by the appropriate chief on such an occasion. On the first day the large oven which is prepared is known as *te fakataurongo*; the next day it is the *umu lasi*. Together with this is provided the food known as the *kafinga*, 'the invitation', for presentation to the mother's brothers of the child. Each man whose son is included in the ceremony brings in a large quantity of raw taro in bundles. He prepares himself also for the exchange of more durable goods.

An essential feature of the occasion is that the *kafinga*, the 'invitations', shall be presented only to those relatives who took part a couple of years previously in the birth ritual of the child. A Tikopia statement is interesting for its clarity on this point. 'The *taumaro* is based upon the infant. When the infant was born, the group of mother's brothers, their women, came here, came here to "put to sleep" (*fakame*) the woman who gave birth, put her to sleep with valuables and with mats, done as it is for the "kindling of the ovens" (i.e. initiation). So, when the putting to sleep is done, we dwell with the infant, and when it has grown big we decide to make a feast. When it is made the "invitations" are set out exactly for folk who came to "put to sleep", but they are not presented to folk who did not come.'

Here is an explicit recognition of the virtues of service as worthy of reciprocity, however long delayed; it is in essence a credit system.

The mother's brothers come with their womenfolk to the house of the child's parents. The women each bring a *maro*, a bundle composed of a pandanus mat, and some pieces of bark-cloth of ordinary type, topped by a piece dyed with turmeric. This bundle is termed *te fatinga-koroa*, and is presented to the women of the parents' household. In return the food of the *kafinga* is handed over. The act of handing over is described by the word *tārā*. A person may ask, 'Has your *kafinga* been *tara* yet?' 'No, I am waiting for its *fatingakoroa*.'

The women make their exchanges outside the house, while the men sit inside and conduct a corresponding series of transactions. I quote from the description of Pa Vainunu.

'We the men sit around waiting for the child to be brought into the house. When the child is brought it comes with valuables, beads and sinnet, and wooden bowls. They are brought and we, the parental group distribute them. When the distribution is finished each of us goes and fetches his exchange from his house. But he leaves in his house the property which came with the child. The things which are to be sent off in return are measured to be exactly the same.' The man who is doing the distribution in the first place says something as follows: 'You look here at this sinnet, at the valuables of our child which came with him, that they may be exchanged completely. He who may wish for any sinnet coil, call out to me that I may give it to him.' Then any man who wants any particular coil will call out, it will be handed to him, and he will hand over another in exchange, as near as possible a replica of that he has chosen. The endeavour is to match each article that has been received as closely as may be. The accumulated exchange material is then presented in a body to the representatives of the mother's brother's group, who divide it up among those who have contributed in the first place.

The *taumaro* is an affair of two days only.

The accounts here given of these ceremonies for the first born infants are of a skeletal kind, and I am not sure that I have been able to give the exact order of events in all cases. No second-hand account makes really satisfactory evidence. Viewed in the light of other ceremonies which I saw, and have been able to analyse in detail, however, the data just given are seen to fit into the general scheme of Tikopia social structure, with its traditional balance between father's and mother's kin maintained by an elaborate system of reciprocal presentations. The restriction of these ceremonies to the eldest child of either sex can be correlated with the general emphasis which the Tikopia lay upon primogeniture; they represent the induction of leading children of rank into the position of eminence which they will have to fill in later life.

CEREMONIES FOR MOBILE CHILDREN

Under the heading of some experiences of childhood a brief account has already been published elsewhere of certain further ceremonies for children up to adolescence.[1] In 1952–3, these ceremonies were still current and the 'kindling of the ovens' (*pungaumu*) associated with them was still regarded as being an important if not indeed essential custom by the Tikopia. This did not mean that every Tikopia child had to have all such ceremonies performed for him but that the custom was available for such as wished to conform to it—or had the food resources to enable them to do so. During my stay in 1952, owing to shortage of

[1] *We, The Tikopia*, pp. 419–21.

71

food, practically none of these ceremonies took place. Later, however, especially in December 1952 and January 1953, during the stay of my research assistant, when food became rather more plentiful, a number of these personal celebrations took place. The occasions Spillius noted were these: a boy's first torchlight fishing expedition; a boy's first daylight fishing expedition off the reef; a girl's first expedition on to the reef to use a scoop net with her mother or other female relative; a child's first ascent of Tufenua, Korofau, Maunga or Reani.

(Later in the life of a person may come the celebration of his or her first visit to one of the huge, precipitous rocks above the lake shore between Te Roro and Uta, and of the first time a man swims in the dangerous waters off Tufenua.)

Another type of performance occurs sporadically, and is not restricted to children of rank, or the eldest in a family. It consists essentially in the 'laying on of hands' by a chief, with the object of securing the general welfare of the child. It is not necessarily for all children, and there is no specific time for it—the parent usually takes advantage of the presence of the chief at some other ritual occasion.

One case that I saw in 1929 took place in connection with the re-sacralization of a canoe of Pa Motuata, father's brother's son to the Ariki Taumako. During a pause in the ceremonies a child of the house was sent to the chief; it crawled forward and knelt before him. He took down from the rafters a bottle of coconut oil, consecrated to one of his ancestors, poured some of the oil into his right hand, extended the hand, and facing out to the eaves of the house, let the oil drip on to the matting. As he did so he murmured a formula, invoking the ancestor to grant health and welfare to the infant. The libation of oil is the normal procedure on such an occasion; not only does it serve as a vehicle for the spoken words, but it also endows the liquid with the power (*manu*) of the ancestor. The chief then turned round, bent over the child, and rubbed his oiled hand gently round its neck, at the same time reciting a formula, interspersed with soft blowing on the top of its head. 'The power of the chief lies in his hand and in his lips,' the Tikopia say.

The simple ceremony was soon over and the child returned, guarded from illness and misfortune for the time being, according to Tikopia pagan belief. On important religious occasions the chief often performs a variant of this rite for adults as well as children. He ties a pair of *ti* (*Cordyline terminalis*) leaves, smeared with consecrated oil, around the neck of each person who comes to him, accompanying the action with a formula for good-health and well-being. The rite is known as *te pe o te rau ti*, the 'throwing' of the *ti* leaf.

In 1952–3 these rites took place on several occasions, being performed by each of the three pagan chiefs, with children and young people among the participants (Plate III).

In addition to all this, there are the elaborate ceremonies of initiation for boys, described in great detail already elsewhere,[1] on the basis of observations made in 1928-9. No such ceremonies of this kind—the *pungaumu* par excellence—occurred in 1952-3. But this was simply due to lack of food resources. The 'firing of the ovens' was regarded as still essential, by pagan and Christian alike, for the attainment of adult life for every Tikopia male. When Spillius left in 1953 one ceremony to initiate the boys of the chiefly house of Taumako was planned, and the preliminary cultivations had already been put in hand. For girls, the ceremony is not regarded as essential. But it is still treated as a normal event, and Spillius recorded several cases concluded recently.

SOME FURTHER THEORETICAL CONSIDERATIONS

I have discussed most of these observances as ceremonies, not rites. By ceremony I understand an interrelated set of actions with a social referent, and of a formal kind, that is, in which the form of the actions is regarded as being significant or important, though not valid or efficacious in itself. A rite, on the other hand, is also a formal set of actions, but the form in which these are carried out is regarded as having a validity or efficacy in itself, through some special quality which may conveniently be termed of a mystical order, that is, not of the workaday world. Like all definitions, this compressed distinction is not wholly satisfactory.[2] However, granted the distinction between ceremony and rite as theoretical action types, in practice they may merge into or alternate with one another, as with the 'fire' ceremony for the child.

We can now take up and give some answer to the problem posed at the beginning. The central point is how is one to explain the intermitted frequency of these ceremonies? Granted for instance that all the ceremonies for Tikopia children described are part of the socialization process, that is, that they widen the social experience of the child and induct him into new social relations. Granted, too, that some ceremonies may tend to introduce the child to new rules or to reinforce his observations of social rules to which his attention has already been drawn. But it is clear that these functions can only be indirect in the case of the child who is *not* ceremonialized, and nominal in the case of the very young child whose ceremonies are celebrated immediately after birth.

---

[1] *We, The Tikopia*, Ch. XIII.

[2] Cf. Introduction to this volume. Like Monica Wilson ('Nyakyusa Ritual and Symbolism,' *American Anthropologist*, 1954, pp. 228–41) I think that a ceremony may be described as enforced by conventional sanctions, whereas a rite is enforced by mystical sanctions. But I would not make the further distinction, as she does, that ritual means a primarily religious action, that is, an action directed to secure the blessing of some mystical power or powers. Such terms imply an isolation of supernatural entities, a positive activity by them, and specific orientation of human behaviour which appear to limit too much the notion of ritual.

Hence if it be held that the ceremonies have social functions, these must be primarily for the other participants, or for the society at large, and not for the principal. But if the ceremonies are a recognition by society of the birth of a child, why are they irregular or intermitted?

Why are some ceremonies performed only for the first child? Here the explanation must lie in some theory of representative status, whereby the first child serves as an exemplar. One can see why this may be so. If the ceremony has as part of its functions the setting of a seal upon the marriage tie, and the assembly of affinal kin in focus upon the fruits of the union, then it is sufficient for one child, the first, to be celebrated. From then on, the kin co-operative process has other occasions to manifest itself. And while the ceremony makes little sense if really directed to the newborn babe, it makes good sense if it be regarded as an early imputation of responsibility to kinsfolk.

It has been pointed out by Chapple and Coon[1] that initiations and other rites for young people have a symbolic content which 'helps to reinforce the prescribed behaviour through an emotional stimulation'. For ceremonies such as the 'fire' in Tikopia, it is obvious that the child is a passive element, and that the symbolic content though ostensibly directed for his benefit is, in fact, an appeal to other, mainly adult interest. In essence, what is done is to set before the kin verbally the media of instruction for the child in socio-economic behaviour and therefore to impress upon them the need that the child be instructed. From this point of view, what purports to be a technical or 'magical' rite for the child may in reality be a ceremony of moral injunction for the kin. Just as the performance of magic in ordinary economic situations may reinforce technical interest and technical observation, so in social contexts it may be part of a moral education.

Yet it may be argued that the Tikopia are in little need of stimulation to train their children in the work they will have to do. This is evidenced partly by the fact that the 'fire' ceremony is performed not only for first-born, but only for *some* of these children. It may be argued conversely that periodic performance is all that is required to reinforce moral behaviour on adults and that there would be no need to perform the ceremony for several infants. Indeed, too frequent performances might dull the moral lesson. Nevertheless, it would seem that we must look beyond immediate affirmations of the text of the formula to the social context. Recital of the formula gives opportunity for exercise of status privileges both by reciter and prompters, and also allows the group performing the ceremony to plume itself upon its performance. Moreover, it is part of the process whereby the structural elements in the kinship system are given expression. This is not by way of reinforcement of the patrilineage system, but by inter-lineage relations. Moreover, there

[1] *Principles of Anthropology*, 1947, pp. 489, etc.

seems a sound procedure in the choice of a relatively neutral occasion for this demonstration, when no conflict of loyalties is likely to be involved. There are clearly two elements involved here. One is the simple quantity of resources available. If food and other goods are very scarce, the economic aspect of the ceremonial is reduced; if they are very abundant, it is raised. But this is only part of the answer. The ceremonial amounts are not always reduced or raised *correspondingly* to decrease or increase in resources. If food is only a little scarce the ceremony may yet be omitted altogether; if it is extremely abundant, the ceremony may yet take place at only very little above the normal economic amounts. When the Tikopia say that such ceremonies are 'proportionate to the food' (*fakatau ki te kai*) they do not mean that there is an exact measure; they mean only that there is a general relation to the amount of food available, in particular as determining whether the ceremony shall occur at all. In other words, each ceremony has attached to it the idea of an *appropriate* level of celebration. This is not always of the same order; some ceremonies may not fall *below* a certain level, but may rise as much above it as is feasible with the resources at command. One may distinguish two types here, then: ceremonies of regular economic norms; and those of conspicuous economic display, without upper limit.

But we have to account also for the intermittent performance of this and other ceremonies. This might seem to be just a correlate of food resources. Performance of any ceremony must take place alongside others and alongside non-ceremonial wants as a demand upon resources. Such demand is not randomly fixed: it is set up for the most part at conventional level—or more accurately, between certain levels. To the extent that the ceremony, one of conspicuous consumption, is linked with status concepts, as are *tau maro*, or *fangainga*, it is hard for reduction beyond a given level to be accepted; the demand is displaced for the time being, and the ceremony postponed or omitted. On the other hand, to the extent to which the ceremony is fulfilling functions of kin integration, reduction may be accepted to a very low level indeed. This has happened in the case of the *asinga* and *fanaunga* ceremonies, where assembly and linkage of affinal kin around the babe seem more important than status demonstration by persons or groups.

The virtual abandonment of some ceremonies by 1952 raises other issues. Food shortage—amounting almost to famine—was certainly an important factor in blocking the *pungaumu* initiation of boys. It may well have been partly responsible for the fact that we saw no 'fire' ceremonies. But there are other reasons in the latter case. One is the new religious ideology. The performance of the 'fire' ceremony, like that of the *pea*, with its appeal beyond the technical and social sphere to traditional Tikopia spiritual notions, runs counter to the modern temper of most

Tikopia, now strongly influenced by Mission views, even when not actually Christian. There are also competing demands for time, in particular among young men who want to work abroad and not remain at home to cultivate food for ceremonies which they are apt to regard as old-fashioned. Does social integration suffer thereby? Up to a point, perhaps yes, but indirectly. Abandonment or reduction of ceremonies for children may reduce interaction between kin in some ways, but it allows increased opportunities for social interaction in other ways. All Tikopia are kin, of some degree. So abandonment of some ceremonies which involve close affinal kin around a babe gives more time for other ceremonial or non-ceremonial activity of the same or more distant kin. *Specific* integration may suffer somewhat, between particular groups, but *general* integration may gain correspondingly. Moreover, it may be argued that so long as some of the major ceremonies, such as *pungaumu* for boys, are retained, attention can focus on them more strongly, and their social functions be heightened. Certainly, enthusiasm for these initiation ceremonies did not seem to be diminished in Tikopia in 1952-3, nor did inter-group linkage in respect of children seem lessened as compared with 1928-9. The social body is tougher and more flexible than would be guessed from superficial consideration of much 'integration' theory of ceremonies.

Ceremonies in celebration of personal achievement also raise some general questions of interpretation. It is common to regard ceremonies of this type as being 'rites of passage', emphasizing the *transition* of a child from one social stage to another. Moreover, it is sometimes argued that there is a disturbance of the equilibrium of the individual which is righted by his participation in the prescribed ceremonial forms. It may be argued that the ceremonies for Tikopia children represent not the celebration of the arrival at any particular *stage* of their social progress but rather the attainment of a new *type* of social experience. With our incurable taste for metaphor, we often use the figurative notion of a person having 'passed through' an experience. This is associated with the time factor, but it is conceptualized not merely as passage of time but as process of development. If, however, we take first an adaptive conception, we may look on many of these ceremonies as celebrations of *accretion* of social experiences. What is the difference? It is that the person is not conceived as 'going through' anything but as enlarging his social personality by virtue of what he has seen or done. There is development, but not by stages. The experience may take place over·a wide time interval or it may be omitted altogether. If it be truly a developmental stage, then, as with the Tikopia boys' initiation, there is no omission of it for any individual. Moreover, individual equilibrium may be disturbed, as by the necessity to undergo some rather arduous physical labour, possibly even with some risk attached. But the ceremony itself does not have the conventional division into an aspect of separation and an aspect of reintegration. The separation is a physical *non-ceremonial* social act; the integration is a physical *ceremonial* social act. Moreover, it may be held too that the ceremony celebrates the *act* as much as the person. This is not altogether borne out by the fact that it is usually a person's first performance of the act that is ceremonialized. On the other hand, a number of similar performances by adults, such as making a circuit of the island for sight-seeing, are ceremonialized by exchanges of food between friends no matter how often the persons may have participated before.

Hence these ceremonies do not serve primarily as mechanisms of transition, nor do they ease the individual's passing from one state of equilibrium to another. They celebrate his having made the achievement, enlarged his experience, and now being of the company of those who have had the experience. They are marks of maturation of the Tikopia individual. But the flexibility in the time of their celebration and in whether indeed they are performed at all, indicate how, to the Tikopia, many of the social indices of maturation are optional and variable, not part of a fixed unalterable sequence.

In sum, theories dealing with ceremonies for children usually assume that *all* children (of the same sex) 'pass through' the same series, and ignore the theoretical questions posed by any omissions. Can a situation of intermittent frequency of such ceremonies be theoretically explained, as regards effects on the child on the one hand and society on the other? In so far as 'explanation' is possible, that is within the general framework of existing anthropological concepts, this seems feasible, along lines such as these. Such intermitted ceremonies 'make sense' in terms of one or more of the following sets of factors: (*a*) a theory of 'representative status' whereby one child stands as exemplar for others, a surrogate for 'childhood' of the family or even of a wider social group; (*b*) variations in resources, linked with concepts about appropriate levels of ceremonial celebration; (*c*) recognition of inequalities in status—ascribed, as through primogeniture or class affiliation on the one hand or achieved, as through expenditure of wealth on the other; (*d*) social stimulus and dramatic interest, through less frequent performance, heightened economic level of those that do occur, and even uncertainty about the performance.

Inherent in part of this explanation is some notion that rhythm or cycle in social events has positive functions, both for accumulation and disbursement of resources, and for attention of members of the society. But this notion is not clearly worked out, and empirical evidence for it is of uneven quality. In support, however, it may be mentioned that many kinds of ceremony are deemed to have an appropriate *interval* of performance, as well as an appropriate economic *level*. If this interval be exceeded too greatly, the idea may grow that the ceremony has been abandoned in entirety, and this idea in itself is a deterrent to those who might otherwise perform it. From such abandonment the integration of society may suffer, but substitute activities may be adopted, and the net effects are therefore difficult to estimate.

CHAPTER 3

PRIVILEGE CEREMONIES[1]

(1951, 1955)

Privilege ceremonies are an important element in the social organization of many primitive communities. By privilege ceremonial is meant a set of activities carried out in a formal way, the performance being conceded as a social advantage enjoyed as of right by a particular person or group. In conventional anthropological theory, the recognition of the ceremonial performance as a privilege tends to serve as one of the demarcation factors in the group structure of the society: the group which carries out the activity or to which the privileged person belongs is thereby marked out from others, and its exclusiveness is enhanced. This gross functional hypothesis can be refined.

The ceremonial which is the subject of privilege is viewed differently by members of the group concerned and by members of other groups. For the former it is something of their own, and therefore tends to be given a maximum value in their estimation of the weighting of social events. It is in effect an extension of their personality, and is defended and prized as such. To the members of other groups, the privilege ceremonial can be something which challenges their position, debars them from participation in a certain sector of social affairs. Against the attitude of enhancement by the performing group may be set then an attitude of depreciation by the non-performing groups. Some privilege ceremonials consist in the performance of a set of symbolic acts on behalf of the society as a whole. But others involve simply the performance of acts with referent only in the group immediately concerned. To a large extent, such ceremonies are socially dispensable. What then is the sociological basis for their continued existence, for the general social concession that they are affairs of privilege?

The explanation lies, I think, in the value of ceremonial or ritual parallelism in providing social incentives. In a society of multiple kin unit structure, for instance, of clan or lineage type, privilege ceremonials are usually well distributed through the groups. If group X has ceremonial performance a, then it will be found that group Y has ceremonial b and probably group Z has ceremonial c. These ceremonials may not

---

[1] Reprinted from *Oceania*, Vol. XXI, 1951, and Vol. XXVI, 1955, under the title of 'Privilege Ceremonials in Tikopia' and 'A Further Note'.

necessarily have any connection with one another; they may not even be ceremonials of the same order. This in itself is of technical interest. The fact that the ceremonies are disparate and are unconnected can be of social advantage. If they were in hierarchical relation, as may be often the case, then the groups concerned have the superiority-inferiority relation between them stressed. If they are unconnected, however, then each group is at liberty to exalt its one performance, to boast about its special validity or character, without check. A group of low status in ordinary affairs can thus lay claim to special position, unique position, in just one thing, not to be matched by the performance of other groups. In this way, privilege ceremonials can provide a partial escape from submission to the general structural alignment in the society, and can mitigate the strains of a hierarchical order of grouping.

The following account gives some data about a few privilege ceremonials of some kinship units of non-exogamous lineage (ramage) type in Tikopia. It elaborates the hypothesis given above, and also takes up some problems of the organization of such activities.

The account is based mainly on hearsay evidence. Even in traditional times these ceremonies were infrequent. Now that some of the groups primarily concerned have adopted Christianity, several of the ceremonies had been abandoned even before I was in Tikopia in 1928-9. Partly for this reason, and partly because of the mutely symbolic, only half-explained, character of some of the acts in the ceremonies, the impression they conveyed to me was of archaic performances. This is backed up to some extent by the mythological associations of the ceremonies, which stress their antiquity, though the time factor emphasized here is of sociological rather than historical importance.

The essential general features of such ceremonies in Tikopia are: the performance of a formal social act of a periodic kind, concerned with the maturity of an individual or a stage in the progress of an artefact; the accumulation and distribution of a mass of food; and the signalization of individual or group privilege by the enaction of some special measure such as a dance, a song or some other semi-recreational, semi-ritual activity. It is socially convenient for such practices to have a collective name. In Tikopia the name may refer either to some object prominently used in the ceremony, or to a term of some honorific value. Normally, it also specifies the kinship unit concerned.

There are many privilege ceremonials in Tikopia, varying in their incidence and in the importance credited to them. Some have already been described in *The Work of the Gods*.

These are of a seasonal order, and are integrated into a closely knit sequence of operations in which all the major kin units of the community have their functions to perform. Other privilege ceremonials are also seasonal, but fall outside the main ritual cycle. Such are the ceremonials performed by sa Taumako in connection with taro, by sa Fangarere in connection with breadfruit, and by sa Fusi in connection with sago.[1]

Apart from these, there are certain ceremonies performed much more rarely, and related to social progression rather than to the harvest of crops. Three important ceremonials associated with specific kin groups are the *Kura* of sa Marinoa, the *Manongi* of sa Korokoko, and the *Pora* of sa Taumako. I shall describe these here.

These names throw little light on the nature of the ceremonials. The word *kura* has several homophones. One means simply 'over there'; another means a funeral gift from a grandparent to a grandchild who is an important participant in the ceremonies. Yet another signifies a valued object, and it is perhaps with this meaning that it refers to the Marinoa ceremony. The term has no reference to the colour red, which is an association of it elsewhere in Polynesia.[2]

The term *manongi* ordinarily refers to the quality of scentedness, sweet aroma as distinct from the pungency of *kona* objects. It is most commonly applied to leaves which when bruised emit scent. By extension, it also refers to the shrubs bearing such leaves, to leaf and flower decorations worn in the dance (usually, but by no means always, sweet smelling). More metaphorically, it means a sweetheart or lover, a common association of Tikopia love-making being dancing and the wearing of flower decorations. In general, then, the term *manongi* can mean a scented object, one of some special interest. *Pora* seems to be simply a descriptive term, without any particular value significance; it refers to the large taro pudding characteristic of the ceremony.

The interest of these ceremonials is reflected in personal names. The Kura of Marinoa is referred to in the name 'Koramua' given to one of the sons of the elder of Marinoa.

I give a brief account of the *pora* first, since I saw one instance of this, in a minor version. The *pora* on full scale is the first of a series of feasts held by the Ariki Taumako after his accession. Every chief in Tikopia tries over the years to hold a set of feasts, but the outlay in food is great, and few appear to complete the series. Only that of the Ariki Taumako is termed *pora*. The basic food for the feast is taro, which is specially associated with the Taumako chief since it is the material representation of his principal god.[3] Hence no other chief performs a rite of that name, or concentrates the food supply for his feast primarily on taro. The chief of Taumako gets his cultivations and those of his clan well planted up in taro, and then if the crop is good, declares that the *pora* will be made. Members of all the clans assemble, each headed by their own chief. On the first day of the ceremonies the taro is dug (*tokonaki*)

---

[1] Sago ceremonies are described in Chapter 12 of this volume.
[2] Cf. H. W. Williams, *Maori Dictionary, s.v. kura.*
[3] See Chapter 11.

by communal labour. On the second day the *pora* is made. This is an enormous pudding. No wooden bowl is big enough to hold it. Instead, a large mat is plaited from coconut leaf, big fronds being used. This mat is lined with the large leaves of Colocasia and other plants ordinarily used for holding food.[1] The taro is scraped, grated and cooked in an oven, then mashed up on the matting, into a pudding consistency. Coconut cream is mixed with the taro mash first, and then oil, prepared on the spot from coconut cream which has been treated with hot stones. A great amount of oil is used, made from specially selected coconuts. Wooden bowls containing the oil stand round the mat, and some people run to and fro with coconut cups splashing the oil on the pudding while others mash it further with pestles. As they work they get splashed liberally with the oil too. In a description of the *pora* this plenitude of oil is stressed, since it is an index of the richness of the feast. Taro is the bread, oil the butter, so to say, of the occasion. Informants took obvious pleasure in telling how when the *pora* is carried to the clan temple the oil in the pudding is so abundant that it runs down on the ground. After the usual rites of offering to the gods and ancestors, the pudding is shared out among the participants, with special shares for the chiefs and other men of rank.

The *pora* I saw was made in connection with the rebuilding of the oven-house of Resiake, the clan temple of Taumako.[2] This was not a very elaborate affair, the people assembled being members of Taumako clan only. The pudding then made as indicated on coconut leaf matting instead of in the ordinary wooden bowls, was known technically as *te taumafa*—the portion—to distinguish it from the full-scale one. Moreover, it was eaten in the oven-house, not in the larger temple of the clan.

The *Manongi* of sa Korokoro is known alternatively as *Te Ruku*, a name applied also to the *Manongi* of Te Akauroro (see later). This ceremony is marked by the exercise of ritual licence in the collection of food which is cooked for the feast. The crowd of participants with those from Korokoro group as their nucleus, go off to the orchards. One of their number is a man carrying a spear. He points silently to a bunch of bananas, a coconut or some yams, and the crowd go and take what he indicates. They make a raid through a wide range of orchards and gardens in this fashion, taking a little food only from each. This is the custom known as *aru*.[3] The food is taken back to the house of Korokoro, and set by the side of a fireplace, which is guarded by two women, each with a circlet of a variety of Cordyline leaf (*ti mea*) round her neck. Their role will be explained later. The crowd then goes off to net fish,

---

[1] See *We, The Tikopia*, 1936, pp. 437, 550; *Primitive Polynesian Economy*, 1940, pp. 222–30.
[2] See *Primitive Polynesian Economy*, Plates V, VI.
[3] *Primitive Polynesian Economy*, pp. 260–1.

doing this in the ritual manner known as *Sa Runga*.[1] Accompanied still by the man with the spear, the people descend to the shore at Siku on the western side of the island, and work along the reef for some distance netting as they go. As a fish is got, the man with a spear sticks it on his instrument, gives a whoop of acknowledgement, and then hands it over to be strung in the usual way. At the far end of the beach, at a place known as Fakafuevaka, the people come out of the water, and begin to walk down the beach. The men carefully adjust their waist-cloths, for they are going to race in competition—'*Te furi ka ta.*' After a stony part of the beach has been passed the man with the spear calls out suddenly 'Hey! the god has arrived.' On this, the men break into a run, without looking behind, while the man with the spear follows slowly. One man after another drops behind. The first-comer to reach Korokoro goes to a row of fire-plough sticks (*sika afi*), previously laid in readiness, seizes a pair and thrusts them in under the eaves on the *mata paito* side of the house. The sticks are seized and held firm from within the house, and the man, bending vigorously to his work, proceeds to kindle fire. Meanwhile, other racers have arrived also, and each does likewise. The first man to get his fire going gives a whoop of triumph. He has the victory (*maro*). The others stop their efforts. A fire is set going both in *mata paito*, near where the chief of the Tafua clan is sitting, and also outside in the oven guarded by the pair of women. On the latter, the vegetable food and fish that have been collected are set to cook.

While the food cooks, the people begin to dance. As they dance, each man has a branch of leafy twigs in his hands. They circle round the fire tended by the two women, and make motions with the leafy branches as if fanning the flames. As they dance, they sing, as is usual at Tikopia dances. But the songs are special to the ceremony, not to be sung elsewhere. They are extremely simple, as are many of the Tikopia esoteric songs. One is:

Tafito: Aku kái, kai kerekére   *Kupu: Taku sikosikó i Rangi*
       Aku kái se vorusía   *Fakaeva tú i te Rongi.*

Translation:

My food is earthy food   My string figures in the Heavens
My food has not been peeled   Rise and stand in the Heavens.

The first stanza refers to the manner in which the food cooking in the oven is eaten. As the first tubers, bananas, etc., are ready, a cook throws them to the two guardian women, sitting silently by the fire; they peel the food and put it in a basket, which is then presented to the chief. But

[1] Practised especially in connection with the re-carpeting of the temple of Somosomo. See p. 63 *supra*, and *Work of the Gods*, 1967, p. 339.

the remainder of the food, as it is cooked, is simply plucked out of the fire and handed to the dancers. With the earthy skin on, it is bitten by them—and if one end happens not to be cooked, it is thrust back into the fire. This process is repeated until the dance and food are finished. Hence the reference to the food not having been peeled. Literally, *varusia*, in its poetic form of *vorusia*, means not scraped, since a shell or knife is ordinarily used to remove the skin by scraping. This departure from the custom in handing out food with the skin still on emphasizes the esoteric character of the ceremony. The dance is very similar to a more elaborate one performed twice a year at Uta, as part of the seasonal ritual cycle.[1]

The second stanza has a more directly religious reference. String figures, of which the Tikopia know a large number of variants, are particularly associated with the kin unit of Korokoro. It is indeed taboo for people of Korokoro to play string figure games in the temple of that name. It is stated that it has been observed that someone doing so was struck by blindness—a typical sanctional myth.

We are now in a position to explain what to the Tikopia is the essential main-spring of this Korokoro ceremony. It is one of the ways in which the group pays respect to some of its principal deities. In the list of deities worshipped by the elder of Korokoro appears the name Ruaeva. This is one of the titles of the pair of deities known as Pu ma in Kafika, and individually as Tafaki and Karisi. They are the premier gods of Tikopia. The spear used in the collection of food is dedicated to them. It used to hang in pre-Christian days ordinarily outside the *mata paito* of Korokoro temple. There is also a connection with Taumako clan, since the central post of the temple 'belongs' to that clan. The spear—which still was in existence when I was in Tikopia—was carved by Pae Avakofe, one of the senior men of Tuamako. The relation of the ceremony to Pu ma comes out also in regard to string figures. There is no specific tale of the origins of this culture item, but the figures are attributed in a general way as having their basis in Pu ma. Hence the reference to the Heavens in the song, and the reason given for the taboo on playing them in Korokoro temple. They are an attribute of the gods. A second song of the *Ruku* takes up the same theme, of Pu ma:

> *Unufe unufe ngaoro*
> *Ifoifo i te Siku e!*
> *Akeake i Fakafuevoko.*

> Caterpillar, caterpillar, crawl.
> Descend at the Siku, O!
> Ascend at Fakafuevaka.

[1] *Work of the Gods,* 1967, pp. 163, 354.

The reference is to the two localities at either end of the fishing beach. But the caterpillar, harmless as it seems, like other creatures in Tikopia, can be a medium of gods. In fact, it is regarded as representing Pu ma on occasions, being used by them in order to take material form. The reference becomes rather more involved when one considers another song of equally simple type about the caterpillar:

> *Unufe unufe*
> *Ngaororo isea?*
> *Ngaororo i te rau taro.*

> Caterpillar, caterpillar
> Whence are you crawling?
> Crawling from the taro leaf.

This is very natural behaviour. But this song is one chanted over a string figure shape known as *unufe*—caterpillar, and reinforces the association with Pu ma.

Association with other deities is given by the identification of the two women at the fire with Pufine ma, twin female deities of great importance in Korokoro and some other groups. It is relevant also to note that the crowd of people going out to collect food is spoken of as *te kauatua*—the spirit crowd—a term which reinforces the esoteric quality of the ceremony.

The Manongi of Te Akauroro, a rite performed in connection with one of the sacred canoes of Taumako, is part of the Work of the Gods[1] but has a close resemblance to the Manongi of sa Korokoro. The reason, in Tikopia terms, is that the former has separated off from the latter; the same name *Te Ruku* is applied to it. In the structural arrangements of the religious system of deities, the canoe is dedicated primarily to Pu ma in their Korokoro title. Hence a basket of food must be sent to the elder of Korokoro on all ceremonial occasions in which the vessel is concerned; the vessel 'has its base in him'. The procedure is much the same as in the Manongi sa Korokoro. The canoe is taken out of its shed, and people go and collect food, as an *aru*. They go 'with hands only', without knife or other implement. They also go fishing, but no net must be used—the fish must be struck with sticks only. The sacred spear—the 'body' of Pu ma—is taken down and pointed at the fish as the tide ebbs—whereupon they turn and come back to the reef, it is alleged. When the vegetable food and fish are brought back, the same competitive race and kindling of fire takes place as described earlier. The dancing and chanting follows the same pattern. A kava ritual also takes place to make the offerings to the gods.

[1] *Work of the Gods*, Vol. I, p. 83.

The *Kura* of sa Marinoa is of the same general type, with *aru* collection of crops, special fishing, and chanting and dance. But the ceremony has different details, and a specific function not shared by the others. This is the creation of the *fafine ariki* of Marinoa. *Fafine ariki* means literally 'chiefly female'. In Tikopia, succession to the normal office of chief is strictly patrilineal; no woman is ever recorded as having been chief of a clan, and the possibility would be scouted by the people. There is no provision for her to perform the body of ritual required of the holder of such office. But in two clans, Kafika and Tafua, a special status existed for one woman in each generation, and she had powers which though limited resembled those of a chief proper. She acquires her title ordinarily as being the eldest daughter, or sister of the chief, who is of course the senior man of the kin unit giving its name to the clan. Marinoa is a lineage of Kafika clan, and its head is one of the senior officials of the clan, supporting the chief in many ritual performances. Here also there is by custom a 'chiefly female'. The eldest daughter of the elder, when she reaches maturity, becomes the *fafine ariki* of Marinoa. A feast is made, the girl has a circlet of Cordyline placed ritually round her neck by her father, and girls and boys put on flower ornaments. The ceremonial of the *Kura* then takes place.

The *fafine ariki* of Marinoa, I was told, does not marry, neither does she take lovers. 'She lives properly.' And when she gets older, it is the custom for her to swim out to sea and commit suicide. Why? 'Her mind is like this: shall she live thus always? She will stop and grow old, and there will be no son to look after her. So she commits suicide.' The father's sister of one of my main informants took her life in this fashion —afraid of men, as another informant put it. This is the customary method employed by Tikopia women in committing suicide. But as usual with Tikopia explanations, there is an esoteric as well as an exoteric reason given.

'This is the basis of it. When she goes to the world of spirits and dwells there, she will live among the *kau kura*, the assembly who have made the *kura*, she will live as a chief among the spirits. But if she marries, then when she tries to take her seat among the assembly as a chieftainess, she is spurned to one side.' The assembly who have made the *kura* is conceived as a crowd of women who are female chiefs as the result of their ceremonial elevation, and who perpetuate the ceremonies and dignities of the earthly life. Chastity enables a Marinoa woman to keep her place there. The *kura*, it is said, continues to be made in the spirit world, and only people who have participated in it on earth—folk of Marinoa and the children of women from that group—attend it. The prohibition of marriage does not extend to the *fafine ariki* of Kafika, and Tafua chiefly groups: from early times, according to tradition, they have married, and a number of the other groups trace descent from them. But Marinoa is a commoner group, not a member of the chiefly houses, and it may be that the prohibition of marriage is a mark of the extra qualification which has to be held for the status of a 'chiefly female' to be acquired. At the same time, the rule is not absolute; one of my informants pointed out to me that one *fafine ariki* of Marinoa, Angarua by name, married a former chief of Tafua.

It is the belief in its religious associations that gives the *Kura* its social importance. In the *Kura* ceremony, the daughter of the elder has more than mortal dignity. She sits on the mat of Nau Taufiti, and is thus the representative of the goddess. The dance itself is held to have originated with the god Rata and his consort.

Rata, who of course is known in mythic cycles from various other Polynesian areas, is localized by the Tikopia. His embodiment is believed to be in the form of a conch shell in the house Tarafanga. In the night this shell crawls from one end of the house to the other to sleep, so that sometimes it is found at one end, sometimes at the other, irrespective of where it may be put. When conch shells are blown on important social occasions, as on the death of a chief, no one will go and take this shell as a trumpet. If he tried to blow it, his lips would be bitten through, so that on taking them away from the shell he would find them falling off into his hand. Even in the Christian households, such beliefs about the traditional gods are still held. This is only one of the tales about Rata indicative of his status in the religious system. His consort, Nau Taufiti, who is one of the deities worshipped by Marinoa and other groups in Tikopia, is known by the title of Pufine Lasi (Great Grandam), and is much feared. This attribution is brought out very strongly in the songs chanted as accompaniment to the dance. The dance is of a very different type from that of the *Manongi* of Korokoro. It is marked by the fact that the participants are restricted in social relationship—only *tautau laui*, kinsfolk in 'good relationship', may attend it. Mother's brothers and sister's children, men and their *nana taka*, unmarried mother's sisters, and women in similar relationship, and persons analogous in situation,[1] go. Men and women face each other in pairs, and the songs are exchanged between the two parties. 'The men sit on one side and the women on the other. It is so that the men are Rata, and the women are Nau Taufiti.'

Such a manner of representation of the male god by the group of men, and the female goddess by the group of women is a symbolic recognition of sex difference and sex potential. This theme is emphasized and brought home in very specific fashion by the songs that are chanted. They are mainly of the type known as *tauangutu*, taunting, challenging songs exchanged between men and women. In some cases they are quite

---

[1] See *We, The Tikopia*, p. 307, for explanation of this term in full.

definitely sexual in their imagery, in the type of song known as *feuku*.[1]

Such songs may well act as a sexual stimulant. 'When night comes, who knows what happens,' said one informant, discussing this point. Yet, as with the songs of sexual theme in the Work of the Gods, the circumstances in which they are sung are such that they are no mere bawdy recital. Their religious context gives them an aura of respectability.

This is brought out by some of the beliefs held in regard to them. It is said, for instance, as of the songs chanted in the Work of the Gods: 'The *Kura* is sung to be exactly right' ; meaning that no error in the wording of the chant should be allowed to occur. A man who is taking part in the singing must keep his mind on the song. If he does not, and makes a slip, then, it is believed, the gods, who are listening, will be angry and make him lose his memory of the song altogether. Some of the words in the song are not those used in ordinary speech; they are supposed to be part of the speech of spirits. In commenting on this, my informant ejaculated 'What, is it a dance song of men? It is a dance song of the gods!' These songs, he added further, are *tauora, oratanga*. The welfare of the kin group is bound up in them. The *Kura* is no longer performed, but in former times if a man (presumably of the kin group) was ill, and the *Kura* was sung, he recovered. And when my informant had concluded reciting me the songs he said that if Christianity was not in the land, he would go to his home and die that night.

In effect the songs contained the life of his group. Only the fact that he was now a Christian protected him from the results of sacrilege.

I now give the text and translation of the *Kura* songs, as I received them from a member of the Marinoa group.

The *matai* (opening song) of the *Kura* is as follows:

I. *Tafito: Kume Kume-te-ua-to!*
   Kume mai ra
   Kove ke ea Kume.

Safe: Oko mai ra ko Pu E!
   Fai atu ke au E!
   Faia atu ke tofuri.

The second song is:

II. *Tafito: Take tu mou ke pou*
   Take tu moku ke pou
   Na Rata kua mako i mua
   E unu moi.

Safe: E unu moi E!
   E unu moi ko te toa
   E unu moi E!

The succeeding songs are:

III. *Tafito: Ta te muri o te unga E!*
   Te maleva na ku penapena
   Na kua laui.

Safe: Moi tungoro kua mofuri.

[1] See *We, the Tikopia*, pp. 428, 520. Songs of this type in a heavily ritual setting, and regarded as sacrosanct, have been described in *Work of the Gods*, 1967, pp. 336, 345.

IV. *Tafito:* *Tou foi pukamaro* *Safe:* *Kau se saere afangio*
Maro fu ke riro. *Fu e ole.*

V. *Tafito:* *E tuku ra* *Safe:* *E loa ne loa marara*
Ka ke rararara *Ka furifuri marie*
Ka furifuri marie *Maseke au.*
Ka fokotutu.

VI. *Tafito:* *Pakalavalava e tiko* *Safe:* *E tiko i e tiko i te ara*
Taki rei ki te rokou. *Saeo e tangata.*

VII. *Tafito:* *Ko Rata, ko Rata memero.* *Safe:* *Fenua, fenua katoa*
Maunga, maunga katoa.

VIII. *Tafito:* *Fetiri moi soa E!* *Safe:* *Te mimi o nau taka*
O tafi toku laso *Te laso e fuo uri.*
Ka nai rei te laso.

IX. *Tafito:* *Te fafine o te ara* *Safe:* *O! Tolo i te repa.*
Kua nofo
Saraua nga pure ke oti
Saraua tamariki ke oti.

X. *Tafito:* *Toku tuo ngokou* *Safe:* *Toku se kalokalo*
Tukuo moi *Na ke tokino*
Toku manava e oreore. *Kua tasese to.*

XI. *Tafito:* *Te kalokalo o te ara* *Safe:* *E au kove i te ara*
Rakeia moi e fofine. *E atangia moi tou tino.*

My informant, an expert of the *Kura*, said that this completed the series of songs.

I. The initial song of the *Kura* is addressed to a female deity, by name Kume. Owing perhaps to the conversion of the elder of Marinoa to Christianity, the name Kume does not commonly appear in lists of the gods of Tikopia. The man who gave me the songs of the *Kura*, and who was of Marinoa group, said that she was invoked in the ancient kava ritual of the group, but not by the ritual elder latest in office. He described her as 'one whom we obey; our origin; the man-cleansing deity'. He said that she controlled the pool in Tarafare, the Heaven of sa Marinoa in the spirit-world. She is one of the deities responsible for cleansing the spirit of a dead person from mortal taint before it can proceed to take full part in the activities of the after-life. Nau Taufiti, a female deity mentioned earlier lowers the dead man in his spirit semblance into the pool, where Kume resides at the bottom. She seizes the corpse—in its spirit form—devours it, and hands up the *ora*, the soul, to Nau Taufiti, saying, 'Here! Now it's yours; I have finished with it.'

Other people gave more specific identification. They identified Kume with Mafurere, one of the two sisters known as Pufine ma, mentioned earlier as involved in the ceremonies of Korokoro. And the other sister is Nau Taufiti, her proper name being Mafutoka, an alternative name being Rautoro. She is generally agreed to be the wife of Rata, though by some people it is said that he married Kume too. This introductory song is supposed to be chanted by Rata to try and induce Kume to incline to him. It must be emphasized that all the names of these deities are regarded by the Tikopia as of great ritual importance, not to be repeated lightly for fear of spiritual reprisals. Pufine ma in particular, are held to be conveyers of disease and evil. Hence the association of the *Kura* with them is significant of its social value.

The translation of the first song is:

> Kume, Kume of the falling rain
> Kume, come hither.
> Where art thou, Kume?

> Come hither, Ancestor
> Do something to enter, O
> Do something to turn hither.

The ancestor in the second stanza is said to be Fakasautimu, adze-god of Marinoa, who is superior to Rata, and whom he is invoking to give his favour.

II. The second song is the reply of Nau Taufiti to her husband, asking him symbolically not to desert her for someone else. She refers to him as the house-post—the man is the post of the house, Rata is her post—and as a Casuarina tree—a tree in the Heaven Tarafare. The post and the tree are also both symbols of the male organ—'You know the spirit of these taunting songs,' said my informant in comment.

> Stand firm, you post
> Stand for me, you post
> It's Rata who has danced in front
> Following me.

> Following me O
> Following me is the Casuarina tree
> Following me O.

III. The third song carries on the sexual theme, with common Tikopia symbolism. The *unga* is the hermit crab, which has its soft rear protected by a univalve shell. Any simple object with a hole in it is a female symbol. *Ta* ordinarily means to strike, but in this context is used instead of *saki* (knock away) because it is more euphonious in

the song. Knocking away the hermit crab's shell reveals the opening—
or alternatively the soft part of the crab—just as removing the skirt of
a woman reveals her genitalia. This is a song of Rata made to Nau
Taufiti.

> Knock away the rear of the hermit crab O
> The maleness there has been prepared
> And now is finely ready.
>
> Sleep snoring now you have turned over (on your back).

IV. The fourth song is also a song of Rata, jeering in usual *tauangutu*
style: the woman's organ is small like a pink Hernandia berry—let her
hide it away:

> Your *puka* berry
> Conceal it and let it be hidden.
>
> Don't walk with your legs apart
> Conceal that which smells.

V. The fifth song continues in the same strain, accusing the woman of
sexual desire and saying in effect: 'When you feel you want to copulate,
go and scorch it at the fire!'—and don't come to him.

> Take it
> And keep on scorching it
> Turn it over nicely
> And sit with legs apart.
>
> It's long, long (the penis)
> Turn it over nicely,
> Your desiring.

VI. The next song is a reply by Nau Taufiti, likening Rata to a large
spider. This animal is believed by the Tikopia to serve as an occasional
manifestation of the god, and a myth embodies a reference to this. The
song continues to jeer at the sex activities of men, using the word *tiko*
(defecate) as a synonym for ejaculation. and referring to their grasping
of women and defloration of them.

> The spidery one excretes
> Come along with your tree trunk.
>
> Excreting O, excreting in the path (with any woman at all)
> Grasped by men.

VII. This song is also by Nau Taufiti, but rather in complimentary vein. 'Nau Taufiti praises the organ of her husband, and likens it to the crests of the mountains.' She admires its size.

> Rata, Rata is red.

> Lands, all lands
> Mountains, all mountains.

VIII. The following song is by Rata, and is a frank *feuku* inviting the woman to lift up his organ:

> Hasten hither, wife
> And lift up my penis
> There is the penis.

> The vagina of unmarried woman
> The penis is dark.

IX. The next song is also one by Rata, this time mocking as it were at a loose woman, who has collected all the lovers available—not one remains, all have gone to her. Her buttocks are black (with rubbing the ground while in sex congress), and all shame her:

> The woman of the path
> Has stayed there
> Has collected the married men to completion
> Has collected the boys to completion.

> O! Buttocks like the oven-covering.

X. The next song is by Nau Taufiti, and uses a theme of a Tikopia folktale, the extraction of the vagina. In this case it is supposed to be replaced by cannibalistic labia—apparently a reference to a type of *vagina dentata* story. The vagina is taken out by Rata and his wife is afraid he will let it drop as he takes it away on his own organ.

> The lips of my throat
> Leave to me
> My belly is hungry.

> My Erythrina flower
> That you have carried away
> I am afraid you will let fall.

This song has many recondite expressions, said to be the speech of spirits.

XI. This song continues the theme of the last, but from the side of Rata. He adopts the metaphor of the Erythrina flower, which is bright red, to describe his penis, and asks his wife to adorn it. She herself is to go with glowing body in the path. The song here follows no logical sequence, but embodies traditional belief about the goddess.

> The Erythrina of the path
> Ornamented by the woman.
>
> You are coming along the path
> Shining hither is your body.

XII. Another dance song, chanted by Nau Taufiti against her husband, was remembered by my informant while he was commenting on other songs. Its place in the series is uncertain. But it uses the same type of taunting epithets about the sex organ as in the last few songs, so may be considered here. Essentially, the goddess likens her husband's penis to a Cordyline root. This root is carrot-shaped and several feet long, and when cooked in the oven goes very dark in colour. Hence she plays up this colour theme.

Tafito: Tou laso, tou laso o te ti vera	Safe: E uri mai, e uri mai
Tou laso fuo uri.	I ou mua
	E uri pakarai, foi pule uri.
Your penis, your penis of the hot	It looks dark, it looks dark to me
Cordyline root	At your front
Your penis dark fruit.	It is extremely dark, a dark cowry shell.

The sexual element in most of these songs, and the attribution of them to the traditional deities of the Tikopia, inevitably led to their abandonment after the coming of Christianity to Faea, where most of the Marinoa people, including their ritual elder, live. But it was clear that by Christians as well as pagans they were regarded nostalgically, partly for their dramatic and recreational interest, and partly because of the distinction they gave to the kinship group which had the responsibility for initiating them and the associated ceremonies.

Now let us pick up some of the general threads again.

The first point to consider is the variety of elements to be found in these few examples of privilege ceremonials. The people of Taumako make a giant taro pudding dripping with oil; those of Korokoro go raiding the cultivations headed by a man with a spear, have a race along the sands and make a fire by friction; those of Marinoa do some of this and also go in for sexual songs and celebrate the accession of a woman as pseudo-chief. There is a pattern to be found, as between the Korokoro and Marinoa ceremonies. All of them share some common features with ceremonies of other kinds, in the Work of the Gods and elsewhere. But some special feature gives individuality and distinction to each. Like the features in the physiognomy of a person, such items in ceremonial help to create and maintain the individuality of a social group. Tikopia society is highly conscious of the differentiation of its major kin units of lineage type, and these ceremonies are thus to be regarded as pertinent structural features.

The second point is the distribution of these ceremonies. I have not attempted to describe them all. But it is noticeable that the groups which possess such ceremonials are some of the more important ones, in economic and ritual status. Korokoro and Marinoa are two of the highest ranking *paito pure*—houses of ritual elders—in the community. The distribution is by no means complete. By no means every lineage of the community has rights to such ceremonial. But a certain structural balance is provided in that some of the more important commoner groups do. In this way they are given status outside the complex ritual cycle, as independent entities, away from control by the chiefly groups.

A third point is that these ceremonies, though controlled by single groups without need of authorization from others, operate with some reference to community resources and standards. In each case it is the religious sanctions that are the final justification for the ceremonies. I say *are* because while Christianity has been adequate to cause the abandonment of these and other tokens of pagan religion among some of the groups concerned, it was clear when I was in Tikopia that the ancient gods were still firmly believed in by all, and this is probably still so.

Both pagan and Christian Tikopia still share the same attitudes of interest in and acknowledgement of the rights of specific groups to conduct the ceremonies. The standards are common in that the gods invoked in one ceremony are shared by other groups. On the economic side, distraint on crops of the *aru* type calls on community supplies. Hence such a ceremony is not just something peculiar to a group, unique, untouchable; it is in some ways part of the expression of community values, one way of using community resources. This representative function is seen most obviously in the case of the songs of the *Kura* of Marinoa, with their highly sexual content. They may have tended to arouse desire in some of the young people when they were chanted. But it cannot be argued for a moment that the Marinoa people have any kind of prerogative of, or special interest in sex. In my discussions there was never any hint that sex had any specially personal associations for them. The songs fall into line with others chanted on various other occasions of ritual significance. The Marinoa group is the custodian of one set of esoteric symbolic materials on the sex theme, not the licensed practitioners of a sex cult.

A final point is that even before the abandonment of some of them, the incidence of these ceremonies was rare. They were widely separated in time. In their recreational and ritual aspects, no time signal is embodied; they might well be annual events, or seasonal like those of the Work of the Gods. The economic aspect, involving the accumulation of quantities of food, demands some care in organization, and imposes a bar against too frequent celebration.

This is particularly the case when there is general distraint on crops of the community. But the regulating factor in the total complex of elements is in some cases at least a stage in the social progression of an individual. A Taumako chief celebrates his first feast, a Marinoa elder confers status on his daughter. From this angle, the ceremony is focused on timing not as a phase of natural sequence, but as a phase of an individual's appreciation of social situations. A chief, an elder, has to evaluate situations from the point of view of the reputation the celebration will bring to him personally, the state of his resources, the support he is likely to command from his kinsfolk and neighbours, and the alternative demands he envisages. The affair has then not only its structual aspect; it has also an organizational aspect which determines up to a point how it will enter the structural field.

A FURTHER NOTE

In the first part of this chapter I have given some material on Tikopia privilege ceremonials, that is, set activities carried out in a formal way with the performance regarded as a social advantage or possession, enjoyed as of right by a particular descent group. This material was collected on my first expedition to Tikopia in 1928–9. In this part I add some notes from my second expedition in 1952.

Earlier I have stated that some of these privilege ceremonials had been abandoned owing to Christianity. It is relevant then to see how far by 1952 the memory of such ceremonies is still retained and whether any of them are still performed. (It may be noted that a major conversion of Tikopia to Christianity about 1923 or 1924 embraced the whole of Faea and that the new faith had been advancing fairly steadily over the island until in 1952 there were only about 200 pagans out of a population of about 1,750.) People of middle age appear to remember quite well the various privilege ceremonials, and those men who take a leading part in social affairs could describe them in great detail. In particular their specific association with particular lineages (*paito*) was clearly remembered. Moreover, it was recognized that they were not simple social and economic performances, but had a religious basis. Each is addressed to one or more gods of the group concerned.

As one man in his middle fifties, a Christian, said to me, 'The kava of each god is different.' As these different kava rites he specified the 'hot food' (*kai vera*) of Kafika, the *putu* of Tafua, the *pora* of Tuamako and the *epa* of Fangarere.

The *kai vera* of Kafika was still performed and I and Spillius participated in this rite. The *putu* is no longer performed. The *pora* of Tuamako was made in 1929 on a small scale when I was present. I gathered that since then it had been made only once, about 1943, by the new Ariki Taumako soon after his accession. The taro for it was taken from the sacred cultivation (*mara*) Fonga Ravenga. But it may be regarded as still a current ceremonial. The *epa* rite which I also saw in 1929, may be regarded too as still current. My informant said, 'this is the kind of time in which it is performed, at the time of an epidemic. But it is not performed at present because of the famine.' The rite takes five days from the unfolding of the small mat, which is the *epa*, to its folding, and the quantity of food to celebrate this was far beyond the strained resources of the people at that period.

In my former account I referred to three other privilege ceremonials. One was that of sa Fusi in connection with the sago. I heard nothing of this in 1952 and to the best of my belief it has been quite abandoned since there is no longer any ritual elder to initiate the performance.

It is interesting to notice how far knowledge of these ceremonials is held by the younger generation. At my suggestion James Spillius questioned various young men on what they knew of some of these ceremonials, and added to my own records the picture is fairly clear.

Of three young men in their middle or late twenties and all Christians, and two youths, both pagan, there was a fair knowledge of the *pora* of Taumako, but very little of the other ceremonials. As regards the *pora*, the young men and one of the youths all knew of it as a giant taro pudding, but they were in general ignorant of the details of its preparation. One of them, an ardent modernizer and in general against ceremonials involving large amounts of food, still felt that the Ariki Tuamako is justified in having a *pora* though only if food is really abundant. He also felt that it should take place not in Uta, the pagan sacred district, but in the beach village without such associations. But being a member of the Taumako clan, he felt that the performance of such a ceremonial would show the strength of the clan. The youngest boy, although he was the eldest son of the Ariki Taumako, did not remember the *pora* performed by his father less than ten years earlier, and his father said that he had not yet told him about it because he was still only a child.

With one exception none of these men had heard of the *Kura* of Marinoa. The exception was a man of the Marinoa group who knew little about it except that the food was collected by compulsory levy (*aru*) and that the ceremonial had some relation to the singing of

THE ARIKI TAUMAKO (1966)
He is the only chief still wearing his hair long

DWELLING HOUSE 'TARAMOA' (1966)
Formerly the home of Pa Fenuatara, it now contains his grave, marked by a headstone. His son and family still inhabit the house

A CANOE OUTSIDE ITS SHED (1966)
The vessel is covered from the sun by a leaf mat

MODERN MALE DRESS (1966)
Tikopia men wear different types of dress according to resources, occasion and taste. (Pa Nukutapu—p. 222—is on the right)

TYING ON A RITUAL NECKLET (1952)
The Ariki Kafika recites a formula for health and welfare

BY THE GRAVESIDE (1952)
The corpse is wrapped in pandanus mats. Women relatives wear bark-cloth of the deceased round their necks in mourning

A FUNERAL FEAST (1966)
Spreading hot stones in the oven

A BURIAL SERVICE (1952)
Father Ellison and Tikopia by the
graveside

A GRAVE IN THE WOODS (1952)
The new coconut leaf mat shows that it is still
cared for

A FUNERAL FEAST (1966)
The oven is covered with banana and other large leaves for the food to cook

A FUNERAL FEAST (1966)
The oven is opened; vegetables and coconut cream are pounded in a wooden
bowl

A SOURCE OF RUMOUR (1952)
Listening to the radio messages from overseas, the crowd speculates

FOOD FOR A MARRIAGE FEAST (1966)
Traditional food outside a new-style house in Nukufero, a Tikopia colony in the Russell islands

MARRIAGE GIFTS (1966)
Bark-cloth, pandanus mats and calico are carried to the bride's kin, in a
marriage celebration at Nukufero

obscene songs. He thought these were different from ordinary songs but was not certain how.

As the Ariki Taumako and I were discussing the *kura*, his son expressed his surprise; he said, 'Now I hear of it for the first time from your speaking about it.'

The *kura* of sa Marinoa has thus now passed almost into the category of forgotten things.

Even my great friend Pa Fenuatara said he had never seen this Marinoa ceremonial, although he had heard of it. He then sang softly to me two songs which he remembered of the *kura*. It is interesting to compare the text of these with that of the songs I received nearly a quarter of a century before from the ritual elder of Marinoa. Each of the two versions is intelligible, but there is considerable variation in them. This illustrates two things: firstly it shows how fallible is memory as evidence, secondly it shows how variation can so easily in such linguistic matters be accepted as part of a traditional cultural equipment. There was no doubt that should the *kura* ever be revived it will be on Pa Fenuatara that reliance for the text of the songs will primarily be made.

(*a*) *Kume Kume te ua e!*	Kume, Kume of the rain
Moe mai ra koe ia Kume	Hither sleep then you O Kume,
Ko Ma—ko Makupu e!	Oh Ma—Oh Makupu,
Fai atu ke au e!	Get ready to come, O,
Fai au o ke tofuri.	Get ready to turn over.

(*b*) *Takaleva te fetararo,*	Take a grip and rise from the shelf,
Kua sa ki muri o te ungo,	The rear of the hermit crab has appeared,
Takaleva te fetāraro,	Take a grip and rise from the shelf,
Ko te māleva na ku penapena	The maleness there has been prepared
Na kua laui,	And now is finally ready.
Pe tefea ko te uti,	Where is the soft flesh
Ke fakatongisio,	That it may be wailed over,
Moe tungoro kua mofuru.	Sleep snoring in your heavy breathing.

The first song is a variant of the opening song of the *kura* (No. I in the earlier account) and refers to the goddess Kume. Pa Fenuatara said he had only heard of her, and apart from the fact that she was a tutelary of Sa Marinoa he knew no more. But his version introduced another goddess, Makupu, a primary tutelary of Sao, and he interpreted the song as a jesting song (*tauangutu*) bringing in the names of those goddesses as an invitation to sex congress with the god Meteua.

His second song is a variation of song No. III of the earlier account. Though there are some differences in wording the imagery of sexual relations is retained. The 'hermit crab' is a symbol for the penis, and the 'soft flesh' refers first to the marine green snail and secondly to the female genitalia. The last three lines refer to the end of copulation, the detumescence and the snoring sleep which follows. This song was said by Pa Fenuatara to have been composed by Nau Taufiti as a jeering song to Rata—an inversion of the attribution given in the earlier account.

The *manongi* of sa Korokoro was likewise almost unknown to the younger generation, who presumably had been either very young or still unborn when it was last performed. One young man had heard of it, but all that he knew concerning it was the way in which the food was collected. Another had not heard of it but was of the opinion that all such things were pagan practices, wasteful, and had therefore died out.

With the elder men, however, it was different. One ceremony seemed to have taken place since my last visit and there were many men, such as Pa Fenuatara and his junior in age the Ariki Taumako, who had seen this ceremonial and retained it more clearly in memory. The Ariki Taumako had in fact participated in the ceremonial before he succeeded as chief. He said that he bore the spear, and he narrated the various events.[1] He said that the ceremony was performed by the present ritual elder. He emphasized the *aru*—the raiding of the cultivations, which was done without distinction, the orchards of chiefs and of commoners being levied upon indiscriminately. He described the fish drive and said that when he pointed the sacred spear at the shoal of fish they stayed still, just circling round in the reef water and making no attempt to escape. He stated, as in the earlier account, that no nets were allowed, only sharpened sticks with which the fish were stabbed; they were not even clubbed. On this occasion 40–50 fish apiece of all kinds were taken, and a small shark in addition. He described also the competition race (*furi*). He came bearing the sacred spear, people called 'Oh, the god,' and the race began. A large banana stem with fruit on it had been brought and stood by the side of the Korokoro house. The winner of the race tore it down and rushed with it over his shoulder to the feast-pile of food, where the fire sticks were, and began to generate fire by friction. All the members of his clan did likewise with their firesticks. The winner was Pa Rongoifo of Niumano. The spark from the sticks was used to kindle the oven fire and then two women, representing the goddesses Pufine ma, sat down to tend it. The food was eaten 'dirty', people peeled it with their fingers as it came from the oven, it was not prepared beforehand. Then came the dance with hair bound up.

Kava was made in Korokoro by the Ariki Taumako, who recited the invocation over the kava stem, and by the elder of Korokoro who bore the libations. By this period the Ariki Tafua had returned to the Church and did not attend. The Ariki Kafika did attend, though he did not perform any kava ceremonial. This was the function traditionally of the Ariki Taufua and the Ariki Taumako on that occasion.

[1] *Supra*, p. 82.

In my earlier account I did not discuss another of these privilege ceremonials, the *ruku* of sa Sao. This ceremonial had been mentioned to me by Pae Sao in 1928 in his description of the funeral ritual known as the 'fragrant path' (*ara manongi*), which was associated in origin region with Sao. He told me that connected with the rite of the fragrant path was a dance performed over dead members of the house of Sao, and he gave me one of the sacred dance songs. He said that when the elder of the house of Sao died, or his brother, people adorned themselves and performed the dance. Siblings and sisters' children were the performers: children of the dead man were prohibited by their mourning rules. As part of the ceremonial, a fire is kindled, and food roasted at it. 'The fire of the dance which is performed is sacred. The women who cook at it, each is girdled by a new bark-cloth skirt. The women dance too— women and men dance at the same time.' The people go and catch fish, then go and decorate themselves for the dance. And as they dance, they come at will, take fish and bananas from the fire, and return to the dance, eating as they go. This custom, so alien to ordinary Tikopia meal etiquette, is termed Te Afi—the Fire. Pae Sao pointed out that the performance of this ceremonial depended on food supply. 'If food is plentiful, then the dance of the *ara manongi* is performed; but if not, then simply prepare the funeral oven, and carry out the rites, with the *ara manongi*, but no dance is performed, because the food for the fire is lacking.' These procedures have obvious close analogies with the *manongi* of Korokoro and other privilege ceremonials. But no member of the house of Sao died during my earlier stay and I had no opportunity of seeing the dance.

In 1952 an old woman of the house of Sao died. In discussions with Pa Fenuatara about these privilege ceremonials he mentioned that he had seen the *ruku* of Sao performed quite recently at the funeral of Nau Taneanu, a member of their house. (Another performance had also taken place at a funeral in Fenuatai fairly recently.) He said that the *ruku* was danced and that another name for it was Fakafenuatau (Pae Sao had told me that Fakafenuatau was the name of the *Marae*—ritual place—where the *ara manongi* was first made manifest). Pa Fenuatara told me that Pa Nukumata, the son of Pae Sao, a Christian, would have the *ruku* performed if I asked him. He said, 'Tell him "get the things of your house performed, friend, that I may witness them".' When I doubted that it would be possible for the ceremonial to take place, mainly because the man was a Christian and might not wish to annoy his ancient gods, my friend continued to press his point. He said—correctly enough—that being a Christian would not inhibit him. As for the food supplies if the man were to object that he had not enough I should reply to him, 'no food? What's the matter, friend—get them performed for me to see.'

Pa Fenuatara then told me the only song connected with the *ruku* that he knew, and described the events. He said that it was performed on the day of the 'fragrant path' and the songs, of which there were many, were learnt the night before. The fire was kindled and food cooked, roasted as with other sacred ceremonies and not put in the oven. Women tended the fire and were called female chiefs—yet they were women of the commoner house of Sao. In other words they represented female deities. Then after the dance people sat round and there was a distribution of food.

I did speak to the son and he told me that the *ruku* would not be made. This was because of the lack of food. But when I said 'never mind about the food; let's have it anyway' he gave two reasons. The first was that the recent death of a child of the chiefly house of Taumako was a hindrance since there would be impropriety in dancing at such a time. The *ruku* could be performed if the Ariki Taumako, in whose village we were living, would allow it. (The Ariki Taumako when appealed to said that it was all right.) The second objection was that the proper people to perform the dance were the bachelors and young unmarried women, and that they were scarce. There was something in this, since many of the young men were away working on plantations and it was not easy to muster a good dance group. The matter was discussed for a day or two while the funeral of the old woman was proceeding, but without result. Our Tikopia friends suggested that if we offered to supply rice the ceremonial would take place. Or that it could be done by preparing a token amount of food, say a single giant taro (*pulaka, Alocasia* sp.). The reply was that it could not be made with a giant taro since the food must be roasted over the fire and the giant taro cannot be cooked this way. Neither could the rice.

From all this, three points seemed to emerge. The first was that a number of people would have been interested to see the *ruku* performed and were not much concerned with the appurtenances or sanctions. They included Christians as well as pagans, and Christians had participated in recent performances. The second point was that the responsibility for its performance and the decision as to whether it should be performed rested in the last resort solely with the senior member of the house of Sao. The third point was that while he seemed to have no objection to the ceremonial as such being performed, to have it take place with inadequate food supplies and an inadequate dance group did not fit his ideas of what was proper. So although personally very anxious to please me—since his father had been one of my closest friends—he felt that he could not give the word, and the ceremonial did not take place.

On the other hand he was very willing to impart to me all the details he could about the *ruku*, including the text of the songs, though he emphasized their sacredness and their importance.

He began as follows:

'Its basis is the fire, which is kindled by two women working in co-operation. Two umbrella palm leaves are set up.[1] Now when their fire is kindled two portions of food are prepared, a portion for the men and a portion for the women. Then after they have danced and danced they come and sit down to eat. Then the portion of the women is consumed by the women and the portion of the men is consumed by the men. The portions, father (he addressed me as such), are not given by the men to the women, nor are portions of the women handed over to the men (such exchanges are often part of the ceremony). When our group of men give instructions that the dance shall be performed, I, father, give the word as to which shall be the initial song and about the making of the food portions. That is the origin of the dance. The food portion of the women originates in the goddess of this house Pufine i Makupu. The food portion of the men originates in the siblings in Torioro—you know whom. So they are held to be the bachelors and the women are held to be the goddesses.'

After emphasizing the sacred referent of the dance, he made known to me a series of the songs, which I reproduce below. I asked him, 'Do not the Mission teachers object to these songs?' He answered in some surprise, 'No, why should they? Because they know that these are ancient things of this house from of old, the basis of this house—customs which are just the same as the customs of the Church. We don't sit down for a long time to sit and weigh things down in mourning, we sit for a long time, then we ornament ourselves—that is the talk (meaning that this is not a long-drawn-out heathen custom which could irritate the Mission). If anyone were to raise objection someone can say "our performances are based upon our own gods, in our own dwelling places which stand here. Their own dwelling places stand there and they can dwell in them." Or again someone of another group can say about the Sao custom, "It is their own performance from of old. Don't you go and raise objections to it because its basis is from the olden times."' In this and similar utterances the head of the house of Soa expressed his view that antiquity in itself gave a title of respect. To some extent this view seemed to be borne out. At least one Mission teacher was quite keen for the *ruku* to be held. When I said that it was unlikely to be performed because there was no food he asked 'What does he want food portions for? The land is in famine' meaning that they should be prepared to perform the dance alone.

If the dance had been performed a sounding board would have been beaten by the head of the house of Sao as his right. He said that in

[1] Compare *Work of the Gods*, 1967, p. 349.

rhythm it would go like the dance rhythms of Uta. Such is the beating for the dances of the gods—they are beaten like those of the Taomatangi.[1]

I asked him why the name of Ruku. His answer was simple. 'That is the name which was given to it by them, the gods, the name of this dance.'

The songs are as follows:

The first song is termed *te matai o te mako*, the 'leading song' of the dance. I recorded this from four informants on separate occasions—from the Ariki Tafua in 1928, and from Pae Sao in 1929, and then in 1952 from Pa Fenuatara, and from Pa Nukumata, son of Pae Sao. The version of Pae Sao himself was:

Tafito: Ko Rangi e tauinoino
*   Rangi Tokerau*
*   E katoa ko tupua.*
The Heavens are inclined,
The Heavens of the North-west
All the deities assemble there.

Safe: Tou surusuru ki te Rangi
*   Tou mako ki ai?*
*   Ki te Rangi nga Kefu.*
Let us adorn ourselves for the Heavens
For whom do we dance?
For the Heavens of the Blue Spirits.

The other versions have obvious similarities, but in places use slightly different themes, and arrange them in different order. The version given me by the Ariki Tafua was as follows:

Tafito: Ko Rangi e!
*   Tou soro ki te Rangi*
*   Rangi Tokerau*
*   Eva atu ou ki oi.*

Kupu: Ko Rangi e!
*   Tau inoino*
*   I te Rangi tamaroa.*

It is the Heavens, O!
Let us press on to the Heavens
The Northern Heavens
I rise up to them.

It is the Heavens, O!
Lying on a slope
On the Heavens of the young men.

That by Pa Fenuatara given me twenty-three years later, was essentially that of Pae Sao, with the stanzas reversed:

Tafito: Tou sorosoro ki te Rangi
*   Tou mamako ki ai*
*   No ki te Rangi nga Kefu.*

Kupu: Ko Rangi e tauinoino
*   Rangi Tokerau*
*   E katoa ko tupua.*

Finally, the version of Pa Nukumata, given me last of all, was identical with that of his father, save that *surusuru* was replaced by *sorosoro*, and the reduplicate form *mamako*, indicating continuity, replaced the simpler *mako*.[2]

---

[1] *Work of the Gods*, 1967, p. 309.

[2] *Surusuru* in the earlier version may have been due to my own mishearing for *sorosoro*. But I do not think so, since I originally wrote *sukusuku*, having in mind the tailpiece of coconut frond as back ornament. This was corrected by Pae Sao, as I understood, to *surusuru*, meaning a leaf ornament in general.

The variation in the different texts of this song is of interest from several points of view. The first is the role of memory in such a pre-literate field. It is clear from these examples that after a generation, granted some stimulation in between, there was a fairly faithful repro-duction of the earlier text of the song. On the other hand, it was not exact reproduction. Moreover, in the version of the Ariki Tafua at the earlier period differences had already appeared, and it was a matter of chance, largely, that they did not persist. The second point is that the privilege in these ceremonials is not in *knowing* songs and procedures (though unique knowledge is sometimes claimed) but in being able to *initiate* them and *direct* them. The Ariki Tafua was of the same clan as Pae Sao, and his senior, but Pa Fenuatara is of a different clan altogether, and has no rights in the *ruku*. This spreading of knowledge, which is an obvious corollary from public performance, has a valuable sociological function in ensuring that details of procedure will not be overlooked, nor songs forgotten by, say, early demise of the head of the title-owning group before he can enlighten his son. But the potentialities of variation in memory show that there is no automatic transmission possible. In a society such as Tikopia one must always look askance at any claim that an item of knowledge bears the stamp of unchanging tradition. The third point about these songs is that while the versions differ, they do so on a set of common themes. There is a kind of pool of ideas: a Northern Heaven (the clan wind-point); it slopes; the spirits are attracted by it and press towards it; men dance in honour of it. Then there is a secondary theme—a Heaven of Blue Spirits (assuming that this is what nga Kefu means in this context); or a Heaven of Young Men, and this is specified within the Northern Heavens. From the point of view of the singing and dancing, it is not really very important in what order these different themes are 'lifted' (*sau* in Tikopia), nor precisely the words used, provided that they can be easily sung. People prefer to use the 'correct' version, which is usually given authority by a person who is in control—obviously for the *ruku*, the head of the house of Sao—or one who is known for his memory for songs. But the sacred-ness of the songs has to do with the decorum with which they are sung, and not with their precise wording.

This first song of the *ruku*, like the two others that follow, is believed to have been composed by the goddess Makupu, after she instituted the funeral rite of the *ara manongi*. She came and sang the song through the medium of Kainarau, a man of the now extinct house of Sekainga, a branch of Sao. The idea of the song is that it is in honour of the Heaven of the Atua i Tafua, which is situated in the north-west, and which all other deities frequent in deference to its lord. The Heaven is not level, but sloping. In the general quarter of the North-west Heaven is Rangi Torioro, the special abode of the Atua i Sao and Makupu herself. It is a fragrant place, with scented shrubs around, chief being the *mosokoi*, which is especially associated with Sao. Hence the second song, from Pa Nukumata:

Tafito: Tu ofeofe ki te vai
  A manongi o te voi
  A manongi o te voi.

Safe: Rangi otou siei kokona
  Ko Rangi Torioro rakei mosokoi.

Stand drooping by the spring
Perfumes of the spring
Perfumes of the spring.

Your Heavens, indeed are fragrant
Rangi Torioro is adorned with
  mosokoi.

The 'spring' to which reference is made is not to assuage thirst; it is really a 'man-cleansing pool' in which spirits of the dead have their taint of mortality removed from them. This happens, with people of Sao, in the second layer of heavens—there being ten in all. This is referred to in the third song:

Tafito: Tu i Rongituarua
  Na ka ofo tu moi E
  Ka ofo tu kove ka poi o mamata
  pe ki oi.

Safe: Au E ki te vai o tamaroa
  Ke uku ko nau toko ki te ata
  tomoroa.

Stand in the Second-layer Heaven
Now come and stand here.
Come you, stand, and go and look
  at whom?

Come you to the Spring of the
  young men
And let the maiden dive into the
  reflection of the young man.

Among the spirits it is as among ourselves—young women desire young men, and are filled with desire for a beautiful reflection.

The fourth song continues the theme of the fragrance of the Heavens of Sao.

Tafito: Tu (i) ke tau ake rei
  Ki te reirei
  Ke fakaroro ki te Rangi Niumoto.

Safe: A Rangi o tupua siei na kokono
  A Rangi Torioro na kokona ki
  te mosokoi.

Stand up and let's ascend then
To make a necklet
And smear ourselves with oil in
  Rangi Niumata.

Heavens of the Gods, how fragrant
  they are.
Rangi Torioro, its fragrance from
  the *mosokoi.*

Putting on necklets of flowers or leaf sprays, and smearing oneself with (scented) oil are favourite ways of preparing for a dance. Rangi Niumata, like Rangi Torioro, is a special Heaven of Sao. This song, it is held, was composed by Rangirakei, a young man whose mother was a daughter of the house of Sao. After his death—before 1929—the song was made known through a spirit medium, Pa Rangitafuri, who announced himself as the spirit of the dead man, living in Rangi Torioro —and apparently liking the life there!

The following song is also believed to have been composed by the spirit of a dead man, Fakasarakau, and to have been communicated by him in the spirit world to a medium, Pa Rarofutu, as a supplement to the set of traditional dance songs. This was after 1929. These songs show two things: that there is a continuity of interest in the *ruku* among members of the kin group concerned, irrespective of when it is performed; and that its sacred character allows human composition of its songs only through mediation of spirit possession. Realistically, it is the living members of the group who add new material to its song cycle, but the sanctions are such that it can be done only in a state of dissociation.

Tafito: Toia fakafua te moana
Maofa taku fau tamaroa.

Safe: Kua tu toku roto
Kau moeria te moana
Kua toto ririfu.

The sea falls in foam
The young man's head fillet breaks.

My mind is set
To sleep in the ocean
That has become terrifying.

The theme of this song is the death of the composer at sea. Like so many Tikopia young men, he had made up his mind to set out by canoe to dare the terrors of the ocean, and had been lost. The song is both figurative and elliptical. The expression *fakafua*, here translated 'falls in foam', refers to the breaking waves in a storm, and is equivalent to the commoner word *peau*. But it is reminiscent too of another word, *fakafua*, which refers to the evil that spirits do to the health of human beings, and so here there is an analogy already with death in the image of the foaming waves overwhelming the craft. The head fillet of the young man, a decoration for the dance, is symbolic of his life, thus severed.

I did not try to record all the songs of the *ruku*. But I give here one which Pa Rangifuri gave me in 1929, saying that it was an ancient song, and used only for the dance of Sao in connection with the *ara manongi*. It illustrates some of the peculiarities of the Tikopia homes of spirits.

Tafito: E momori tangata ora
Ka momori ki Rangi
Tarifoki na kakaina.

Safe: Arofi moi ko Rangi
Fekaikai ki ei
Ko Rangi kou tinifo
Taki vae tasi
Taki rima tasi
Ka ketu moi.

The living man is conveyed	The Heavens gather around
Is conveyed to the Heavens	And together eat of him
He is brought and will be eaten.	The assemblage of toothed Heavens
	Each with one leg
	Each with one arm
	Come hobbling along.

The 'living man' is the soul of a person recently dead, who is conceived as being devoured by two grim spirits in the Heavens, and recreated in a purified form according to the usual fate of souls. The rather gruesome picture in the second stanza describes what are held to be the inhabitants of one of the Heavens of Sao—a crowd of cannibal spirits, each with one ear, one nostril, one arm, one leg, and termed collectively Te Kau ti-nifo, which can be fairly literally translated 'the assembly in control of teeth'. The song and its ancillary details should probably be regarded as part of the horror embellishments, symbolic of various aggressive impulses, which are found in many mythic systems. Akin to the Rangi Kau ti-nifo and its inhabitants is the Rangi Nga Sape, also under the control of Sa Sao, a Heaven of the club-footed, to which go all the lame and crippled. Lest it be thought that this song of 1929 was merely the product of a single individual's fantasy, it may be noted that in 1952 I was given similar details by Pa Nukumata, who had evidently got them from his father. A Heaven of club-footed spirits is then a standard item.[1]

At the end of our discussion, Pa Nukumata, who it will be remembered was a Christian, said to me: 'I have given you all now and left myself a beggar (literally, a bat); there is not a thing hidden.' By this he meant that he had imparted to me the most secret and sacred knowledge he possessed. I think this was true, especially since most of it was confirmed from other sources, and it fitted into the general framework of Tikopia religion.

This further note on a small sector of Tikopia ceremonial has not only added a little fresh ethnographic data; it has also confirmed the sociological analysis made on the basis of material from a generation earlier. We have here one of the many examples of combination between community advantage and individual advantage—the community gains occasional drama and social embellishment, without the responsibility of decision and organization; the individual gains status from ownership of esoteric material and from control of its use, while the group which he represents gain the same in a secondary form. But the inroads of Christianity on ritual and belief have meant that many young people are now ignorant of past ceremonials. Yet many older Tikopia in 1952

[1] It is possible that the Rangi Nga Kefu of the first song is in the same category. I have translated it literally, and did not get any special significance for it. Pa Nukumata said, 'I don't know what it means, are they spirits?' Then answered himself, 'They are spirits.'

—both Christian and pagan—still attached much importance to traditional practices and the body of ideas associated with them. They were still interested in the special character and dramatic quality of some of these privilege ceremonials, and regarded with respect their specific association with named descent groups and the control over their performance exercised by the representatives of these groups. In their turn these representatives were still proud of and jealous of this control and of the knowledge they bore. Moreover, communal interest and individual control had to meet in provision of resources for the ceremonial, both in food and in personnel.

These privilege ceremonials are a 'survival'. But those of them which have survived have done so not simply because of public interest but also because the competing social pressures have not yet spent their force. In the completely Christian field of Faea there are no such rites nowadays. They could occur in Ravenga with pagans, or with Christians in spheres in which their traditional interests still are active. A limitation to their operation is set by the major religious system which takes charge of subsidiary activities. Again, precedent is extremely important as an element in continuity. The *ruku*, which might have been performed in 1952 had it not been for the shortage of food, may fail of performance when next a member of the house of Sao dies, largely because no performance took place in 1952. In a situation of some uncertainty as to the morality, the expediency and indeed the fashion of ceremonial, any omission on what would otherwise be a structurally appropriate occasion is an important organizational gap affecting future decisions.

CHAPTER 4
BOND FRIENDSHIP[1]

(1936)

In his *Sacraments of Simple Folk* Dr Marett has drawn attention in his usual stimulating manner to the importance of the *covenant* as a form of co-operation in primitive society. He distinguishes it from contract by its voluntary nature; it is an agreement resting on moral obligation. This raises the question as to what can be the basis of such free-will association of individuals.

Much attention has been paid to that form of covenant popularly known as 'blood-brotherhood', which adopts a dramatic means of emphasizing the creation of the tie, and is particularly prevalent in Africa. But in other parts of the world there are less striking forms of covenant between persons to their mutual advantage, which illustrate some aspects of the sociology of co-operation. In Tikopia, a Polynesian island of the Solomons, there is an institutionalized form of friendship which constitutes a life-long bond, reinforced and expressed by reciprocal obligations, mutual trust and periodical exchange of gifts. Two persons so linked are known as *tau soa*, a term which may be translated as 'bond-friends', *tau* being the particle of linkage, and *soa* the ordinary word for friend. The term of address in Tikopia to a person who is not a kinsman, or whose kinship bond is not particularly relevant at the moment is *soa*, strangers and small children are thus spoken to, and a wife also uses this term in reference to her husband, especially after his death; her widow's lament for him is, in fact, called by this name. But the fullest implications of the term are reserved for the institutionalized friendship, and it is easy to discover in a given case what is the connotation. A common linguistic usage aids the distinction. If a man speaks of another as '*tatou soa*', 'our (inclusive) friend', then it is normally a courtesy mode of reference; if, however, he speaks of him as '*toku soa*', 'my friend', then there is probably an institutionalized bond between them.

This regularized form of association takes place between men; I heard of no such bonds being set up between women, and their friendships remain of a comparatively unorganized order. The bond is usually made in the days of bachelordom. The young men are used to going

[1] From *Custom is King: Essays Presented to R. R. Marett on his 70th Birthday*, ed. L. H. Dudley-Buxton, London, 1936.

about in bands, fishing, cultivating and dancing in groups, and as the result of temperamental compatibility demonstrated in these everyday affairs, particularly amicable relations develop between a pair of them. One proposes that they be *soa* and, if the other agrees, the affair is ratified by an exchange of food and other gifts. The ceremonial binding of the friendship is symbolized by chewing betel together. A single areca nut and a single betel leaf are divided by one of the pair, a share handed to the other, and both chew at the same time. This expresses the conventional attitude of bond-friends, who should share their possessions when necessary. '*Soa* eat equally' is the popular saying— one should never let the other go hungry if he himself has food. This initial rite is the *noanoa o te tau soa*, the tying of the bond-friendship. It is not necessarily performed publicly; the presence of other people is immaterial to the rite. Witnesses are not required since the fulfilment of the covenant in concrete ways lies at the discretion of either party, and cannot be enforced by any appeal to external authority.

The tie thus created is reaffirmed from time to time in material fashion. Small presents of tobacco and areca pass from one *soa* to the other, and visits are exchanged between them. One goes to stay in the house of the other, remains for a few days and, on leaving, repays the invitation. 'Friend! I am going on ahead to my dwelling; you follow, that we may sleep there together.' Periodically the friendship is expressed anew in more formal style. Each man prepares food and carries it to the house of the other, care being taken to give food of good quality. 'It is prepared properly, because it is carried to the friend' is the stock comment on this gift. Usually food alone is presented, but a coil of sinnet, a paddle or an ornament may be attached to the basket as an extra mark of appreciation. This piece of property is reciprocated. This exchange takes place in the monsoon season, after the cycle of ceremonies known as the 'Work of the Gods' is performed, and the land is free for dancing and general festivity. Nowadays this falls about Christmas-time, and there is a tendency among the Christian Tikopia, who form about half the population, to equate this bond-friend gift with the giving of Christmas presents, with which idea it fits extremely well. But Christian and heathen alike assert that the custom is an ancient one in Tikopia. The exchange bears the name of *te fakaraunga nga tau soa*. Any man may have several *soa*, so that some days of arduous work are often necessary at this time to enable him to meet the economic responsibilities which the relationship entails. He is recouped, of course, in kind, so that there is no net loss.

The obligations and privileges of bond-friends are not very clearly defined apart from the periodic gift-exchanges, but they are of considerable importance. A *soa* assists his friend in economic affairs when called upon, or even without being summoned, particularly when there are large quantities of food to be prepared for a ceremony. He gives his friend a refuge if he has quarrelled with his family or is in danger of his life. If he learns that his friend is planning to slip away on an overseas voyage he will try and accompany him, at the risk of death on the face of the ocean or in a foreign land—it may be deliberately to seek death with his friend. 'Bond-friends will die in the one grave,' is the popular expression of such attachment. This code of fidelity is by no means adhered to rigidly, but there are many incidents narrated by the Tikopia which show how the tie between bond-friends has expressed itself in individual cases in such ways. These serve also to set the ideal of the bond before the youth of today.

The relationship of the *tau soa* is of particular value to a young unmarried man since it provides him with a confidant in his sexual adventures. The *soa* does not necessarily act as go-between in an intrigue, though he may help in approaching the girl, but he assists in concealing the matter, in throwing other people off the scent. He is asked: 'Was not your friend with a girl last night?' or he hears his friend accused of being in her company. He says: 'Oh, no! He and I slept together·' He denies scandal and laughs at rumour directed against his friend. His privilege it is to be told the secrets and to keep them. 'The *soa* knows and does not tell' is another stock comment passed on the relationship. When one of the pair has married this aspect of the friendship loses its force, and so, as the natives say, the ties 'loosen'; the mutual confidence and assistance remain, but are exercised in less exciting channels. The Tikopia institution has obviously much in common with that of Samoa,[1] though unlike that of the latter community the assistance in sex intrigue is not the primary aspect of the relationship.

In some societies a covenant of friendship between men involves a special bond of linkage by marriage, as between their children. This is not the case in Tikopia, and the existence of such a bond would in fact defeat much of the intent of the relationship, since the system of taboos between affinal kin which is in force would inhibit a great deal of that freedom and confidence which is the basis of the covenant.

The primary function of the institution of bond-friendship in Tikopia is fairly easy to perceive—it provides a man with a confidant outside the immediate kinship circle, one on whom he can rely for aid against all else. A secondary function is that it assists in bridging the gaps created by the sense of solidarity of the members of the major social units; it is one element in the network of personal bonds which tend to mitigate the effects of existing clan and district feuds. With a number of important men of rank the bond of friendship overleaps clan affiliations. Pa Rangifuri of Tafua clan is *tau* soa with Pa Nukuomanu of Kafika on the one hand and with Pa Rangitisa of Taumako on the other; the Ariki

[1] Margaret Mead, *Coming of Age in Samoa*, 1929, pp. 90–1, 97.

Tafua is *tau soa* with Pae Avakofe of Taumako; Pa Fenuatara of Kafika
is *tau soa* with Pa Sukuporu of Tafua. In Tikopia there is no convention
whereby the bond-friend is made an adopted member of the clan, or an
exchange or fusion of identities is simulated. Such a merging of the
two parties would tend to destroy the value of the relationship, which
consists in having one's friend *outside* one's own group, and a separate
entity.

The fact that the attachment is ratified usually during late adolescence
or early manhood indicates perhaps that it fulfils a need for emotional
expression in an extra-familial sphere at a time when psychologically
and socially the individual is not yet ripe for a permanent heterosexual
relationship. In this connection it may be noted that the bond-friend
association is regarded as one of social linkage and implies no sexual
relationship. Homosexual practices do apparently occur at times between
some bond-friends, but are regarded by the community at large with the
same distaste as is expressed for other cases. Ordinarily the meetings
between *soa* are of too casual and public a character to support an
interpretation of definite homosexual arrangements, as a regular
feature. Moreover, the function of the *soa* as a guardian of his friends'
secrets of intrigue with women bears out the non-sexual character of the
relationship.

The linkage between bond-friends is interpreted solemnly, not only
by the partners, but by the society at large. 'Great is the weight of the
bond-friendship in this land,' people say, in a general discussion on the
subject. The obligation to honour the bond is of a moral order, and a
betrayal by a *soa* is condemned as wrong by folk who hear it. But there
is no religious sanction involved, no introduction of the concept of
breach of taboo, no action believed to be taken by spirits or ancestors.

Children as usual imitate the behaviour of their elders, and lads will
designate each other as a 'friend', and make small exchanges apparently
without understanding the full significance of the arrangement. Sometimes there is merely the verbal simulation of the tie. A small boy came
out of an oven-house carrying a double handful of *uso*, the white spongy
interior of a mature coconut, which had been given him to eat. 'Bring it
here! We two are *soa*,' called another boy to him. But the little fellow
guarded his treasure and made no response.

Occasionally, bond-friendship arises in a curious way. This was the
case with Pa Fenuatara and Pa Sukuporu. The latter is much the older
man, and the friendship is of quite recent origin. Pa Sukuporu had set
up a *tapu* sign in his orchard to protect his coconuts from being utilized.
One day he went to the spot, plucked a nut, pierced the eyes and drank
of it. The ghostly father of Pa Fenuatara—not his own father, but
a half-brother of the chief, long dead, from whom he bears his name
—came and stood by the side of Pa Sukuporu, took the coconut and

threw it away. The man plucked another nut and put it over his shoulder to go home. As he went the spirit kept influencing his mind to carry the nut to Pa Fenuatara, its namesake, but the bearer went on to his own house. When he arrived he lay down as if dead. The news was brought to Pa Fenuatara, in Te Roro, by Pa Nukumarere, a well-known medium. Later the same spirit entered into Pa Nukumarere and announced his identity, saying that he wished the two men to be *tau soa*. The message from the spirit-world could not be disregarded, though it was of an unusual kind. Pa Fenuatara came to the house, and Pa Sukuporu revived: hence he owes his recovery to his friend. The bond of friendship was then forged between them by means of presents, and remains firm. There was no other special reason why they should be linked.

These two have composed songs in praise of each other, as the practice sometimes is. That of Pa Fenuatara is:

> I go to my friend O!
> I call in to him on my way
> To the finest of men
> I seek food for you.
>
> It was brought to me in the east-wind season
> I feasted
> Upon your sweets
> I knew of your wealth.
>
> O your aroma, friend,
> Came first to me
> Then I peered over
> Into your basket.
>
> And for our division, friend,
> Of the scrap of betel leaf
> Chewing the morsel equally
> We two.

The first stanza refers to the habit of a man of deviating from his path to call on his friend on the way home, and lauds him. The second and third stanzas commemorate the food presentation of the *fakaraunga*, in which Pa Sukuporu had taken the initiative that season. The 'aroma' is a term of praise for the gift, as also is 'sweets'. The food of the *fakaraunga* is spoken of as *a kara o tau soa*, 'sweets of friendship'. The difficulty of adequate translation is seen in the word 'know', which conveys here also the idea of being sensible of, appreciating, benefiting from as well as ordinary recognition. The last stanza refers to the ceremonial act which first bound the friends together.

The laudatory ode of Pa Sukuporu stresses particularly the high position of his friend, who is the heir of the principal chief of the island.

> My friend is the moon of Ravenga
> The chieftain of men
>
> My friend is a power in the midst of Kafika
> The prime fragrance of my friend
>
> Was plucked for me
> I ate bitter things from other orchards.
>
> Now you are the power in the land
> Excellent man
> Lofty person, my friend.

In this composition Pa Sukuporu obviously remembered that his friend was the heir to chieftainship! Both songs are good examples of the Tikopia style, with its imagery, its compressed manner of expression, and its alterations of the normal verbal forms.

There appears to be a sincere affection between many bond-friends. This finds expression in laments composed by one on the death of the other, and termed *soa*, the same name as for a friend. Said Pa Fenuatara: 'If you are a bachelor, and go and die at sea (a common fate of young men), and I am another, if I am living on shore, then I make a dirge for you, a *soa*.' Most pathetic of these songs is one composed for a lad, Tanuma, who died in the southern islands, by his friend Vakataua (known by the name of 'Ben') who was an old man when I was in Tikopia.

> My paddle from the stern of the canoe
> My paddle from the bow
> Has slipped away
> Buried beneath far skies!
> Now if it had slipped away at sea
> That you might sleep in sweet burial—
>
> The unclasping of our hands
> Friend!
> But to be buried in the earth
> Indeed you have parted from the crew.

The 'paddle' is, of course, the friend: the 'sweet burial' is death at sea, a fate which has overtaken so many a young voyager that it seems the only proper end for an adventurous spirit. This lad died on a foreign shore, and his body was interred there: so he was separated from his companions. Here is the expression of the Viking spirit which animates even the Tikopia of the present day, and makes them most daring and foolhardy sea-rovers.

Strangers are frequently taken as bond-friends. This is done partly from the tradition of caring for the welfare of visitors, partly from the wish to share in any property that the strangers may have brought, and very largely from the desire to become their social impresario, to be clothed in the novelty of their presence, to have first claim upon news which they have of other lands and remarkable phenomena.

According to Pa Rangifuri this privilege is reserved primarily for men of rank. 'When men from foreign skies come here they stay only with the chiefs and the executive officials. No commoner makes a friend for himself.' If a man of no particular position should anticipate a man of rank in this the latter would say to him: 'Why did you make a friend of him? Are you a chief or executive official?' Such statements represent perhaps the view of a man of rank as to what should be the norm rather than the norm itself, but it is true that most arrivals from overseas in recent years have been befriended by men of importance.

The pattern of bond-friendship is one of mutual assistance, but occasionally the trust may be betrayed. An old tale describes a tragedy that occurred between two friends.

Two bond-friends, Pa Fatumaru and Pa Raropuka, who lived in Uta, went to Fongatekoro to net birds. They tied a length of sinnet to a support, and descended to the ledge. When the sport was over they climbed up and went back to Uta. Again they descended, and this time the man of Fatumaru went to a different spot. Pa Raropuka returned, climbed up, untied the rope and went away. When the man of Fatumaru came back the rope had been untied, and he stayed there, with no path on a sheer cliff face. As he stayed he began to suffer from thirst, so he called on the rain to fall, and drank. After he had been there five nights he collected eggs until he had accumulated a quantity by his side. Then Pa Raropuka appeared. But Pa Fatumaru broke the eggs, and averting his face, bathed it in them. Then he lay down. The *nono* (a small black midge-like fly) went to him and clustered on his body. Pa Raropuka came, tied the sinnet cord and descended to him. When he went there the other was stretched out and covered with flies. He thought that he was dead. He left him lying there and went off to snare birds. As he went, Pa Fatumaru arose, climbed the cord and went to the bluff top. Then he untied the cord and went to Uta. And when Pa Raropuka had finished his sport with the birds and returned, he was gone. He sat down to weep. He wailed and wailed, and had to stay there. But Fa Fatumaru went and called on the sun to shine. It shone, Pa Raropuka suffered from thirst, and at last died. When Pa Fatumaru felt that he was dead he went off to the bluff. He observed that the other was dead, and stiff like a tree trunk. Then he went and snared birds. After he had his sport with the birds he returned to Uta. But the bones remained there, in a cave. 'My grandfather saw the bones,' said my informant.

This tale is an indication that bond-friendship was not always proof against other considerations. It was explained that Pa Raropuka had it in mind to possess himself of Fatumaru, the family orchard of his friend, hence his desertion in the first place. 'They of old, bad were their doings,' was the comment. This is in the same strain as the many other struggles for land that seem to have gone on in past Tikopia history.

One final observation of a theoretical order may be made on this institution. A. M. Hocart[1] has expressed the view that covenants such as blood-brotherhood, and, presumably, bond-friendship, are nothing but two-party rituals in which the proper purpose of creation and the pursuit of life and welfare has been replaced by an alliance for commercial or other social purposes. Such a hypothesis of degeneration receives little support from the Tikopia evidence. There is no suggestion by the natives themselves—to whom, as Hocart rightly insists, we should always appeal for an interpretation—that 'fertility' or 'life' is sought by bond-friendship, there is no moiety organization correlated with the institution. There is, on the other hand, the very definite asseveration that practical ends of confidence and assistance are served by it, and it obviously provides a convenient 'cross-bearing' in the society from the obligations of membership in family and clan. To interpret this bond-friendship as merely a specific minimization of a more general form of covenant for the creation of ritual opposites seems to ignore the very real and immediate advantages of a psychological, economic and social kind which an institutionalized friendship provides, and the moral sanction which attaches to the performance of material, non-ritual services.

[1] 'Blood-brotherhood,' *Man*, 1935, 127; 'Covenants,' ibid., 164.

CHAPTER 5

SUICIDE AND RISK-TAKING[1]

(1961)

Ever since Henry Morselli suggested that in the 'so-called voluntary actions' of suicide there could be discerned regularities and uniformities which could be related to social factors, and Emile Durkheim brilliantly demonstrated some of the major relationships,[2] there have been many attempts to correlate suicide behaviour and frequencies with states of society. In the enormous literature that has grown up there have been a number of studies of specific anthropological interest, including the general works of Steinmetz and Wisse, and localized analyses of varying detail, such as those of Voegelin, Fenton, Elwin, Carstairs, and Bohannan —to mention only a few.[3] These studies contain very valuable material, especially on the aetiology and mechanisms of suicide, its distribution, and the social reactions and events connected with it. But while one can accept Durkheim's general thesis about the social determination of suicide rates, there are still some difficulties—which I shall explore in this paper—about aspects of the theory which has been built upon it.

Durkheim's argument, in outline, was that in two types of suicide, anomic suicide and egoistic suicide, the social controls have been weak— in the first type because the individual has become detached from social institutions, and in the second because society itself has left the resolution of his personal affairs to him as a voluntary matter. In a third type, the altruistic suicide, the controls of society have been so ordered as to encourage and virtually dictate the individual's action.

---

[1] From *Psychiatry: Journal for the Study of Interpersonal Processes*, vol. 24, 1961.

[2] Henry Morselli, *Suicide: An Essay on Comparative Moral Statistics;* London, 1881. Emile Durkheim, *Le Suicide: Etude de Sociologie;* Paris, 1897 (translated by John A. Spaulding and George Simpson as *Suicide: A Study in Sociology;* Glencoe, Ill., 1951).

[3] S. R. Steinmetz, 'Suicide Among Primitive Peoples' *Amer. Anthropologist* (1894) 7:53-60. J. Wisse, *Selbstmord u. Todesfürcht bei den Naturvölkern;* Zutphen, 1933. Erminie W. Voegelin, 'Suicide in Northeastern California,' *Amer. Anthropologist* (1937) 39:445–56. William N. Fenton, *Iroquois Suicide: A Study in the Stability of a Culture Pattern;* Washington, D.C., Smithsonian Inst. Bur. of Amer. Ethnology, Bull. No. 128, Anthrop. Papers No. 14, 1941. Verrier Elwin, *Maria Murder and Suicide;* Bombay, 1943. G. M. Carstairs, 'Attitudes to Death and Suicide in an Indian Cultural Setting.' *Internat. J. Social Psychiatry* (1955) 1: Winter, 33–41. Paul Bohannan, editor, *African Homicide and Suicide;* Princeton, 1960. See also Marcel Mauss, 'Sur un Texte de Posidonius, Le Suicide, Contra-prestation Suprême', *Revue Celtique*, Vol. XLII, pp. 324–9, 1925, for a novel type of suicide.

SUICIDE AND STRENGTH OF SOCIAL CONTROLS

One argument that subsequent theory has made is that suicidal behaviour is correlated positively with strength or completeness of social controls. Nadel[1] has argued with respect to the Nuba that where there is less latitude for misfits, the suicidal predisposition is fostered; where individuals deviating by choice or accident from normality are least able to find legitimate alternative ways of living in the group, they must lean most strongly toward ultimate escape by suicide. Straus and Straus,[2] using a comparative case study from Ceylon, hold that in a closely structured society, where reciprocal rights and duties are stressed and enforced, the identity of the individual merges with the group, and altruistic suicide occurs, even for seemingly trivial causes. But in a loosely structured society an offender can be reabsorbed into the family group and the society, or at any rate interpersonal relations are not so rigid that suicide ensues.

I find such propositions superficially plausible but not entirely satisfactory. In effect they fail to utilize some of the distinctions and the flexibility which Durkheim introduced as regards categories of persons concerned, and combinations of suicide types. Nadel regards a correlation between social rigidity and suicide incidence as an 'intrinsic and logical one'. I regard it as a tautology. If by definition suicide is an escape from society and its judgements, and if the society is so rigid that no other avenues of deviance from normality are open, the two variables are already interdependent, and the correlation is spurious. The *behaviour* of suicide is an index of social rigidity, but the *incidence*—that is rate—of suicide is an index of the degree of deviance in the society. With societies of equivalent rigidity in norms of conduct, there may be different degrees of deviance, depending, for example, upon the character of personal goals, variation in the resources available for satisfying them, and so forth. The model for theories of a direct relation between suicide and social rigidity seems to be of a rather simple mechanical kind—society is seen as a kind of vessel with apertures, and with a constant internal level of pressure from deviant behaviour. In the case of the most rigid system, only one aperture is open, and pressure can be reduced only by use of the single outlet—that is, suicide, which therefore has a high rate. In less rigid, more loosely structured systems, there are presumably more apertures, and the rate of outlet through the suicide aperture is correspondingly lower.

I do not think that this simple conceptual model is a travesty, but there are objections to it. The first is that the notion of a social system

[1] S. F. Nadel, *The Nuba;* London, Oxford Univ. Press, 1947; pp. 172–4, 226, 480.
[2] Jacqueline H. Straus and Murray A. Straus, 'Suicide, Homicide and Social Structure in Ceylon', *Amer. J. Sociology* (1953) 58: 461–9.

which is rigid overall, in every particular of judging conduct and repressing deviance, seems unrealistic. Even in societies with a very elaborate and precise moral code, and very full mechanisms for dealing with breaches of the code, there still seem to be avenues for personal expression of deviant tendencies. Some of these may be in the direction of developing evasion techniques, or of the formation of deviationist subgroups, if the society has enough magnitude. Others may be in the direction of more positive outlets, possibly of a sublimatory kind, in the fields of art or religion.

A second objection lies in the type of argument which has been put forward with some cogency by Henry and Short,[1] to the effect that suicide varies *inversely* with the strength of external restraint over behaviour. They point out, as did Morselli and Durkheim, that suicide is often a correlate of less responsibility—for example, of bachelors as against married men, of people of advancing age as against younger people. Even if it be found difficult to accept their general proposition comparatively, there is another alternative. In a society with more permissive, more flexible rules and treatment of deviance (and for brevity I am speaking here as if 'deviance' can be used as a unitary term, despite the differences in kind and degree), suicide incidence may be a semi-independent variable. It is conceivable that for reasons unconnected with the rigidity of social norms, suicide might be a preferred way of dealing with a situation, because of assumed finality. If the character of the problem for an individual be seen not in the rigidity of society but in the very fact of having to cope with existence in society, then, however easygoing the society, the individual may still prefer to escape from it altogether. Moreover, it could be argued that to some types of individuals—for instance, adolescents—it is not the rigor of social norms that is appalling, but the lack of firmness. They may commit suicide because they lack guidance, not because they have too much of it. As Kluckhohn has pointed out, the speculation that adolescent suicide occurs more often where marriage is late and premarital sexual expression is severely punished would be vindicated only if examination of the facts proved a higher rate in the more repressive societies and a lower one in the more permissive.[2] Empirical data may of course bear out the contention that lack of guidance leads to crime or some form of deviance other than suicide; yet though suicide and murder are usually seen in inverse relation, they are to some extent alternatives, as Elwin has mentioned for the Bison-horn Maria.[3]

Again, in a loosely structured society, in which considerable variation of individual behaviour in general is sanctioned, there may be

---

[1] Andrew F. Henry and James F. Short, Jr., *Suicide and Homicide;* Glencoe, Ill., 1954.
[2] Clyde Kluckhohn, *Mirror for Man*; New York, 1949; p. 170.
[3] See Elwin, footnote 2.

118

different views about the propriety of suicide. In one such society suicide may be strongly condemned, or, as among the Zuni or Tallensi,[1] it may be regarded as silly. In another, it may be tolerated, and if not actually praised, may be tacitly approved, as a solution of personal difficulties. As Durkheim argued, the presence or absence of a religious sanction may not appear to affect greatly the actual volume of suicide. But it may be an indicator of the significance of more general social attitudes with more effect.

I put forward these views to indicate that it is logically possible for suicide to vary semi-independently with permissiveness, but I intend to offer later what may be concrete support for this theory. I would argue that the whole question of the incidence of suicide is much more complicated than is indicated by propositions such as I have cited earlier. Analysis is further complicated by one more element—the characterization of 'suicide' itself. Most definitions of suicide refer to the death of a person through his intention to commit the act of self-destruction. Such a definition by intent is necessary for clear theoretical classification. Yet empirically the classification is in a sense *post hoc*. Where death has eventuated through an act initiated by the dead person, intention to self-destruction must be presumed. But where a similar act has been initiated, but for some reason death has not eventuated, there is often a question as to whether the person really intended to destroy himself and was prevented, or was feigning such intent and wished to be prevented. Some deaths classified as suicide were possibly acts which their initiators hoped would be prevented, but through miscalculation or other accident were not. As Weiss has pointed out, attempted suicide is often a different type of action from successful suicide.[2] Such situations are well known—for example, the rate of attempted suicide is much higher for women than men in Western society, though the incidence of actual suicide by men is higher. Involved in the suicide attempt is a distinct element of risk-taking. It is part of my argument that such risk-taking may be built into the structure of ideas about suicide, and may then have a bearing on the sociological interpretation of the volume of suicide.

SUICIDE METHODS IN A 'PRIMITIVE' COMMUNITY

I will illustrate this point of view by data from Tikopia.[3] With less

[1] M. Fortes, *The Web of Kinship Among the Tallensi*; London, 1949; p. 168. But some Tallensi do commit suicide, as from grief at the death of a favourite child; and some may threaten suicide as a means of compulsion (p. 91).

[2] James M. A. Weiss, 'The Gamble With Death in Attempted Suicide,' *Psychiatry* (1957), 20:17-25.

[3] For suicide, see *We, The Tikopia: A Sociological Study of Kinship in Primitive Polynesia*; pp. 473, 536; *Social Change in Tikopia: Re-Study of a Polynesian Community After a Generation*; 1959; pp. 55, 66, 309-10, and *Elements of Social Organization*, 1951, pp. 74-5.

than 2,000 people in all, Tikopia is politically part of the British Solomon Islands Protectorate, but has been so isolated that until very recently little effective administration has been given it and social control has been the responsibility of the local chiefs. The rate of suicide in this community has been relatively high. My figures on incidence relate to the period between 1929, after my first expedition, and the end of 1951, shortly before my second expedition (in March 1952). Though not official, the figures may be taken as fairly accurate, since they were obtained primarily by comparison of the names in my sociological censuses at the two dates, and inquiry as to the cause of death of every person who appeared in the 1929 census but had not survived until 1952. The data on the second expedition were collected and analysed with the help of my colleague, James Spillius. Many of the people concerned had been known by me personally very well, and information about their deaths was obtained not from a questionnaire but as ordinary news, with much descriptive detail. Uncertainty in the classification of a death as suicide is therefore not due to lack of information about manner of death, but to uncertainty as to whether the death was intentional. The special physical circumstances of Tikopia offer, as it were, a wider arc than usual within which the ascription of death as self-destruction or not may swing.

Tikopia attitudes toward suicide are closely connected with their attitudes toward death in general. Summarily stated, these attitudes express regret concerning death rather than fear of it; the Tikopia view death realistically, both as a social and a personal phenomenon. There appears to be much sincere feeling expressed at the loss of close kin, but there is also much mourning of a more formal kind. The absence of the dead person, the social loss, receive ample emphasis: the personal terrors of physical dissolution do not seem to occupy much attention. The transient character of human life is accepted together with the idea of the continuity of the soul, consequently the timing of the moment of cessation of bodily functioning is not necessarily treated as a matter of critical importance. To take one's own life is merely to anticipate the inevitable end. In some circumstances, death has an aesthetic attraction. Judgement is primarily concerned with the circumstances of the death, rather than with the fact that it may have been self-inflicted.[1]

No term in Tikopia is the exact equivalent of 'suicide', but the expression *fakamate* (causing to die) is used reflexively and conveys the idea of devoting oneself to death. The descriptive terms for the various ways of putting an end to one's life are commonly used. Tikopia have sometimes chosen odd ways to commit suicide. About the oddest was

[1] Tikopia attitudes toward death are illustrated in *We, The Tikopia*; pp. 20-1, 287 ff. Attitudes toward homicide are illustrated by a case in *History and Traditions of Tikopia*; 1961; p. 149.

that chosen by Pu Sao, who, having broken wind in a public gathering, in his shame climbed a coconut palm and sat down on the sharp-pointed, hard flower spathe, which pierced his fundament and killed him—a bizarre case of making the punishment fit the crime. But the normal Tikopia ways of committing suicide are three, differentiated broadly according to age and sex; hanging (mainly by middle-aged and elderly people); swimming out to sea (women only, especially young women); putting off to sea by canoe (men only, especially young men). Hanging (*noa ua*, tying the neck) is usually fatal. The person makes a noose in a fishline or other fairly thin cord, ties the other end to a house beam, and then rushes to the end of the house, the violence and tightness of the noose apparently bringing death very quickly. The method is not completely reliable. One man looped a noose around his neck at the top of a coconut palm and leapt off, but the rope broke; he fell, but lived. In swimming out to sea (*kau ki moana*), the women, though good swimmers soon seem to be overcome by heavy seas or by the sharks that are common off the coast, and mortality from such suicide attempts appears frequent. In accounts of Tikopia's past this method is mentioned very often, and the laconic *ne kau* (swam) is often used in discussions of a genealogy, indicating the fate of many unmarried young women.

Resort to either hanging or swimming out to sea may be classed (with a qualification discussed later) as a suicide attempt, since if straightforwardly accomplished without interference the result is death. But resort to putting off to sea in a canoe (*forau*) is more difficult to interpret. The Tikopia term in general indicates a sea voyage, and any canoe voyage from Tikopia is a hazardous undertaking. Tikopia is a mere dot in 40,000 square miles of ocean, with the nearest land, Anuta, equally isolated—only half a mile across and 70 miles away; larger land is more than 100 miles away and in some directions many hundreds of miles. With the alternation of storm and calm, especially in the monsoon season, to try to make a landfall from Tikopia is a great risk. Many would-be voyagers fail, and the chances for survival average considerably less than even. Yet spurred on by the desire to see the outside world, Tikopia men, especially young men, have been ready to take a chance. In many cases it is difficult to separate an attempt to escape from Tikopia to see the world, with a serious chance of not surviving, from an attempt to escape from Tikopia society with an intent to perish or an attitude of not caring whether one perishes or not. All these cases covered by the term *forau* involve a fatalism which is very strange to the Westerner. In effect, judgement of the canoe attempt as a suicide attempt or not is based by the Tikopia primarily on the conditions in which the person puts to sea. Secrecy—often helped by a night departure—at the start of most such voyages is normal, to avoid being stopped not only by sorrowing relatives, but also by the canoe owner, who does not want to lose his property. But if a person puts off alone, in a high sea, after a scene in which he has been enraged or gravely embarrassed, in a tiny canoe ordinarily used for lake traffic, with no sail or provisions, then the interpretation is that he is a probable suicide. If, in contrast, he puts off with other members of a crew, in a quiet sea, with no emotional scenes preceding his departure, in a large seagoing craft, with some sort of sail and provisions, then the interpretation is usually that he has made a deliberate ocean voyage. Yet it is possible for a man to take sail, club, bow and arrows, coconuts and other food, but not intend to use them. When far out at sea—perhaps having been afloat for days—and tired of life, he may overturn his canoe or break it with his club, and go down to death or be devoured by the sharks. The odds against survival, of the individual hothead especially, are so high that it is reasonable to characterize *forau* of this individual type from which young men did not return as 'suicide-risk' or 'suicidal' adventures in the pejorative sense of the term. But even in this connection, there is a qualification, especially in relation to the Tikopia 'rescue service', which will be discussed later.

In discussing Tikopia suicides, I give what seem to be predisposing conditions, but I am not implying thereby that I have provided all the elements for the final understanding of any case. Still, social factors are clearly apparent both in the choice of method and in the attendant circumstances. In suicide at sea, an almost complete sex differential is manifested: a woman swims to her death, a man takes a canoe. Yet Tikopia men in ordinary circumstances swim as well and as freely as do women. Again, by report a curious fastidiousness is sometimes displayed in committing suicide. A person dying by hanging, it is said, excretes freely. If the deed is committed without premeditation, the interior of the house is in a mess: in the person's dying struggles mats and the interior of the house become covered with excrement. People coming to release him are disgusted, and before mourning begins women must clean up the disorder. For this reason, I was told, a person who is thinking of suicide by hanging may refrain from food for a day or so, in order 'that his excrement may not be laughed at'. It may seem to us unnecessary to be so finicky about the manner of dying, yet this has a crude logic. If part of the reason for destroying the body is to preserve the social personality intact—by safeguarding it from disintegrating despair or shame—then the person does not want his reputation to suffer by his death. Suicide in Tikopia is thought to merit a certain dignity.

The physical details as such of the suicide do not seem to worry the Tikopia. For a suicide at sea, the common fate is often discussed thus: 'The death of a woman, to be eaten by sharks; when a man voyages out in a canoe, he goes on and on, his canoe overturns, he too is eaten by sharks.' The details may be quite horrible to Westerners, but the Tikopia face them in a matter-of-fact way.

Attitudes Toward Suicides

The Tikopia attitude towards suicide of others is in general one of mild disapprobation. Among pagan Tikopia in 1952, according to information given by Pa Fenuatara, there was some religious sanction for this opinion. The gods dislike a man to kill himself by hanging, because their function is to take the soul at death, and a sudden death gives them no time for preparation. If a man commits suicide, his soul goes off and wanders about, and its ancestral spirits in the heavens must search for it to bring it safely to its spirit home. But if a man commits suicide by going off to sea in a canoe, or a woman by swimming out to sea, the result is 'a splendid death', a 'sweet death', to which the spirits do not object, and from which they can catch up the soul of the dead person. When the canoe of a man is engulfed at sea, he cries out to the spirits of his mother's lineage, who come and bear off his soul. The same is true for women, but in some groups there are special privileges. The Ariki Kafika—the chief—told me that when the women of his lineage swim out to sea they are clasped in the arms of their Female Deity, who pulls them down. They drown but are not eaten by sharks, while the goddess takes their souls. Similarly, the women of the allied lineage of Porima are protected by their Deity of the Woods, who spits in the eyes of the sharks.

Among Christian Tikopia in 1952 the orthodox view was that the soul of a suicide does not go to paradise, but to Satan. The Bible says it is wrong for a man to die this way, and the Church is opposed to the practice. But the common view seemed much more tolerant. Spillius was told that if a man commits suicide, the priest should make the proper prayers at the altar to ensure that the soul goes to Heaven, but the families of suicides in fact seemed to go to little trouble to see that this was done. As Pa Raroifi said, the special prayers and services of the priest would cost the family a mat as a gift to the priest, and once the body of the man was in the ground people did not worry about him unless his ghost started to walk.[1] I myself have no record of any such special prayers.

In common with its condemnation of suicide, the Church also condemned the *forau sora*, the secret voyage, holding that if a man wishes to undertake an overseas voyage he should wait for the Mission vessel or some other powered craft. The souls of people belong to God, and they should await the will of the Lord in respect to their time to die. Hence the more pious Christians held that the *forau* custom should be abandoned. Yet it is significant that the incidence of *forau* seemed to be much

[1] See Chapter 15.

the same among Christian and pagan young men, and that among those who took canoes secretly in this way were two sons of the Mission priest, one of whom was lost at sea. In other words, the compulsive character of competitive adventure among the young men seemed to override all Christian teaching. The sanctions of the Church had not yet been effectively internalized and integrated into the personality.

By 1952 no effective political sanction had been imposed on Tikopia canoe voyaging. But since at various times these voyages have given much trouble to the administration in searching for lost men and re-patriating survivors, it is likely that before long some hindrances may be placed in the way of Tikopia risk-voyaging, and going off in a canoe may be declared an offence. Unless alternative outlets are provided at the same time, however, it may be very difficult to implement such a control.

In general, then, the Tikopia viewed suicide as no crime, and the Church's doctrine that suicide was a sin was not influential enough to inhibit many Tikopia from risking their lives and some from deli-berately sacrificing them. The disapprobation of suicide and the strenuous efforts to save those who had attempted it were based on social more than on religious reasons:

Suicide Rates

To consider Tikopia suicide rates more closely I give in the accom-panying table the deaths between 1929 and 1951 from the three main methods as closely as could be ascertained by years:

TIKOPIA SUICIDES* AND POSSIBLY SUICIDAL VOYAGES, 1929–1951

Year			Suicides According to Method		
			Hanging	Swimming to Sea	Canoe-Voyaging
Unclassified	...	...	3	1	26
1929–42	...	...	...	0	0	7
1943	...	...	...	0	0	6
1944	...	...	...	0	1	10
1945	...	...	...	0	0	2
1946	...	...	...	0	0	1
1947	...	...	...	0	3	6
1948	...	...	...	0	0	11
1949	...	...	...	0	0	8
1950	...	...	...	1	7	4
1951	...	...	...	2	0	0
Total	...	...	...	6	12	81

* Occasional suicides by odd methods are not included in this table.

Disregarding for the time being the deaths from canoe-voyaging, and considering only the indubitable suicides from hanging and swimming out to sea, for a mean population of 1,500, over a period of 23 years, the annual rate of suicide was 0·8 persons, or for comparative purposes, 53 suicides per 100,000 population. Even if in a mass suicide of six girls in 1950 by swimming out to sea, only the principal girl be counted (and her followers be put down to misadventure), the rate would still be about 37 suicides per annum per 100,000 population, which is considerably higher than that for most Western countries, where the yearly rate is between about 10 and 30 per 100,000 population.[1]

Now consider the deaths from sea-voyaging. The loss of 81 persons in 23 years includes three females who accompanied their male kin, either on an ordinary voyage overseas, or as part of a crew in a searching fleet, and at least five persons who died from exhaustion or other illness after landing on a foreign island. But the majority of those who perished must have set out under conditions so hazardous that their prospects of survival were slight, and their fear of self-destruction small. Since the Tikopia keep no precise annual records, a breakdown of the figures by years was not exact. But at least 30, and probably considerably more, were in the five years 1944–48, when the new experiences of the war had stimulated a high level of interest in overseas adventure. Despite their intense, almost obsessive interest in the novel, scarce goods of the Western world, the Tikopia did not develop a millenarian movement of the kind known as a 'cargo cult',[2] in which fantastic preparations were made to receive an expected bounty from heaven. A combination of reasons was probably responsible, but it may have been partly because of the outlet for their craving presented by the possibility of a voyage overseas. They could go to meet the millenium; they did not have to wait passively for it to arrive. In this connection it is significant that of the 55 persons whose loss could be dated with reasonable accuracy, about 40 were probably under 30 years of age when they died, In such young men the lust for adventure was greatest. But they tended also to be the more easily emotionally disturbed. From evidence about the nature of the flight and the preceding circumstances, it is clear that probably at least a dozen of these *forau* were deliberate suicidal attempts, and that the rate of effective suicide should perhaps be put at between 60 and 70 persons per annum per 100,000 population.

Types of Suicidal Situations

I have no systematic material of a quantitative kind on the causes of suicide in Tikopia, mainly because in many cases, often long after the

[1] For example: England and Wales, 10·6 (1947); United States, 11·5 (1946); Sweden, 15·0 (1930); Switzerland, 26·1 (1930); Austria, 39·9 (1930). From Straus and Straus, footnote 4; p. 462.

[2] See Chapter 6.

event, it was not possible to get from the surviving kin any very clear-cut statement of all the reasons which led a person to self-destruction. It was evident, for instance, that many young men put off to sea following some degree of emotional disturbance, but the relatives and friends were not always sure exactly what the circumstances were leading up to this, and it was often impossible for me to discern how much shame, resentment, and frustration were intermingled. But the major types of situations apparently involved in suicide can be indicated, with ostensible cause.

One type of suicidal situation is that involving loss of spouse or other close relative. Pa Mukava, youngest son of the Ariki Tafua of 1929, some years after my first visit committed suicide on the death of his wife. 'He killed himself for his wife; he hanged himself. When she died, he wailed and wailed that day, his grief was great; then he went to hang himself—on the same day.' A similar case was that of Pa Nukusoro-kiraro; his wife died and he hanged himself on the same day. In 1929 I was told how one of my friends had earlier tried to commit suicide on the death of his son. In the darkness of the funeral house one of the mourners had felt someone crawl past. On inquiry, people discovered that the father was gone. One mourner, guessing that the father had gone to hang himself, ran out and saw him standing in a nearby canoe shed with a noose about his neck. The mourner dashed over, lifted him up, and yelled to the others, who released him, worked over him and revived him. Three points characterizing this type of suicide are: action is taken by the grief-stricken person quite soon, with no more than a few hours for reflection; the method chosen is often hanging, which is fairly quick and certain; if the suicide is prevented, usually no further attempt is made.

Another type of situation is chronic or severe illness, including mental illness. In despair at the infirmities of old age (including, I was told, the disintegration of his body, so that his skin began to stick to the mat on which he lay), Pa Saukirima, the rather dour head of the lineage of Fusi in 1929, hanged himself in his house one evening, using a tough rope which had bound up a bundle of tobacco. Other suicides were by mentally ill people, as is illustrated by the following:

The mother of Pa Ranginiumata was lunatic, and swam out to sea. A canoe party including the Ariki Kafika heard shrieks, eight or ten times, and then silence. Paddling to the spot, they found a basket with water bottles floating (a woman's equipment) and sharks poking up their heads from the water. The sea around was smooth and blood-stained, though waves were breaking elsewhere.

With regard to suicide from insanity, it is questionable how far the Tikopia would accept the old 'suicide while of unsound mind' formula of the English coroner. In general, the Tikopia draw a definite distinction between the suicides of insane persons, and those of persons who in their view have made a free choice voluntarily and consciously to take their lives. Here is an illustration:

Pa Rangitoko went crazy, chasing children, fighting people who tried to restrain him, and trying to enter houses at random. People tied him up at night by his wrists and ankles, and his wife, in fear of him, went to live with her daughter. This went on for a long time, with periods of lucidity intervening. At last his head cleared, and after living alone for a time, he wanted his wife to return. But his wife, still afraid that it might be a trick of the spirits to induce her to come back in order to wreak harm on her, did not come. His body pitiably wasted from lack of food, the man hanged himself, in the daytime, in his house.

I asked if his suicide had been brought about by spirits, since he had been so crazy. The reply was: 'Oh! It was his own doing! His being affected by the spirits, his shrieking, his madness, were over. When we used to come to him, he threw things at us, he fought us. But when his mind cleared, his wife didn't come and prepare food for the two of them, so he became angry, hanged himself and died.' Here then the Tikopia interpretation was that resentment against his wife took the form of an aggressive act against himself, a commingling of anger and despair. In such a case, too, the suicide is partly revenge against the person who has offended one.

But while the Tikopia distinguish suicides due to insanity from ordinary suicide, they are sometimes inclined to attribute the obsessional aspect of suicide to a temporary disturbance of the balance of the mind. They may even use the same expression (*vare*) as is used for insanity, although it is susceptible of a range of translation, and can also properly be interpreted in the relatively mild sense of plain silliness or stupidity. For instance, an old dirge voiced by a man for his sister can be rendered as follows:

> My sister, my nourisher
> You jumped into the sea
> Nor did you glance aside to shore
> The foolish thought was conveyed to your mind
> And you went to your death—whither?

Here the brother does not imply that the woman was actually insane, but stigmatizes her idea of taking her life as stupid. Akin to this is the view traditionally taken when Tikopia chiefs at times insist on risking their lives on overseas voyages. A chief, especially the Ariki Kafika, the premier chief, should not voyage abroad for trivial reasons, such as a lust for adventure. If such a chief will not be held back by pleading and argument, but determinedly goes on a *forau* and is lost at sea, then it is thought his mind has been made up for him by the spirits. The expression is, 'His mind has been caused to be bound by the spirits.' His mental balance has been disturbed and his judgement affected.

Another type of situation sometimes leading to suicide is domestic discord. Not long before 1928 Nau Saraniu hanged herself because her husband was guilty of continued infidelity with a widow. In another case, some time after 1929, Pa Korofatu took a second wife, but fought with her so strenuously that both of them rushed off in opposite directions and committed suicide, separately, by hanging. After the death of the Ariki Taumako, some time in the 1940s, the wife of Pa Nukuvakai insisted on keeping all the food taboos of mourning rigorously. Her husband tried to feed her with pudding and other good quality foods, but she refused. He objected, saying, 'Are we not married? And don't we eat together? Stay in your taboos. But I'm going, and you can stay and keep your taboos for me.' By this he meant that she could now start mourning for him instead. He did not steal away secretly but ostensibly joined a searching fleet looking for three young women who had swum off to sea. Then he slipped away to pursue his own suicide attempt, and it was only discovered later that he had had a row with his wife. 'It's not certain if he died at sea, or if he died on shore—he went in a small canoe and with no provisions.'

The last case illustrates the pattern of many Tikopia suicides—the person feels himself or herself offended and frustrated, and flounces off in a rage, often hurling back some pointed 'last words' to make the survivors regretful. I did not actually witness any such departure, and it was not clear to me how far the subsequent reports tended to dramatize the final situation, or simply to reproduce in brief form the admittedly dramatic quality of much Tikopia behaviour. While in general Tikopia manners are urbane, and the Tikopia are adept in concealing their thoughts, they often seem to lack self-control when frustrated. This is very much a matter of social conditioning, and their anger sometimes appears to an observer to be histrionic, and rapidly appeased by the recognized techniques of status enhancement. Yet they are capable in such conditions of radically destructive acts. The Tikopia well recognize and regret their propensity to take umbrage. As one of my informants said, 'This land is bad. Someone is angry, he goes then and hangs himself. Someone else is scolded by his family, thereupon there's a hanging.'

Under the general heading of suicides from domestic discord may be placed the consequences of revolt against parental authority. If a son is struck or strongly rebuked by his father, he may go off to sea with the intention of seeking his death. When the father finds out, he will wail

for his son, and then go out to sea in search of him. If he finds the boy
he will bring him back, forgiven, the incident purged. If not, he may
return back to mourn in his house, or he may go on in his canoe to meet
his own death. Such is the Tikopia stereotype. Actually, while most
fathers go in search, few appear to have followed their missing sons to
death. But by traditional account many sons have flung off in suicidal
rage after reprimand from their fathers. Similarly, girls subjected to
parental wrath are recorded to have reacted by swimming off to sea.
Such suicide attempts by young people are part of the expected norms
in Tikopia and, being feared by parents, help at times to mitigate
parental discipline.[1]

Another type of suicide situation is shame at the unavoidable consequences of an act, which occasioned the curious death of Pu Sao, and
also the mass swim out to sea, both mentioned earlier. The physical
basis for the shame may vary through a wide range of circumstances.
But with young women a common reason is pregnancy, if the lover
either will not acknowledge himself as responsible, or will not marry
his mistress. The circumstances of the mass swim were as follows:

A granddaughter of the Ariki Kafika, Fakasuariki, 'swam out to sea
because she was pregnant and ashamed'. She knew the father of her
child, but, it was said, his family refused to allow him to marry her
for reasons not known. She was afraid that, if she revealed his name,
he might be killed by the men of Kafika lineage, as he was a commoner
and she was a woman of a chiefly family. Her father and mother were
ignorant of her pregnancy, but her companions among the unmarried
girls knew. When she decided to swim off to sea, many of them
followed her. From Tuatekoro, the base of the cliff between Ravenga
and Namo, they plunged into the sea. Some of them, perhaps a score
in all, were held back on the beach by brothers and fathers who had
obviously been alerted by the unusual sight, and others were pulled
out of the sea. But not all could be rescued. It was midmorning on a
sunny day, but with a very high wind and heavy, breaking seas.
Those girls who succeeded in getting out beyond the reef were soon
lost. A searching fleet of ten canoes put out, but failed to find any of
the girls who had evaded the first pursuit. One vessel of the fleet,
containing three men and a girl as crew, was lost in the search, and
one young man who had swum out to try to save his sister was also
lost.

This tragedy cost eleven lives, six of them with intent. The cause of the
suicide of the girls who followed Fakasuariki may be broadly set down
as loyalty, although from another point of view it may be termed
anticipatory grief. Such loyalty is a complicated sentiment. In part it

[1] For details of parental-filial relations see *We, The Tikopia*, pp. 178–86.

rests upon the notion that a person of high status should have a *following* when entering upon a new and critical experience (such as a voyage abroad, or a religious conversion), and in part here upon the peer-group attachment which obtains among young men or young women. Loyalty in another form is demonstrated by the traditional accounts of the death of bond-friends at sea, in which one will tie his wrist to that of his friend so that they may both perish together.[1] Still another type of loyalty suicide, according to Tikopia account, occurs when a sick, elderly man, either because of food shortage, or because he believes that the time has come to hand over the responsibilities of office to his son, will refuse to take food, and starves himself (*fakapakupaku*) to death. It is difficult, however, to class such behaviour simply as suicide, if only because the Tikopia are very sentimental about family relationships and may be inclined to attribute to suicidal starvation what is in fact mere physical weakness or inability to take nourishment. A type of suicide which may be linked with this category is that carried out from respect for authority. Such cases have occurred when an offender is ordered off to sea, in a canoe; or when a man of rank confronted with a woman who does not wish to marry him, has ordered her to swim to her death rather than allow her to marry another man. Such virtual executions have been regarded by the Tikopia as justified, and even the victims have acquiesced with regret rather than protest against their enforced suicide.

In this analysis my aim is not to make any particular psychological contribution, but to try to relate individual action more closely to social process. One might classify the motives for suicide in Tikopia into four general categories of a psychological order: (1) grief or despair, such as in suicide because of unrequited love, or love for a dead spouse; (2) anger, such as that resulting from domestic discord, including revolts against parental authority; (3) shame, such as occurs in the case of pregnancy of an unmarried girl; and (4) loyalty, such as is evident in suicides from friendship and peer-group attachment. How far do these relate to the sociological categories, for example, of Durkheim? Tikopia suicides hitherto mentioned do not fall easily into his 'anomic' type, characterized by loss of integration of the individual with society. Tikopia social values—as distinct from religious values— have been fairly well preserved, and even the upheavals consequent on the famine of 1952, or the loss of confidence in the state of Tikopia society when the division between paganism and Christianity seemed most acute, saw no outbreak of suicide. But anomic suicide is not unknown in Tikopia; at least one case is recorded in a previous famine of a man's taking his family in a canoe to sea rather than face starvation on shore. In general, suicides from motives of grief or anger may be

[1] See Chapter 4.

regarded as falling under the heading of 'egoistic'; with regard to those in the category of response to shame, although they are in part egoistic, the strength of the shame may be related to the strength of the identification with the norms of the society. Suicide of the loyalty type clearly comes under Durkheim's 'altruistic' category.

Yet I find classification in his terms difficult. Every suicide is in some respects an egoistic act, yet nearly every suicide displays some regard for the norms of society, and a recognition that the person is not in a position or not willing to adapt to these norms. 'Detachment from society' or 'integration with society' seem very crude phrases, grossly oversimplified, for the description of states of interaction of the potential suicide with other members of his society.

Durkheim's notions of the relation of the suiciding individual to society are too naïve. His statements, for example, about obligatory altruistic suicide, in which 'society' compels some of its members to kill themselves, raise a question of basic classification. If the individual has no choice, but is forced to his death as a duty, as in the case of a Tikopia criminal ordered off to sea, would not this be classed as execution rather than suicide? Even with the voluntary or 'optional' (*facultatif*) altruistic suicide, Durkheim misses an important point: that some *conflict* of obligations is usually involved. 'Society' is not united in praising the suicide; some sections of it may praise him, others —for example, members of his family—may condemn him, or at least anxiously try to stop him. Out of such situations of conflict the suicidal intent and much of the drama of the event arise. I would argue that at least for societies of the primitive order of Tikopia the potential suicide situation is one of much greater flexibility and even uncertainty than is usually stated in the theory of the subject.

One may first look at the suicide situation of going off to sea, either by swimming or in a canoe. As Halbwachs did,[1] I have drawn attention to the difficulty of classifying the empirical material in terms of knowing the actual intention of the person who died. Somewhat the same difficulty arises about Durkheim's famous principle of detachment, in so far as it refers to the initiative taken by the person concerned. Successful suicide is the only real detachment from society. People commit suicide in order to become detached from society; they need not, as Durkheim seems at times to have argued, first become detached from society and then commit suicide. If a person makes an attempt and does not die, is it because he was detached and made an error of judgment, or because he was not sufficiently detached and his nerve failed? Something like this quandary exists with the Tikopia. The problem is connected with what Weiss has termed the 'lethal probability' of the means used. For Tikopia the lethal probability of going off to die at sea, by

[1] Maurice Halbwachs, *Les Causes du Suicide*; Paris, 1930.

either swimming or canoeing, is high, but not one hundred per cent. There are two major possibilities here. One is that the potential suicide has time, if not often much opportunity, to change his or her mind, and come back to shore. The Tikopia themselves are fully aware of this possibility, and take it into account in their calculation of motivation and outcome. One of my Tikopia friends put the matter in this form:

> This land is sacred (in respect of) the women—a man does not make fighting gestures to a woman (this is not strictly true). A woman who is reproved, scolded—an unmarried woman only is scolded by a man—desires to die, yet desires to live. Thereupon she goes to swim out to sea. Her thought is that she will go and swim, but be taken up in a canoe by men who will seek her out to find her. A woman desiring death swims to seawards; she acts to go out and die. But a woman who desires life swims within touch, behind the breakers. She goes and goes, and arrives at Tai here (the speaker was thinking of her starting from Ravenga a mile away) to emerge on shore. She then comes and deceives her relatives, 'I went and swam, swam, swam, to seawards, there, but I did not die.' Great is the mind of women!

The second major factor adding to the uncertainty of the situation is the searching fleet. The Tikopia have a very lively understanding of the whole situation of going off to sea, and a very energetic attitude toward rescue expeditions. As soon as news of a suicide swim or voyage is known, a searching fleet of canoes is organized and hastily paddles out in chase of the fugitive. If the attempt is really serious, the fleet's chances of success are not very high—the escapee goes off at night, or in a high wind, which militates against the likelihood of his being spotted and caught in those huge ocean wastes. But if the potential suicide rushes off in a rage at once, when sea conditions are good, or if his or her absence is noticed at once, or if the searching fleet is lucky or guesses well the effects of wind and current, the person may be recovered. For many of these attempts, especially by people who set off in daylight or in good conditions of wind and sea, it is very difficult indeed to decide just what combination of motives and chances lay behind their calculations—or whether they made any conscious calculations at all. They may have thought that they stood a good chance of being picked up, and could return in restored equilibrium; they may have thought that their chances were slim, but were prepared to risk their lives for their reputations; or they may have thought that it was impossible for them to be located and stopped. All those who die are classed as suicides. Of those who are rescued, some can be classed almost certainly as intended suicides, some almost certainly as fakers; but for most of them the issue

must remain very much in doubt. And it may be that this doubt is inherent also in the view of the escapee himself.

To illustrate these points, including the vivid appreciation of such
a situation by the Tikopia themselves, I give the history of such a
'suicide' attempt.

Rather than live with a wife who had been forced upon him because
it was understood that he had made her pregnant, Fakasauakipure, a
man of Tafua in Namo, went off to sea in a commandeered canoe belonging to the Ariki Taumako. I was with the chief when the news
came to him. He was sympathetic to the man, who was a matrilateral
kinsman of his, and did not vent his displeasure upon the man's kinsfolk, as they had feared, but sent his son over to reassure them.[1]
The Tikopia were sorry for the man on account of his flight to
sea, but against him for the desertion of his wife. His family wept
for him.

At this time the general fleet of canoes was engaged in diving for
greensnail, and it was thought that the news had not reached them. In
any case, since the Namo people had already sent out a searching fleet,
it was thought by senior men with whom I talked that many of the other
craft would not leave their work and in fact few, if any, did so. The
Ariki Taumako showed an adequate practical grasp of the situation.
He asked whether the searching fleet was large, and on learning that
it was, commented, 'Great is the number of the fleet! Oh! Then they
will secure him.' He said that if the canoes of the fleet would spread out,
starting from different places, they would have a better chance of seeing
the wanderer.

The man's flight and the search made good material for gossip, and
people sat out on the beach until late that night discussing the case.
The next day the chief and others were very ready to talk about such
voyages and the action taken by the rest of the community in regard to
them. First the constitution of the searching fleet was discussed. 'The
married men mingle at intervals,' it was explained; when the fleet
responds to the news that someone is missing, the canoes are not
allowed to start with crews of bachelors only, 'because their mind is
different'. If left to themselves, fired by the spirit of adventure, and
stimulated by the example of the man who is gone, these young men
might quite likely start off on a voyage of their own. Hence the married
men interpose themselves in ones and twos in each crew. The bachelors
try to dissuade them, saying, 'Go and get a canoe for yourselves.' But
the married men insist, for they know the minds of the young men. A
very large fleet goes out in search only if the son of a chief has gone.
In this case, 'Not a person may remain on shore,' say the Tikopia in
hyperbole. When such a fleet goes out, a woman may sometimes go

[1] For more details on this case see *We, The Tikopia*, pp. 245–6.

with it—for instance, a mother wailing for her son may jump aboard and sit in the bottom of the canoe. She does not paddle, but merely wails. If the man is found, she may be of use in inducing him to return, for often he objects strenuously to being brought back.

If the weather is uncertain, the searching fleet goes out until the cliffs are lost to the sight and the hill of Korofau and the peak of Reani alone show above the sea. But if the weather is good and the sea is calm, they go out until Korofau is lost and Reani (about 1,200 feet high) alone remains. They do not go out of sight of land altogether. All day they search, but if the man has had a long start they may not find him; at nightfall they abandon the attempt and return.

The attitude of the fugitive was also analysed by my informants. They gave three possible variations of motive for the voyage: an attempt to reach some other land in order to have the thrill of being a voyager and seeing the world: a deliberate attempt at suicide as a means of wiping out disgrace; or a feint at suicide, the man hoping to be pursued and caught before he got too far away. It was pointed out, too, that when a man is alone on the face of the ocean, anger and shame are apt to burn themselves out, and the initial urge to self-destruction might change to a desire for life. The putative situation of such a fugitive was outlined thus: if the man has affection and sympathy toward his island and his parents, then when he is out at sea he thinks of them, rests on his paddle and wails, 'Oh! Alas, my land! Oh! Alas, my parents! Oh! Alas my children!'—or similar thoughts. Then he stops his paddle and drifts or starts to return. In this case he will probably be picked up by the searchers. But if a man is intent on his purpose he plies his paddle steadily, and soon gets beyond reach, so that he is not found.

There was much discussion of chances. It was said that Fakasaua-kipure had supplies, two pairs of coconuts. The Ariki Taumako said that even if he stayed at sea for a couple of days, if he drank from time to time to clear his throat and to strengthen his arms for the paddle he might be all right. People had found him missing in the morning, and had sought for him on shore without success. When they discovered that the canoe was gone they knew he was at sea. When it is known that for any reason a man has become angry, a watch is kept upon him; if he says he is going anywhere, another man follows to prevent him from taking a canoe. But in the present case, since the man had lived with his wife for some time, apparently amicably, and then had vanished suddenly without warning, no one was prepared.

Reference was also made to the actions of his kin on shore. Wailing was begun in his house after his departure was discovered, and should he finally not come back, the mourning ceremonies would follow a prescribed course, which was described to me. The *forau* continued to be a principal topic of conversation in the villages of the district, with much speculation on the man's fate. The Ariki Taumako said to me, 'I have sympathy for him, for the man who is drifting. We do not know if he is paddling, or if he is sleeping.' He illustrated each action in turn with his hands—paddling and then, with arms outflung, a man sleeping stretched over a thwart. General opinion was against the chances of his return. It was argued that if he had gone to the south, he might, considering the conditions of wind and sea, reach another land. But if he had gone to the west, he would simply drift in the ocean spaces. Discussion also turned on the action of the chief's son, who, sent by his father to Namo, had gone in anger, inclined to smash one of the canoes there in revenge. Returning home without having done so (he discovered the canoe he proposed to smash belonged to his own clan), he was reproved by his mother, 'Why do you show anger? Look at your father! He is full of sympathy for the man. Why should you be angry about the canoe? Is it a man?' It was reported that the allegation of the woman's pregnancy had been untrue, and to that extent the man had been justified in rejecting her; but she was not criticized for having been the cause of his going off to sea.

The return of the wanderer put an end to speculation. Shortly before sunset, three days after he had gone, his canoe was sighted a long way off shore. There was great excitement. For a time he was lost to sight again, and it was not certain whether it was a canoe or a fish. The chief's wife said uncertainly, 'Perhaps it's a spirit!' Finally Fakasauakipure's identity was established. Five canoes, hastily dragged down to the water's edge, ranged out for a couple of miles, with the rays of the setting sun full upon them, and at last they saw him. The nearest canoe closed in, and two of the crew jumped into his craft and paddled it back to shore. As they came into the shallows, people crowded down on to the beach, and some went into the water to press noses with the wanderer in greeting. He did not speak. He saw a chief, the Ariki Fangarere, seated near the edge of the beach, went over to him and pressed his nose to the chief's knee in token of abasement, was raised up by the chief, and pressed noses with him. The man who first reached the wanderer now led him off to his house by the wrist, in a conventional friendship sign, and put a new, dry, bark-cloth garment on him. The wanderer was then offered food, which he refused. Meanwhile the Ariki Taumako had been waiting in his canoe-yard to see the wanderer and hear his tale. He and his entourage examined the canoe, which had been carried up, and exclaimed about how the outrigger, which had been weak, had been strengthened with coconut fibre. They speculated whether the man had sat in the bow or the stern. Then the chief got impatient and angry at the delay, and stalked home, while children were hushed lest they annoy him further. The kind of remarks prevailing in the conversation were: 'Our friend is alive! If he had disappeared it would have been bad!' 'It is good that the man has lived.' 'It is good that he has come in.'

Later the wanderer, accompanied by his brother and his friend, entered the chief's house. The chief greeted them crossly, saying, 'Why didn't you come before?' 'Shall he come wet to you?' answered the friend (a cousin of the chief) with spirit. As soon as they came in the door, the voyager and his brother began to wail. The voyager then crawled to the chief, who was seated in the centre of the house, lay at his knee, and pressed his nose against it. The chief raised up the bent head, and Fakasauakipure pressed his nose to the chief's face. Then, still lying at the chief's knee, he began to wail a dirge—the continuance of the formal token of abasement and apology. After a little chief said, 'Sit still! Sit still!' and the man stopped and went to sit at the side of the house. By this time a crowd had assembled.

Then he began to talk. First he mentioned where he had been—out to the south-east—and then he spoke of the fish (he was not sure if they were sharks or not) which had come and rested their snouts on the canoe outrigger. First he called on the Eel-god to chase them away, and then on the Taumako ancestor, upon which the fish disappeared. 'Ah! If you had called on him first!' said the chief's wife; and the chief added, 'He it is who has given you to us again.' One of the first questions the chief asked was whether the man had lost sight of land, to which he answered in the affirmative; later the chief asked if he had seen any of the searching fleet, to which the answer was no. There were also several practical questions about mending the canoe. I noted particularly that throughout this discussion, which lasted a long time, the whole attitude was of interest in the man's journey—there was no reproach for the desertion of his wife, or for the trouble he had caused. The man himself related his experiences with considerable dramatic flair, and the audience listened quietly, with the chief doing most of the questioning. There was perhaps a kind of personal identification for each of the audience with the man who dared the unknown and suffered alone in the ocean wastes. A day or so later came a gift of atonement from the man's family to the chief for the abstraction of his canoe. I am not sure whether the customary rescue-payment was made to the first men to reach the wanderer and jump into his canoe.

Sociologically, two points of importance emerge from all this. The first is that the returned 'suicide' voyager by these procedures is completely reintegrated with society. His effort at detachment has failed, but he has succeeded in resolving his problem. He is once again absorbed and an effective catharsis has been obtained. The second point is that since a returned adventurer becomes the centre of attention, a certain premium is attached to attempting a dramatic sea flight of this kind. The stakes are high: they involve a real gamble with death. But if a man can go out, stay away for a while, and then return, he has a wind-fall gain in immediate social status. Yet cases of return from a distance would appear to be very rare; usually if a man is not found in the course of the day, he is lost to Tikopia—although in rare instances he may fetch up on another island.

From the point of view of suicide interpretation, what such a person is doing is gambling on natural hazards and on his credit with society. If either Nature or society is against him—if the weather is bad, or the searching fleet lethargic—he loses his life. As the figures on ocean voyages indicate about a four to one chance against survival in 1929–1952, this is suicidal conduct, although not suicide in the accepted sense of the term.

What I am saying, then, amounts to this—that except where the lethal probability of the means employed is known to be almost complete (for example, with some poisons), there may not be a clear-cut line between the categories of suicide and non-suicide, between intending to kill oneself and not. There may be instead a scale of intention-*cum*-risk-taking. At one end, no intention to lose one's life, and little risk; at the other end, the intention to kill oneself and the most grave risk of accomplishing it, or little risk of being prevented. In between there may be many degrees of partly formed intention mixed with reluctance to die and hope of being saved, with yet enough resolution to face the risk and abide by the outcome.

All this bears on the question of the rigidity or permissiveness of the society and the incidence of suicide. It is quite clear that no correlation between social rigidity and suicide rates can be effected without taking into consideration the efficiency of the rescue procedures. Whatever the rigidity of the society, if the rescue procedures are good, then the incidence of suicide may be relatively low, even though attempted suicides may be many. Moreover, the fact that the rescue procedures are good, and the suicide incidence low, may mean that the society is a firmly structured one. If the rescue procedures are poorly organized and ineffective, this may mean a more permissive, less rigid structuring of the society—associated with a higher, not a lower suicide rate.

Tikopia society may be regarded as firmly structured, even rigid, in some respects, as in the procedures concerned with lineage organization and chieftainship, and the sense of social obligation is high. Yet in other respects it may be seen as a fairly permissive, tolerant society, with many alternative avenues of escape for offenders. Some kind of outlet for deviance is provided by spirit mediumship, which allows considerable personal expression outside the overt structural framework. Where frustration and aggression emerge in social relations, the Tikopia have well-developed techniques for smoothing over difficult situations and allowing aggrieved persons to retain their status. The expression *fakamatamata laui* (making the face good) refers to such techniques, which soften the rigour of social rules. In pregnancy, an unmarried woman has precedents for abortion or infanticide, or for bringing up her child out of wedlock—although this last is not common. For offences against a chief, a man usually has the alternative of fleeing to another district and thence in time making his ceremonial apology. But the sea flight, with all its terrible risks, is part of the pattern of Tikopia behaviour, associated for men, at least, not only with the commission of offences but also with adventure and freedom of a positive, praise-worthy kind and the fascination of pushing back the limits of their universe. It is a case not of there being no other avenues of self-expression or expiation, but of seeking this avenue as a first resort rather than a last.

There is also a further factor linking the incidence of suicide and the permissiveness of Tikopia society. According to traditional Tikopia custom, the punishment for the most extreme offences was for a chief's executive officer to drag the offender's canoe to the sea, and order him into it, to set out and either perish in the ocean or fetch up on a foreign land. The chances of survival being so small, the order was virtually equivalent to a demand for self-execution. Conversely, if a person offended a chief, he might announce or imply an intention to go off to sea. After allowing time for the intention to mature, a man of rank might step in and order the offender to stop. He could then acquiesce in obedience to the command, yet with the dignity of having been prepared to expiate his offence with his life. Into this situation enter some of the most delicate elements of Tikopia personal diplomacy. The person who had let it be known that he intended to put off to sea had no certainty of being stopped. Perhaps no one would take the initiative in getting him to desist, either because the responsibility was left by each man of rank to the others, or because there was not enough enthusiasm for his retention. In essence, then, the person placed his future in the hands of society. To what extent a given offender relied on not being allowed to proceed, it is impossible to say. But the whole situation of suicide attempts has this uncertainty of intervention as one of its parameters.

This may be illustrated further by a case which occurred during my first visit to Tikopia. A son of the Ariki Tafua fell seriously ill, and for a few days showed no signs of recovery, despite strenuous efforts by his family and others. The Ariki Tafua then attempted to commit suicide by hanging, to try to compel the gods to pay attention to the plight of his son. He was prevented from accomplishing his objective by two men, coming to him with a gift of food, who happened to enter the house just as the noose was settling over his head. They rushed to him, and while one supported him the other removed the fatal cord. I happened to visit the old chief shortly afterwards, and found the household plunged in gloom. The chief soon began to speak, addressing his gods, upbraiding them for not curing his son and asking them to take his life instead, since he was an old man and could be more easily spared. It was a very serious, dramatic occasion. Shortly afterwards the old man did fall ill, it was believed in response to his appeal to the gods. But he was finally cured, and meanwhile his son had recovered also. The attempted suicide and the illness of the chief were the talk of the community, and great attention was paid to him, including ceremonial visits to him by the other chiefs. But I found that while the attempted suicide was treated as a very grave matter, some people questioned whether the chief's action had perhaps been quite so spontaneous as it seemed—possibly he had chosen his time carefully, when the sound of approaching footsteps had notified him that rescue would be at hand. But this was no more than a breath of suspicion. Even had it been correct, the chief would have been taking a risk, since the newcomers might have been slow to take in the significance of the situation. But the mere existence of this suspicion indicates how far the notion of suicide as the outcome of a gamble is built into Tikopia conceptions.[1]

In general, then, I would argue that the incidence of suicide is not a simple variable that can be correlated directly with another single feature of the society. From the Tikopia evidence it may be that not only the manner but also the fact of suicide is socially determined. The promptness of mobilization of other members of the society and the efficiency of their rescue organization have a definite bearing on the incidence of suicide. Moreover, the incidence of suicide is affected through the classification of acts. Where risk-taking assumes a proportion great enough to amount to a virtual throwing away of one's life, and there appears to be a complete intellectual and emotional acceptance of the virtual certainty of self-destruction, the sharpness of the boundaries of the suicide category become blurred. Rigidity or permissiveness of the society, alone, then have little meaning in the interpretation. The Tikopia have a propensity to violent conduct in a variety of social situations in which their social status is threatened. There are a number of alternatives for the resolution of these situations. Even where the initial move is left to the person primarily affected and is in the direction of self-destruction, there are still some alternatives open. These are a product of natural forces, social forces, and the decision of the individual himself. Suicide, even if narrowly defined as persistence in conduct calculated to lead to self-destruction, is not a

[1] An analogous argument has been presented in a much more general context by E. Stengel. 'The Complexity of Motivations to Suicidal Attempts', *Journal of Mental Science*, Vol. 106, pp. 1388–93, 1960: *Suicide and Attempted Suicide*, London, 1964.

simple response to lack of alternatives, but to a selection of one alternative against others, for a complex of social reasons. The suicide of a person is a social act, to be understood only in the context of other social acts both of the person himself and of other members of his society.

CHAPTER 6

RUMOUR IN A PRIMITIVE SOCIETY[1]

(1956)

In a small-scale 'primitive' society of the type usually studied by anthropologists, what is the currency of rumour, and how do its processes compare with those of rumour in more sophisticated societies? These questions have not yet been studied. Rumour is a subject of which most anthropologists in the field seem to have had much experience, generally and as affecting themselves. But, curiously, they have written little about its formation, its incidence, and its social repercussions. This essay is meant to open up the problem by analysis of data from the Polynesian island of Tikopia in the Western Pacific. It is also hoped that the material will be of interest to psychologists.

What are the main characteristics of rumour? They are these: talk or report of hearsay kind, not original expression; general currency or spread of such report through a social group; assertions of doubtful accuracy or unverified.[2] For an anthropologist many questions are involved in rumour. What is its material or content in a primitive society? What themes are most commonly involved? How far are they of individual, how far of social concern? Are these themes few and repetitive, or do they show a wide range of variation? Is the treatment of them relatively prosaic, corresponding fairly closely to ordinary verified experience, or is it experimental, with much fantasy? Other questions arise regarding the originator of rumour, the agents who spread it, and the efforts made at its verification or dis-proof. There is also the time factor—are rumours ephemeral or persistent; are they slow or do they come in rapid succession?

Finally, what is the functional significance, if any, of rumour in

---

[1] Reprinted from *The Journal of Abnormal and Social Psychology*, Vol. 53, 1956. I was encouraged in the publication of this essay by discussion with Gordon W. Allport, Jerome S. Bruner, David M. Schneider and other colleagues at a meeting of the Anthropology Colloquium and Social Relations Colloquium at Harvard, where the material was first presented.

[2] I drafted this essay originally without seeing the interesting analysis by G. W. Allport and L. Postman, *The Psychology of Rumour*, New York, 1948. But the above criteria, which seem to represent the lowest common denominator of the concept in popular usage, fit fairly closely Allport and Postman's more precise definition: 'rumour is a specific (or topical) proposition for belief, passed along from person to person, usually by word of mouth, without secure standards of evidence being present' (p. 9).

relation to the structure and organization of the society where it occurs? Its negative, disruptive functions often seem fairly clear; the very use of the term is ordinarily pejorative. But can any more positive social functions be discerned in its operations? Does rumour ever promote group solidarity without apparent scapegoat-creation or other social damage? Does it provide individual defence mechanisms against group pressures? Can it be a means of group mobilization for social action? In the following brief account I try to provide interim answers to some of these questions.

As a general proposition, I would hold that rumour has not just purely negative social functions, and that it is not simply the product of idle curiosity or fantasy, but serves as a social instrument, helping groups or individuals to gain their ends.

REPORTING, INVENTION AND RUMOUR

When I was in Tikopia in 1928–9 and in 1952, though I did not make any detailed study of rumour, on both occasions I noted many of the rumours encountered and their relation to social affairs. My assistant in 1952–3 did this also. Our records are the basis of the following analysis.

First consider the question of accuracy. The line between *news*, ideally the reporting of verified events, and *rumour*, the reporting of unverified events, is a very difficult one to draw, as every newspaper recognizes. At some point between eyewitness and recipient of news in any society there must be some degree of trust in the veracity and the accuracy of the informant. This is one of the requirements of social living. If there should be no trust, then nothing but eyewitnessing of events could serve as a basis for action. If there should be trust but no veracity or accuracy, then social living would soon break down through lack of correspondence between account and subsequent experience. In any society, however, there can be only an approximation to the ideal. Facts offered to the eye may be incomplete, the observer may see only part of the event which he wishes to describe. And particularly if any attribution of *intention* be included in the report, the interest of the observer himself may lead him to misrepresent it. With the recipient then, there always tends to be some amount of reserve as to the correctness of report. All this is a statement of sociological first principles. How does it apply to the case of Tikopia?

In Tikopia, a vast amount of ordinary news is passed on by word of mouth daily. This is so especially within any village, and between villages in the same district. Folk are continually travelling up and down the beach and along the inland paths, and exchange of news is part of regular social intercourse, as it tends to be in any rural area. Between districts there is less contact. Formal visiting is not very frequent between their inhabitants. When it occurs, as for a dance festival or some other large-scale ceremony, or when a vessel arrives from overseas, the visitors are apt to remain separate from the local residents, to hang about together under the trees or to sit together in a house. But even then there is plenty of exchange of information between the parties. And in everyday life people of different villages throughout the island meet a great deal, as in the cultivations, which are dispersed, not concentrated in district ownership. The great amount of accurate reporting arising from these social contacts must be set as a background to the prevalence of rumour.

The Tikopia have an avid interest in all such news. They are eager to hear about events in the outside world and also about events, including movements of people, in their own community. An arrival from one side of the island at a ceremony on the other is usually asked first for the news. When in 1928–9 I came regularly over a gap in the hillcrest from my house in Faea to the temple of the chief of Kafika in Uta I used to be asked every day by him at once 'Any news from Faea?'—and I had to tell him about the fishing, any illness or death, what the local chief there was doing, and so on. In July 1952, when the same old chief was spending the night at his sacred glade in Somosomo inland, I joined him there early next morning. 'Is there not any news from the strand?' he inquired immediately. 'No' was the reply, to his evident disappointment. The term which I have translated as 'news', *taranga*, is also that generically for 'speech', illustrating the verbal nature of communication in Tikopia.[1] This interest in news is presumably a correlate of the small size and isolation of the community. The colour and richness of Tikopia personal experience are derived largely from consideration of the minutiae of social existence in their tiny area. Yet this intense curiosity is matched to a surprising degree by an effort at detachment. The news is received as conveyed by individuals, but often treated as if it stemmed from a generic social source.

As may be expected from a linguistic usage which identifies news with speech, the Tikopia make no clear-cut categorical distinction between news of verified, accurate type and rumour, unverified and often inaccurate. But indication of some differences is often given by the expression *a taranga o faoa*, meaning 'speech of the crowd' or 'speech of people in general', or by the introductory phrase '*E ati . . .,*' 'It is held that. . . .' The very fact that no precise attribution of origin is given implies an element of vagueness and the possibility of inaccuracy. Such an expression conveys a derogatory note, a judgment or evaluation in advance of investigation—or at least a suspension of acceptance of the

---

[1] Only recently and still very rarely have Tikopia communicated by letter or other indirect means, such as radio. (During the ten years since this was written, such communication has increased very greatly.)

story as correct. It also dissociates the speaker from the statement in advance. An analogous expression is *'Faoa e muna . . .'*: 'people say . . .'. These are the nearest equivalents to our 'Rumour has it . . .'.

Despite the lack of a very specific Tikopia expression for rumour as distinct from news, there is a very great interest in the truth of accounts received. The question is often asked, is the story true (*maori*) or false (*loi*)? Is it correct (*tonu*) or not? Such an attitude may be also expressed when a story is passed on. The narrator in telling it may add: 'We don't know whether it is true or false,' or 'We don't know whether it is correct or not.' This indicates not only suspension of judgement on the veracity or on the accuracy of the account; it also indicates that the narrator himself is not committed, and cannot be held responsible for the story afterwards. Moreover, action may be suspended until verification is received. An example of this occurred in October 1928. It was reported early in the morning that Pa Maevetau, a man of rank in Rofaea, had died. I was living in Matautu about half a mile away at the time and noted that all the people waited to hear if the report was true (*maori*) or not. Then confirmation came by ceremonial whooping and firing of guns from Rofaea—a token of some important event. Immediately there was great excitement in Matautu. People went about whooping; they dropped all work; and prepared to form mourning parties. An immediate decision was taken to postpone a dance which had been arranged.

Some further features of the Tikopia speech background are relevant to the discussion of rumour there: the people's interest in story-telling; the accuracy of their memory; their capacity for recognized fantasy and invention.

The Tikopia are great narrators. They delight not only in hearing news as items of information: they also delight in giving and hearing a presentation of news in elaborate aesthetic form, with dramatic emphasis. They dwell on incidents, the narrator taking time to explain in particular his own emotions and thoughts as an event takes place. Such narratives are normally presented as a record of actual events. In this the reproduction of remembered items may be often extremely accurate. In 1952 I heard a Tikopia describe to others many details of my movements in 1928–9. A stone on which I had sat under a tree in a pause in a walk twenty-three years before was pointed out. A funeral gathering was told by one man of a song which I had not finished writing down at his dictation then (the remaining stanza was dictated to me on the spot) and so on. And in 1928 I was given details of the visit of HMS *Mohawk* thirty years before, including loss of one of her anchors off Tikopia—a story which on checking recently (in 1955) I found to be quite correct. The Tikopia are fully capable of accurate accounts from memory.

As regards fantasy, there are a number of Tikopia traditional stories of 'folk-tale' character, some brief, many long and elaborate. These are recited informally and often fragmentarily, on no set occasion. One may be told when a group of people are resting after a ceremony, when members of a household are waiting to go to sleep at night, or when a grandparent is looking after a grandchild. Such tales, though their truth may be a matter of suspended judgement, or they may even be regarded as fiction, are usually not regarded as specifically *invented*. Only once did I hear a man tell a story which, with some amusement, he declared to be an invention of his own.

Where the element of personal invention does come out in a very marked fashion, though not so acknowledged by the Tikopia themselves, is in the dissociated state of spirit mediumship. In this condition a Tikopia medium, especially if in a light state of dissociation, may give a long narrative dealing with the adventures of a spirit. But this is regarded by Tikopia as falling in the category of a true recital, granted that spirit mediums as individuals are recognized as being capable of untruth or unverified and inaccurate pronouncements.

On the whole, it may be said that the Tikopia recognize no great field for free fantasy—with one exception, that of song. Here a person is allowed free rein to his inventions and the way in which human relations are handled in songs has often considerable subtlety. There is also a wide range of analogy and symbolism in the songs (cf. *We, The Tikopia*, pp. 196–7, 289–302, 520–3). But they are apt to be stereotyped and they lack the soaring of the imagination which characterizes songs in some other primitive communities. In perceptiveness about human relations the Tikopia are highly skilled, but they are not very fertile in imagination in fields outside their immediate experience. Even within such experience they do not seem to indulge in much deliberate fiction or in much speculation about possible differences from ordinary behaviour. On one such occasion one of my friends observed in a classical style, 'If mosquitoes were as big as the birds which fly above, when they fed on men, we should disappear.' But this is the only remark of the kind which I recorded. I think it would be fair to say that free fantasy of an *intellectual order* is not common among the Tikopia. What is common is free fantasy of an *emotional order*, and this forms the basis of much humour.

GENERAL TYPE OF EXPERIENCE USED BY TIKOPIA RUMOUR

An important question in considering rumour is what type of experience does it use? Allport and Postman have pointed out how in the formation of rumour psychological processes of levelling of detail by omission and, conversely, of sharpening of detail by selective retention, are very relevant. Assimilation (by cultural and individual selection of perception, memory, and reproduction) also converts an incident into narrative material for more general transmittal. Such processes would seem to be valid as a description of what happens in Tikopia.

But since a great deal of such process is assisted or even short-circuited by common acceptance of *signs*, it is pertinent to ask what the Tikopia do. In our Western culture some signs are selected from natural phenomena, others from cultural phenomena. Black clouds are a sign of rain; the whistle of a railway engine in open country is a sign that a train is approaching a level road crossing. Both natural and cultural signs may have social implications. Rain affects human crops, and an engine whistle affects human traffic across the railway lines. But with us, ordinarily a 'natural' sign is an indicator of natural occurrence, and a sociocultural sign, an indicator of social occurrence. So is it also with the Tikopia. Among natural indicators, black clouds likewise are held to denote rain, other types of clouds denote wind, and so on. As cultural indicators, smoke rising from trees gives a sign that an oven is being made ready for a ceremony; or gunfire announces the death of a man of rank. The Tikopia have great interest in such signs or indicators. (They have a term *fakamailonga*, as a generic term for indicator.) But a point of interest in Tikopia perception and reproduction is that some natural events are interpreted as signs of social occurrences. A certain kind of ribbed cloud structure denotes to the Tikopia not merely a kind of weather but also the approach of a vessel which is as yet invisible below the horizon. Similarly a rainbow or the sound of thunder can be a vessel sign. Even a sneeze can be so interpreted.

An important point about these natural signs or indicators is that while from our Western point of view a social interpretation of them is unrealistic or non-empirical, from the Tikopia point of view this has a fair degree of empirical validity. Hence stories based upon them are relevant to the classification of rumour, but marginal in that classification. A story of a ship coming, based on the sight of a rainbow, is to be treated as a positive error, or mistaken attribution, in which the elements of interest-guided perception lie farther back, as it were, and have become culturally pre-selected and standardized. Moreover, in general, such indicators as rainbows, cloud formations, sneezes, are taken not as a basis for the spread of stories but for speculation. They indicate probabilities, but of no high degree. People do not pay them much attention, but wait to see if the prediction is justified. Often the person who makes the identification. himself regards the sign with some scepticism, or refers to it in terms of possibility—'Is it perhaps that. . . ?'

It may be noted that despite the keen interest the Tikopia show in the arrival of vessels, and their tendency to seize on indicators of approach, they have not utilized dreams for this purpose. Yet they use dreams fairly freely as indicators for foretelling the sex of a child, or a catch of fish. This may be related to the fact that whereas rainbows, clouds, and even sneezes are patent to outside observation and are checkable, the occurrence of a dream relies solely on individual statement. Hence the signs which it gives are apt to be construed as of individual rather than of public significance—that the person concerned will have the experience predicted. That occasionally a dream may provide the basis for rumour is shown by a case where after a dream a man spread the story that a shark caught by a fishing fleet had been caught by his clan; it turned out that he was wrong. But ordinarily dreams are signs of personal, not public, occurrences.

But if neither cultural signs nor dream experiences provide the stuff of rumour, it is different with the material provided by dissociation. Statements issued by spirit mediums are heard publicly and are regarded not as individual pronouncements of the human personality, but as information or instruction from the spirit world. Hence they are deemed worthy of serious belief. They are the basis of many rumours. In 1928, as the result of the statement by a spirit medium, it was widely believed in Tikopia that if I attended the pagan religious rites I would take away their sacred power of bringing rain and fertility to the crops. Luckily, when I first attended I came in a heavy shower of rain, no other deleterious consequences occurred, and the rumour soon died down. Apart from such types of material, rumour in Tikopia is based for the most part on misinterpretation of ordinary physical events of a cultural order. Examples of this are given later.

A word may be said here about the agents of rumour in Tikopia. Children there are widely blamed for creating and spreading rumours. In this as in many other primitive communities, they have a very positive role. Often going around in gangs, they form a ubiquitous and semi-autonomous social element of limited experience and without much responsibility. There is no doubt that they do in fact generate, spread, and elaborate many rumours, particularly those concerned with approach of vessels and movements of people. But to some extent they are a conventional scapegoat, to whom authorship of rumour is often shifted when its falsity becomes manifest. Many rumours are the work of adults. Support to this, apart from absence of children as narrators, is given by the fact that such rumours are often clearly in an adult sphere of interest. Women seem to be authors of rumours as well as men.

CONTENT OF TIKOPIA RUMOUR

Externally, the content of rumour in Tikopia is concerned with two basic subjects; the movement of vessels in relation to Tikopia, especially their arrival; and the fate of Tikopia abroad. Internally, it covers a wide range, from the timing of ceremonies and doings of men of rank (including anthropologists) to quarrels, and reasons for illness. In all, from my own records in 1928–9 and 1952, I have extracted thirty-eight specific rumours, and from the records of Spillius come another thirty-six, making a total of over seventy rumours noted over a period of about twenty-eight months. This is a minimal figure since we did not set out to record rumours on all small details of behaviour, or other relatively ephemeral matters. (Practically all these rumours were false.)

The lack of data on minor rumours, relating to ephemeral issues, means that our material does not represent a complete cross-section of Tikopia rumour. It is not completely representative for another reason —it is biased in the direction of rumours affecting our own movements and intentions. This is natural—for operational reasons it was important to know what was being said about us or matters in which we were concerned, so as to study how to handle the situation. Such rumours usually came rapidly to us—we were speedily asked, as a rule, if they were true. In addition, our doings in themselves were the object of the greatest curiosity and speculation to the Tikopia, since the anthropologists have been the only Europeans for over a century living on Tikopia for any long period. But I think that by one channel or another, most of the major rumours on Tikopia during our stay reached us—that is, most of these which not only tended to alter the social behaviour of the recipients significantly, but also affected the organization of social affairs on a considerable scale.

Examples of minor and of major rumours will illustrate some of the procedures in rumour formation in Tikopia.

Minor rumours. One evening I was told that my assistant was not returning to our house in Ravenga that night, but was going to sleep in the dwelling of his friend, the chief of Tafua in Faea, where he had been during the day. The message was brought to me and others in the house of the Taumako chief in the village where we lived. It came through a small girl, who had been listening to the gossip around the bearer of a note from my assistant to me; the messenger had come to my house, and was waiting for me under a tree when I got back. When I read the note, it turned out to be merely an announcement that my assistant was going to be back late for dinner. This is typical of much Tikopia rumour. The delay in the arrival of my assistant; the arrival of a messenger from Faea—these are put together with a false inference that the intention is stopping the night. The inference is not so stupid or far-fetched as a Western observer might think. A Tikopia on a visit to the other side of the island would not normally send a message back to say that he would be *late*. He might send one of his companions, a child or young person, to return ahead of him, with instructions to say that he was following. But a special messenger would be sent almost certainly only to tell his family that he was staying the night away. So Tikopia custom gives some plausibility to the rumour, and the force of the interpretation was added to by the sight of a written document, held by them to be a weighty thing. But in addition there is the element of interest in novelty. There is more fun in speculation about someone's staying the night away than in his returning home. A rumour of similar exaggerative type came to me when a man fell from a breadfruit tree. Some boys told me that evening that he had broken his leg above the ankle. But his nephew, who went and saw him, told me later that he had hurt his back and grazed his shin, no more. The comment in my notebook at the time (November 1928) was that 'rumour is quick to exaggerate in Tikopia'.

One further subject of minor rumour which may be mentioned is personal illness. Rumours in this field range widely from assignment of cause to attribution of credit for treatment and cure. One instance of this was a rumour that the illness of my assistant on a certain occasion was cured by a spirit medium who, in fact, worked no cure since he came to our house for quite another purpose. As regards causes, rumours frequently involve flights into the realms of spirit action, a subject too elaborate for discussion here.

Major rumours; movement of vessels. A major and continued subject of rumour was the movements and arrival of European vessels. The isolation of the island makes the coming of a vessel—in normal times, only once or twice a year—an event of great importance. For a vessel to call is a time of excitement, news, valuable exchange, gifts, and perhaps arrival and departure of persons. It is much desired, for economic as well as social reasons. Hence there is much inducement to false identification—a tiny cloud on the horizon looking like a smudge of smoke, a distant unidentified object, and a cry of 'The ship! The ship!' rings out. Such is the novelty-interest and wish-fulfilment type of rumour

During the second expedition to Tikopia there were at least a score of rumours of vessels recorded. This was partly a function of the strain and emotional intensity of the period—owing to hurricane and drought a food shortage had developed into a famine, and prospects of food relief were a vital question. It was also related to the presence of our radio telephone set, with fairly frequent messages.

Here are some typical cases. On June 5, 1952, a rumour began to spread in our village about 9 a.m. 'A ship has come.' Large numbers of people, men and girls, went off to the other side of the island to see and to trade. A ship was indeed expected that day with food supplies, so it was very likely that some person might deceive himself into believing that he had seen its smoke on the horizon. But what was interesting was the lack of sceptical verification. The Tikopia have been deceived innumerable times by such rumours. And each time afterwards they talk about '*Te loi o faoa*'—the falsehood of the crowd. But they seem just as gullible next time. On this occasion we questioned our retainers as to the accuracy of the report. One of them said that a villager, one of our neighbours, had gone along and verified the story; it was quite true. I asked if the vessel was still far off. He replied, 'Oh, she is standing inshore.' But about 10.30 a.m. the news came back that the story was entirely untrue. The disgruntled crowd streamed back.

Four days later the vessel arrived with food supplies. Ten days later again, when many of the supplies had been consumed and there was some wistful hoping that further food might arrive, another rumour began. It was said that a Government vessel would come that day or the next; that my assistant and I had announced this after hearing it on the radio telephone. People should sit in their houses, we had stated, and not go to the woods to get food; simply sit and wait for it to be brought by the vessel. Popular support was given to this story, by the fact that for the last two days the peculiar cloud formations supposed to be indicative of approaching vessels had been observed. We ourselves had had our attention drawn to them—for instance by the old chief of Kafika. The basis for this rumour about the ship apparently was that in a news item from the Solomons on the radio the day before, it had actually been mentioned that a Government vessel was proceeding from Honiara, the capital of the Protectorate, to Gizo, a port in the West. This is in the opposite direction to Tikopia, and more than 600 miles away, but someone in the crowd which always assembled whenever the radio was in action[1] had evidently caught a part of the message and garbled it. A day later the rumour took a further form—of criticism of my assistant and me, and of the radio, for (it was alleged) giving wrong information! It was said that we ourselves had *started* the story of the coming of the Government vessel to Tikopia and then it turned out not to be true!

Movement of persons. Another set of rumours was concerned with our alleged movements. One was that I had tried, a year or so earlier (the time varied in different accounts), to return to Tikopia. (This was in accordance with a statement I was alleged to have made when I left in 1929.) But, it was said, I had been prevented by the Government or by some other agency after having got part of the way, and turned back. The bases for this rumour were dual. On the one hand I did, in 1929, express a *wish* to return to Tikopia, though I had said I was uncertain if I ever could. On the other hand, I had actually paid a visit in 1951 to New Guinea. I had no intention on that occasion of attempting to reach Tikopia. But the airline to the Solomons was by way of New Guinea. When in the end after my arrival I told some Tikopia about this earlier

---

[1] See Firth, 'Social Changes in the Western Pacific', *Journal Royal Society of Arts*, Vol. CI, p. 810, 1953, and Plate VII.

trip it provided the basis for the story of a thwarted start for the island. Again, in May 1952, the story became current, that in one case I, and in another my research assistant, was going to Vanikoro, another island about 120 miles away, in a Government vessel to buy tobacco and return with it to Tikopia. The basis for this was an acute shortage of tobacco in the community at this time; several people had half jokingly suggested to us that we should send out an order for more or go and get more—without regard, of course, to the finance involved. Such rumours are of the wish-fulfilment type. Their genesis lies basically in an attempt to give concrete form to a strong desire. But others, also related to the movements of persons, are essentially an anxiety expression.

The vessel on which the first shipment of relief food supplies was brought also took away a number of Tikopia who had been recruited as plantation labourers. About seven weeks after they had gone the rumour spread that disaster had overtaken this labour force—though no details were given even as to whether it was on sea or on land. Further, it was alleged that my assistant and I had received this news on the radio-telephone and had concealed it. (Hardly necessary to say, this was complete fiction.) As a variant of this was the rumour that two men of this force, cited by name, had died. About a week later the story assumed a different form, that two men had died—one of those cited earlier, but the other of a different labour shipment, at Vanikoro. Again, it was said the report had come by radio, but that we had not made it known.

On the one hand, these rumours were reflections of the fear of Tikopia for their kinsmen away at work, which past experience had shown usually resulted in several deaths.[1] On the other hand, they were also expressions of the resentment of some Tikopia at our restricted use of the radio-telephone as a news instrument. Here was a magnificent source of news, we were the only channel through which it could come, and instead of furnishing them with frequent information about their kin or any other matter in which they were interested, we just listened to weather reports and more general news which they did not understand, and selfishly engaged in business conversations of our own! Such was the attitude, not very clearly formulated. Indeed, we guessed at this view, rather than actually heard it expressed.[2] Such rumours, fairly directly related to fears and hopes for kin, are a reflection in part of the Tikopia family structure and its system of sentiments.

[1] See, *We, The Tikopia*, p. 42.

[2] We did make what inquiries we could about the labourers—including report of several deaths—and transmitted news about them, apart from keeping the Tikopia informed of matters of public interest. In particular also, we kept in touch with the Government in Honiara about the approaching food famine. This, even apart from matters concerned with the organization of the expedition, was difficult owing to serious weather distortions and breakdowns, which only the devotion of my assistant to the instrument was able to remedy. Most Tikopia seemed genuinely appreciative of this service, and made this known to us.

Another rumour with personal referent was concerned with the recruitment of the labourers. At the time when the vessel called I was asked by a man of rank why my assistant was barring men of the district where we lived from being 'written down', i.e. having their names entered in the recruiters' book. I asked what he meant. He said that my assistant was 'writing down' names of men of the other district. Later, two other men of our village said much the same to me. The genesis of this rumour was an ordinary field inquiry to ascertain the motivations and attitudes of those men who were offering themselves for recruitment, or who had stated they wished to go. Since the vessel had anchored off the coast of the other district, and its boatswain, a most active recruiter, was a Tikopia man from that district, he tended in the first place to recruit or approach men who were his own neighbours or kin. But the traditional suspicion between the people of the two districts coupled with the very limited knowledge of English possessed by most Tikopia, and their ignorance of recruiting procedures and how to get themselves on the list, gave rise to the view that favouritism was being exercised by my assistant.

Rumours based on other fears may have a broader sociological referent. One of these involving alleged movement of both vessel and person was associated with the receipt of relief food supplies—which came mainly in the form of rice. A rumour in July 1952, after the first relief vessel had been gone some time, was to the effect that one of the most respected and best known of the European priests of the Melanesian Mission stationed elsewhere in the Solomons had objected to this rice being sent, saying, 'Shall it be food for pagan religious rites?' He said (it was alleged) that if another food vessel was sent he would see that it 'sank at sea'. He had been on Tikopia nearly half a century before, and was known by a number of Tikopia men. One of my old Tikopia friends who had seen this man as a boy asked me, 'Is he someone the spirits desire? He has "power".'

In this rumour there emerge several themes characteristic of Tikopia religious thinking. The first is the opposition between Christian and pagan. In this case it is projected on to the distant priest, in actuality a saintly man, wholly innocent of such thoughts as the sinking of relief ships. The second is the translation of that opposition into terms of the outstanding economic preoccupation of the Tikopia—food, and its use. The close association in Tikopia thought and action between religion and food is seen in the whole pagan cycle of the 'Work of the Gods', as also in the Christian argument that the pagan religion is wasteful of food by its offerings and ceremonial accumulations and feasts. The third theme is that of the possession of supernatural power by men of rank. The European missionary's suggested 'sinking' of the vessel alluded to was to have been done by supernormal techniques, and not by physical sabotage. Hence, the question of my friend as to whether the missionary was 'desired' by the spirit meant, did he have their support?

Violence and social strife. Traditional structural elements were reflected in another type of rumour concerning the treatment of thieves. The rumour became current, as the food situation worsened, that if the rice shipment did not arrive the chiefs would have given orders that thieves would be killed. I told one of the chiefs of this. He laughed and said 'Oh, no!' He explained that what had been said was that anyone who thieved consistently should be carried off to work in the Solomons. This, in fact, was the policy of the chiefs, and they did succeed in having several thieves recruited as labourers. But one traditional punishment in such cases was banishment to sea, which was virtually equivalent to execution.[1] The rumour here was doing two things: it was reviving this extreme punishment in anticipation; on the other hand, it was assimilating it to the general type of physical rough handling to which thieves, in fact, were traditionally subjected.

A little later we had a repercussion of this rumour in the form of a message from the Government of the Solomon Islands Protectorate, stating that it had been reported on Tikopia authority that if it had not been for the arrival of relief supplies the chiefs would have taken the matter into their own hands and killed thieves. We were asked for comment. We replied that the story was without foundation. But almost at once two other radio messages came from Tikopia police constables at District Headquarters addressed to their kinsfolk on the island. Each was from a son to his father. One was: '*I heard news stop People there thieving stop advising you and the family not to follow them.*' The other was: '*I heard news about there stop look after people do not do any harm to them.*' These messages were interesting from several points of view. They used the father's personal name in address, thereby breaking one of the stringent Tikopia taboos. They were in English through an intermediary. They were certainly the first time that Tikopia had ever used radio as a means of communication with one another. But the most significant point in this context is that both these young men obviously believed in the possibility that the rumour was true. This was partly a reflection of their belief, later shown to be well founded, that violence was not far from the surface of Tikopia public affairs in such a time of severe strain and crisis. It was also partly an indication of the extent of their credence in what was, at that time, a far-fetched suggestion.

As the famine crisis developed rumours of violence became more frequent. They took such forms as this: 'An aristocrat was going berserk and was going to take his club and kill commoners.' 'Two

[1] Firth, R., Authority and public opinion in Tikopia. In M. Fortes (Ed.), *Social structure: studies presented to A. R. Radcliffe-Brown.* Oxford, 1949.

prominent executive officials were going to kill thieves.' 'Executive officials were about to fight among themselves in a struggle for power.' Each of these had become, indeed, a none-too-remote possibility, and each followed the traditional Tikopia cultural pattern.

The rumour about the chiefs having thieves killed involves the conception of the chiefs as a primary source of public order in Tikopia. But it implies more—opposition of interests, as well as the coincidence of interests between chiefs and their families, on the one hand, and commoners on the other. This was exemplified in another rumour—that the chiefs were going to band together and drive out the commoners to seize their lands. This is a theme of long standing in Tikopia. I was asked about it rather anxiously by leaders of the commoners in 1952, but it was then only a fear and demand for reassurance, not a concrete rumour. Later, when my assistant was alone in the island and the food situation had degenerated still more, it became rumour. At his instance there was a meeting of chiefs and executive officials in the Ravenga district where he lived, to discuss plans for the distribution of a further food supply being sent as relief. This meeting was interpreted by a spirit medium of the other district, Faea, as a meeting to decide on the long-talked-of expulsion of the commoners of Faea, to make them set off in their canoes, leaving their homes for ever. As a result the men of Faea bound their heads for war, took down clubs and conferred, excitedly, determined to resist. On their return, the executive officials of Faea were met by armed parties. Seeing how the situation stood, they circulated among the villages explaining what had really occurred. But to allay the fears of the commoners my assistant was asked to go over to Faea in person, and make a normal appearance as a demonstration that nothing untoward was happening. On his way over he was asked on two or three occasions, half jokingly, by women working in the cultivations, if it was true that the aristocratic families were about to expel them from Tikopia. Here the dormant solution of traditional type was evoked once again in time of real crisis.

RECAPITULATION AND FUNCTIONAL IMPLICATIONS

I have shown that with the Tikopia, the content of rumour is closely related to their experience, and that while the total range is wide, the main themes are relatively few and repetitive. While the mode of communication itself is almost wholly verbal, Tikopia rumour has shown itself capable of seizing upon a new medium, the radio, and of incorporating it by fictitious citation into rumour content. Psychologically, the processes of formation would appear to be similar to those current in more sophisticated societies. But sociologically, the types of experience used vary considerably from those used in the West, e.g. in the public reliance placed on the pronouncements of spirit mediums.[1] It is difficult in Tikopia, as elsewhere, to identify the agents of rumours. But occasionally an original utterer can be identified, usually, it would seem, someone with a power-axe to grind. The Tikopia practice of tending to avoid or disclaim public responsibility, however, reduces the possibility of this. As regards spread of rumour, its currency in time, and the credence given to it, there is wide variation in Tikopia. But most rumours are ephemeral. They tend to follow one another in fairly rapid succession, especially when the issue is one of immediate emotional significance—as a famine, or the fate of absent kin. When they persist or reappear, it is because they correspond to some deep-seated structural cleavage. But for the most part they diffuse quickly through the whole community. Whether they do so depends in part on the possibility of check (willingness to check being in itself an index of some scepticism) and in part on whether the rumour is of major or minor import.

I now draw some further implications. To begin with, one can classify Tikopia rumours into two main divisions: those which are prosaic, fairly simple enlargements or explanations of ordinary experiences, and those which are fantastic, of the extraordinary kind. The former, dealing on Tikopia with the coming of ships, the movement of people, the death of workers abroad, the cure of illnesses, are set in the common cultural mould. They represent some of the fruits of speculation about the alternatives of action. Some are fairly simple cases of wrong inference through not having access to all the premises, of which one or more are concealed from superficial observation. An example is the interpretation of a written note as my assistant's intention to stay away for the night.

In them, the instrumental factor[2] is at a minimum, though it may be present to some degree in giving opportunity to the rumour-monger for ego-assertion. Check is quickly applied and currency is short. In other rumours emotional elements are more marked. There is hope for excitement and novelty, or food supplies, in the rumoured arrival of a ship; there is anxiety, as in the rumour of a death. Here, the instrumental factor is more marked and more complex. To some extent it may be argued that the rumour serves as a tension release. By anticipating the event, or possible event, it tones down the emotional excitement and makes it easier to bear. To put speculation into concrete verbal form and give it as a statement, not question, may give subtle reinforcement to the personality by reduction of the unknown to event-shape, to occurrence. Such rumours can be scotched on check—but they tend to revive again.

---

[1] A Western analogy is the statements of soothsayers, astrologers, etc.; but reliance upon them for public action is marginal.

[2] This is analogous to what Allport and Postman have called 'expressive significance', though it is more related to concrete action (p. 169).

There is quite a close relation between these last kinds of rumour, and Tikopia religious speculation involving details of spirit behaviour. Rumours that labourers have died overseas, their deaths being reported by radio, are very similar to stories that spirit mediums tell of the end of men who have gone on canoe voyages, their deaths being reported by spirits. Results in social action would be in general the same—preparation of the family concerned for the funeral ceremonies. But there is one significant difference, that with the radio there is opportunity for immediate check. Application by messenger to our house speedily enabled the family concerned to discern rumour from truth, and to avert their mourning. In ordinary Tikopia life, when no anthropologists with radio are resident, there is no such chance of check, and the pronouncement of the spirit medium is normally taken for reality.[1]

In rumours of the fantastic, the untoward event, the extraordinary, other elements are perceptible. In a rumour of a tidal wave, of the suicidal voyage of a man of rank, of the intended violence of chiefs, there are the fruits of speculation of alternatives to action in nature or in the society, as before. But the instrumental factor is much more evident as a move in the field of social action. It may be indirect or direct. A case of its indirect operation is that of a hurricane and tidal-wave rumour. By this, the rumour-monger, it is fairly clear, was making a bid to regain for himself and his family—the leading missionary element—some of the control of public opinion which they had lost. The ostensible subject of the rumour had little or nothing to do with the object desired. But to be in the position of the author of the warning of disaster is tantamount to a claim to the special knowledge, and hence the power, that no one else possesses. A case of rumour with a direct instrumental factor is the story of the meeting of chiefs and executive officials to decide on the expulsion of commoners. This was a false interpretation of circumstances. But its effects were cathartic, the crystallizing of possibilities which had been before men's minds for some time. It was power potential made concrete. Moreover, it could be anticipatory. Rumour may have a proleptic function. The effect of the rumour was to bring out the commoners with arms prepared to defend their lands and homes. This was not necessary. But *if* the thought had been in the minds of the chiefs that action of expulsion was desirable *then* the effect of the rumour was to trip the wire in advance, to bring the matter to the surface of discussion and obtain reassurances as to its impossibility. To change the metaphor—rumour may be said thus to draw the teeth of intention.

In the case just cited, the instrumental factor was hardly likely to have been consciously employed, after due deliberation. But at a time of crisis a man of rank may allow it to be inferred that he intends to *forau*,

[1] Cf. *infra*, Chapter 14.

to take his canoe and voyage away, to die or survive as the fates decide. This implication is to be distinguished from an announcement of intention, but grades into it. The result is a rumour which spreads through the community, often in exaggerated form. The final outcome of this is to mobilize a force of public opinion against the rumoured action. Other men of rank will see that the suicide voyage is not undertaken.[1] And on the other hand, action is usually taken to correct the position to which the man of rank originally took objection. A further instrumental use of rumour here is as a test of public opinion. By making no public announcement of intention the man has not compromised himself, and can withdraw if no counteraction eventuates, i.e. if the public are not seen to be behind him. The 'kite-flying' function of rumour can occur in a primitive society, as well as in a sophisticated Western society.

Hence rumour may be said often to have a positive social function. Its social effects do not necessarily involve any individual or group in scapegoat-suffering. It becomes an organizational mechanism or social instrument in the hands of individuals, seeking to remedy or improve a status position for themselves and the groups they represent. It may tend to maintain rather than destroy a social structure. In this sense the proleptic function which such a rumour may exercise acts as an element of conservatism. But it is a dangerous instrument. Whether its use be conscious or unconscious, rumour in a primitive as in a civilized society is rarely neutral. The fact that it is interest-based almost necessarily gives it destructive potentialities. Whether these are absorbed more easily in a primitive than in a civilized society only further comparative investigation can show.

A NOTE[2] ON THE THEORY OF 'CARGO' CULTS

In the course of this examination of the nature of rumour in Tikopia, and some of its effects, I have been led to consider some aspects of the theory of cargo cults.[3]

There is no cargo cult or cargo movement in Tikopia. When I began to consider the subject, my first reaction to such a thought was the unlikelihood of any such movement arising in Tikopia. It seemed absurd. The Tikopia have too well integrated a society. Although they

[1] 'Authority and public opinion in Tikopia', p. 184.
[2] Reprinted from *Man*, 1955, No. 142.
[3] These movements have been called 'cargo cults' because they usually include the notion that quantities of European goods will arrive as 'cargo' from overseas in ships or aeroplanes, usually by spirit agency, for the benefit of the native people. There is now extensive literature on these cults—see Ida Leeson, *Bibliography of Cargo Cults and Other Nativistic Movements in the South Pacific*, South Pacific Commission, Technical Paper No. 30, Sydney, 1952, for early work.

are divided in religion between paganism and Christianity, each of the religious systems has a strong framework which would not allow of the emergence of a new mystical system. The Tikopia are too pragmatic in their attitude to the acquisition of Western material goods by work and by exchange to lend themselves to any fantastic notions of aeroplanes or visiting ships bringing special cargoes to them. And yet the idea, as I shall show, is not so far-fetched.

It seems to me fairly obvious to assume that cargo cults tend to arise as a resultant of several factors in operation together; a markedly uneven relation between a system of wants and the means of their satisfaction; a very limited technical knowledge of how to improve conditions; specific blocks or barriers to that improvement by poverty of natural resources or opposed political interests. What constitutes a *cult* is a systematized series of operations to secure the means of satisfaction by non-technical methods. Yet the implications of technical methods may, as I have shown,[1] approach cult behaviour if they are used more to give immaterial than material satisfaction.

A gap between wants and the means of their satisfaction may be assumed for all human beings. What is characteristic of a cargo-cult situation is where the gap is markedly very wide *by comparison* with a much narrower gap observable in another cultural system. In other words, the situation is one of relative magnitudes, established by comparison. Such disparity is very apt to be established in modern conditions of technical and economic development in under-developed countries. For the most part these have sufficient untapped resources to provide a field for development, offering a market for labour or for goods, enough to give the impression of lessening the wants-satisfaction gap. But there are some areas where the resources are exceedingly scanty, or for other reasons the means of development are very limited. Moreover, in primitive communities an increase of communication facilities may lead to a rapid expansion of wants. It may spread information about the outside world more rapidly than avenues for differential acquisition of wealth and status becomes available. Communication development might thus produce a cargo-cult reaction if there does not seem to be possibility of parallel development in the economic and political spheres.

Poverty alone does not stimulate a cargo cult. On the other hand economic enterprise in itself does not mean that such a cult may not develop. Some individuals, especially if they are willing to leave their group, may be able to match their wants and their satisfactions to a tolerable degree. But if such individuals have a strong sense of communal responsibility (e.g. founded on a wide-range corporate-kinship system), such prosperity may be inadequate for them if it be theirs alone. Again, even although a group may advance economically to a considerable

[1] See my 'Social Changes in The Western Pacific', 1953, p. 816.

degree, a moderate economic prosperity without political control may not be enough for them.

Is the development of a cargo cult inhibited by a strong centralized government, e.g. where there is a well developed chieftainship? The answer would seem to be, not necessarily. Among the Maori, and among the Fijians, both with highly developed chieftainship, movements analogous to cargo cults, or movements of a Messianic kind, have risen. Such cults have found leaders from among traditional chiefs as well as from new leaders of a charismatic type.

Does an integrated religious system of traditional type inhibit this development? It may do so. A strong ancestor cult of unbroken type may block the development of ideas that ancestors can bring new kinds of property. A cargo cult usually seems to come where there is a dual framework in religion as in other social matters. But a cargo cult may arise in an area where no foreign religion has penetrated, and indeed where white men have not yet arrived.[1] What is basic here is the spread of information by new communications so that new wants have been generated, but without access to the goods in adequate supply to meet them. What is important from the angle of religion is the catalytic agent. There must be some generating mechanism, some purported channel, which allows of free invention beyond the existing religious ideology. One such ideal channel is a spirit-medium cult. Here fantasy and wish fulfilment are given easy expression, and according to the cultural system, with relatively little control. But it is not necessary to have a spirit medium—a Christian priest will do if he is willing to take an extra-dogmatic role of creative interpretation.

How does this refer to Tikopia? I have said that there has been no cargo cult in Tikopia. But cargo cults feed on rumour. In Tikopia there have been at least two rumours which may be regarded as prototype cargo-cult phenomena. One of these concerns what the Tikopia termed 'the goods of Pa Fenumera'. Some time after I had arrived in Tikopia in 1952 I was asked if it was true that I had brought with me the goods of Pa Fenumera and given them to another man. I was puzzled. The man whom I had known in 1929 as Pa Fenumera had been dead for some years, and there had never been any communication between us since I had left the island in that year. It then turned out that in the view of Tikopia the spirit of this man had been equipped after his death with special powers in recognition of the special functions he used to perform in the most sacred pagan religious rites. Indeed, though in life he was only a commoner he had been elevated to aristocratic status in the spirit world with the title of 'The Chief of the North'. A spirit medium had announced that he owned certain European goods abroad, and that he

[1] R. M. Berndt, 'A Cargo Movement in the Eastern Central Highlands of New Guinea', *Oceania*, Vol. XXIII, pp. 40–65, 137–234, 1952.

had put these goods in my charge to bring them from Australia, and to deliver them to him in Tikopia. Presumably. I was to have given them to the human medium through whom his spirit spoke. Some goods which I had given to one of my other friends had been tentatively identified by the general public as those for which Pa Fenumera had asked. Hence the query to me. Hardly needless to say there was no truth in this story, and after my denial I heard no more of it. What it illustrates, however, is the possibility of an incipient 'cargo' theme arising—namely, putative wealth of Western type, eagerly desired from overseas, destined for a Tikopia and turned aside by a European agency. If the Tikopia had not known me so well and presumably trusted my word, the rumour might have got much greater currency.

Another later rumour was of the apocalyptic type which often is an accompaniment of, or alternative to, a 'cargo' movement. This was traceable to a member of a missionary family who misinterpreted a wireless message about a hurricane. He alleged that Honiara, the capital of the British Solomon Islands Protectorate and the Government, had been destroyed by the hurricane. He also said that a tidal wave was coming to sweep Tikopia, and that all the inhabitants, except presumably the elect, would be killed by it. This rumour began to circulate towards the end of a period when Tikopia was being affected by the edge of a hurricane centred several hundred miles away. Hence, it was widely believed. In the hope of survival, some people started building houses inland; fifteen to eighteen dwellings being completed before the end of the violent winds. They also began tearing out their crops near the beach, in order to save these or at least to have a last feast if they should die. This rumour affected only the district where its author lived, since people of the other districts were more closely in touch with the radio and could check daily upon its reports. In fact, these reports were to the effect that the Government meteorologist, having plotted the course and velocity of the hurricane, had given information that it would not affect Tikopia further, and that, indeed the, centre would miss the island by 100 miles if it advanced. Honiara, of course, had been unscathed, nor was there any tidal wave, The notion of complete destruction embodied in the rumour, and the fact that it sprang from a missionary family, suggests a basis in Biblical narrative. But it was reminiscent of an apocalyptic cult movement in its effects of causing people to build houses to escape disaster, and to destroy crops for a final feast if they were destined to perish.[1]

In both these cases the development differs from that of a typical cult movement; in fact there was no organized development in the first case, and it was of very limited range in the second. In part this was probably due to the position which my assistant and I held in the Tikopia polity.

[1] I am indebted to my research assistant, J. Spillius, for record of this case.

We were in constant communication with the people, spoke Tikopia freely, disbursed a wealth of goods and information, and, we could say without hesitation, were generally trusted by the people. Our actions and explanations on most matters were usually accepted. Yet despite this the rumours obviously had some considerable circulation before being stopped. In other words, there can be a *'cargo'-cult type of behaviour*, without it attaining the organized coherence of a movement or cult development. One important element in such development would seem to be a charismatic leader. He must be more than a catalyst; he must be able to fuse together the various elements available and apply them to the common goal. On the other hand, in so doing he is likely to enter a field of competing status relations. Here an organized chieftainship is likely to inhibit the implementation of his ideas—unless one party already established in the field can use his talents to its advantage.

The simple introduction of improved means of communication is in itself not enough to deal with the effects of such 'cargo' rumours. As with our radio in Tikopia, these means in themselves may even provide the starting point for more elaborate rumours. The only remedy may be to improve communications still further, but by personal and not simply mechanical transmission of information. Moreover, education on the one hand and the provision of avenues of employment and political expression on the other would seem to be important alternatives to cargo-cult development. Again, while it would be incorrect to say that the Tikopia type of social structure with well developed unilineal descent groups and chieftainship with strong political authority necessarily prevent the development of a cargo cult, they do seem to serve to some extent as inhibiting factors.

CHAPTER 7

THE MEANING OF DREAMS[1]

(1934)

The investigation of the nature of dreams, their importance and their significance in the life of primitive peoples, is a subject in which interest has grown in recent years. This is due particularly to the stimulus given by C. G. Seligman, who has collected much information relating to a number of 'typical dreams' in various parts of the world and provided valuable suggestions for their study. It is perhaps then appropriate that an essay in a volume dedicated to him should be concerned with one of his favourite topics. Though to my regret it was not convenient for me in my field-work in Tikopia to follow in entirety the methods of procedure indicated by Seligman, which would have added greatly to the interest of this account—the method of analysis by free association was not used—I have been able to bring together illustrative material which corroborates to a considerable degree some of the results he has obtained. This article through the exigencies of space consists mainly in a statement of the general character of dreams and dream interpretation in Tikopia; the adduction of full texts and detailed discussion has had to be postponed till a later occasion.

On first acquaintance with the Tikopia one would be inclined to think that dreams would not play any great part in their life. They press the observer by their practicality, their concentration on the material side of things, their indifference to matters which do not serve some directly useful end for them. They are by no means devoid of artistic feeling, but they normally waste little time in enhancement of their possessions; their bark-cloth is abundant, but coarse and plain; their woodwork skilful and effective, but rough. A thing passes muster, however uncouth, so long as it is efficient. The European who thinks to create an impression, in traditional style by the display of some trick or piece of mechanical ingenuity as 'white man's magic' finds himself put out of countenance. These people are not taken in by super-natural explanations: the thing is clever, they admit, they cannot do the like, but it is made by men's hands; how then does it work, and what is its use? 'Tough-minded' in fact!

[1] From *Essays Presented to C. G. Seligman*, ed. E. E. Evans-Pritchard *et al.*, London, 1934.

There is some excuse, then, for wondering if such flimsy stuff as dreams is of any interest to them, and whether they ever allow their conduct to be influenced by such immaterial considerations. Casual observation in this direction is not encouraging, but closer acquaintance reveals that beneath the crust of materialism and practicality lies an active belief in a world of spirits and immaterial forces, potent for good or evil, a firm conviction of their interference in the affairs of humanity, and a sensitiveness to any phenomena, however trivial and bizarre, which might portend action from the other side of the veil. The Tikopia dream, and they regard their dreams as significant of supernormal influences, though they do not attach equal weight to them in all circumstances.

Our study of the matter may be begun by indicating the type of replies elicited by concrete questioning when the subject is first opened. The question is put, 'Does a person when sleeping look on other persons, meet them, have speech with them, go fishing or to the woods, and on waking find that he still lies on his bed mat?'

It is admitted by the Tikopia that such a thing happens: it is called *te miti*.

'Do *miti* occur often?'

'To some people, yes; to others, no!'

'These *miti*, are they true?'

'Some are true, others are false, others are dreams only' (*te miti fuere*)—without significance, that is. As the inquiry proceeds further a mass of information is revealed which indicates that considerable attention is often paid to dreams, and the diagnosis of them is thought to throw light on the affairs of the normal waking life. Nevertheless, dreams in Tikopia do not obtrude themselves on the ethnographer. Unless he makes specific inquiry it is possible for him to be for a considerable time in close contact with the people without hearing a dream told to a group of listeners or advanced as a reason for following some line of conduct. There is no taboo against making known one's dreams; they are told willingly and openly on request, in good narrative style, with the native attention to detail and command of dialogue, sometimes with a strong affective reaction. But no systematic scheme of telling them exists, no formal technique of interpretation has been elaborated. Dreams when related are told casually, on waking or at odd moments of leisure during the day. Many of them, though vividly remembered, are not reported in public at all. Some dreams, too, have no significance assigned to them. It may be said, indeed, that the weight attached to a dream varies as the emotional intensity of the personal situation at the time, that a dream receives attention and credence largely in so far as it can be related to some question immediately at issue within the social horizon of the dreamer. It is this correlation of dream interpretation with the situation of the moment that explains the inconsistency frequently to be found in assigning a meaning to such experiences.

The Tikopia explanation of the cause of dreams varies according to the precise nature of the experience, but rests at bottom on the general theory of the mobile soul. Every person has a *mauri* or *ora*, an intangible entity normally invisible to the waking eye, which may for convenience be designated the spirit or life principle—the Tikopia terms being generally used synonymously—and this is capable of leaving the body during sleep and wandering abroad. *'Tou mauri ku poi tatafau'* 'Thy spirit has gone strolling' was an explanation made by one informant. In this condition the *mauri* has experiences which are transmitted to its mortal owner and constitute the stuff of his dreams. The Tikopia have no clear theory as to the relation between spirit and body at this time; they are separate, yet the adventures of the spirit part become the responsible agent, the property of the whole, and a person in narrating his dream uses the pronoun 'I'. Both spirit and body, in fact, are treated as the Ego. Other persons seen in dreams are *prima facie* the *mauri* of such persons, though here an important qualification has to be made as will be seen below.

Dreams of visits to distant places are readily explained by the mobility of the *mauri*, which can flash about at will, annihilating space, while the same power also allows it to journey to Rangi, the Heavens, and have contact with persons long dead. These are represented by their own spirits known as *mauri* in their lifetime, but now as *atua*. The recognition of another person either living or dead in a dream encounter, however, is not necessarily taken to mean that it is his own spirit entity which is present. Many dream experiences are the result of the interposition of *atua* of another kind, spiritual beings who have never belonged to human kind and lived upon earth, but who for their own purposes, generally malicious, counterfeit familiar forms in order to deceive the dreamer. We shall return to this point again.

The problem of mobility of the spirit of the dreamer in time does not arise for the Tikopia, since any experience which might be considered as an incursion into the past or future is sufficiently explained by the thesis of spirits of the dead living in the present in Rangi, or the powers of counterfeit possessed by non-human *atua*.

A question of primary interest is the nature of the dreams which Tikopia have, what constitute the 'typical dreams' of the culture under review. I did not conduct an elaborate inquiry on these lines, but such investigations as I made show that many of the same types of dream context are found among the Tikopia as among ourselves. In this my material agrees with the general conclusions of Seligman.[1]

Dreams of physical oppression of the nightmare variety occur, and

[1] *Man*, 1923, 120.

are believed to be due to unidentified *atua* of the non-human category. Such a spirit comes to a man as he lies asleep, steals up and presses him down, sitting on his chest or on his belly. The presence of the *atua* is made known to the sleeper by a heavy feeling on his body, as of a great weight laid thereon, and to onlookers by his uneasy movements. He turns uneasily, grunts, and may even call out in his sleep. If his movements are violent his neighbours waken him and question him. Such experiences are regarded as definitely unpleasant, and may be remembered for years afterwards. Thus one informant, a young married man, the son of a chief, told me of such an adventure he had when he was a child. He went to Maunga Faea, a locality much frequented by spirits—*e tapu*—and there chewed betel, chewed betel in great quantities. Then he slept and an *atua* came to him and sat on his chest. He shrieked in terror, the spirit disappeared, and a few moments afterwards he woke. He was surrounded by people who, as it turned out, had awakened him, and to them he cursed vigorously, objurgating his ghostly visitant. In this case the physiological prelude to his experience was probably the amount of betel consumed, but such a reaction is not recognized by the natives. The betel may have caused the sleep—or stupor, as it apparently was—but the spirit-haunted spot was the cause of the nightmare. To the Tikopia a dream experience is a reality—not identical with the reality of waking life; contrary to some anthropological opinion, there is no confusion between them—but an adventure of the spirit. It may be deemed true or false as a portrayal of events, the figures of the dream may be considered to be masquerading for purposes of deception, but their spiritual character is never doubted.

In fact the experiences of people in dreams are regarded as proof of the existence of spirits, and much of the information regarding the method of locomotion of these, their appearance, speech, and habits, retailed as common knowledge, is derived from the dreams in which they play a part. In discussing the movements of *atua*, Pa Fenuatara, a particularly intelligent informant, said, 'Persons in this land see them in a dream, in sleep at night.' Dreams are valuable circumstantial evidence for the reality of the spirit world.

A spirit afflicts a man in sleep for various reasons, pure spite being the commonest, but one explanation given is more charitable. The spirit comes to the sleeper because, it is alleged, it finds itself on a strange path in its wanderings, it does not see any light thereon, and says to itself, 'The way is dark, I will return to men.' Then it approaches a person and touches him.

An outcome of the belief that a person is always liable to molestation by strange spirits is the habit of the Tikopia of not sleeping with an axe or knife by his side. An *atua* may come to him and deceive him, pretending that it is a man coming to fight him. Then the sleeper, alarmed, seizes the weapon and blindly slashes with it, to the danger of property or life. He may cut a house-post, or even injure someone. The absence of intent in such a case is well recognized by others. 'He strikes blindly only, and indeed that person is foolish, he is sleeping.'

Dreams of personal activity of a violent order, with an unpleasant affective reaction, are not infrequent among the Tikopia. The dream of running with clogged feet, impelled to flee yet held back by invisible restraint while some being, either man or spirit is in pursuit, is well known. The Ariki Taumako, a chief of vigorous and somewhat dour personality, who formerly had several experiences of this type, assigned the cause of the clogged feet to the subject's sleeping with knees drawn up—*e me peru*. If a man sleeps with his legs straight out—*e fora*—and is chased by a ghost in a dream, then he is free to run, but if he is in a bent position, his flight must be impeded. This logical explanation, it will be noted, does not appeal to physiological factors as the cause of the dream but only as a factor of limitation within it; the dream itself, the spirit encounter, is an independent matter already assumed.

The remark of the Ariki that he *formerly* experienced the dream of clogged feet is significant. According to his own statement he no longer has this. The same is true of the dream of jumping from a cliff. As a commoner (*tangata vare*) not yet elected to the chieftainship, he often experienced this sensation in sleep; nowadays he is not subject to it 'because I have become a chief'. The differential liability of commoners and chiefs to dreams of nightmarish type or to bad dreams as a whole is acknowledged to be general. It rests upon the responsibility which the chiefs feel for the lives and prosperity of their people. Unpleasant dreams they regard as portents of evil, and a chief having had a vivid experience of this kind is considerably disturbed, and speculates as to its meaning. 'Sleeps the chief, dreams badly, wakes with a start then, and thinks what it may be, a man will die, or a hurricane will strike?' The precise form of the misfortune is uncertain but some disaster is indicated. There is no doubt that the chiefs take their responsibilities seriously in this as in other respects. With common people, however— as with a future chief before his election—there are no cares of such magnitude, and a bad dream is not regarded as necessarily ominous, and is treated more lightly. This difference in the weight attached to the dreams of chiefs and commoners is in line with distinctions made in many other social spheres. Whether chiefs actually do practically cease to have such unpleasant dreams—which would indicate a high degree of co-ordination of their mental and social norms—I am not prepared to say. I have only statements made privately as above.

Dreams of violent action of a kind common to other cultures, including our own, are general in Tikopia. A person is walking up in the hills, and either jumps or falls over a cliff, and wakes with a start; he is afraid and runs; he goes for a walk and sees people fighting, or he himself has a struggle and kills a man. The significance given to such dreams varies with individual preoccupation, and they may be entirely neglected.

The dream of losing a tooth has no stock meaning. 'A man may dream that a tooth has dropped out, he wakes up, but no! the tooth is still there. There is no meaning to it.'

Certain types of dreams are, however, regarded as being of more importance than others, and definite interpretation may be assigned them. These are concerned particularly with the pursuit of fishing, and the sphere of birth, sickness, and death—all, it may be noted, aspects of human life peculiarly liable to chance, and therefore apparently where some degree of assurance in advance is welcomed.

Birth dreams embody a certain kind of personal activity, of a neutral order. A woman dreams that she goes to the stream, fills her water-bottles, and puts them in a basket on her back. It is believed that this indicates she will conceive and bear a girl-child. Or if she goes out fishing with a *kuti*, a small scoop-net used on the reef by women, then the same interpretation is attached. Dreams of a similar type associated with pursuits of sea-fishing portend the conception of a man-child.

'She who sits there, will sit in pregnancy, will bear a male.' This dream has the same result, whether the woman has previously conceived or not. Any one of the *kano o paito*, the relatives, is competent to give an indication of this kind; a person in the family dreams of So-and-so, and announces the next morning that she will bear a child. The husband of the woman is also an eligible subject for such dreams.

Dreams of death also occur. Seremata, a young bachelor and expert fisherman, for example, dreams on occasions that he sees a canoe approaching shore with some of his relatives in it. The canoe runs in on a breaker, then swings and overturns—an accident which happens in real life. This he accepts as an indication that someone of his relatives will die, and waits accordingly for the news.

Death dreams in Tikopia have, as one might expect, a tragic, gloomy or disturbing context. They are not of the irrelevant type found in some native communities. There is usually a fairly close correlation between the affective character of the dream and that of the real experience supposed to be foreshadowed by it. Dreams of personal action, as of being chased by a spirit or of falling from a cliff, do not usually share this character of portents. They are regarded as events completed at the moment, not to be resolved in the future—perhaps since the final issue of the dream is really successful. Unpleasant scenes witnessed in a dream foretell undesirable events.

Another variant of the canoe dream is one in which the omen is given by the nature of the fish caught. Seremata says: 'A man sleeping sees a canoe coming in with fish. He is looking at a good thing if it has brought hither fish in plenty, but if it is concerned with a shark, a shark the body of which has fallen in, is emaciated, is like a sick man, then the dream is bad, a man of his family group, or he himself will die.' The association here between the gaunt appearance of the fish—'with ribs showing' is the idea conveyed by the term *maki* in the original; the same word is also used as a substantive, denoting epidemic disease—and the appearance of a sick man is very clear, especially when reinforced by this simile used by the narrator himself.

Again our informant remarks: 'I will be asleep, and will see my father, who is dead, enter. I look at him, and his body is good, that is he comes well-intentioned; but he comes and his body is bad, it is unsightly, as it were, like that of a person who is ill, that means he is angry, he is on the point of coming to afflict the family group. If I decide to narrate this to my relatives I do so; but if not, I sit then and observe the signs.' Here the omens are derived from the physical appearance of the spirit dreamed of: the native term *para* here translated as 'unsightly' denotes such conditions as wrinkled, rough, scaly skin, a disintegration of the flesh, an unpleasant condition of the body, which is held to be a reflex of the state of mind of the *atua*. For some insult or neglect, real or fancied—it would hardly be pure malice, from one's own father—he intends to visit disease or death on some member of the family circle.

As already indicated, however, dreams of evil are not always significant of illness or death; here as in other dream interpretations there is considerable variation. Thus, quoting Seremata again: 'I will be sleeping in Ravenga here, my relatives are dwelling in Faea. I sleep, the funeral of one of them takes place, when it is light the following day I go then to him, I go, go, he is sitting there, no! a deception merely.' Such dreams may be a correct forecast or may correspond to no reality. As he says, 'There is no sign for it that I know.'

There is one notable exception to the general rule that dreams of unpleasant events are to be construed as pointing to misfortune. This is in regard to fishing, particularly from a canoe at sea. The convention is that contact with human excrement in a dream is the sign of a good catch on the following day. Pu Rangifau, white-haired and frail, but once a famous ocean-rover and deep-sea fisherman, speaks of such a dream in his quaint style: 'The canoe is pulled, pulled then on to a bad place. A person sleeps, looks at the fish of the canoe being obtained. It came to rest then at the place which is bad. The person wakes and says, "Talk of the land about my dream! I slept then of the canoe which will slip ashore hither." We speak to him, "That there, a fish dream is that thing." Goes to sea, brings hither the fish, is correct the person who sleeping had his dream. The canoe is set in a filthy place, that is a fish dream; we know that a fish dream is that thing.'

This statement, though cryptic, describes the dream of a person in regard to his family canoe. He dreams that he sees it at sea, fishing, then, paddled inshore, and having shot the breakers, hauled up on land where it comes to rest on a spot defiled by excrement ('a bad place'). Waking, he narrates his dream to the household, who identify it as a token of a good catch, an interpretation which later events justify.

To dream that one's hand is smeared with ordure is also a fish dream indicating that one will haul up a shark at the next trip of the canoe to sea. The interpretation of unpleasant material, excrement, as signifying success, and abundance of fish is a curious piece of symbolism and difficult to explain, though the psychoanalyst might be able to provide a solution. The suggestion of association with ordure is unpleasant to the Tikopia in ordinary life, as is shown by the commonest form of curse. 'May your father eat filth.' In esoteric formulae, however, the higher gods are requested to excrete upon the land and into the sea, this being explained by the natives themselves as a deprecatory metaphor for the granting of fruits and fish as food supply. The identification of fish with excrement in this case may give point to the dream interpretation, though I have no confirmation of this from natives, for whom this association is an unexplained convention. One may wonder to what extent the knowledge of this convention actually produces the appropriate dream, and how far such dreams occur to fishermen in contrast with other members of the community. On this point I have no precise information, but the impression I received was that this was the dream of *tautai*, sea-experts, who had it more frequently than others. It was mostly with such men that these dreams were discussed.

The degree of rigidity in attaching a stock meaning to dreams is of importance. With fish dreams, as elsewhere, there is no absolute interpretation which is automatically adopted by the dreamer. Out in a canoe on the lake in the early morning I once heard Pa Fenuatara tell of a dream which he had had the night before, in which he had trodden into excrement and defiled his foot. This was at the time of the sacred fishing expedition in which all the clans engage in competitive spirit, striving as to who shall bring home the first shark. But Pa Fenuatara was in doubt as to the meaning of his dream. 'A fish dream, for certain,' said one of the paddlers. 'I don't know!' said Pa Fenuatara reflectively and continued to ponder over it for some time.

Each dreamer is liable to be uncertain as to the significance of his experience, until events have proved the correctness or otherwise of his surmise. He submits his dream to the opinions of others but accepts their judgements tentatively, holding his own verdict in suspense to await results. Dreams may be true or false, and as Seremata says, there are no signs by which we may know them—until they have been confirmed or refuted by the passage of time.

Inquiry into the reason for the falsity of dreams brings us back once again to the Tikopia theory of the motive power of dream experiences in general. They are the result of spiritual manifestations, of one's own spirit entity the *mauri* in contact with the external world, the *mauri* of other persons, or *atua*, the spirits of the dead, or beings outside the human range altogether. Some *atua* are well-disposed and truthful, as those of one's fishing-canoe, who are allied with the family and send fish-dreams to replenish the family's larder. Others are mischievous or ill-natured, such as the spirits of the woods, of the earth, and of the ocean-floor, beings who, never having borne the vesture of humanity, have no social affiliations with men, and desire to wreak on them an injury where possible. Hence they are responsible for dreams which do not mirror the future from a true angle, they misrepresent the situation and deceive mortals. It behoves a man always to be on his guard, lest by accepting the conventional interpretation of a dream too readily he be tricked and led into a snare. It is for this reason that persons, however ready to attach a definite meaning to the dreams of others, are usually cautious regarding the explanation of their own, until such time as events seem to justify a conclusion.

At the same time the doctrine of truth and falsity of dreams allows the belief in the virtue of dreams as omens to remain intact. Any dream the immediate sequel to which violates the general convention of interpretation is at once diagnosed as a lying dream, one sent by ill-disposed spirits to deceive the dreamer and confuse his course of action.

This brings us to the consideration of dreams of sexual intercourse, from which general category dreams of incest need not be here distinguished. Such experiences are not infrequent, among married men as among bachelors, and among women also. The object of the dream may be an unknown person, a fellow villager or a member of the immediate household. The explanation advanced by the Tikopia is the same in each case. If it were possible to discuss them in detail, it could be shown how dream experiences of a sexual type are held to be inspired by malignant spirits who take on the form of a person of the opposite sex, even of a near relative, and invite to connection. The mind of the dreamer is swayed to compliance, and on awakening the deed is realized.

This principle of dealing with such dreams on the basis of spirit-impersonation has two important functions. In the first place it tends to avoid any serious emotional disturbance occasioned by the thought of having violated a taboo—a man knows that he has not had relations, even in the spirit, with his mother, his clan-sister, or the wife of a friend, but with a stranger, an impersonator of these. There is no moral judgement involved, no feeling of guilt or shame. The dreamer has committed no offence, not even in thought; he has been duped and constrained by false spirits in familiar shape. His reaction is one of anger, he curses. He does not remain silent and sad. In this he is in a more satisfactory position than the dreamer of the Trobriand Islands, as described by Malinowski.[1] The Trobriander believes in the reality of the dream-form and is severely disturbed. He is fain to explain its incestuous presence by the hypothesis of magic accidentally misapplied, but cannot escape the emotional consequences of his dream act. The Tikopia is more free: while the Trobriander excuses the fact, he denies it. The Tikopia knows nothing of magic which works through dreams. It may be noted in passing that if a young man dreams of having had connection with a girl he does not regard that as an index of real desire on either part. If he approached her in the flesh with such a tale he would be laughed at as a clumsy liar. Fancy trying to attract a girl by pretending that he has had relations with her in a dream! What a story! She would tell all her friends and he would be laughed to scorn. Even if his tale were true it would be a female spirit from abroad, not that of the girl herself who came to him. Such is the opinion of my native friends on this point.

The theory of spirit-impersonation removes one from the necessity of accepting seriously dream encounters which are undesirable. On the other hand it goes deeper into the layers of the cultural strata than does the point of view of many peoples. Sexual intercourse in a dream is intercourse with an *atua*, who is possessed of considerable powers, and the result is a loss of vitality on the part of the dreamer. The consequence is not inevitable, and the event itself decides, but illness may easily follow a dream of sexual congress, incestuous or otherwise, owing to the malignancy of the impersonating spirit. In practice, such a dream is usually produced to assist the diagnosis of an existing case of illness. It is even probable that such dream experiences are invented or transmitted *ad hoc*, as when a close relative of a chief a few days *after* the beginning of his illness related an ominous dream alleged to have taken place the night *before* the first signs of sickness were observed. The mechanism of this dream diagnosis and the cure cannot be discussed here. It is sufficient to indicate that dreams of sexual intercourse, including those of incest, take their place along with other manifestations of spirit activity in providing an explanation for illness, and by consequence a point of departure for healing activities. By spirits can spirits be fought, and the whole technique of the treatment of disease begins from this general basis. The sexual dream has thus a significance far beyond that of a mere experience in sleep; it is an important link in an institutional chain.

As a point of general interest it may be noted that the idea of the Tikopia that a dream may be a false reflection of events owing to

[1] *Sex and Repression*, 1927, p. 96; *Sexual Life of Savages*, 1929, pp. 331–4.

deception practised by spirits bears against the criticism which Durkheim has advanced against Tylor's theory of animism. Durkheim argued that the savage could speedily find out that dream experiences were untrue, an illusion of the imagination, by comparing notes when awake with the person thought to be encountered in sleep. The inconsistency would soon prove to him that his dreams were not to be relied on as evidence, and any idea that he might form as to the existence of a separable soul, a double of himself, could receive no corroboration therefrom.[1] The doctrine of the Tikopia anticipates this criticism by postulating the existence of further spirits of a mischievous order, on whom may be laid the onus of dreams which are not in accord with fact. The spirit of the dreamer himself takes part in these experiences—this is basic—but the behaviour of other participants in the dream can never be checked because though identified as friends and relatives it is possible for them to be mere impersonations. The dream as an adventure of one's spirit double can never be invalidated by other testimony and the native faith in the existence and power of the human spirit to wander outside the body remains unshaken.

In conclusion a further word may be given on the interpretation of dreams of the portent type. In discussing the place of dreams as omens in a primitive community a stock meaning for each is often given by the ethnographer, the suggestion being that these meanings are constant for all dreams of the same type. There is no such rigidity in Tikopia society. Similar dreams may be rendered in different ways on different occasions, according to the problems of the moment, the stand-point of the dreamer, and the course of action he desires. In other words, there is considerable elasticity of interpretation, stock attributions of meaning are few, and the value that is set on a dream tends to be a function of the immediate practical situation of the dreamer and his relatives. This flexibility of the dream interpretation is one of the factors in preserving the belief in dreams. If a dream makes an impression it is told to the family circle and its meaning sought. At any given time there is a certain background of social interests against which it may be set; a fishing expedition, the future of a newly-married pair, and a quarrel over the boundary of an orchard, for example. The dream is discussed in this general context, and its bearings as an omen decided. But its interpretation is dependent on human fallibility: members of the family circle may disagree regarding it. Hence when its promise as originally understood is not fulfilled, the reason is found in a false attribution. The anticipated result did not follow, it is said, because the dream really referred to another situation.

When a dream is not borne out in fact the dreamer may say it has lied, whereas other people repudiate this suggestion, saying that the dreamer has merely construed it wrongly. To reinforce their contention they can

[1] *Elementary Forms of the Religious Life*, 1926, p. 57.

usually point to different interpretations of their own, slighted at the time, but now vindicated.

By admitting the fallibility of human understanding of the message vouchsafed by spirits, credence in the genuineness of that message may be retained unimpaired. Thus an institution or a belief persists in society, turning its very failures as weapons against the human agents who might be tempted to call its validity in question.[1]

[1] I hope to publish further material on dreams in Tikopia, collected subsequently and illustrating other aspects of Tikopia problems.

CHAPTER 8

AN ANALYSIS OF *MANA*:
AN EMPIRICAL APPROACH[1]

(1940)

Despite sixty years of discussion and a bulky literature the controversies that have raged round the meaning of the Oceanic term *mana* and its related concepts are still far from settled. Much of the obscurity and confusion has arisen through the fact that elaborate theoretical discussions have been constructed on the basis of inadequate factual data.

In examining the meaning of the native term the investigators have tried to arrive at their results by varying combinations of the following three methods:

(a) By attempting an exact 'translation' of the word concerned and trying to get a precise verbal equivalent for the native idea.
(b) By examining the relationship in native thought between the '*mana*-idea' and other concepts of the same native community; —that is, by obtaining linguistic explanations of the '*mana*-concept' from the natives themselves.
(c) By studying the actual usage of the word as employed in the course of normal behaviour and activities, and obtaining native linguistic comments on such usages.

The difficulty of obtaining any reliable empirical data in the last two categories makes it inevitable that nearly all armchair discussion has centred round the dictionary definitions supplied by the first category. The results have been unfortunate.

Certainly in past discussions concerning *mana* nearly all the initial emphasis has been laid on trying to find some European verbal equivalent for the Oceanic concept. The diversity of the resulting translations may be an indication of the confusion that has arisen in fixing the meaning of the term. But it may also be a reflex of the assumption that there is in fact any general *mana*-concept that is common to all Oceanic communities. Such an assumption may be quite unjustified; there may be genuine significant differences of connotation between different communities.

The following selection from the various meanings (not all exclusive)

[1] Reprinted from the *Journal of the Polynesian Society*, Vol. 49, pp. 483–510, 1940.

that have been attributed to *mana* shows the confusion; it also illustrates the theoretical preconceptions of the various authors. *Mana* has been translated as:

> Supernatural power; influence (Codrington).
> Magical power; psychic force (Marett).
> Impersonal religious force; totemic principle (Durkheim).
> Divine force (Handy).
> Effective; miracle; authority; prestige, etc. (Tregear).
> True (Hocart).

Lehmann in his useful collection of material on the subject gives numerous other examples. More recently, Handy and Driberg have sought an analogy for *mana* in electricity,[1] while Hogbin has compared it with luck.[2]

The difficulty of describing the concept exactly is brought out by Hubert and Mauss,[3] who characterize it as 'not only a force, a being; it is also an action, a quality, and a state. In other words the term is at once a noun, an adjective and a verb.' This seeming grammatical confusion has been responsible for much laborious theorizing. The elaborate arguments that seek to determine whether the nature of *mana* is 'personal' or 'impersonal' seem to turn largely on the question as to whether it is more nearly correct to say that an object 'is *mana*' or 'has *mana*', though as Lehmann has pointed out this distinction is not

[1] Handy, *Polynesian Religion*, p. 28; J. H. Driberg, 'The Secular Aspect of Ancestor-Worship in Africa', *Journal of the Royal African Society*, Vol. 35, No. 138, January, 1936, pp. 4, 8.

Driberg likens *mana* to 'an abstract Power of natural potency, formless as ether . . . It has been likened in its manifestations to electricity (though perhaps radium would provide a better analogy) . . .' 'Like radium it gives out energy indefinitely without diminishing its own extent or potency, and each spark is capable no less of infinite sub-division without loss of potency.' This sounds like a denial of the second law of thermodynamics, but even if the proposition could be defended by modern physics I doubt if it very much helps us to appreciate the meaning of *mana*.

[2] H. Ian Hogbin, *Oceania*, Vol. VI, p. 265.

[3] H. Hubert and M. Mauss, 'Théorié générale de la Magie', *L'Année Sociologique*, 1902–3, pp. 108 et seq. Their otherwise excellent analysis is, however, obscured by a mystical element which they bring into it, thus:

'L'idée de mana est une de ces idées troublés, dont nous croyons être débarrassés, et que, par consequent, nous avons peine à concevoir. Elle est obscure et vague et pourtant d'un emploi étrangement déterminé. Elle est abstraite et générale et pourtant pleine de concret. Sa nature primitive, c'est à dire complexe et confuse, nous inderdit d'en faire une analyse logique; nous devons nous contenter de la décrire . . .' (p. 109); and again:

'L'idée de mana se compose d'une série d'idées instables qui se confondent les unes dans les autres. Il est tour à tour et à la fois qualité, substance et activité.' The confusion and instability, however, seems to be the result of the anthropologists' analysis rather than a property of the native idea; indeed as this article will show the concept in Tikopia at least is entirely non-mystical, has always a concrete referent and is quite capable of being handled in a non-intellectual way. The complexity of the concept only begins to arise when anthropologists insist that *mana*—'c'est également une sorte d'éther, impondérable, communicable, et qui se répand de lui meme' (op. cit. p. 112).

material in many Oceanic languages. By some writers the notion of *mana* as 'a vague and impersonal fluid' has been represented as in opposition to assertions that it is derived from spirit entities.

The type of inference drawn for anthropological theory from the material on *mana* has been almost as varied as the differences in translation. A. M. Hocart has made an important contribution to the study of *mana* by stressing that the Polynesian conception is a practical one connoting prosperity and success, and he has also drawn attention to the fact that *mana* tends to be attributed particularly to the leaders of the community, their chiefs and priests. His inferences, however, are essentially of an ethnological order. He is concerned to show the archaic character of the Polynesian idea and its place in the history of religion as intimately connected with the doctrine of the divinity of kings.[1] A. Capell, again, in a recent article has attempted to trace the linguistic history of the word, taking its primary meaning as 'effective', with the general implication that the efficacy goes beyond that encountered in everyday life. With this one agrees. His conclusion is that *mana* is a prevailing Polynesian concept, but that 'exactly similar ideas prevail amongst the American Indians, but naturally under a different name'. He holds that the Polynesians brought the word *mana* with them from Indonesia, its incidence in Borneo and the Celebes being of particular significance here. He agrees also with Pater Schmidt that *mana* had its origin in and with mythology, developing in dependence upon an ancestor cult.[2]

R. R. Marett, who by his own statement is entitled to rank among the 'prophets of the gospel of *mana*', has stressed the view that *mana* and allied notions constitute the category that most nearly expresses the essence of rudimentary religion. His thesis that *mana* is the nearest expression of the positive emotional value which is the raw material of religion is too well known to need further discussion.[3]

Recently Ruth Benedict has revived this view in another form by stating that *mana*, *wakanda*, etc., have as their fundamental concept the idea of the existence of 'wonderful power, a voltage with which the universe is believed to be charged', and always the manipulation of this wonderful power and the beliefs that grow out of it are religion.[4]

In contrast to these latter views is that of B. Malinowski. He argues cogently that on the empirical material the *mana*-concept is too narrow to stand as the basis of magic and religion, and holds that the concepts

---

[1] 'Mana Again', *Man*, 1922, 79. It may be remarked that such attempts at recovery of the 'original notion' from which others have been derived rests implicitly upon a projection of a sequence in the mind of the analyst into the phenomena analysed. This sequence may or may not have been followed historically.

[2] 'The Word Mana: A linguistic study.' *Oceania*, IX, 1938, pp. 89–96.

[3] *The Threshold of Religion*, 2nd Ed., 1914, pp. xxiii–xxvii, xxxi *et passim*.

[4] In *General Anthropology* (ed. by F. Boas), 1938, p. 630.

of *wakan, orenda,* and *mana* are simply 'an example of an early generalization of a crude metaphysical concept, such as is found in several
other savage words also'. He adds the very necessary warning that we
have hardly any data at all showing just how this conception in Melanesia
enters into religious or magical cult and belief.[1] As will be seen, the
argument of this article agrees in essentials with Malinowski's position.
Controversy over the meaning of the term started soon after Codrington had published his somewhat abstract rendering of Melanesian
ideas on the subject. This was a set of statements which he might never
have given in this form if he had known that they would be treated as a
classical text by distant scholars, subjected to microscopic analysis, and
made the foundation of a system of primitive philosophy. The theoretical
structures of Marett, Durkheim, Hubert and Mauss on this basis have
in fact added much more to our understanding of primitive religion in
general than to the clarification of the concept of *mana* itself.

Indeed, treated in this manner, the word *mana* becomes something of
a technical term describing a specialized abstraction of the theoretical
anthropologist and, as such, may have little in common with the same
term as used in native phraseology. This fact indeed is appreciated but it is
still assumed without serious inquiry, even by the latest writers on the
subject that, quite apart from the technical usages of anthropology there
is in fact a *mana*-concept that is common to all parts of Oceania.[2]
Scientifically speaking, any such general connotation of the term could
only arise by inference as the result of the careful comparison of material
from different communities; but in point of fact little adequate material
exists.

It is true that the term *mana* had been known from Polynesia long
before it had received attention from the neighbouring Melanesian area.[3]
In the Maori literature in particular there are some data available which
have received less than their due.[4] F. R. Lehmann and E. S. C. Handy
have analysed the concept of *mana* from the available literary material
on Polynesia.[5] But while this material is important, it is unfortunate that
specific research into this problem was not carried further in the original
field-work. Moreover, too often it is the European's own conception of

---

[1] 'Magic, Science and Religion', in *Science, Religion and Reality* (ed. by J. A. Needham),
1926, pp. 72–3.

[2] Marett, *Threshold*, p. 99; Hocart, *Progress of Man*, p. 185; cf. R. Lowie, *Primitive Religion*, 1924. p. 76.

[3] W. Williams, *Dictionary of the New Zealand Language*. Paihia, 1844, where it is translated as 'power, influence'. A later edition by Bishop H. W. Williams (1917) gives 'authority,
control, influence, prestige, power, psychic force', and verbally 'to take effect'; the causative
whakamana, 'to give effect to, to give prestige to'.

[4] For example see W. E. Gudgeon, 'Mana Tangata', *J.P.S.*, 14, 1905, pp. 49–66.

[5] Lehmann, *Mana*, Leipzig, 1922; Handy *Polynesian Religion*, 1927, pp. 26–34. Some
pertinent observations are also given in R. W. Williamson's *Religion and Social Organization
in Central Polynesia*, edited by R. Piddington, 1937, p. 110.

the meaning of the term that has been placed on record and not an exact translation of texts spoken by the natives themselves. Again, the observation and analysis of actual native behaviour in situations where *mana* has been used as an explanatory concept is at a minimum. It is particularly to be regretted that Codrington, who knew his Mota people well, did not base his exposition on the analysis of examples which he actually recorded or observed, but instead composed some of them for his purpose. There always remains a doubt whether a native would really have thought out and performed an experiment in the way he describes.

The aim of the present article is to supply a body of empirical material from one particular area, Tikopia. By giving a contextualized description of the native usage of the *mana*-concept I hope to clarify its precise meaning at least for this particular community. By implication the material here put forward will also set certain negative limitations to the *mana*-concept in its more general connotation.

To my mind the proper understanding of the general notion can only emerge out of a careful consideration of particular usages such as are here recorded, and I would add that for our final appreciation of this general notion, if it exists, particular factual details may be irrelevant.[1] Thus, for example, the elaborate discussions that have been carried on by Codrington, Lehmann, Hocart and others as to whether or not *mana* is in the last resort dependent upon a spirit agency appear to me to be marginal to our understanding of the concept of *mana* itself.

I am concerned here first with the problem of definition of the term, and then with some other problems of the relation of the concept of *mana* to the economic and religious structure of the Tikopia.

In defining the meaning of the term I present material of three kinds: formulations obtained from men with whom I was specifically discussing the term, and to whom I put questions about it; citation of ritual formulae in which the term *mana* appeared incidentally as a standardized item in another context; and examples of the exercise of *mana* given in discussion of the behaviour and qualities of chiefs, comparison of past and present prosperity, illness, or other events in the life of individuals.

In presenting this material I give in translation statements of my informants, together with a few Tikopia texts as recorded in my notebooks. (In the original article, several other vernacular texts have been quoted as samples. Comparison of the translations with the texts will allow the accuracy of my rendering to be judged.) It will be obvious

---

[1] Note . . . '. . . if it exists'; Hogbin's material from Ontong Java and Wogeo suggests that the *mana*-concept is far from being common to the whole of Oceania, and hence he questions the validity of attempting to build up any general theory of primitive religion on concepts of the *mana* type. (*Oceania* Vol. VI, p. 274.)

that definition of such a term as *mana*, which is not the direct description of an act of behaviour or of a material object, must rely primarily on linguistic data. But it is important to note that this linguistic material is of varying value for interpretation. Statements given in response to direct questions of the order of 'What is *mana*?' are acceptable only when reinforced, as in this case, by material of the other types mentioned above, where the formulation arises from the interest of the native himself in explaining or discussing another topic, and so is much more part of a standardized attitude than an abstraction.

MANA AND MANU IN TIKOPIA

It may be noted in the first place that the Tikopia use two words, *mana* and *manu*, for the one idea. The problem of definition is complicated by the fact that the sets of phonetic combinations giving *mana* and *manu* in Tikopia have a number of different equivalents according to the context in which they are used.

Mana may mean:

1. Thunder.
2. Father (short for *tamana*).
3. For him, her, or it (pronounced with first vowel long).
4. Efficacious (equivalent to *manu* in the sense discussed in this article.)

Manu may mean:

1. An animal, particularly a bird (the first vowel being stressed but short).
2. Efficacious, etc. (as here discussed; the stress on the second vowel).
3. The name of an *atua*, a spirit-being resident in the heavens, identified with a star, and forming the subject of an important myth-cycle concerning storms.

As a preliminary explanation it may be pointed out that most of the Tikopia explanations of *mana* or *manu* are given by reference to the behaviour of their chiefs, and to prosperity, success, and welfare. A Tikopia chief is regarded as having a peculiar responsibility toward his people. He is considered to be able through his relations with his ancestors and gods to control natural fertility, health, and economic conditions, in the interests of his dependants. Material evidence of his powers is given in native belief by the condition of the weather, of crops, of fish, and of sick persons whom he attempts to cure. Success or failure in these spheres are symptoms of his *mana*.

I give now a series of statements in detail to illustrate the empirical presentation of the idea by Tikopia. The views expressed by Pa Rangifuri, eldest son of the chief of Tafua, may be first considered. The subject arose between us during our discussion of initiation-ritual prompted by a case then in progress. He said that initiation originated with the god of his clan and that in olden times if the sun had shone fiercely for a long time then the rite was performed to induce rain to fall—'to seek *manu*'. I enquired 'What is this *manu* that is sought for?'

He replied, 'If something is to be done indeed for the seeking of *manu*—(for example) you speak for the rain to fall; the rain falls; you sought *manu* by it; great is your *manu*; speech of praise is that, praise for the man (to have it said 'great is your *manu*'); he (the man seeking *manu*) speaks to his deity as my father is used to speaking to the deity of Tafua, thus:

'I eat ten times your excrement, Rakiteua,
Drench down upon the land.'

That means the rain to fall; thereupon when we see that the rain has come we say: 'the *manu* chief'. If we say also 'the chief is *manu*' it is correct. If he asks for the breadfruit to come, for it to fruit, and then it fruits, we say 'he has been *manu*'; the asking of the chief has been made *manu*'. If no breadfruits fruit it is *mara*. He is termed a *manu* chief, a *manu* man. He asks for different things, *manu*!

'When we look at the land to which food comes constantly then we say "the land is *manu*". But when we see that no food comes that is the *mara*.'

I wished to find out if my informant regarded *manu* as something generally distributed, and inquired if it were to be found in rocks and trees everywhere. He answered, 'O! It is not there in stones. It is not there in trees. It is there only in food and in fish. We who dwell here, when we desire food, the chief requests the god to give hither food for us. When we look upon the *taro* and the yam which are living, and the breadfruit which has fruited there, it has become *manu*, the *fakamanu* has come. It is not there in all things, it is only in food and fish. When the fleet goes to sea and brings hither fish, that is, the reef has risen (figurative expression for the rising shoals of fish), it has risen and is *fakamanu*.'

Somewhat later Pa Rangifuri and I returned to the subject of *manu* and he began by discussing it in relation to the position of a newly-elected chief. He said 'The new chief beseeches the chief who has gone for some *manu* for himself, that he may crawl to the gods and the assemblage of ancestors. Indeed it is! That *manu* may come for him whatever may be done for him, the orphaned person cast down on that spot.' (This is a technical phrase used of himself by a chief in addressing the gods to signify his humility and need.) 'The chief who has departed, listens to the new chief, beseeching him indeed, calling out to him:

> 'I eat ten times your excrement
> You crawl to the gods
> For some *manu* for me
> My hand which touches a sick person may it heal
> (When he touches, that his hand may be *manu*)
> When I wail for anything that it may be *manu*.'

'Then the chief who has departed goes, performs his crawling to the god, and stretches out his hand to him "Here! Give me some *manu* that I may go and give it to my next-in-line (successor)." It is given him by the god, whatever it may be, a bundle of leafage or the fruit of the coconut or a fish, or whatever be the desire of the chief who is beseeching him. Thereupon he comes again to sit in his place. He stretches out his hand to the new chief who is sitting among men (in the world of men). "Here! There is your *manu*." The *manu* is given hither after the fashion of gods; not a man looks upon it; he observes only the food which has become good, the *taro*, the yam, the coconut, all food has fruited well indeed.'

Pa Rangifuri stated that when an old chief dies his *manu* goes with him—the sun shines, water dries up, food is scarce, and so on. This is the 'parting of a chief'. Hence the new chief whose vegetable resources have been cut off sends a request for *manu* for himself.

I put a question as to whether there could be *manu* alone independent of these material things. He said, 'there is no *manu* alone of itself, there is *manu* of the rain, *manu* of the food, but no *manu* only. We look at the rain which is about to fall, that is the *manu* which will come, come to the new chief. *Siei se manu mosokoia, te manu o te ua, te manu o te kai, kae siei se manu fuere. Ono ko tatou ki te ua ka to, tera te manu ka u, au ki te ariki fou.*'

Some other explanatory material, obtained in other contexts, shows also this essential pragmatic aspect of the concept. Pa Rangifuri on another occasion gave me a formula used in a net-rite which I had just seen. It appealed to a spirit, Keretapuna, to turn to the net, to act as sea-expert, that the net might be filled with fish, and ended '*Ke manu ko te kupenga*'. When I asked for the meaning of the term *manu* he said. 'The *manu* canoe, the *manu* net, are those which catch fish. The canoe which has no fish for it, is not *manu*.' '*Te vaka manu, te kupenga manu, e au te ika ki ei; te vaka sise ni ika mana, sise manu.*'

Pa Motuangi, of Kafika, said of his mother's brother the Ariki Tafua '*Toku tuatina, matea na mana; ka fai te kava, ka to te ua; ka fai te kava ki te ika, ka tari mai; tari mai te ika.*' 'My uncle, great is his *mana*; if he makes the *kava*, the rain will fall; if he makes the *kava* for fish, they will be carried hither; carried hither are the fish.'

Again, I was discussing with Pa Te Arairaki of Kafika the canoe-rites of the Work of the Gods, and the celebration of what is termed 'Evil Things', an offering to the gods of the fish secured. He said, *'Ka tu te vaka i te toki, au mai te ika e toto i te tunga te toki; ena na tunga toki. Tena e manu. Ko te toki e tu e manu, kae siei se tunga toki, e manu foki; te ika fuere e au mai te atua ke kai.'*

'When the canoe is cut with the adze, the fish comes hither bleeding from the cut of the adze; there is its adze-cut. Now (it) is *manu*. The adze which cuts is *manu*, but if there is no adze-cut, it is also *manu*; the spirit simply brings hither the fish for food.'

On another occasion, at a yam-rite in the Work of the Gods, I heard the Ariki Kafika ask for *manu* from the gods Pu Ma, that the breadfruit might 'run', that is, that the fruit might be properly formed.

The term *manu* is used in a variety of ritual formulae in which spiritual beings are asked for practical results. Pa Rangifau gave the formula recited when the noose-method of fishing for *para* is used; in this he is an acknowledged expert

Tou soa Ariki tautai	Thy friend, sea expert chief,
Fatia tou mangai	Let thy tail be broken
Ke rere o kai manu	To dash and eat in *manu* (fashion)
I tou raro vaka	Below thy canoe
Inu tau poa.	Eat thy bait.

To explain here the significance of 'friend', used in a special context implying that damage is sought, or the identification of spirit and fish, would demand a lengthy discussion. But the significance of the term *manu* is clearly the production of a practical result of securing the fish.

Again from Pa Vainunu I received the formula recited by a chief in investing a person with a cordyline-leaf necklet to secure his welfare.

Te rau ti ka tutaki atu	The cordyline leaf is being joined
Ki a ke, Pa e!	To you, Father (his ancestor)
Tutaki manu	Join with *manu*
Motusia ki atea ko te fefea	Be parted away things of whatever kind
Ma te urungaruru . . .	And headaches . . .

'Things of whatever kind' refer here to the various types of illness or misfortunes that might afflict a person. Kavakiua of Taumako gave me the formula used by a chief to cure sickness. The chief calls on his father

'Au o fakamana i oku rima Pa e,	'Come and make effective my hands,
Ma te tauru rakau	Father,
Takina ki atea	And the bunch of leaves.
Ko te kafo . . .'	Be dragged away
	The fever . . .'

182

Pa Fenuatara, eldest son of the Ariki Kafika, explained *manu* as follows: 'In this land *manu* is there in the lips of the chief. In his speech whatever he may ask for, if a chief is *manu* then when he asks for fish, they will come; when he speaks requesting a calm it falls. That is a *mana* chief. But a chief who is *mara* there is no *mana* for him. The chief whose *kava* is wrong is *mara*. There is no *manu* for him. If he asks for a calm, no calm falls; if he asks for rain, no rain arrives; that is because his things (rites) are wrong.'

I asked if *mana* lay simply in the chief as a man. My question made him laugh. He replied:

'No, friend. His *manu* is given hither by the spirits. When he asks it of the spirits, if the spirits wish to give it hither, they give it, and therefore I say that the chief is *manu*. A chief who is *manu*—the spirits just continually rejoice in their desire towards the chief.'

I asked also if *mana* lay simply in the words recited. He replied:

'There is no *manu* in speech, it is simply asking. Now if I bewitch a man, I sit and look as to what may be his day upon which he may fall. If he is not ill that is the spirits are not turning to him, they do not wish my speech that I uttered. I am not *manu*.' This too shows the dependence of *manu* on the will of the spirits or the gods.

Several problems of definition are raised by these texts. The first is that of linguistic usage, as to whether *manu* and *mana* represents the same or different ideas. It will be seen in the texts above *manu* is used more frequently, but that *mana* sometimes occurs side by side with it. I asked Pa Rangifuri about this, and his reply was 'A *manu* man, a *mana* man; a *manu* chief, a *mana* chief; great is his *mana* and great is his *manu*—such speech goes just the same; it is praising speech indeed.' And Pa Fenuatara and Pa Motuangi also said that the two words meant the same thing.

A simple Tikopia assertion about the identity in meaning of the words could not be accepted without question. But I found that in actual usage by my range of informants, as can be seen from the texts, that either term is uttered with apparent indifference. The speaker switches from one to the other, obviously using them as synonyms.

A word closely allied in meaning to *manu* is *mairo*, though I heard it used mostly in reference to the healing of the sick. In discussing the 'laying-on of hands' on a sick person the Ariki Kafika said 'The hand of a chief is *mairo*; it touches and it heals. *Mairo* is *mana*. He is a *mana* man.' He explained further that if the invalid rallied at the touch of the chief but then died when the chief had gone, the people would say, 'Indeed, the hand of the chief, of course, was *fakamairo*,' meaning that it was this touch alone which had given the invalid sustaining power for the time being. Another statement points also to the equivalence of *mairo* with *mana*. 'The hand of a chief is *mairo*; it touches a sick person, he gets well.

He (the chief) calls to the gods to *fakamairo* his hand since he is going to the sick person.'

Further material on the linguistic usage was obtained from Pae Sao. Our discussion began on the *kava* ritual, which as an important elder he himself regularly performed. He spoke of chiefs and elders making appeals in set phraseology to their gods and ancestors to give them *manu*. He then proceeded to explain, 'The *manu*—that calm may come and rain may come, that the *kava* made to the gods may be *mairo*. The *fakamairo* indeed of the *kava* are the tokens of the *kava*. That is, it has become calm and it has rained.' Later he added, 'A ritual elder, a chief, is *mana*, is *manu*; the name of the chief is *manu* and *mana*.'

The position in Tikopia thus is that *manu* is the general term with *mana* as a synonym of it and *mairo* used less commonly, mostly in connection with healing. The usage of *manu* in Tikopia instead of or additional to the common Polynesian *mana* is puzzling. It is possible that the use of *manu*, in the sense we are discussing, is due to the fact that in this island *mana* is the ordinary abbreviation for *tamana*, father, with equal stresses also. This is speculation and I have no Tikopia opinion to support it.

Both *manu* and *mana* are quite flexible in syntax. Either can stand as a substantive or an adjunct, and can suffer some verbal modification. Some simple examples of the usage of *manu* may be given, extracted from the material quoted in this chapter.

Te manu ena i te ngutu te ariki.
The *manu* is there in the lips (of) the chief.

Na manu e sori mai i nga atua.
His *manu* is given hither from the gods.

Muna atu kuou te ariki e manu.
Speak away I the chief is *manu* (I say that . . .)

E faia toku mana ne manu, ne nofo ko ia, manu rei.
Because my father was *manu*, did live he, *manu* then.

Ku manutia ko te kaisianga a te ariki.
The request by the chief has been *manu*.

Ono tatou ki te mei kua fua, tera ku manu, ku au te fakamanu.
When we look on the breadfruit which has borne fruit, there it has become *manu*, the making-*manu* has come.

An interesting verbal modification of the term *mana*, which has a similar range, came from the spirit medium Pa Tekaumata, who after giving me a formula he was in the habit of using said: '*Tena tenea nokofakamana ki oku nea.'* ('That is the thing used to give *mana* to my affairs.') Here both frequentative and causative prefixes have been attached to the word.

To students of Oceanic dialects this flexibility of the grammatical function of the word will be no novelty.

There has been some discussion as to whether it can be properly said that a man *'has mana'* or he *'is mana'*. In Tikopia both types of translation would be valid. If the flexibility of the word in syntax be borne in mind an analogous situation in English would be of a man 'having' success and 'being' successful.

From the descriptive statements given above it can be seen that *manu* covers a category of socially approved phenomena. It signifies positive results attained. So when a man is said to possess or to be *manu*, this is a judgement in his favour. As Pa Rangifuri said, this is 'speech of praise'.

Standing in opposition to this active and socially-welcomed sphere of interest is the term *mara* which connotes absence of visible results and is not a judgement of approval. A chief who is *manu* is regarded as fulfilling his duty to his people and deserving their praise. A chief who is *mara* incurs their tacit censure because the visible lack of fertility reacts upon their well-being, which is his charge, and this is regarded as being due to some defect in his relations with his ancestors and gods. No action of any kind is taken against such a chief; his people merely grumble and speculate among themselves.

The alignment of *manu* with these positive effects might seem as if *manu* signifies the activity-principle in nature. But it is correlated always with concrete situations, falling of rain, growth of food, advent of calms, relief of sickness. In fact its very existence is inferred by such concrete results. Again and again I hammered away at my informants trying to find what was the meaning of *manu* itself apart from the evidence of it in crops, fish, and the like. But all my inquiries for the *Ding an Sich* came to nothing. Always it was insisted that the crops and the fish *were manu*. Now obviously my informants were not facing the logical and metaphysical issues squarely here, but their indifference to the existence of such issues is extremely significant. To the Tikopia, *manu* I am sure has not the connotation of an isolatable principle, a force, a power, or any other metaphysical abstraction—though it may be conceived of as a specific quality. The interpretation in terms of such abstraction can only be the work of the anthropologist. The Tikopia is content with concrete description of the results of activity and does not pursue the intellectual problem as to the nature of that activity.

It is well to reinforce this point by consideration of more material obtained not as the result of questions about *manu* but volunteered in an entirely different context.

When the seasonal dances were being performed in Marae, I participated in them. The songs chanted dealt mostly with the gods. When I asked why the dances were performed, the answer was given: 'They are performed for the *manu* of the gods. All the chiefs sing to the gods that they may perform hither the *manu* for the land to be well.' It might seem here that we are dealing with a native concept of the physical activity of man giving a stimulus to the activity of nature and using the theme of appeal to the gods as a medium of expression. But reference to the tradition of origins of the dances and to the beliefs about the gods show that though this be true as a sociological abstraction it is unjustifiable if put forward as a Tikopia idea. In Tikopia belief the gods give *manu* when the dances are performed because they see that the traditional ways of behaviour which they instituted are being faithfully followed; and they are pleased. Moreover, dancing is their primary amusement in the heavens and they are moved to interest and approval—and even to active participation when they see this practice being observed on earth.[1]

Another linkage of the idea of *manu* with physical activity is given in the formula which is recited when a sacred adze is being used on a new canoe being built by a chief. From the Ariki Taumako and from a number of other people at different times, I was given texts of the formula and the explanation of it.

> '*Manu!* for your *marie*
> *Manu!* for your *para*
> *Manu!* for your *varu*
> *Manu!* for your bonito
> *Manu!* for your flying fish
> *Manu!* for all your fish on the starboard side
> *Manu!* may an orchard stand for you on the reef
> *Manu!* let them rise from the foam of the ocean
> *Manu!* flick behind harmful things.'

Here again the pragmatic context of the term *manu* comes out very forcibly. The primary function of the canoe is to be an aid in securing fish and the kinds of most important fish are mentioned. The *marie* is a species of shark, while the *para* and *varu* are also types of highly prized large fish. The 'orchard' is a metaphor for the fishing bank, and again it is fish which are adjured to rise from the ocean foam. The last line is an exhortation to ward off those spirits of the ocean which are evilly disposed. Although it is not stated in the formula, this is an invocation to the tutelary deities of the vessel and of the sacred adze. The best translation of *manu* here is 'be effective' or 'be efficacious'. This example illustrates the use of the term *manu* in practical association with the citation of its material manifestation, the belief in the spiritual beings

[1] cf. *Work of the Gods in Tikopia*, 1967, p. 282.

who vouchsafe it and a manual act of canoe-making—all this in a ritual context.

Another manual act believed to be accompanied by *manu* was described to me by Pa Fenuatara in connection with the initiation of a boy of rank. The chief of his clan pours some oil into his hand, announces it to one of his deities and then rubs it on the boy's chest. This is to take away his fear of the approaching operation. Pa Fenuatara said of his own case 'I felt his hand strike my vitals. I was frightened but I felt as though he had given me food and that I was full. Great is his *mana*. Then my fear quite left me.' In this case the Kafika chief was a very old man and so did not attend the lad's initiation. The ceremony was performed by the Ariki Fangarere instead.

Other material was obtained in discussing traditional events. Pa Torokinga, an old man, was telling me about his ancestor, the chief of the ancient group of Nga Faea, who were driven off to sea by their enemies. He said 'Great was the weight of my ancestor the chief. His hand pointed to a man, the man slept down below (in death). His god indeed abode in his hand. He was *manu*. When he went down to the reef-waters and called to the fish to come to land they came—the *ature* (mackerel, which are netted on the reef). Long was the abiding of the fish; the land ate and ate and ate. He went and waved his hand at them to go; they went. Great was his weight. He spoke to a tree, the tree died. He spoke to the breadfruit, it came, it fruited.' Pa Torokinga told me that his ancestor, on the day he went out to sea (driven away) loaded his canoe with food, took down a length of bark-cloth, beat the sea with it, and tied it trailing to the stern of his canoe. 'The drawing away of the fish to go out to sea. The fish went completely. The reef was bare, there were no fish.'

From Pa Motuangi of Marinoa I was told of the time when two rivals both occupied the ritual position of elder of the house at the one time. In this dual reign both performed their own *kava* ceremonies and both sacralized their canoes for sea-fishing. When the rival fleets went to sea, fish were caught by the vessels of one elder named Vaiangafuru (my informant's ancestor) while those of the other caught nothing. 'He made fish for his own fleet but not for the fleet of Pu Fangatafea which came in bare from the ocean. That is, Vaiangafuru was *manu*.' I asked what was this *manu* and got the answer 'A man who is not slept upon by the gods, that is a man who is not *manu*. It is exactly alike (*taufangatasi*), the *mana*, the *manu*.'

Pa Vainunu of Kafika was one day describing to me various types of ritual chant, and gave as an example one composed by his father, a former chief. The song referred to the 'making bitter' of the lake. At certain times, apparently, the lake waters became affected so that the fish rose to the surface in large numbers, died, and were collected by the people who carried them home to cook. Pa Vainunu with filial loyalty maintained that this did not happen nowadays, whereas in former times it occurred, because his father was *manu*. 'The lake which stands there is not bitter in these after days because another has dwelt. When my father used to live it was bitter, from time to time it was bitter, because my father was *manu* as he dwelt, he was *manu* then. When he disappeared among the gods he disappeared with his own *manu*, and the land which stands here has become different. Because he called to his god; but they who dwell here do not know. The two of them, he and his god, have the same name. The name of the god is Mourongo, and my father had Mourongo as his second name. My ancestor Mourongo sat at the *kava* bowl as an *atua*, and prepared the *kava*. He listened to my father calling out among men but he himself heard him from the realm of spirits. My father called out:

> "You Mourongo,
> I eat your excrement
> Turn hither to me who am calling out
> Shake the *kava* pith into the lake
> To be bitter that the land may eat."

Then the *kava* bowl was prepared and shaken into the lake; it was shaken in the realm of spirits. And my father the chief called upon the god and therefore his calling was *manu*. The fish went and sucked the *kava* pith, went to drink of it, sucked, were poisoned, and died.'

Pa Vainunu gave another incident after this to illustrate his father's *mana*. He said, 'My father, great was his *manu*. He called out to the gods and his words were true. Look you upon me; I will tell you. It was his building of the sacred canoe which is drawn up there, Tafurufuru. As his building was going on the people went to hew out the vessel and he called for the fish to run hither. They ran then on the day on which the vessel was hewn out. The fish ran hither and the canoe was hewn while people went to bring hither the fish from the sea. They awoke on another day and brought them hither, awoke on another day and brought them hither, while the vessel continued to be hewn. The canoe was finished, but the fish continued still to stand. But when the chief who dwells here stood in his place he did not act thus and the fish did not run hither.'

Here we have the recital of a miracle performed as an accompaniment to an important act of a chief—for the hewing of one of his sacred vessels is one of the marks of his career.

In the above text reference is made to the *truth* of the words of a chief when he called upon the god. The meaning of this is that his appeals to them were validated by results, not falsified by lack of results. The association hinted at here is between correctness of the formulae used, influence with the gods, and validity of one's case. Such association was illustrated by a discussion I had with Pa Motuata and Kavakiua who spoke of their father's brother the late chief of Taumako. They said: 'Great was his *mana*, because he did not speak in lying fashion. He used to speak truly only; he spoke for calm—it fell; he spoke for rain—it rained at that moment.' From the first part of the sentence it seems as if the possession and exercise of *mana* were contingent upon the practice of truth and the leading of a virtuous life. From the remainder, however, the actual position is clear that the truth is an inference from the results of the appeal and not a prior condition to those results.

This series of examples, drawn from a range of informants in different social groups, show how any Tikopia explanation of *mana* is presented in concrete terms, and on the other hand how concrete results which are more than those produced by ordinary efforts are interpreted in terms of *mana*. In all these examples as mentioned already the reference to *manu* was introduced in the course of explanation of the particular circumstances.

One question which arises is that of the origin of *manu*. From some remarks of the Tikopia it might appear that they believe that it was essentially an attribute of human beings. Pa Rangifuri said, 'The *manu* is there in you, there in your hand which touches and your outer lips.' And, as mentioned earlier, Pa Fenuatara said, 'In this land the *manu* is there in the lips of the chief.'

The statement that *manu* resides in the lips and hands is an explanation of its immediate location. It is there for the time being because these are the agencies through which it is liberated. It is the lips which utter the formulae, the hand which is laid upon a sick person.

To the Tikopia the only real source of *manu* is in the spirit world. *Manu* does not mean the exercise of human powers but the use of something derived from gods or ancestors. One further example is the case of an ancestor of the Fangarere people named Rakeimaitafua. He was a *tama tapu*, sacred child, of Tafua clan, that is, his mother was of that group. One of his descendants Pa Fenumera described him to me thus: 'The coconuts came through him, his *manu*; the breadfruit and the chestnut. Things of the earth, the *taro* and yam, rose up above by his *manu*. He was *manu*, he sprang hither from Tafua, therefore the breadfruit and the coconut rose through the *atua* of Tafua; he made *mana* for his sacred child.' This point of the origin of *mana* from the gods was made over and over again in different ways by my informant. Pa Porima, for instance, asked the question, 'Kafika is *mana* through what?' And answered himself immediately, 'It is *mana* through Tafaki and Karisi who used to be chiefs among men, who used to be chiefs formerly in Kafika.' These two are the principal deities of the clan. The statement of Pa Rangifuri about *manu* being handed over by a dead chief to his successor has already been quoted. Pae Sao, discussing the same point from another angle, that of the relation between a dead elder and his son, said that sometimes the father out of pique would withhold his *mana*. 'It is clenched in his fist, the *manu* of the *kava* is denied to his son. The *manu* is clasped by his father and diverted away by him that it may not enter to his son.' This, Pae Sao pointed out, is proven by the fact that no rain falls and the sea remains rough, hence the son knows that his father is displeased with him and so addresses him in deprecatory fashion to induce him to relent. The *manu* of the *kava* may be affected in other ways, as by some imperfection in the form of the invitation or in the list of names invoked. It is held that an ancestor or deity whose name is omitted turns his back in anger upon the performer of the *kava* which is thus rendered ineffective. In other words he refuses *manu* to it. Pa Rarovi complained to me that when his father died he was only a child. He got his *kava* from the Ariki Taumako and Pae Avakofe. But he was not sure if he received it rightly or not. He imagined that certain names were hidden from him because at first his *kava* was not satisfactory. Later, on the advice of Pae Sao he inserted other names into his lists and received good results in the shape of rain, or clear skies, when he demanded them.

When we were discussing the relation of a chief's activities to the state of the wind and of the weather, Pa Fenuatara said 'A chief who is wrong in his *kava* is *mara*; there is no *manu* for him. He requests a calm, but none falls; he requests rain but no rain arrives. That is because his things are wrong.' The expression 'to be wrong in the *kava*' means to omit from the list of deities invoked some important names, or to use expressions incorrectly. A reason given for this is that before his election the future chief has not listened properly to the instruction given him by the reigning chief or other elders. He may have been too intent on fishing, or on work in the cultivations. Then, when he performs his *kava* and omits a name, the spirit concerned is offended, turns his back and refuses to hand on *manu* to him—that is, to give any practical results to his invocations.

An example of a chief calling upon his dead father for *mana* arose when Pa Rangifuri gave me a formula used by the Ariki Tafua in cases of illness.:

'Fokimainiteni!	'Fokimainiteni!
Koke ono mai ki toku rima,	You look on my hand
Ke fakamana i toku rima,	To give *mana* from my hand
Ka po ki te ngaengae	When it touches the sick person
Ke tu fakamaroi	That he may stand firmly
Ke laui ki te ngaengae.'	That the sick person may be well.'

The method whereby *mana* is conveyed to a chief is described thus: 'The gods take and place it on the head of him who has asked for the *mana* to be given to him.' Hence according to this theory the *mana* lodges in the top of the head of the man. According to the Tikopia it never resides in the belly. But the Tikopia ideas are not very clear on the matter of the relation of *manu* to the spoken word. On the one hand it is said that *manu* resides in the lips and might thus be expected to go out in speech, to exercise its effect. On the other hand, as just stated, it is held that the spoken word which invokes the gods is only a request for them to give *manu*. This position can be resolved by the thesis that a man first asks his gods for *manu* which, vouchsafed to him, he then emits on other occasions to do its work.

A summary of the statements quoted will help to bring the Tikopia concept of *manu* into relation with the points discussed in anthropological theory. To the Tikopia nature does not work independently of man; fertility is not merely a concatenation of physical factors but depends on the maintenance of a relationship between man and spiritual beings. *Manu* is discussed largely in terms of concrete results, natural phenomena such as crops, fish, and recovery from disease. Not only is its presence judged by material tokens, but at times it is represented as being in itself a material object—as when a dead chief hands it over to his successor or keeps it clenched in his fist. On the other side *manu* is connected with the personality of human beings, and is exercised through human agencies. It is not spoken of as a universal force inhering in all natural objects. The Tikopia view of *manu* may be regarded as an element in a theory of human achievement. Its thesis is that success above a certain point, the 'normal', is spirit-given. It connects an end-product empirically observed with a set of human desires by a theory of spirit-mediation and a technique of verbal utterance. To the Tikopia the end-product is frequently equated in summary statements with the means whereby that product is obtained. 'We look at the rain which is about to fall, that is, the *manu* which will come.' But the separation of means from ends is also done. 'The *manu* of the rain,' 'the *manu* is given after the fashion of gods; no man sees it; one observes only that the food has become good.'

The difficulty of rendering a term such as *manu* in translation is that of comprising under one head a number of categories which we ordinarily separate. Uncertainty in natural phenomena, differential human ability, dependence upon spirit entities, are the three primary factors in the *manu* situation. A possible translation of *manu* or *mana* in Tikopia would then appear to be 'success' or 'successful', which can embody reference both to the ability of man and to tangible results. This term is valid only if it be remembered that for the Tikopia success is not merely a matter of human effort. It is essentially success in certain spheres, those which affect human interests most vitally—food, health, and weather-control, but in ways with which ordinary technique cannot cope.

Another possible translation of *manu* is 'efficacy' or 'to be efficacious'.[1] Here the emphasis again is on the fact that the activity works, that it performs the function for which it was intended. But since the efficacy is believed to be only partly due to human endeavour, any translation must also by implication embody a reference to the extra-human causes of the result. The difficulty lies in comprising in the one term both the result of activity and the native theory of the reason for it. Any single word in English cannot therefore express the fullness of the native concept.

Most of the translations proposed for *mana* fail to give the reality of the native attitude, because of their abstract nature, and their introduction of categories which may have no counterpart in the native system. 'Supernatural power' for instance does represent one aspect of the concept but it leaves out of account the essentially material evidence of such power, and directs attention to the means rather than to the end-product. It ignores also the vital factor that such power does not exist *in vacuo* but is exercised by human beings or personified material objects, for human benefit. 'Psychic force' is a highly intellectualized rendering of the same idea and neglects the native theory of origins.

I could not find in Tikopia any secular connotation of *mana* as 'authority' or 'influence'. Where this meaning occurs, as it apparently does among the Maori, it appears to be secondary, an inference from the more basic significance already discussed. The possible difference of meaning of *mana* in the various Polynesian communities may lead some critics to the conclusion that the *mana* or *manu* of Tikopia is an atypical concept. But this is not a justifiable view until a body of empirical evidence comparable with that here presented has been analysed for those other communities. From the material already available it seems to me that the same factual definition of *mana* of Tikopia probably could be applied elsewhere in Polynesia, though in some cultures there is an extension of meaning into the social sphere. However this be, it is clearly inappropriate to talk of *mana* at this stage as if it represented an identical system of ideas for the Oceanic field.[2] So far as Tikopia is concerned however, we have now arrived at a factual definition of *mana* (*manu*) in terms of the following characteristics.

1. *Material events*, e.g. crops, fish, death of bewitched persons, cure of sickness, relief from fear.

---

[1] The translation given by Bishop Williams (*Maori Dictionary*) 'to take effect' appears to be an appropriate one: his *whakamana* is also apt.

[2] My research in Kelantan, Malaysia, has shown that a very similar factual definition can be given to the Malay word *keramat*, translated by R. J. Wilkinson as 'saintly; working miracles . . .' (A *Malay-English Dictionary*, Mytilene, 1932). That it also can bear meaning akin to *mana* is shown from the remark of a Malay friend of mine to me 'I think Tuan must be *keramat*—Tuan said "tomorrow you will get fish"; and I did.'

2. As a *personal attribute* of chiefs, though by way of illustration an informant may refer to himself.

3. Implying the *volition* of spiritual beings who grant to or withhold the *manu* from the chiefs.

4. Involving *value* judgement: in contrast to *mara*, *manu* and *mana* always have a positive connotation.

The concept of *manu* as being a personal attribute primarily of chiefs raises the problem of the relation of the concept to political and religious organization. To what extent does currency of this concept tend to maintain the organization and in particular the role and status of chiefs?

Viewed from one angle the linguistic concept of *manu* is a means of formulating the responsibilities and privileges of chiefs; it gathers into a single concept a series of disparate occurrences; material events, and the acts and influence of chiefs. The *manu* theme is thus part of the definition of a chief's job.

But the metaphysical control said to be exercised by the chief over goods and production by virtue of his *manu* must be correlated with the factual control exemplified by the chief's receipt of first-fruits and baskets of food, and with the ritual control exemplified in his priestly functions.

On the one hand the concept of *manu* tends to sustain the role and status of chiefs and to exaggerate their actual power: it is associated essentially with a chief, it is there in his lips and in his hands, it is given to him (and not to others) by his chiefs and ancestors. In this manner economic and social results which in a great part at least arise from natural phenomena (e.g. seasonal change, recuperative powers of the human body, etc.) are concentrated upon the person of the chief and thus redound to his credit.

But on the other hand, in contrast to this, material failure as well as success is projected on to the person of the chief and his reputation may suffer through events entirely outside his control. Thus though a man may be, from the outsider's point of view, an effective chief, with a sense of responsibility to his people, hard working and keen to give a lead to the economic affairs of the clan, and assiduous in the performance of ritual, yet so far as the possession of *manu* is concerned he may be put at a disadvantage merely through a succession of bad seasons. Thus from the practical point of view the *manu* of a chief is no thorough test of his efficiency. I say no *thorough* test because, as with the Ariki Tafua, attribution to *manu* to him by reason of large catches of fish may well be based in reality on his better powers of organization, or his superior judgement of place and time for fishing.

It may be noted also that even where a chief is rated low in *mana* this value judgement is not implemented in economic terms; there is no refusal, for instance, to give him the customary first-fruits or other food-acknowledgements. One reason for this is that his condition is not necessarily permanent; he may become *manu* again soon. Another reason is undoubtedly the social repercussions which any such refusal would involve. Thus projection of failure on to the person of a chief does not endanger the institution of chieftainship as a whole; all chiefs are not suspect because one is *mara*. It may be postulated that a breakdown of chieftainship in Tikopia from this angle would need a fairly thorough demonstration that success in agriculture, fishing, and medicine could be obtained on a wide scale in the face of resort to gods and ancestors.

POSTSCRIPT

In Tikopia in 1952 I made no extensive inquiry about the concept of *mana*, but found that such statements as were made to me on the subject in the course of conversation accorded with the pragmatic attitude described above, and referred to food supplies and to recovery from illness. For example, the Ariki Kafika, referring to the great lack of breadfruit said, '*E mara; pe ne manu, ku fua,*' meaning that people and things were ineffective; if they had been effective the breadfruit would have fruited. Pa Maneve observed, while we were eating pumpkin (a very second-grade food in Tikopia eyes) '*Te onge nei, e mara; pe ne manu, te kai ku laui.*' In this statement he was linking the famine with infertility; otherwise the food would have been of good quality. He went on to assign responsibility for this state of things to the chiefs, whom he accused of sorcery through envy. The Ariki Taumako spoke of the significance of the dart-match as contributing to the setting of the breadfruit and development of a good crop—'*te sakiri manu o te mei*'; 'the seeking of efficacy for the breadfruit'.

I was told again that *manu* and *mana* were 'the same speech—branching', and again was given *mairo* as their equivalent, with special reference to healing. A woman medium said, '*E mairo toku rima; e mairo, tera ku maroro i te ngaengae. E mana, e ora te tangata.*' 'My hand is *mairo*; it is *mairo*, that is (a person) is made well from illness. It is *mana*, the person is living.'

The view that *mana* is essentially an attribute of chiefs was not completely maintained; spirit mediums were also included as possessors of the *mana/mairo* quality, through the powers given to their laying on of hands by their relation to spirits. The inclusion of spirit mediums in the *mana* category was probably not a new development, though I did not specifically note it before; it is in conformity with the basic principle that *mana* is derived from spirits.

CHAPTER 9

THE SOCIOLOGY OF
'MAGIC'[1]

(1954)

The classical forms of magic hardly occur in Tikopia. There are almost no spells of the conventional kind, believed to be effective through the peculiar power of the vocables uttered. There are few special substances of virtue, such as the 'medicines' of common African type or the talismans of the Orient. There are no beliefs in witchcraft of a personal order, based upon a psycho-physical disposition or endowment of the actor. Can Tikopia be said to have any magic? I do not think the question in this form is important—except in its bearing on the historical and semantic problems of anthropological thought in this field. What then can I discuss? To me, what is of interest is to examine certain types of social action, and social situations, in Tikopia: the fact that these resemble in some respects actions and situations ordinarily discussed under the head of magic gives a useful framework for theoretical comparison of elements which appear relevant for sociological analysis. That is why the inverted commas appear in the title of this article; they indicate that as with Tikopia totemism[2] we are considering a variant from a generally accepted pattern.

THE PROBLEM IN TIKOPIA

What are the kinds of social action and social situation to be discussed here? Briefly, they are those in which a specific object is sought, with immediate or proximate time-place co-ordinates, by a particular person, by means in which a form of words is regarded as an integral part of the activity. My emphasis upon *a form of words* is intentional. It may be that in some forms of African magic the essential virtue of the performance is regarded as abiding in the 'medicines'. But even here it seems that explanatory or descriptive speech is necessary. Malinowski's theory of the compelling word is inadequate for general currency, but he was right in holding that a basic clue to the understanding of magic lies in the verbal element, expressing the human

[1] Reprinted from *Sociologus*, n.s., Vol. 4, pp. 97–116, 1954.

[2] Cf. Chapter 11 *infra*. W. H. R. Rivers held that there was a complete absence of anything that can be called magic in Tikopia, but he obviously had not grasped the true position. (*History of Melanesian Society*, I, p. 315, 1914.)

desire and will. In Tikopia the set form of words in such a context is known as *tarotaro*. This term distinguishes a verbal formula from ordinary speech, which is known as *taranga*. In reply to a question, the answer has been given me '*Siei se tarotaro: a taranga fuere*' 'Not a verbal formula; just words only.' *Tarotaro* is not used to signify all set forms of words; distinct terms such as *mako*; *fuatanga*; *oriori* indicate forms of words in dance song; dirge; and praise chant respectively. Not only is their content different; they are distinguished by the difference in their occasion of use and purpose.

The Tikopia word *tarotaro* has an obvious affinity with the Mota (Melanesian) word *taro*, which has been adopted by the Melanesian Mission as the term for prayer, and as such, is used in common Tikopia speech. It is possible that formerly Tikopia usage would allow the term *taro* to be used of a pagan formula, but nowadays the distinction between the two terms is kept clear. The term *tarotaro* is not confined only to 'magical' formulae; it is used for the formulae of the kava and other occasions which are part of the great ritual cycles which one must call religious.[1] The Tikopia make no distinction as regards category of formulae *per se*. But for analytical purposes one may differentiate, as they do between the situations in which formulae are recited. There are those of a generalized nature, where the objects sought by the form of words are health of the people as a whole, calm weather, good fishing, fertility of crops; and those of a more immediate specific character, such as a catch on a fishing expedition, the recovery of someone from an illness, or the death of a person. Generally speaking, the formulae recited to attain immediate specific objects do not form part of an operational series or cycle, whereas those with generalized objects do. But there are borderline cases, as with the *fifinga vaka* formula recited by a chief as his canoes put to sea after the seasonal technical and ritual overhaul, with the object of their getting a bumper catch of flying fish that night; or the *raufangota manu* formula recited by the chief at the most critical stage of turmeric manufacture, to secure a proper yield of this elusive and prized pigment. Both of these situations are part of the great ritual cycle of the Work of the Gods.[2] It is by supplementary terms, some referring to the technical processes involved, some referring to the object sought, and some of special coinage, that the Tikopia distinguish their formulae. *Tarotaro to te futi*, formula for planting banana; *tarotaro o atu*; formula of bonito, are self-explanatory. *Tarotaro fifinga vaka*, formula of sprinkling canoes, refers to the dipping of a flying-fish net into the sea and shaking it, as a sign for the recital to begin.

---

[1] For example see *Work of the Gods in Tikopia*, 1940, pp. 131, 132, 338. (In Tikopia there is a homophone *taro*, meaning the *Colocasia* plant. In Anuta, *taro* is used for formula.)
[2] Op cit. pp., 54, 353.

Tarotaro penu toki, formula for clam-shell grating, for enticing sharks, refers to the technique whereby, it is believed, these fish are attracted to the hook. *Raufangota manu,* 'deep-sea fishing for power', the basic turmeric formula, embodies the symbolic analogy of drawing in the pigment from afar, as one catches fish on a hook; it is a search with and for special powers for a very important end.

I am concerned here with the *tarotaro* as one of the elements in the type of situation to be discussed, and shall not examine in detail the linguistic expressions used therein, though examples will be given to illustrate points of sociological interest. The main questions to be considered are: In what light are these formulae and associated non-verbal practices regarded by the Tikopia—what is believed to be their effect and by what agency are they thought to operate? What Tikopia are believed to use them, do use them, are regarded as having a right to use them? What is the relation of such use and belief to the structure of Tikopia society? Can any differences be discerned in the various types of situation and practice? Considering that I worked on Tikopia both in 1928-9 and in 1952, did I see any changes in the 'magical' field on my second visit, and if so, were there any differences between different types of 'magic'?

KINDS OF 'MAGIC' AND THEIR PRACTITIONERS

To facilitate this discussion the Tikopia practices can be classified roughly under the same heads as I used for the classification of Maori economic magic: *'magic' of production; of protection; of destruction*[1]. (This can be done, since in a broad sense the aim of all magic is the increase, maintenance or decrease of resources, material or immaterial.) Examples of the Tikopia 'magic' of production are the formula for inducing plants to grow when they are set in the ground; the formulae for catching fish. An example of the 'magic' of protection is tying on of the ritualized Cordyline leaf necklet to preserve a person in good health. An example of the 'magic' of destruction is sorcery directed against persons or food.

In Tikopia there are no 'magicians' as such, that is, people who specialize in the recital of formulae and performance of associated ritual for practical ends, as their major occupation. Every performer of 'magic' is something else as well—a fisherman, a chief, a spirit-medium. But the social position of the 'magical' performer tends to vary according to the type of 'magic' performed.

In theory, the 'magic' of production may be carried out by any

[1] Raymond Firth, *Primitive Economics of the New Zealand Maori,* London, 1929, pp. 242-68. Cf. my analysis of the economic aspects of ritual in *Primitive Polynesian Economy,* 1939, Ch. V. For simplicity the rituals of conservation or increase there referred to (p. 170) have been included in this article under the heads of 'magic' of protection and production.

member of Tikopia society. With few exceptions, anyone who has the knowledge can recite the formula and perform the appropriate actions, irrespective of status in the social order. In practice, nearly all 'magic' of production is performed by men, since nearly all the tasks for which it is appropriate are those normally done by men. Only in such matters as preparation of *soi* (an aerial yam), or collection of crabs is there scope for use of 'magic' by women. There are however, practices, of oral education and a theory of entitlement which set some limits to the practical application of 'magical' procedures. Education in esoteric as in exoteric matters in Tikopia is not highly formalized and is apt to be spasmodic and irregular. A possessor of knowledge normally expects to hand it on to his eldest son or grandson, or possibly, to his sister's son; but there are few effective sanctions for this, and early death or lethargy are apt to intervene. Hence knowledge of productive 'magic' is very uneven. Some people try to use 'magic' without having been properly taught, but especially in the more important spheres, they lay themselves open to scorn for doing so. Lack of specific entitlement in itself is not regarded as rendering the 'magic' invalid, but increases the probability that it is in fact incorrect, and so useless. The theory of entitlement is directly relevant, however, with productive 'magic' which, like that of the *fifinga vaka* or *raufangota manu*, forms part of regular series of performances. Here the normal person to perform the 'magic' can only be he who is entitled to carry out the series as a whole, that is, the chief of the clan. In exceptional circumstances of illness or senility of the chief his heir might officiate, but simply as a substitute. But granted this uneven distribution of 'magical' competence in this sphere, the 'magic' of production may be said to be the property of the society as a whole. There are various social reflections of this. The esoteric content of these types of 'magic' is low; most of it is not particularly 'sacred' and much not at all so. There is no secrecy about it; its use is taken as very much a matter of course. It is not obligatory, but a matter of discretion by the person primarily concerned. Often, the occasion is one when the person is operating single-handed or in a small weakly co-ordinated group.

The 'magic' of protection is much more limited in its practitioners. On the one hand, there are those who have a specific status entitlement—ritual elders of lineages (*matapure*) and especially chiefs of clans (*ariki*)—to care for the welfare of their group members. But while Tikopia is rigid in its adherence to the principle of patrilineal descent, it does not confine spiritual benefits so closely, and custom allows help to be obtained by resort to another than one's own lineage or clan head. (This custom has an advantage in that it is part of the mechanism of organization in practice and theory to deal with failure.) On the other hand, 'magic' of protection can also be performed by persons of another social category, the spirit mediums (*vaka atua*). For practice in this capacity no particular status is required, only the ability to enter a state of dissociation and give the appropriate social responses. Here is an opportunity for women. No woman can be chief or a ritual elder,[1] but it is not uncommon for women, of ordinary as well as chiefly families, to be spirit mediums. Nor is this thought abnormal, or disapproved of, and they attend male as well as female patients. The 'magical' procedures of protection and healing are more highly specialized and individualized than those of production. Much of them is common knowledge in the society at large, but the practitioners are regarded as having the special entitlement by status or capacity which secures them from imitation. No one would use a procedure he had just 'picked-up', as he might with some 'magic' of production. There is a higher degree of esoteric content, a greater degree of systematization, a more complete 'performance'.

The 'magic' of destruction is in a different position again. To some extent it is a reflex of the 'magic' of protection; he who protects and heals can also kill. Its practitioners therefore tend to be the same. But there is the conditioning factor of sorcery everywhere—not only that it is apt to be carried out in secret but that belief tends to outrun performance. While performers of 'magic' of production are known from casual contact without concealment, and those of the 'magic' of protection almost necessarily perform with some degree of publicity (in pagan conditions), the performers of 'magic' of destruction are careful to keep their doings hidden. Consequently there is much suspicion, but little evidence. But unlike the conventional witchcraft complex, there are actual procedures which people can follow in the belief that they will bring destruction on others. For reasons to be mentioned later, these procedures are primarily at the command of men of rank in the society. Known possession of such weapons is part of a complicated set of relations between the lineage of the chiefs and the commoners. But before considering this further we must examine the question of how Tikopia 'magic' is thought to operate.

Closely associated with Tikopia 'magical' belief is their belief in supernormal power of the *mana* type. Though they do use the term *mana* for such power, the word far more commonly used is *manu*. I have explained the connotation of this term from detailed evidence already elsewhere.[2] It is sufficient to say here that the conception of *manu* has as one of its functions a let-out in the case of non-success of a 'magical' procedure. A formula is recited and the appropriate actions performed, but the desired results do not follow. The implication can be that the *tarotaro* is not *manu*; either the phrases are

---

[1] The status of 'Female chief'—*Ariki fafine*, is a special one, with social functions, and ritual significance, but without the political control and ritual duties of the normal male chief.
[2] See Chapter 8 *supra*.

wrong, or if they are correct, they lack the appropriate force—they are not 'heavy' (*mafa*). Alternatively, it may be argued—usually by someone else than the performer—that the *tarotaro* is all right, but it is the performer who is lacking in *manu*. (Some such explanation is clearly necessary in the major religious field of the Tikopia, to account for poor crops, etc., when a chief has performed what are obviously the same rites, with the same formulae, as on previous occasions when harvests have been good.)

The concept of *manu* relates to the quality of operation of Tikopia 'magic'. The agency of operation involves a twofold conception: that natural objects are sentient and capable of response to human urging; and that spiritual beings can be induced to intervene in the process. But their relative importance varies greatly according to the situation. At one end of the scale, as in planting a banana sucker or in the simplest forms of fishing, the formula implies direct action; a spirit being is concerned little or not at all. As the individual object becomes more valuable, or can be thought to be capable of contrary will, the entry of the spirit being is posited more clearly. An important point in comprehension of the Tikopia 'magic' is that the spirit being cited though often anonymous, is never of unknown identity. In all forms of sea 'magic' he is commonly addressed as 'Sea-expert chief' (*Ariki tautai*), a term concealing the identity of a named ancestor who acts as tutelary deity of the family canoe. In other forms of 'magic' he may be addressed as Ancestor or, particularly if he is a non-human deity, given his name or title. It is with this that the range of control of the various forms of 'magic' is associated. For ordinary 'magic' of production, especially those where the entry of a spiritual being is at a minimum, any member of the Tikopia community is eligible as a user, since he always has some ancestor at call. But the more important the 'magic' the greater the power needed to implement it, the more weighty the spirit being required for intervention, and consequently the higher the rank of the possessor and user. It is for this reason in particular that the 'magic' of personal destruction is believed to be primarily in the hands of chiefs and lineage heads who are ritual elders.

Some content may now be given to these general statements by a brief set of notes, selected from my empirical observations in 1928–9. I begin with fishing.

'MAGIC' OF FISHING

The Tikopia have a great body of knowledge about fish, distinguishing many types by name according to size, colour and other characteristics and linking this with information which they have accumulated about their various habits. To catch these various kinds of fish they have a wide range of technical implements: hand nets and seine nets, nooses, fish spears, bow and arrow, poisoning, lures, and various styles of hooks. In nearly every case there is some ritual which accompanies the technical act. Only in the case of fish spear and of bow and arrow there is, as far as I am aware, no ritual. It may be suggested as an hypothesis that this is due to the fact that the prey in such case can be seen immediately before the strike; there is an immediate relation between activity and result. But in most kinds of fishing the connection is not so immediate; there is a gap between the activity and the behaviour of the fish. In particular, the fish sought are not continually visible.

The major ritual act of Tikopia fishing is oral recital (*tarotaro*). Unlike many situations into which magic enters elsewhere, fishing rarely has any act beyond the purely technical one to serve as a vehicle for the spoken formula. The technical process itself serves as a substitute for a manual rite. The series of ritual formulae in use vary according to the type of technical procedure and of fish to be caught. They usually embody some reference to the technique, to the name of the fish and to its habits. The formulae vary also greatly in length and elaboration. Those used in crab catching or in reef fishing are short and simple; those for deep-sea fishing and for the catching of bonito are long and make use of elaborate metaphorical expressions.

The major formulae are far too detailed for full examination here. I therefore take for analysis a few of the simpler types of fishing, in catching small crabs, in using a rod and line at the edge of the reef, in diving for greensnail, and in line fishing from a canoe.

I went out one day with Seremata to be shown how to catch *rukuruku*, a small species of pink reef crab. This is not a common article of diet, but is sought for when the surf is so heavy that fishing on the reef edge or in canoes is impossible. First of all we looked for bait. A small univalve shell fish, *te sisi*, was broken with a stone and the flesh tied to a string which hung from a tiny wooden float. The end of the string, immediately beneath the bait, was made into a small slip knot. Walking along the reef at low tide, the fishermen selected a deep pool and threw the float into it. The float was termed the *vaka*, the same word as is used for a canoe. We were seeking small fish, *raukatea* and *tukuku*, to be used as further bait for the *rukuruku*. Before the float was thrown out, the fisherman told me the formula to be used. He explained that this float method was used principally by children for taking fish for food rather than by adults for getting bait. He said also, 'All the children know the formula.'

'*Tou vaka tena raukatea*	'That is your canoe, raukatea,
Ukufaki ki raro	Dive down below
Fakateretere ki tai	Speed to seawards
Fakateretere ki uta	Speed to shore
Oia ku ravea.'	Oia, it has been caught.'

But although the formula was given to me in full, when he threw the float out, the fisherman recited only a part of it.

The tiny fish which was finally snared was tied on to a stick and we went out to the edge of the reef where the crabs hide in holes in the coral rock. The bait was set before a hole into which a crab was observed to retreat and gently played to and fro. At the same time a formula was gently sung:

'*Rukuruku e, rukuruku e,*	'*Rukuruku, rukuruku,*
Pakio au o kai e	Be struck, come out and eat
Ngauroro ifea	Whence are you crawling
Ngatorotoro i o rauakoe.'	Crawl from the reef.'

This little song is described as a formula (*tarotaro*) which is sung after the fashion of a dance chant. As the crab crawls out to grasp the bait, it is grabbed with the other hand. It is said that if there is only one small crab in sight at the beginning of the song, by the time it is finished a number will be seen closing in from all sides (this, however, I did not observe). 'They have listened to the formula.' If no crab emerges in response to these blandishments, it is said 'it refuses'. Here is the concept found generally in Tikopia fishing that the formula acts upon the fish through its sense of hearing. It is treated as a sentient thing, capable of acceding to or refusing the command.

When a fisherman goes out with rod and line to the edge of the reef he seeks a variety of fish, the commonest of which are *api* and *nefunefu*. Each of these has its appropriate formula. I consider only the first-named. The fisherman takes with him bait in the form of shell-fish or scraps of other fish. As he stands at the edge of the reef or channel, he scatters some morsels on the water and cries: 'Climb hither the *api* of the channel here', then he baits his hook and casts his line. As he does so, he calls:

'*Api na api uri ma na api tea*	'*Api*, its dark *api* and its pale *api*
Mi ki roto vae tau fakapoke	Gather together and divide your
Pe ruru, pe ruru, pe ruru	pudding
Riaki ki runga tou sukusuku	Eat quickly, eat quickly, eat quickly,
Kai ifo i te mata matau	Turn up above your tail
Mori ki raro.'	Bite down on to the head of the hook
	Bear it down below.'

This is a very typical fishing formula. First of all, it calls upon the fish by name, specifying different varieties. It then commands the fish to assemble and tempts them by speaking of the bait figuratively as 'pudding'. That food is very agreeable to the Tikopia; fish are credited with the same tastes. The expression *pe ruru* is said in a shrill falsetto tone, and is heard more as '*prmm prmm prmm*'. It means that the

fish are invited to bite quickly and the words convey an analogy with
tying up (*ruru*) a leaf package of pudding when a person has eaten
his fill. They are uttered when the fisherman sees that the *api* are
attracted by the bait. He then goes on to adjure them to turn their
heads towards it, bite and strain on the hook (so that they may be
securely caught).

The man who gave me this formula, Pa Nukutai, said, 'Men of Namo,
men of Ravenga, men of Faea, speak in the one formula.' A father makes
known to his son the one formula.' This suggests a rigidity, an invari-
ability in the Tikopia ritual. But this is by no means the case. There is
no belief in Tikopia that the form of the words is so exact that a slip in
the recital will invalidate their effect or bring misfortune upon the
reciter. The Tikopia use in all cases what I have termed *free formulae,
not fixed formulae*.[1] There is a great deal of individual variation in the
words recited. Two days later I was given by the same man the *api*
formula again. But this time he inverted the order of the first two phrases,
substituted another word (*mangai*) for 'tail' and left the words *pe ruru*
till the last. From another man, Pa Teva, I received a much longer
version, which embodied the same points but elaborated them, stressing
particularly the theme of the provision of food for the *api*. He added
another theme.

'Te *tapu* has been long in its standing Seize your staff, bind up your hair,
The *tapu* stands to be breached   And strike your lips down below there
Where is the man who will breach   That your belly may be secured.'
the *tapu*?

Here the *api* is represented as having been prohibited from partaking
of food by reason of a taboo, but is told that the time is come for this to
be temporarily laid aside.[2] Carrying on the theme of the fish as a person
he is invited to prepare himself and rush off to a feast, to fill his belly.

Pa Teva concluded his formula, saying 'It goes and goes thus, but
the point to which it is fixed is '*pe ruru pe ruru*'. By this he meant that
these words form a central phraseology of the formula and should not
be omitted though the reciter can go on elaborating figurative expressions as he wishes.

I obtained these two formulae in ordinary discussion on shore. In
actual practice, as with the *rukuruku*, the fishermen did not use every
one of the expressions which they gave when talking, but recited only
a selection of them, and sometimes contented themselves with merely
a brief phrase. Thus the words *pe ruru* are basic to the *api* formula in
that the fisherman may frequently recite them alone.

[1] Cf. *Work of the Gods in Tikopia*, Vol. I, p. 11.
[2] The meaning of the 'breach' (*asi*) of an economic *tapu* is explained in *Primitive Polynesian Economy*, p. 206.

I now turn to diving for greensnail. A fine day is chosen and a crew of men take out a canoe, paddling out fifty yards or so beyond the edge of the reef. The canoe is then turned broadside on to any breeze that there may be, to offer a lee. The crew have with them some pieces of mature coconut flesh. They chew this and spit it into the water, uttering phrases of a formula as they do so. When I first saw it I thought that this was a ritual practice, but it was explained as *fakamarino*, 'sea smoothing'. The oil of the coconut does in fact give a more glassy surface through which one may look down to the sea bottom. As the canoe drifts, the crew look keenly down. One cries 'There is an *alili* (greensnail)' and jumps overboard. Competition is keen to secure the shell fish.

During one of these expeditions in which I participated I was given at sea the formula to be used. It is as follows:

'*Tu fatu kanofi*
Takitu tarua, takitu tatoru
Matou mataki i ei
Ko ai te uku ka nai ukufia
Ngaoro pe te sisi
Fakasa fakataata tou fau i katea
Tou vaerangi taurekareka
Ariki tautai
Furifurisia o fatu akau
O raro na
Ke tu ma fatu kanofi.'

'Stand a fleshy shell
Standing each in twos, standing each in threes,
May we look upon it.
Who will dive and bring it up?
Crawl like a *sisi* (small shell);
Appear and make pale your whorls to starboard,
Your beautiful sky.
Sea-expert chief!
Let there be turned up stones of the reef
Below there
To stand with fleshy shells.'

The expression 'fleshy shell' is a synonym for the greensnail. It is adjured to be in groups on the sea floor, crawling like the *sisi*, which small mollusc is found in great numbers in the reef waters. The reference to the sky is supposed to be an aesthetic inducement to the snail to allow itself to be brought up (diving needs calm weather).

Here again, though I was given a complete formula on the spot when the members of the crew were actually looking over the side they at no time recited the full set of phrases. From time to time they called out, '*Alili* O, light be your whorls'; 'Friend, *alili* O, crawl over', and similar expressions. I asked if the snail and fish listened to the words that were spoken. Pa Teva replied, 'We do not know; it lives in the ocean. The speech is simply made. One fish hears, another not.' But here comes in an extra element. Introduced into this formula is a mention of the Sea-expert chief, the generic term for the tutelary spirit of the canoe. The spirit is being asked to turn the snail upwards so that the white under surface may be more easily visible from the canoe. (Apparently snails are often seen to occur in such position.)

A final example of fishing 'magic' may be given from hand-lining at sea. I went out one morning with Pa Rangifuri and three of his kinsfolk. He himself was in the bow, as is usual with a principal fisher-man. He baited his hooks with pieces of fresh flying-fish, then carefully hung a coral boulder on the tip of one of the hooks and lowered the line overboard.[1] As the line was being lowered the fisherman uttered frag-ments of a formula, a few sentences at a time. These were said in much the same tone as ordinary conversation, high-pitched and in a voice of command resembling the address to a wilful or disobedient child. There was no particular attitude of reverence or awe shown; the sentences were spoken in the interludes of ordinary talk. The expression most often repeated was '*kai ko ni ika*'. 'bite, some fish', and this was the burthen of the recital throughout. Another set of phrases frequently used was:

'*Vero manu, vero,*	'Lower successfully, lower
Poipoi tu atu ki raro tou fatu	Go and stand there below, your stone;
Fakato	Make it fall down;
Taomia atu ki raro se ika mero.'	Be pressed down below a red fish.'

Here are three common elements: the appeal for success (*manu*)—made by implication to the canoe spirit; a command for the sinker to go down to the bottom and not to slip off *en route*; and a command for a fish to take the hook. From time to time the people in the canoe who are not fishing may also encourage the fish with scraps of the formulae. Thus suddenly the steersman calls out, 'Bite, a red fish.' (*Ika mero* is a synonym for a common fish, the *marau*.)

On this occasion the first place fished proved barren and the canoe was moved off elsewhere. Here too at first there was no success; two fish were hooked but were lost as the line was drawn up. I noticed that at this point sentences of the formula were uttered with greater frequency and some degree of exasperation. The fish were nibbling but

---

[1] The reason for this detachable sinker is that when it reaches the bottom it slips off and the line is left free. It is uneconomic in that it involves time in collecting suitable boulders from the reef before going out, but it allows the line to be hauled in rapidly. The Tikopia have developed no form of permanent sinker, except for reef-edge fishing.

would not bite further. The fisherman tried to make them bite by jerking on his line, but fruitlessly. Angrily he exclaimed, 'Fish won't stay on.' We discussed the reasons for the lack of success. The fisherman first said disgustedly, 'I don't know.' Then after a couple had been hauled in he advanced unsolicited the reason for the previous non-success—the wailing of people at a funeral party on shore, which had distracted the ancestors responsible for looking after the canoe and bringing in fish.

FEATURES OF TIKOPIA 'MAGIC'

These examples bring out the main features of the Tikopia productive 'magic'. The essence of the 'magic' is the formula. There is no accompanying manual rite[1] or magic substance which acts as vehicle for the application and transmission of the words to their object; the place of such is filled by the technical act itself. Ritual utterance and technical or ordinary social utterance are closely integrated. The formulae used are of 'free' not fixed type. A differentiation must be made between what may be called the *traditional* or *professed formula*—the educational medium handed on to others—and the *operational* or *working* formula, which is actually used on the job. Yet the difference between the traditional formula and the operational is not constant for every type of activity. Comparison of formulae for bonito-fishing and shark-fishing with those of ordinary handlining would have shown that in the former cases the formula as actually recited tends to correspond more closely with that which is regarded as the accepted version outside the immediate fishing context. But in all this the principle of *selective utterance* is important. This operates in two ways: those not fully conversant with the traditional formula will use the phrases they know, which tend to be the obvious commands; while those who are fully conversant take from it only a few phrases when they are at work. Such phrases are often highly elliptical or evocative. With this freedom is linked an absence of belief that a slip in recital means danger to the reciter. With it is linked too the notion that the words are not automatic in their action; they are rather of 'persuasive effect', as lawyers might say. They impute an element of choice in the object addressed. Moreover, the notion of direct action of word upon object is combined with the notion of indirect action, whereby the entry of a spirit being provides an additional factor of elasticity.

From this two further conclusions can be drawn. One is the importance of the recognition of an intermediary category between spell and prayer. If spell is the *mandatory* or compulsive word, and prayer the

---

[1] Save in shark-fishing, where the grating of clam shells is believed by the Tikopia to be as much technical as ritual, and a few other border-line cases.

invocatory or *propitiatory* word, the Tikopia formula is, above all, the *hortatory* word. It neither commands nor beseeches, it urges compliance. (There is a fourth category, the descriptive or *explanatory word* in ritual situations, as illustrated, for example, in the information given about a patient to a spirit medium in a state of possession.) The other conclusion is that the hortatory word is often cathartic in function. The Tikopia formulae of productive 'magic' are a verbal complement to manual action, with some analogy with the kind of speech often addressed in Western culture to animals and machines with which we have to do. The words uttered are an outlet for interest and physical energy. They may not increase the confidence of a fisherman that he will be successful; they may not offer any direct contribution to the organization of the activity as a whole; they may not help to fill any gaps in his knowledge of the marine environment. But if form has value, these set series of expressions, with traditional sanction, may be economical of energy in situations of stress.

A similar cathartic function could be indicated for the Tikopia 'magic' of protection and 'magic' of destruction, which there is no space to describe now. Here technical procedures are at a minimum, and the formulae, with their accompanying ritual procedures, may be regarded as in part providing catharsis for tensions on the part of the performer. The phrases uttered in the 'magic' of protection are akin to the soothing, generalized, rather trite expressions for health or recovery in common use on social occasions. The phrases uttered in the 'magic' of destruction have affinity with the curses which consign a person to the nether powers. The line between cursing as a social act and cursing as a ritual act is indeed not a simple one to draw in Tikopia. One of the main differences is the specification in the latter case of a particular spirit being by name—often chosen to be of opposite sex to the intended victim.

But this cathartic function is primarily individual. Socially there are other functions, both manifest and latent. These can be most easily considered by comparing the condition of 'magic' in Tikopia in 1928–9, as discussed so far, with that in 1952.

A COMPARISON OVER TIME

When I revisited Tikopia after the absence of a generation I found that the 'magic' of production in its traditional form had undoubtedly declined. The situation had changed in two respects. In the general field of fish ritual, while the three pagan chiefs still continued their appeals for fish as part of their kava rites, they now had more competition. The mission teachers, more numerous and more powerful than before, took a more prominent part in praying for fish, while spirit mediums were more active in 'asking' their familiar spirits to help. All parties claimed successes. There was a tendency therefore for the traditional ritual balance to be disturbed, with confusion as to who were the people primarily responsible in producing fish, and who were primarily entitled to do so. (The answer was by no means clear-cut.) In the more specific field, there was less use of individual *tarotaro*. Formulae seemed to be rarely if ever used for *api* or for greensnail. Two well-known fishing experts, Pa Teva and Pa Motuata, from whom I formerly got the 'magic' of shark-catching, told me that this has now been discarded. A few men rub clam shells together to bring the shark, but recite only a phrase or so of the long traditional formula. A man will say, 'Bite, a fish!' Or as he feels the tug of the shark on the hook he may call out, 'Keep still! Put on your breast pendant'—a reference to the symbolic way in which the hook is represented to the fish as an adornment for his neck! Some men grate the clam shells but recite no *tarotaro* at all—in some places they don't know it. The other most elaborate form of fishing 'magic', for catching bonito (*tarotaro o atu*) had also a much reduced currency. A very few men of middle age were expert bonito fishermen, and knew the formula. The moderns as a whole, it was said, did not know it. By 1952 the chase of bonito had been practically given up. But one fisherman who had tried often and abandoned it because of lack of success, illustrated the position. He said he did not know the formula; his grandfather, a noted expert, had never taught it to him. If he knew the formula, he said, he would go and try again—but he didn't know if the bonito would respond to it or not. On the other hand, when the Ariki Tafua (a young man and a Christian) went out after bonito in 1952, he used the formula ardently and consistently—though without success. This mixture of ignorance and semi-sceptical, semi-trusting attitude towards the 'magic' of production was characteristic of many of the younger men in 1952, in contrast to the fairly solid belief of 1928–9. Among the older men, belief in spirit control was still fairly definite. After our talk on shark 'magic', my informants, who were both Christians, asserted that the tutelary deities of the canoes were still active. When I asked Pa Teva the same question as I did twenty-four years before, does the fish hear the words of the formula, the reply was 'I don't know. But it is held that the deity of the canoe hears.' 'Is it true?' I asked. 'It is true. When some shark is hauled up, there is the cut of the adze—there on the body of the shark. That is the deity of the canoe who has gone and cut the fish so that it will die, to come and bite on to the hook.' 'But do the canoe deities still go to sea?' 'They go. The deity of one canoe arms himself with a spear; another deity of another canoe furnishes himself with an adze; while the deity of another vessel furnishes himself with an arrow. Even when a sacred canoe has been de-sacralized (when the owner has become a

Christian) the deity doesn't stop, because his name has been attributed to the vessel.' Such views were confirmed by other men. While the younger people might be often sceptical about the existence, or at least the powers of spirit beings controlling fish, their elders still believed.

The problem is then, why should the 'magic' of production have declined? One answer commonly given, and partly true for the bonito, would be that the techniques of production have changed. But this is not so for Tikopia production in general, yet. Most forms of fishing and other craft occupations are still practised as before. We must look then to sociological, not technological reasons. Of these there would seem to be several. With many young people, grown up entirely in the Christian faith, belief in traditional spirit beings may not have been obliterated, but it is peripheral, not nuclear, in their thinking. Brought up to believe that the fruits of the earth come from God, they may still think that *atua* have some influence upon fertility and yields, but this is not strong enough to make them take trouble to learn formulae. On the other side, their elders may not have changed their basic convictions, even when converted to Christianity; but while they do not think 'magic' is invalid, there is sufficient uncertainty for them about spiritual responsibility for crops and fish to absolve them from the obligation to see that the younger generation are taught formulae. Apart from such shaking of the educational tradition, the general widening of Tikopia cultural horizons, including the growing appreciation of how other peoples abroad use techniques, without 'magic', has tended to decrease interest in formulae as aids to production. On the other, it is significant that in many cases brief, expressive phrases have been retained and are uttered in the midst of work. Here is the exercise of the outlet or cartharctic function in attenuated form.

It will have been noted that a decrease in the 'magic' of production is associated to some extent with the provision of an alternative, in the form of generalized prayers by mission teachers. This provision of alternative is seen more clearly with the 'magic' of protection. In traditional Tikopia ritual the 'magic' of protection is epitomized especially by the wearing of an oiled leaf circlet, put round the neck of a person by a chief or ritual elder with a formula for health and welfare. This is still done in pagan circles, and has the sociological function of serving as a demonstration of a ritual relation, and up to a point, a political relation between the person so invested and the man of rank. Practising Christians do not normally have such investment. But a similar function for them is fulfilled by the wearing of the Cross. Both it and the leaf necklet are described by the same general term *feao*, a ritually protective token. A conversation I had with two Christian lads in 1952 will illustrate the point. The Ariki Taumako, one of the three pagan chiefs, was about to hold an investiture one morning, I asked the lads if the leaf circlet was effective, was it 'correct'? They answered that is was—'the blocking of anything foolish', i.e. of maleficent influences. 'Then why don't you two go and get your circlets?' I asked ironically. 'The dark crowd'—i.e. it's a pagan affair. 'Have you got your own protection then?' 'Yes! the necklet of the Church.' The Cross on a chain round the neck was their *feao*, their spiritual protection against physical ills. Such a Cross can be made by anyone, they said, from the appropriate materials—copper and a white metal such as aluminium or stainless steel. When it is made it does not need to be taken to be blessed by the priest; it is simply hung on the neck. But when the person goes to bathe, or to excrete, it should not be taken, but hung up in the house. If it should be taken to such contaminated places, ill results would occur.

Certain traditional formulae of protective 'magic' seem to have practically died out. In 1929 I was given a protective formula known as *te pongi* by two experts in such matters. In 1952 the brother's son of one of them and successor to the ritual affairs of the lineage, did not know the formula, and did not even know what it was—he had heard of it rather vaguely, but thought it was something performed at sea. But in another direction, that of spirit mediumship for healing, there seemed to have been some enlargement of role. There were three reasons for this. Firstly, the relatively smaller part played by the rituals of the pagan chiefs in the total Tikopia sphere gave those of the spirit mediums more importance. Secondly, in the loosened state of Tikopia ritual allegiance, they were relatively freer agents, operating outside the authority of the chiefs to a greater extent than formerly. Thirdly, whereas in 1929 spirit mediums were tolerated within the Church, a sharpening of the doctrinal and political issues of Christianity versus the traditional beliefs had by 1952 made their position more controversial. Another reason too perhaps, was that by 1952 the limitations of Christianity as a means of preservation of bodily health were more clearly realized than in 1929, so that many people, Christian as well as pagan, tended to turn in time of sickness to others than the Christian priest and teachers. In the absence of developed medical facilities on the island, they turned to the spirit mediums. Mediums alleged even that some Christian teachers themselves had done this.

To sum up, for the 'magic' of protection, a generation of experience brought substitution rather than abandonment. The situation as regards the 'magic' of destruction is more complicated, since the moral criterion enters more deeply. For the traditional 'magic' of production and 'magic' of protection the issue is fairly clear-cut. For pagan Tikopia they are good, for Christian Tikopia they should be, in theory, bad—though in practice many regard them as at least neutral. But the 'magic' of destruction as a general category is bad for all Tikopia. It is only in special circumstances, as a punishment for evildoing, that a person will justify its use, either by himself or others. Yet its use is less easy to pin down. A person is easily seen to perform 'magic' of production or protection; hardly anyone ever knows if someone performs 'magic' of destruction. Controversy about the former is primarily in terms of their validity; about the latter, in terms of its existence. Its validity is hardly questioned by Christian or pagan. It would seem as if the more remote the matter is from ordinary experience, the greater faith in it.

In 1928–9 I heard various accusations of sorcery, levelled on the whole against men of rank, including two chiefs. The Ariki Tafua, in particular, was alleged to have practised sorcery against men of his own clan, in order to secure their lands. In 1952 my impression was that such accusations were at least common. One spirit medium, a woman, cited three cases of patients of hers who had been made ill by sorcery. Another spirit medium, a man, gave sorcery as the reason why the shoals of fish—mackerel and another small pelagic fish—which he claimed to have brought inshore did not always come in over the reef, where they could be caught. He commented, 'If I knew the man who worked sorcery on the fish, I would tell you his name, that you might write it down, but I do not know. A man who practises sorcery, his mind is evil, he's a bad man.' He was a Christian, as also were his family, who shared his views. Another case concerned a girl in the village where we lived. She fell ill, probably with the influenza which was then beginning to be epidemic. By various village people, including her father, she was said to have been affected by sorcery, because she had accused two men of chiefly family of having stolen some of our food. When she told us this, she said she was afraid of being beaten by these two; her illness, she believed later, was a spiritual affliction from the same source.

SORCERY ALLEGATIONS SYMBOLIZE SOCIAL RELATIONS

The reasons for sorcery are mainly those of economics or of personal status; desire for land; wish to punish for theft of food; jealousy of competitive achievement; resentment at a personal affront. What is particularly interesting in Tikopia, in contrast to some other societies, is the allegation of sorcery against men of rank, even chiefs. Its use by them on occasion is hardly to be questioned. Every chief and ritual elder, even the Christian ones, still regards himself as having such control over spiritual beings as to kill or render ill by their agency, if occasion demands; and from time to time plausible occasions do arise. But more to the point is that they are thought by many other people to act in this way. My old friend Pa Fenuatara, himself the heir of a chief, said of the former Ariki Tafua 'the chief who used to ensorcell; this land was lost'—meaning that many people lost their lives through his black art. Other people said the same. A spirit medium in dissociated state accused the Ariki Kafika, saying that he had picked up the news in a spirit resort, that the chief had appealed to spirit beings of his clan for help in sorcery. An earnest Christian, a poor man, said that the famine in Tikopia was due to the infertility of the crops, brought about by the sorcery of the chiefs. If food plants such as bananas are introduced, they become jealous if those of a commoner bear fruit in advance of their own, and work sorcery. All the chiefs do it, including the Ariki Tafua, a Christian. 'It happens. A chief is jealous; sorcery is there in the jealousy.' 'How do you know it is the chiefs?' I asked. 'It happens all the time. A chief sits, sees whatever it may be, is jealous, ensorcells. He doesn't tell anyone. Sorcery comes from the chiefs, from of old. Truth abides in this land in their utterances. Thereupon is the food bad. A commoner has no power in his lips.' (By this he meant that the 'magical' utterances of men of rank alone were effective; no ordinary person could affect the food. But to this there may be exceptions.) 'What about Faea?' (the Christian stronghold). 'In Faea they have all been baptized, but the mind of man remains always the same.'

And yet with this, two other kinds of view must be contrasted. One is that of most chiefs, who denied that they work sorcery. Pa Fenuatara also said this, in apparent inconsistency with his earlier statement. They are only said to do so by the people, he argued. But this was only a momentary merging of ideal and real. He said also, that there is a notion that a chief who practises sorcery on people so that they die, is in the end stricken by the 'tail' of his own weapon—the words turn round, bite and impact on the man himself. The other view, expressed in 1928 by the Ariki Taumako and in 1952 by a ritual elder, but common to all men of rank, was that if a man uses sorcery regularly, the spirits he employs become attuned to evil, and won't respond to requests for good, helpful activity. Here then are two sanctions, which allow for an occasional, spontaneous exercise of the sorcerer's art, but weigh against the calculating person who frequently resorts to sorcery as a means of gaining his ends.

In all this, one could see more plainly, if space allowed further analysis, the interplay of interest-groups in Tikopia society. But I have given enough data to show how with their 'magic', which is only part of a greater ritual system, the Tikopia operate at a symbolic level (which they have endowed with reality) a complex, dynamic scheme of personal and social relationships. Whether this relieves them from some of the burden of facing reality directly, it is hard to say. But it is clear that after the lapse of a generation, they are still attempting to deal with most of their problems in analogous, though not identical ways.

CHAPTER 10

RITUAL ADZES IN
TIKOPIA[1]

(1959)

This essay is intended as a sociological contribution but it may help to emphasize the social relations of technology in a Polynesian culture.

Nowadays Tikopia use modern steel tools, but traditionally their main working tools were of giant clam (*Tridacna*) shell. These tools were of adze form with blades of various shapes, including some which would be described as chisels and gouges were it not for the fact that they were adze-hafted. The ordinary shell adze blades were between three inches to four inches in length, quadrangular or triangular in plan and thinly quadrangular or ovate in section. They were made from the medium-sized clam shells found at the edge of the Tikopia fringing reef or on the sea bottom not far out. The name for adze in Tikopia is *toki* in the general Polynesian style. It is interesting to note that the Tikopia name for clam is also *toki* and for clam shell *penu toki* (the term *penu* being a general Tikopia word for husk or shell of anything). The Tikopia are quite conscious of this verbal equation of adze blade with clam, and regard it as due to the traditional relation of tool to material. (Yet originally the material may well have been named for the tool it furnished.)

SHELL ADZE BLADES

The religious associations of the clam did not affect the ordinary working tools made from the shell, which were quite secular in their use. But certain of the Tikopia shell adze blades were known as *toki tapu* (sacred adzes). These were of two categories. The *toki tapu*, sacred *par excellence*, were much larger than the ordinary working adze blades, measuring from eight to nine inches up to more than twelve inches in length and two inches or more in thickness. Moreover, they were not quadrangular in section, but almost oval. The second category of shell *toki tapu* were those of intermediate size and known as *pipi*. They were regarded as 'supporters' to the major sacred adzes, and were not of such size and importance as the major blades; they seem to have been larger examples of ordinary blades.

[1] Reprinted from *Anthropology in the South Seas*, pp. 149–59. 1959.

In addition, there were two other categories of ritual adzes in Tikopia. One category was comprised by a number of stone adze blades known as *toki uri* (black adzes), since the stone was in general of a very dark colour. The fourth category of ritual adzes were steel implements, in particular those known as *toki fakatu* or *faingata*.

I use the past tense in speaking about these objects because, now that the Tikopia since 1956 have apparently become complete Christian, these sacred objects will have lost their primary religious functions. If still regarded as *tapu* it will be because of belief in their residual ritual effect (see later).

The three major sacred adze blades secured from Tikopia on my expeditions were due to the advance of Christianity. One I obtained in 1929 from the brother of Pa Ngatotiu, who was then ritual elder of his lineage, in exchange for a large bush knife. Pa Ngatotiu's eldest son, who was himself ritual elder in 1952 explained to me 'The sacred adze was something sacred which was rejected by my father because the land had become different, the land had stood for Christianity. My father never made his *faunga vaka* (canoe rites). My grandfather alone did so. "Te Uruakau" (the name of his sacred canoe) which stands there had its ritual performed by him.' Pa Ngatitou said that his father rejected the rituals—and the sacred adze which was never used—at the death of the grandfather. Presumably then it was for this reason that the sacred adze could be given to me without arousing suspicion and hostility. Another sacred adze was obtained by Spillius from Pa Fatumaru, also one of the ritual elders of Taumako. This man, because of his friendliness, and presumably seeing the trend of religious affairs, was willing to dispose of it. A third adze of large size was given to me broken and apparently had lost its ritual quality. I have no data about it.

Before the complete overthrow of paganism by Christianity, the different categories of ritual adzes had various technological and religious functions.

THE MAJOR TOKI TAPU

Traditionally, before the coming of iron and steel tools to Tikopia, these large sacred adzes seem to have been the prime canoe-building tools of the Tikopia. From a rational point of view one can presumably link their sacredness in part with the fact that only clams of exceptional size could provide a working blade of the length and thickness required. The elaborate ritual surrounding these adzes may then also be regarded as an enactment at symbolic level of the technological and social value of these crucial implements.

Tikopia tradition assigns the origin of these large adze blades to the most remote period of Tikopia society, the time when 'the gods went as men and men as gods'. According to Ariki Kafika, the origin of these *toki tapu* was Pu Ma: 'Their own adzes that they prepared; their adzes that they rubbed down.' (The rubbing-down process is that of smoothing a rough piece of clam shell into shape on a sandstone rock.) The alternate origin for them was given me by Pa Vainunu who said that there was no detailed legend in regard to them, but they were made by Pakora—the Atua i Porima—and his two sisters. Both accounts agree in stating that the sacred adzes were given by these gods to the Atua i Kafika, the culture hero from whom so many Tikopia institutions are said to have originated. Later the adzes were distributed by various chiefs of Kafika, two to the progenitor of Taumako chiefly line, two to Pu Tafuaroa, whose mother came from Kafika, and one to Fakaarofatia, the progenitor of Fangarere, who was also a sister's son of the Kafika chief. One of the large adzes remained with Kafika.

Generally speaking, the adzes had no names, but were simply referred to as *toki tapu*. Those of Tafua, however, were said by the Ariki Kafika to be called Te Ngutusivi and Te Otaota; the origin of these names was unknown.[1] These major adzes were treated as having great sanctity. They were kept each in the prime temple of the clan, hung up on a shelf at the side. As I myself saw, they were given the greatest respect and their very presence helped to contribute a great deal to the awe in which that section of the temple was held. Their role and significance in the elaborate canoe rituals in the Work of the Gods I have already described.[2] The adze of Taumako in particular was treated with the greatest deference. The Ariki Kafika told me that whereas when his adzes were taken down no particular customs were observed (beyond ordinary ritual), when the leading adze of Taumako was taken down for any special reason from its shelf, the whole clan brought food and valued property to the chief lest they die. This was because of the particularly dangerous powers of the Eel god who, according to Tikopia belief, was in charge of the Taumako adze.

When in pre-European times—the eighteenth century and earlier—these large adze blades were presumably actually used in canoe-building they had to be properly hafted. The type of haft (*kau toki*) used had a characteristic notched ornament.

The lashing is of coconut sinnet and is of ordinary wrap-round type known as *rii*. Spillius described the process as he watched the lashing being done by Pa Fatumaru in 1952 as follows:—A strip of bark cloth is laid as a bed for the blade and a strip on top so as to 'catch' the lashing of coconut sinnet cord (*kafa*). The short end of the

---

[1] For more detailed stories of the distribution of these adzes, see *Work of the Gods*. 1967: pp. 59–61.

[2] *Work of the Gods*, pp. 69 et seq.

sinnet and a long piece of cord are crossed underneath the haft and the short end brought up and over. The long end is tightly bound around and over the short end. After eight bindings the long end is taken to the second tooth of the haft underneath, carried through and over again. A new piece of cord, this time of hibiscus, is added to the two ends, and binding over and under with a cross at the back continues until five teeth have been used. In joining the hibiscus cord (*uka*) to the coconut sinnet, the loose ends are left sticking up like horns.

This wrap-round lashing was of a type used for common working tools. But the more craftsmanlike type of lashing, which was also aesthetically much more pleasing, was that known as *sumu*, in which the cord was elaborately bound in a criss-cross design. This type of lashing was used *inter alia* for the most prized working tools and also to bind the ridgepole of a house to the central uprights. The general term for lashing (*fau*), when used in the form *fau toki tapu*, referred to this particular kind of lashing. The lineage of Avakofe were the acknowledged experts in this. It may be noted that in the lashing of Tikopia traditional adze blades, it was said that it was equally good for the bevel (*kina*) to be on the upper face (*tua*) or under face (*aro*) of the adze. It was said that in canoe-making the blade might be turned either way according to the work to be done. If the work would be spoiled by striking with the bevel on the under face (giving too much 'bite'), the blade would be reversed.

The general aura of ritual surrounding the use of the *toki tapu* meant that any technical process of preparation was ritualized. When a new haft was to be put on, I was told in 1929, it was a great ceremony like that of the *faunga vaka*. The adze was brought to the canoe yard in the beach village. The special canoe with which the adze was associated was brought out and the normal rites performed. The new haft might be made by a commoner, but it should be lashed on by the chief. In accordance with the Tikopia custom of linking a technical renewal of equipment with a periodic performance of ritual, the putting on of a new haft on the sacred adzes was done normally when a sacred canoe of a chief was being built. After the election of a chief, his first sacred canoe to be built was known as *singa kau toki*, a title which itself referred to the renewal of adze hafts. For this occasion, the hafts of the major *toki tapu* were renewed. The second sacred canoe the chief built was known as *tanga tapu*—literally, 'sacred building'. For this occasion the hafts of the supporters (*pipi*) to the primary sacred adzes were renewed. When a chief built a third sacred canoe—known as *tanga lasi*, literally, 'great building'—the hafts of any adzes that needed it were renewed.

For canoe building adze blades must be sharpened. So an important ritual feature of the sacred canoe building was the formal sharpening of the sacred adze. After the log had had some of the rough work done on it, it was dragged to the building place. That same day the chief went off with his sacred adze to sharpen it. The sharpening stone (*fuanga*) lay at Fakaseketara, near the path to Maunga on the eastern side of the island. The sacred adze blade was rubbed on the stone until it was cleansed. Coconuts were plucked from the orchards of Maunga and a rite of revivification (*fakaora*) was performed at the sharpening stone. Before the sharpening operation, the blade was loosened from its lashing, the old haft thrown away and the new one lashed on. It was from this removal of the sacred adze haft that the initial sacred canoe of the new chief took its title. Such was the account of the traditional practice as given me by Pa Vainunu in 1929.

A somewhat similar account was given me by the Ariki Kafika, but he was referring to a later period when his own practices were conditioned by the fact that steel tools had long replaced shell blades as working equipment. He emphasized that the adze blade was not actually sharpened. The sharpening stone was carpeted with coconut fronds, and the coconuts of revivification were oriented towards the adze. The chief went and sat by the adze. The coconut shell was filled with water from the sea and brought with pumice (*fatu manu*) to him. The piece of pumice was dipped in the water and rubbed on the edge of the adze blade while the chief recited the formula to the tutelary deity of the adze. The blade was then washed with water and laid down, while coconuts were pierced and libations poured from them. The people present then consumed the coconuts as an ordinary meal. The chief then shouldered his sacred adze and carried it back again to the temple. The chief said that meanwhile the new haft of the adze had been prepared, and it was relashed by the lashing expert (*tufunga faufau*), not by the chief himself.

Later, the adze was used in order to initiate the hollowing out and shaping of the canoe hull. In former days it was used as an actual working implement, but in later days (i.e. early nineteenth century onwards) it was applied only ritually. A simulated cut was made in the timber while the appropriate formula was recited, appealing for success for the fishing which would be done by the canoe. The chief then put the adze on his shoulder again and took it off to his temple. The kava rite was then performed. If it were the adze of the Ariki Kafika that was being celebrated, the other chiefs did not go to the ceremony, but remained in their houses. Each opened up the end of his temple and some repairs and replacements of thatch were done. This was an old custom with no very specific association. Symbolically, it seems to have indicated a form of ritual release from constraint, and some revivification. In value terms it was a special mark of distinction indicating the solemnity of the occasion.

STONE ADZE BLADES

Adze blades of shell were obviously common in traditional Tikopia life and hundreds of them have survived. Only a very few, however, of special size and quality, constituted the *toki tapu*. Stone adze blades on the contrary seem always to have been extremely rare, and all of them seem to have been regarded as *toki tapu* to some degree. On my first visit to Tikopia I was given five of these adze blades, including two by the Ariki Kafika and one by the Ariki Tafua, this last a fine black specimen highly polished and about three-and-a-half inches long. On the second expedition, Spillius and I collected about half-a-dozen more of these implements, ranging from a tiny blade two inches long to a very solid one six inches long. These were received from various sources in exchange, none of particular significance. In general, they belong to Duff's Type 2, Variety A, though one is of Duff's Type 4, Variety F.[1]

A question of great importance is where did they come from? Most of the blades are of close-grained black stone, apparently fairly hard and capable of taking quite a high polish. Three, however, including the smallest are of a greenish rock, apparently somewhat softer. Opinion differed as to the origin of the blades. A usually very good authority, Pa Fenuatara, said in 1952 that the material was local. But I think he was referring only to a small greenish stone blade. Certainly the great majority of opinion in Tikopia was that the stone blades in general were of foreign origin—sometimes rather vaguely attributed as Tongan. What seems to be clear is that they were of long standing in Tikopia. If they had been made locally one would have expected some knowledge of a quarry, and of this I got no indication. Moreover, one would have expected them to have been much more numerous. Until more definite evidence is obtained, I am inclined to think they are correctly attributed as imports.

Pending petrographical comparison of the material of the adze blades and of local rock, one can hazard only a tentative opinion. But Dr W. Campbell Smith, of the Department of Mineralogy, British Museum (Natural History) very kindly examined for me seven Tikopia stone adze blades and his opinion was as follows. Sections cut from two of these implements showed that they were made from volcanic rocks, fine-grained basalts of a kind that occurs on many volcanic islands. One implement, a grey basalt of 158·2 gm., had a density of 2·95; the other, a black basalt, of 266·9 gm., had a density of 2·93. Four other adze blades were of similar material with densities from 2·85 to 2·95.

In the brief description of the geology of Tikopia given by John C.

[1] Roger Duff, *The Moa-Hunter Period of Maori Culture* (Canterbury Museum Bulletin No. 1) Wellington, 1950: Figs. 35, 47.

Grover,[1] he records lava flows and andesitic dykes. It would therefore
be possible for basaltic volcanic rock such as that from which the adze
blades are made to have been found on Tikopia itself. The seventh
adze blade is a dark green rock, apparently a schist (density 3·07,
weight 27·2 gm.). No such metamorphic rocks are recorded by Grover
on Tikopia. On the other hand, Dr Campbell Smith points out, it is
known that there are metamorphic rocks in the central part of Guadalcanal and on San Cristoval. Specimens of these rocks were collected by
H. B. Guppy (1887) and are in the collections in the Department of
Mineralogy of the British Museum (Natural History), and metamorphic rocks are also mentioned by Grover as occurring on these two
islands.

These stone blades have been regarded by the Tikopia as in the
category of *toki tapu*. But their sacredness seems to have been by no
means as intense as that of the major shell blades and their place in
Tikopia ritual is not quite clear to me. In 1929 I was given these blades
as objects of great importance with some aura of *tapu*. But the fact that
they could be handed over to me by chiefs indicated that they did not
play an integral part in any major Tikopia ritual. (I saw none in use in
any of the very many rites I attended.) By 1952, their *tapu* seemed to
have decreased even more. Several of them were handed over in public
on barter nights when we had let it be known that we were willing to
exchange fish hooks, beads, calico, knives, etc., for Tikopia specimens.
When a man produced one of these objects from his waistcloth there
was a murmur of some interest and surprise—perhaps some feeling of
shock—but there was no expression at all that sacrilege had been committed. (No major shell *toki tapu* could ever have been handed over in
that public way.) Yet it was agreed that these blades were *toki tapu*. Pa
Fenuatara gave me a description of how they were used. He said that a
black stone blade was 'the splitter of the coconut in Uta' (*te fai o te
tafa ı Uta*). He first gave me a vivid description of how the ritual elder,
Pac Sao, used his shouldered adze—the hafted plane-iron—during a
rite. He said that Pae Sao during his ritual of the kava had the adze hung
over his shoulder as he sat in his house. He held up a green coconut in
his left hand, cut off the top, threw it out as an offering to the gods and
then poured the coconut liquid in libation. When the nut was empty he
reversed the adze and smashed in the nut with one blow.[2] Meanwhile,
Pae Sao's black adze blade lay, not hafted, in a small basket by his side.
In this case he was using the modern implement to do the ritual work of
the old stone blade; the modern was a surrogate. Pa Fenuatara said that
toki tapu of this stone type were in the possession of the house of Sao

---

[1] *Geology, Mineral Deposits and Prospects of Mining Developments in the British Solomon Islands Protectorate*, London, 1955, pp. 58–61.
[2] Compare similar procedure in the *Work of the Gods*, 1967: pp. 80–5.

and perhaps of Fusi and Farekofe—these being the lineages of certain ritual elders. The chiefs, including the Ariki Kafika, also had such blades, but according to Pa Fenuatara the chiefs actually used the larger stone adze blades. The blade was held in the hand with the cutting edge uppermost and this was then driven into the coconut to smash it. Pa Fenuatara added that the small grey blade given us by the younger brother of Pa Ngatotiu was also a *toki tapu*—this indicated that the lineage of Ngatotiu had also possessed such an implement. When I said that this blade was too small to have been used in the hand, he said that it would have been hafted.

It would appear that some lineages possessed more than one of these blades. A blade about five inches long, brought by a member of the house of Sao, was said by Pa Fenuatara to be different from the stone blade used by Pae Sao in his kava rites. About three months later than this conversation, Pa Nukumata, heir of Pae Sao, brought me a large black stone blade which he said he had dug up on the ritual side of the ancestral dwelling of Sao in Uta. This is very likely to have been the sacred blade used by Pae Sao. Apart from the one reference by Pa Fenuatara, I did not get any specific indication that these stone adze blades were ever hafted. It is possible that they were used primarily as ritual objects either in baskets or set out in mats when the kava was performed, their efficacy being regarded as due to their presence, not to their specific technological employment. But whereas the major shell blades had each very specific tutelary deities, stone blades seem never to have had such specific associations with spirits. Their virtue lay in their more general ritual quality of *tapu*—rather analogous to the 'sacred objects' (*anea tapu*) used in the Work of the Gods.[1]

STEEL ADZE BLADES

In 1929 and again in 1952 there was a very keen demand by the Tikopia for steel adzes of the ordinary European type, known as *kamuro*. These were wanted primarily for canoe building and for dressing the larger house timbers, and the Tikopia demand, even by 1952, was far from being satisfied. These ordinary adzes were prized mainly for their blades since the Tikopia often preferred to have their own hafts. But except in one case (see below) these adzes, though highly valued, were in no sense *tapu*. It was different with the second form of steel adze, that made by hafting adze-wise a plane-iron blade. For these blades too there was a very great demand. For the most part these plane-iron adzes were not treated as ritual implements. But as already indicated to some extent, in some lineages with chiefs and elders at their head having specific ritual functions, these plane-iron adzes had come to be assigned very

[1] Op. cit.: pp. 51–3.

important roles. In the Work of the Gods in relatively modern times the chiefs shouldered such adzes when they marched around the lake shore.[1]

As a descriptive term these adzes were called *toki fakatu*—a reference to the sharply upstanding angle between blade and handle. In their ritual function they were known as *faingata*—literally 'doing the cutting'. According to Pa Porima in 1929, he, Pae Sao and Pa Saukirima (of Fusi) had such adzes. Characteristically he said that they were possessed in the realm of the spirits, as in the realm of men, indicating the parallelism often conceived to exist between the spirit world and the human world. He said that only a few ritual elders had *faingata*—for example, Pa Rarovi, one of the most senior, had not. The association here was with the possession or not of tutelary deities of specifically evil qualities. Certain lineages were believed to have the control of such deities, others not, and those without such control did not have specific ritual adzes. What was the reason for this? Because in Tikopia view the *faingata* as a ritual implement had as one of its essential functions the capacity of causing the illness or death of a person against whom its powers were directed. These powers were of peculiar virulence when one of these evil deities was invoked. At the back of this conception again is a rather vaguer association—that the lineages possessing this supernatural agency were those generally considered to be of greater antiquity in the land. But this association must not be pressed too far and requires much more detail for adequate examination.

Pa Porima said that the *faingata* of olden times had clam shells and that these were later replaced by iron blades. An elder possessing one ordinarily had it hung in his house. If a theft occurred in his cultivation he shouldered the *faingata*, walked to the tree which had been robbed and struck the trunk with a cursing formula, drawing the attention of the deity (*atua*) to the theft and asking vengeance thus:

> Pakora (name of deity)!
> Turn to your ritual adze.
> Let that one be cut by it
> Be cut by your ritual adze
> Let him be cut by your black face.

The 'black face' refers to the dark colour of the iron blade. An alternative phrasing in olden times, said Pa Porima, was 'Let him be cut by your white adze' (i.e. clam shell blade).

The elder then returned, laid the adze on a sheet of bark-cloth and performed his kava, orienting the ritual towards the adze. In order to make this rite efficacious, meanwhile the kinsfolk of the elder prepared

[1] Op. cit.: p. 36, cf. *Social Change in Tikopia*, 1959: pp. 106–8.

food from which offerings were made. This would cause the thief to fall ill and perhaps die. No member of the household spoke abroad of this kava lest the thief got to know and took counter measures. After a space of some days a second kava rite was performed and by this time—so the story ran—the thief would be dead. The term for this special kava was said to be 'the thieving from the chiefs and the elders'.

Although the *faingata* was *tapu*, it could be used for ordinary work, as a *toki faisanga*. It might even be lent to another man to use, but he would be cautioned not to hand it over to a third party, but to look after it carefully. The plane-iron adzes are thus a very interesting example of a tool of which the ritual qualities, if not the sacredness, could be turned on and off, as it were, according to need. This was possible because of the Tikopia capacity to conceptualize the physical and ritual aspects of an object separately or in combination as the social situation demanded.

I have stated that no ordinary steel adze, save one, was sacred. This was the adze used as the leading implement in the canoe work of Tau-mako. It was known as the *Matatoki* (or *matua toki*), the principal adze. This served as the working representation of the sacred adze in Uta. The specific implement belonged to Pae Avakofe and by him was handed on to his son, Pa Tarikitonga, with instructions that he hand it on in turn to his son, Pa Nukutapu. In 1929 I learned of the general ritual significance of this implement when a sacred canoe of the Ariki Kafika was being repaired by Pa Tarikitonga. It was believed that the principal adze of Taumako could kill borer in canoe timber and stop decay. The basis of this in Tikopia eyes lay in the fact that not merely sacred shell blade adzes but also this actual working implement had as its tutelary deity Pusiura, the fierce malevolent spirit ordinarily incarnated in the grey reef eel.[1]

In 1952 I learned more about this adze. Pa Nukutapu told me that he was now afraid to use the implement. He said 'Nowadays I have not built a canoe with it, I have become afraid, because the god is evil.' He said that the adze was kept hung up in the ancestral house Toa near the beach, above the grave mat of Pae Avakofe, his grandfather. He then modified his statement a little to say that in fact he had used the adze fairly recently, but only under special conditions, but he had now definitely decided to discontinue. 'The idea is that the adze is taken down only when a timber is becoming rotten. It is taken down, announced to the gods and cut into the place which is going bad, so that it may be well again. For ordinary canoe building the adze was taken down and about ten cuts were made with it to begin the work. If the timber was seen to be in good condition then the adze was taken away again to be hung up. If it was seen to have a bad patch, then this was cut out with the adze.' At the same time invocation was made to Pusiura and, he said,

[1] For details see *Primitive Polynesian Economy*, 1939: pp. 121–2.

the idea was that the god not only killed borer but also converted poor wood into good, repairing by supernatural means the rotten place in the timber. He thus re-affirmed and elaborated the belief of his elders in 1929. 'But,' he said, 'I am abandoning it.' He said he was going to use from then on only a new adze which I was giving him. 'I object—I object because of the activity of the spirits; because of the activity of the evil god.' I asked him how he came to get this idea. He replied 'Nowadays things have become different. The reason is that I do not throw food offerings for them. When food portions are set out I do not throw. It was only my father who when he lived used to throw offerings of food as food portions of the adze.' I asked 'Why do you not do so?' 'It's my own idea. My mind is like this. Because he turns to his own people to strike them. Therefore I have abandoned him. It is good for an aged man alone to speak continually to him and to throw food offerings continually to him—and for a chief to do so. That indeed is good. When I go to build a canoe I make his food portion, and I go and carry it to the chief for food offerings to be thrown by him. On the day on which the tree is first cut I prepare the oven, I make his food portion, I carry it to the chief and he throws, to recite formulae for the tree to be good.'

I then asked my friend, 'But if you desert the god, won't he turn on you?' He replied, 'I don't know. Now on a day on which Rakei-maranga (a spirit possessing a medium) will come I shall tell him that I am abandoning the adze on account of my abandonment of the gods— I shall build canoes thenceforth at my own pleasure.' I asked him if the god had already harmed his family. He replied, 'I keep on thinking of my children and I say to myself that the god is evil. I have affection too for my grandchildren. My wife and children have been affected. My wife has been bewitched by him severely. She is sore in her ribs and her belly flows. As she descended to the seashore, there came rushing to her the god. He came and his head was split. There were three days on which he rushed at her in the sea. She was afraid and she ran up inland. She threw stones at him but he did not go. Thereupon I sat and sought in my mind among the stories that had been told. Thereupon I abandoned the adze.' This somewhat cryptic account refers to the Tikopia belief that this feared Taumako deity, incarnate in the reef eel, manifests his hostility towards men by aggressive unusual action. What Nau Nuku-tapu had seen was apparently a particular reef eel which had approached her on several occasions and which she had remarked because its head had been split by a cut with a knife or other implement. She had never seen this phenomenon before and, taken in conjunction with the approach of the eel to her, regarded it as an evil sign. Her husband said to me, 'Split in his head he goes in his evil. He is turning evilly. He goes to a person with his head split. It is not certain just what this means, but he is going evilly among us men. He wreaks ill on a man or on a woman.'

At the time of our conversation his wife, who had been obviously ill, probably with some form of influenza which was then common in the island, was feeling much better. I asked if she had dreamed at all of the deity. He said 'Yes, for two nights or so.' She dreamed that the deity took on the semblance of the Ariki Taumako. The figure, apparently that of the chief, appeared on the ritual side of the house and asked her for some biscuit for himself. Her husband said he could not remember whether she gave it biscuit or not. He said that this was a custom of the god to take the form either of the Taumako chief or of his brother or of some other member of the chiefly lineage of Taumako with which he was ritually associated. When he took on the form of a man in this way, it was an evil sign. My friend added that the deity was an evil one indeed. By comparison the god of Sa Kafika was good. Their lineage was fortunate.

As a final proof of the ferocity of this god, Pa Nukutapu mentioned to me the idea still current in Taumako that the deity demanded a sacrifice from any man of the lineage who aspired to be recognized as a *toa*, that is a strong man and a warrior. He said 'In former times in our chiefly house a man who wishes to develop as a *toa*, it is good that he kill a man for himself; to kill a food portion for himself. The man as he kills announces this: "Here, that is your food portion, Pusiuraura." But if he does not, the god comes and strikes him. The god comes and strikes and kills the *toa*. For this reason died my father, Pa Veterei who is buried in Nuku—because not a man did he kill for himself. If he had killed a man he would have lived.'[1]

The general notion at the back of this specific statement was essentially the same as that in the case of the large shell sacred adzes—that the implements of prime technological value were associated with powers more than normal. In this case the adze which was the chief tool of the acknowledged master-building family, was thought to depend for its efficacy upon a supernatural being. But this efficacy had its price. Just as the effectiveness of an adze was epitomized by its sharpness, so the power of the god behind the adze was epitomized by his fierceness. What Pa Nukutapu was saying in effect was that he preferred to run the risk of lowering his technical standards rather than have these maintained at the cost of much nervous strain.

CONCLUSION

A distinction between implements of technological use and of ceremonial or ritual use is well known. But it is often assumed that these

[1] Further information about Pa Veterei is given in Rivers, *The History of Melanesian Society*, 1914; I, p. 314; Firth, *We, the Tikopia*, 1936: p. 515. (Pa Veterei is the man making coconut cream in Rivers, 1914: Plate XXI.)

represent two quite separate sociological categories. These examples from Tikopia show how the two categories are not necessarily exclusive in their application to any specific implement. The Tikopia have shown considerable flexibility in their ideas. They ritualize their most important tools, dedicating them to the supernatural beings held to be responsible for all major Tikopia cultural achievements. But the Tikopia were able to replace these implements by others of superior efficiency without wrecking their scheme of ritual associations. They removed the traditional tools from their technological function completely, and assigned to them a wholly symbolic value. At the same time they brought the new implements into ritual association while allowing them to be used in ordinary tasks. This ability to combine technological function and ritual function, emphasizing the one or the other as the situation demanded, shows the capacity of the Tikopia to conceptualize and abstract elements of different quality in their social situation.

CHAPTER 11

TOTEMISM IN POLYNESIA[1]

(1930–1)

In the islands of Melanesia and on the New Guinea mainland some form of totemism is frequently an important feature of the native culture, but in Polynesia this institution is considered to be of minor interest. Controversy indeed has arisen over the question as to whether totemism really does exist in this area. Categorical statements on this point are inconclusive, as the classification of the data has varied in each case according to the weight attached to one or other of several theoretical principles. Some writers, impressed by the relationship of social groups to animals and plants, insist that they are dealing with totemism; others, paying more attention to the connection of these natural species with supernatural beings of the native pantheon, consider that 'pseudo-totemism' is a more adequate description. Fundamentally, however, one point is certain. The material innocently offered by Mariner, Turner, Brown, Gardiner and others, and re-examined by Frazer and Tylor, the theoretical study by Rivers on the basis of his additional information, the recent review of the data by Handy, and still more comprehensive, by Williamson, demonstrate clearly that in western and central Polynesia, at all events, there is a peculiar association between certain animal and plant species and the religious interests of the people. This association is stated by most writers in terms of a native belief that the animals and plants are used by deities as a form of visible incarnation.

A divergence from the general standpoint is made by Rivers, who treats of the various natural species as if they were deities in their own right and does not introduce the concept of exterior abstract beings at all. Whether this is due to the inadequacy of some of his material, or to the subordination of his inquiry to the precise argument of his thesis of culture interaction in Melanesia, it is unnecessary to determine.

THE PROBLEM OF TOTEMISM

In consideration of this difference in views, and the rather summary nature of the evidence supplied by many authorities, it may not be amiss to review the whole problem afresh, and to attempt to get a more definite

[1] Reprinted from *Oceania* Vol. I, 1930–1.

idea of the precise quality of this ritual association which undoubtedly exists in Polynesian culture between man and selected species in Nature. Several questions must be considered.

It is essential to know whether on the human side the relation is one in which people are involved as a group or only as individuals, and, as regards the animal or plant, whether each species is concerned as a whole or single members of it alone are considered; whether the natural object is regarded as a representative or emblem of the human group; whether there is any idea of identity between a person and the creature or object and of descent of the one from the other; and whether the interest of the people is focused on the animal or plant *per se*, or it is of importance primarily through a belief in its association with ancestral spirits or other deities. And in the latter event it is very necessary to understand something of the native concept of the relation between the species and the supernatural being. In the present study an attempt is made to analyse the precise native attitude involved. To this end new data are brought forward from what may be regarded as a critical area, where the phenomena of this type of 'totemism' are most marked— namely the island of Tikopia.[1]

The conditions in this one community do not allow of generalization for Polynesia as a whole, but since the survey of evidence in the later part of this article shows that the situation in the other island groups seems to be parallel to that in Tikopia, the existence of a similar basic attitude elsewhere is suggested.

ANALYSIS OF DATA FROM TIKOPIA

The social organization of this community as briefly described in Chapter 1,[2] consists of four large patrilineal kinship groups (*kainanga*), which for convenience may be termed clans, though they are not necessarily exogamous in marriage relations. Each of these is governed by a chief (*ariki*) who in his capacity of religious head of the group and performer of the principal *kava* rites stands in a special relation to the gods (*atua*). These comprise the spirits of his ancestors, the dead clan chiefs in order of precedence, headed by a number of major deities, sometimes distinguished as *tupua*, who have never lived on earth as men. Each chief has as his council and assistants in religious affairs a small number of *pure matua*, elders, who hold their rank by virtue of their position as heads of the most important families in the clan. Each *pure* has

---

[1] 'The clearest evidence for the existence of totemism in Polynesia is derived from Tikopia,' W. H. R. Rivers, *Journal of Royal Anthropological Institute*, XXXIX, 1909, p. 160. This article gives references to the theoretical works of McLennan, Tylor and Sir James Frazer, which need not be repeated here.

[2] See also *We, The Tikopia*, 1936.

his own *atua* to whom he performs ceremonies, but in a more limited sphere than his chief. There is to some extent a parallelism between the arrangement of social groups in the community and the arrangement of deities in the religious scheme.

The nature of Tikopia totemism can be understood only after reference to the attitude of the people towards the living objects of their natural environment as a whole. To the Tikopia, the primary matter of interest, apart from the classification into animals, plants, fish, etc., is the distinction between things which are eaten (*e kai*) and those which are not eaten (*sise e kai*). The former may be dealt with first.

CLANS AND PLANT FOOD-STUFFS

The diet of this island people consists almost solely of vegetable products and fish, but within these limits is extremely varied. There appear to be very few species in either domain which though edible, are not utilized as food. Of the great majority which figure on the bill of fare nothing need be said here; the four chief vegetable items, however, demand consideration—the yam (*ufi*), the taro (*taro*), the coconut (*niu*), and the breadfruit (*mei*). Each of these is affiliated with one of the clans of the island and is regarded as being in a sense their special property. Following the native mode of speech in which the term *fakarongo*, meaning primarily 'to listen', or secondarily 'to obey', is employed to denote this relation, it may be said that the yam 'obeys' sa Kafika, the coconut 'obeys' sa Tafua, the taro 'obeys' sa Taumako and the breadfruit 'obeys' sa Fangarere. The role of controller of the plant is often assigned in ordinary conversation to the chief of the clan. Thus as an alternative statement it may be said that the yam 'obeys' or 'listens to' the Ariki Kafika—and so on; the meaning is the same in both cases, since in all ceremonial matters and in much else as well the chief is the representative of his clan. The term *fakarongo* as used in this connection implies no conscious obedience on the part of the plant, no imputation of personality, but simply that jurisdiction is exercised over it by the particular chief in question. This control relates primarily to religious ritual, the chiefs of Kafika and Taumako having certain very sacred and important duties to perform in connection with the seasonal planting of yam and taro respectively, while the Ariki Fangarere celebrates ritually each crop of the breadfruit as it comes to maturity. The Ariki Tafua has no such definite obligations or privileges connected with the coconut, which is probably to be correlated with the fact that this palm has no well-marked fruiting season, but bears almost continuously throughout the year, several different stages of the nut being represented in its crown at any one time. The precise ceremonies by which these various food plants are assisted to develop, or are welcomed at harvest, are of more interest in relation to the economic life of the people. Those for the yam are described in *Work of the Gods in Tikopia*.

There is no restriction of any kind on the growing of these food-stuffs by members of a clan other than that which exercises special jurisdiction over them. Every man of the island community has his patches of taro, usually, though not invariably, his clump of yams, and always his breadfruit and coconut trees. But when the appropriate time comes it is left to the members of the affiliated clan, headed by their chief, to perform the due rites.

The utilization of the product of any of these plants for food, again, involves little in the way of special treatment. Taro and yam tubers are prepared for the oven by scraping, breadfruit is either roasted whole on the coals or chopped into sections for cooking with other foods, all of which are efficient methods and most suited for a simple meal. More complex means are adopted when it is desired to prepare more tasty food, as *susua* or *ngaruenga*, the pudding formed by mixing the pounded flesh of the fruit or vegetable with coconut cream, a dish of which the Tikopia are particularly fond, and for the diverse preparation of which they have a number of ingenious recipes. The scraping of tubers is done with a hinge of the *kasi*, a sharp-edged bivalve shell, which is coming to be replaced more and more by the small European knife. There is no restriction on the members of any group from using the knife on their clan plant. As Rivers makes a definite affirmation on this point I took pains to obtain accurate information, but neither my own daily observations nor the express statements of authoritative informants, as the Ariki Kafika, gave any colour to his opinion. In the case of Tafua alone does a prohibition exist. The people of this clan may not cut the *muri niu*, the back of the coconut, i.e. the end away from the stalk, as is commonly done by others for drinking, but pierce (*suki*) the eyes; and to extract the flesh afterwards they break the nut with a stone, or crush it between the hands if it is young.

The association of each clan with its food plant rests in native belief on the relation between the plant and the principal clan deity. Each of the four groups has its main god, who is regarded with great reverence and is termed sacred (*tapu*) in the highest degree. He possesses a variety of names; one or two of these are widely known, but the others are supposed to be the property of the chief alone. To meet the needs of ordinary reference the descriptive terms 'Te Atua i Kafika', 'Te Atua i Tafua'—the Deity in Kafika, the Deity in Tafua, and the like are employed. Often, again, euphemisms are in vogue, as '*Ko ia e nofo i te vai*'—'He who lives in the water', for the God of the Lake, represented by the freshwater eel, '*Te atua e poi i roto tai*'—'The deity who goes in the shore-waters', for a sea-god represented by the grey reef-eel, or more simply, '*te atua*', the spirit or god, or '*te tupua matou*', 'the deity of ours', where the significance is clear. A more accurate statement then from the native point of view is that the yam, taro and other food plants belong primarily to the chief *atua* of the respective divisions, and that it is through this that the clan and chief exercise their interest in them.[1] Hence the seasonal ceremonies mentioned above have a very definite aim: they induce the deity to continue his policy of productivity and to send once again the crops by which his people live. The association of the clans with the principal food plants of the island and the performance of rites to ensure a continuance of their fertility is comprehensible in that the importance of these foodstuffs is thereby maintained in the eyes of the people, their cultivation is invested with a certain religious sanction, and their economic interest is thus reinforced.

The specific social partition, however, whereby each clan is definitely responsible for one type of plant, rests on different grounds. In the native belief it has its foundation in an incident, in reality of a mythical nature, which is held to have happened in the distant times when men were gods and gods were men, and when the principal deities themselves were the representatives of the clans in the land. The story in the best-known version is that an *atua*, by name Tikarau, came to the land of Tikopia from foreign parts. On his arrival a feast was made, and a huge pile of food, *te anga*, was set up in the marae of Rarokoka in Uta. Emulation then began between the local deities and the visitor as to who would be the victor in trials of strength or speed. According to the usual tale a hopping match was instituted, and a circuit of the lake was begun. The contestants had passed round the seaward side, left Namo behind, and had entered on the path through Te Roro, when Tikarau slipped and fell. He made pretence of having injured his leg on one of the rocks which strewed the way, and began to limp. Suddenly, however, he made a dash for the glade of Rarokoka, where the provision for the feast lay, and grabbing up the heap, fled to the hills. With the Family of gods in close pursuit he made for the crest, but arriving at the spur of Marepa he slipped and fell once more, so that a deep groove in the hillside at the present day is known as 'The Place of Falling of Tikarau' (*Te Singanga o Tikarau*). The Family of deities, coming up, were just able to grab, one a coconut, another a taro, another a breadfruit, and others a yam, before their opponent, gathering himself up, bolted to the edge of the cliff, and being an *atua*, launched himself into the sky and set off for the far lands with his ill-gotten gains. He retained the bulk of the feast, but the Family had been able to save for Tikopia the principal food-stuffs, and transmit them to posterity. Thus the Atua i Tafua had seized a coconut, whence his clan now control that fruit; the Atua i Taumako

[1] Cf. also a somewhat similar situation in the Marquesas. E. S. C. Handy, *Native Culture in the Marquesas*, B. P. Bishop Museum Bulletin, 9, 1923, pp. 262–3.

230

had grasped a taro, which is now the vegetable of that clan, the Atua i Fangarere had gripped a breadfruit, which is now controlled by his group, while Pu Ma, deities of Kafika had obtained the yam, which is now under the jurisdiction of this clan.

The tale is thus a myth of a type common to many primitive peoples. Its general function is to provide a foundation for existing socio-economic relations.

The partition in sphere of interests to which it refers, to be understood clearly, must be studied in conjunction with the whole religious system of Tikopia. There it is seen that in every important aspect of life there is a division of function among the four clans, each, headed by its chief, having its own part to play in the total scheme. It is not easy to frame a satisfactory generalization, but after an intensive study of the culture of the Tikopia I am drawn to the conclusion that the small size of the island and the dense population, in association with the intricate ceremonial so characteristic of all Polynesians, and the conflicting interests of the major groups have done much to favour the minute division of social and religious duties and privileges which one observes. On the other hand the need for social unity within this limited area has tended to promote also the rather remarkable complementary functions and interlocking ties which link clan with clan.

One problem which may arouse interest is the definiteness of the clan association with the principal food plants, and the absence of such specific linkage with the chief species of edible fish which have no such clan affiliation. This is probably to be correlated with the greater fixity of the plant species. the fact that their propagation, their growth and their harvest are more under human control, and that they are clearly localized at all times; fish on the other hand are much more liable to variation, and are present to human ken as a rule only in immediate connection with their capture.

The variation in restriction on the use of taro and yam and breadfruit on the one hand, as contrasted with that of coconut on the other, appears to be related also to practical considerations. A coconut may be conveniently opened for drinking as well by piercing as by cutting—in Tikopia the former method is often employed by people not of Tafua clan even when a knife is at command—but to forego the use of a tool in preparing vegetable food means a greater disability. The alternative to scraping of tubers is peeling off the skin and adherent dirt after the food is cooked, which is much more tedious than the use of shell or knife beforehand, and is a method employed only at a religious ceremony of the most sacred type. Hence whatever be the actual circumstances which gave rise to the prohibition on the use of the knife on the coconut, and the permission for it in the case of taro and yam, it can be equated with certain rational elements of technical process.

A prohibition which is of definite value in the economic life of the people is that against injuring the growing food plants. Disputes in the woods over boundaries are not infrequent, and one method of expressing disapproval and defiance of one's opponent is to destroy food-stuffs at the spot in question—to cut down the banana trees, root out *pulaka* (*Alocasia*) and the like. But it is *tapu* on such occasions to interfere with the principal crops. Yam vines must not be slashed, taro is immune as are also breadfruit and coconut trees. This has an obvious utility. The prohibition, however, to the Tikopia lies in the supernatural sphere. They are sacred, and destruction of them would involve the vengeance of the gods. For not only, as explained hitherto, are these food-stuffs the property of their respective deities; they actually represent them corporeally in whole or in part. Thus of the yam the Ariki Kafika, its guardian, said: '*te ufi, te tino te Atua i Kafika*', 'the yam, the body of the Deity of Kafika'. The taro is likewise the body of the Atua i Taumako. The breadfruit is the head of the Atua i Fangarere, while the coconut is the head of the Atua i Tafua. Hence the *poroporo* rite for the new season's crop of breadfruit is understood by the Fangarere chief and his people as being by way of atonement for the violence which they and the rest of the community do continually to their deity by splitting open his sacred head in order to place it in the oven. Splitting the *mei* (breadfruit) is not breaking a specific rule of *tapu*, presumably because there is no other convenient way of dealing with it. The cutting by Tafua clan of the rear end of the coconut is barred since in so doing they would cleave open the back of the head of their chief god. In this case presumably, the *tapu* continues operative since the alternative—the piercing of the eye—is as simple and effective. It must be noted here that this hypothesis does not pretend to give an explanation of the *tapu* as a whole along rational lines—its roots lie elsewhere—but merely to indicate a possible basis for its differential application in this particular field. The attribution of the two kinds of tubers, as the 'bodies' of their respective *atua* and of the breadfruit and coconut as the 'heads' of theirs, is clearly derived from the differences of shape and interior quality of the two types of food-stuff.

THE TERM 'ATUA'

None of these plants are in themselves considered as sacred, nor are they ever—in spite of Rivers' statement[1]—termed *atua*. They are controlled by the principal *atua* of the respective clans, and figuratively are spoken of as being the bodies or portions of the anatomy of these supernatural beings, but they are not *atua* in themselves. No Tikopia

[1] Rivers, op. cit., *J.R.A.I.*, pp. 161–2, *History of Melanesian Society*, I, p. 304.

ever termed an edible food plant an *atua* even when speaking of it on the magico-religious or mythic plane.

A brief reference to the connotation of the term will make this clear. As in other Polynesian communities the word *atua* in Tikopia applies primarily to a supernatural object; whether of human or non-human kind. It is used to indicate: (i) Specific supernatural beings as spirits of the dead, ancestors and important deities who have never been men. Each of these has an individual personality, one or more names and often a number of individual attributes of appearance and character. (ii) Supernatural beings of the 'wandering ghost' type, known to Tikopia as *atua vare*—common or foolish *atua*. These are regarded as having personality, but are nameless, have no specific characters and have no continuity in the native social scheme. By this is meant that while as a class they continue to exist, as individuals they are significant only at the moment of manifestation. Such *atua* are in great numbers everywhere, in the bush and along the paths, and are especially prominent at dusk. Every now and again a human being has an experience with one of them, which then, unidentified, sinks back into the void. Of this type are the *atua fakafua*, the bringers of disease. Hosts of unnamed sea beings, *atua o te moana*, exist, parallel to those on land. (iii) Individual objects associated with supernatural powers or invested with supernormal attributes, as certain stones, trees or weapons regarded as being beyond the ordinary are classed as *atua*. (iv) Individuals of a natural species held to be inedible are occasionally spoken of as *atua*. The usage in this last case is somewhat outside the ordinary range of applicability of the term. Here there does not seem to be any element of the supernatural involved, but simply an unfitness for human consumption. The terms *atua* and *kai* (food) in this connection are in fact mutually exclusive. A native referring to the *tarasea*, a small seaweed-eating fish which jumps on to the rocks with the wash of the waves and wriggles off again as they recede, said: '*Te atua, sise e kai, pakupaku fuere e fai*,' 'The *atua*, is not food, bait only is made.' The fish is not regarded as sacred in any way, nor is ritual observed with regard to it. The term *atua* here bears no sense of the supernatural; it is simply the converse of 'fitness for food'. The same applies to small crabs, sea anemones, bêche-de-mer and other marine creatures on the reef, as well as to iridescent lizards, spiders and some insects. This purely mundane application of the word *atua* is not invariable but may be heard by the observer if he wanders round the reef with fishing parties and discusses the varied fauna to be found there.

I have drawn attention to the use of this term on the purely normal plane, as correlative with 'inedible', because the speech and behaviour of the Tikopia in such cases do not appear to be concerned with any elements of the supernatural. It must be acknowledged, however, that in many instances the two types of meaning (iii and iv) above seem to shade into each other; it is indeed as if the connotation of *atua* as 'inedible' were derivative from its significance of 'supernatural', since to the Tikopia creatures which are unfit for human consumption are not of the normal order of nature. This last is by way of speculation only, since it is impossible to obtain from the natives themselves a precise statement on this matter.

One point, however, may be stressed with certainty, that any object which is regarded as an *atua* may not be eaten, and anything which is fit for human consumption cannot be in itself an *atua*—though it may, as we shall see, become associated temporarily with *atua*. Hence it can be seen from an analysis of the significance of the term, that the yam, taro, coconut and breadfruit cannot be called *atua*, as is also made abundantly clear from the observed usage of the natives. Rivers' treatment of the whole question of totemism in Tikopia is in fact vitiated by this basic error—that unknowingly he has confused the material object with the supernatural being for whom it is a symbol, or a vehicle of expression. He thus attributes to the plant or fish or bird the actions, the qualities and the sociological importance which really belong primarily to *atua* of the type of personal beings.

The relation of the four principal plant food-stuffs to the social order is in quite a different category from that of animals. In the latter case it is not the edible, but the inedible elements which are associated with supernatural beings. The facts are clear. The taro, the yam, the coconut and the breadfruit are of great importance in the native life. They are closely and directly linked with their respective clans, a complex series of rites is performed in each case to ensure their productivity, and the members of each clan, as of the others, may eat the clan plant. With birds and sea creatures the converse is the case. Species used as food are linked with no social group, and any increase rites are of a more generalized type. It is the inedible kinds which are associated with clans and clan gods, they have little attention paid to them, and, naturally enough, are not the subject of any increase ceremonies. Even when one of the creatures is killed, no ritual procedure is carried out to avert ill results. If we are to speak then of these phenomena as constituting totemism it must be acknowledged that there are in Tikopia two distinct types of the institution—the positive, relating to plant food-stuffs, with emphasis on fertility; the negative, relating to animals, with emphasis on unsuitability for food.

There is no question of association of plant and animal species in any form of 'linked totemism'; they are on entirely different planes of religious interest.

The animals and marine creatures which enter into the ritual relation embrace a variety of species, and certain corresponding differences of behaviour towards them are exhibited by the natives. These may now be considered in detail.

'ATUA' AND LAND ANIMALS

The simplest relation occurs in the case of certain crabs, lizards, insects and such 'small deer'. This class comprises creatures such as the *kaviki*, the ghostly pale little land crab, which lives in burrows in the sand, often under the house floor, whence it emerges by night and stalks rustling over the coconut matting, to engage in battle or love affairs. to the annoyance of the humans whom it disturbs. The *kalamisi* or *karamisi* is a kindred animal, a crab of a reddish-brown or yellowish hue, somewhat hairy-legged, the favourite residence of which appears to be the crotch of a branch of a tree. Both these species of crustacean are termed *atua*, being inedible. At times it is thought they are entered by itinerant spirits, often of the malignant disease-bringing kind, against whom man has continually to be on his guard. When such a ghostly being is thus its denizen the crab is noticeable for its interest in human beings. An actual native statement will illustrate this point. My informant said:

'*Te atua fakafua e au o uri i te kaviki—sise e tupu ki ei—au ki te tangata e me, nai utia rei. Popo rei ko te tangata ki te kaviki, sau mai fafanga.*' (The spirit making disease comes to enter in the crab—not changes to it —comes to the man is sleeping, by it pinched then. Grasps then the man the crab, takes up, breaks apart.)

The significance of this is that the disease-bringing spirit is thought to enter for its own purpose the body of the crab, which thus animated, crawls over to the sleeping man and pinches him with its claw. The man awakes, reaches out for the creature, grasps it and drawing it to him, maims it. The term *fafanga* belongs to that class of words known to the Tikopia as *taranga pariki*, 'bad speech'—it is an indecorous expression. It means primarily 'to open out', but is applied in particular to the action of a woman preparatory to intercourse. With this suggestion always in mind the term is barred from use in the presence of affinal relatives or indeed in the polite conversation of married people in general. It is used in the text above since the talk was conducted among a group of *tamaroa*, unmarried men, where expressions are more free. In the present instance it refers to the action of the man in bending back the legs of the crab, thus breaking them—the common method of disablement, after which the creature is thrown away. The statement is of interest in that it specifically indicates one mode of relation between spirit and material object; the *atua* on this occasion does not change (*tupu*) into a crab, i.e. assume the form of one; it enters into (*uru*) the body of an already existing crustacean. A further point may also be noted, that the crab, even with its ghostly inhabitant, is harshly treated and repelled, the presence of the *atua* not acting as a deterrent.

The European cat, introduced according to native tradition during the early part of last century by a Tikopia voyager, is also regarded as providing an occasional abiding place for similar spirits. The animal is named the *sukuroa*, or 'long tail'. Thus:

Te atua e uru foki ki te sukuroa, e ata ki ei, e poi tangi saere i nga tafa fare e au te atua poi o uru ki tenea e varea, tena e tangi rei. Poi o tangi saere i vasia paito. Rongo mai ko te tangata, uru mai ena ko a fatu, puke atu, sau mai, pepe rei ki ei. Pa i ei ka mate, mate; ka ne ora ko ia ka rere. (The spirit enters also into the long tail, impersonates it, goes crying walking at the sides house comes the spirit goes to enter into that one is maddened, thereon cries then. Goes and cries walking in between houses. Hears the man, goes out, there are stones, grasps, takes hither, throws then at it. Thud on it will die, dies; but lived (did) it, will run.)

The account of this disturbance of slumber and the consequent reaction by stone-throwing needs little further explanation in any society where cats also 'walk abroad crying' at night. To a Tikopia, however, persistence of the animal in this pastime indicates that it is literally possessed by a devil, which has driven it insane and inspired it to annoy mankind.

THE CONCEPT OF THE 'ATA'

The term *ata* is frequently used to describe the relation of the supernatural being to the animal which is its manifest form. In its most concrete sense *te ata* is the *shadow*, as of a person cast by the sun. *'Te ra e poi i runga, kae te ata rei i raro.'* 'The sun goes above, while the shadow then is below.' It is also used of a *reflection* as of an image seen in a pool of water. The appearance of a spirit in material animate form is also described as its *ata*, which is best translated in this connection as its *image*, or *simulation*. The native expression is that *'te atua e ata ki te manu'*, 'the spirit simulates the animal', meaning that it takes on this form. Thus of the white tern it is said *'Te akiaki e ati te ata o nga atua, e ati nga atua e oro feurufi ki ei.'* 'The tern is called the *ata* of the gods; it is held that the gods go and enter into it.' The word *ata* is used only when the concrete materialization is that of a living creature; in other cases the spirit may have as a permanent resting-place an object such as a war club, a spear or the sacred centre post of a clan house. These are alluded to as *fakatino*, embodiments (*tino*=body) of their respective deities. The *fakatino* is a permanent concrete symbol of the supernatural being, a definite individual object of known locale; the *ata* is the form which he simulates at will, and may be any individual of a given species. The significance of the rendering of *ata* as simulation or impersonation is borne out by the Tikopia belief in regard to dreams. Untoward incidents in dreams in which friends or relatives play a part which does not accord with their character and position in real life are explained by the natives as due to the agency of malevolent spiritual beings, who assume the representation of the person in question, adopting his or her form and features. This deception is described thus: 'The spirit comes in a dream, impersonates the brother, or the sister.' Incestuous dreams are explained on this basis.

The terms *tupu* meaning primarily 'to grow', and *fiti* 'to spring' are also used to indicate the process of conversion of the spiritual being to its material manifestation. In this sense they are most closely translated by 'change'. Thus it is said:

'*Ko nga atua i fenua nei e ata ki a manu e orooro fuere; e ati e ata, ka e tino ki ei; e fiti ki ei, o mai o oro ki a tangata.*' (The spirits in land this simulate animals going simply; is called simulate, but body (to) them; change (to) them, come hither to go to men.)

In freer rendering, 'The spirits in this land simulate the animals which simply wander about; the term used is simulate (*ata*) but they actually take on their bodies, they change into them, and come here in order to visit mankind.'

Another statement:

'*Te atua ka poi fakafua, te atua a te kere; e tupu ki te unga, ki te karamisi, ki anea vare. Te atua e tupu ki ei, kae poi rei te karamisi, tenea vare fuere.*' (The spirit will go making disease, the spirit of the earth; changes to the hermit crab, to the red land crab, to things common. The spirit changes to it, but goes then the red land crab, the thing common simply.)

The significance of this is 'The spirit who wishes to go and convey disease, a spirit of the earth (i.e. one of the nameless host who inhabit the ground) changes into the form of a hermit crab, or of a red land crab or into any common creature. (The word *vare* conveys a tinge of contempt, since it is also used to mean 'stupid', 'foolish' as well as 'common'.) The spirit changes, for example, to the red land crab. but as for the crab itself, it still continues to be simply an ordinary creature.'

This analysis of the linguistic usage, including the presentation of a rather cumbrous literal rendering of the native text, is necessary to reveal the precise nature of the relation between the supernatural being and the 'totem' animal. The animal, in fact, is of quite secondary interest in the socio-religious scheme. It is the spirit, the *atua*, which is of fundamental import, and the animal, in native eyes, is of moment only in that the *atua* utilizes it as a fleshly vessel by entering its body, or on the other hand simulates it by assuming its form. To put the case quite simply; it is the spirit in the animal or the spirit in the form of the animal who commands the respect and the 'totemic' interest of the Tikopia; the individual animal as such or the species as a whole has no particular ritual value. It is merely 'anything common'—*anea vare*.

Now that the central feature of the situation as understood by the Tikopia has been stated the position of the various animal species may be examined more closely.

Tikopia say that all birds and animals are *ata* of various *atua* which appear in this form to mankind. To this general statement there are certain exceptions since a few kinds of bird are not regarded as serving *atua* as a vehicle for manifestation, and are eaten freely. The great majority of species, however, are associated with supernatural beings.

But not all animals of the one kind are so characterized. Some may be acting as media or materializations of the spirits, fraught with religious interest and perhaps with peril, while others of the same species remain simple and harmless creatures. The problem then arises of how to distinguish the one type from the other—to separate the spirit in animal shape from the mere animal. This problem has had to be faced by the Tikopia and an attempt made at its solution, since while on the one hand it is impracticable for him to respect and give licence to every member of every animal species which he encounters, it is imperative, from the point of view of religious belief to observe a becoming reverence to such creatures as may be possessed by supernormal attributes. The broad test is based in a rational manner on the behaviour of the animal itself. If it behaves strangely in a manner not characteristic of its species then it is an *atua* in animal guise; if it acts in normal fashion then it is an ordinary individual and may be treated as such. A Tikopia said to me:

'*Koke e poi i te uruao, e ono ki te manu ku rere mai, tera te atua kua uru i ei, ku ata ki ei. Tera tau fangatasi ma te ika. Te atua ku poi o sakiri te ika ka u ki ei, o tino ki ei.*' ('You are going in the woods, look on an animal has run hither, that the spirit has entered in it, has simulated it. There the same relation with the fish. The spirit has gone to seek the fish will come to it, to body to it.')

The point of this statement is that if a person walking through the woods sees a startled bird fly away from him or a swamp hen run, then it is simply a creature in natural form; if, however, it comes towards him and exhibits none of the fear which is to be expected in the circumstances, or if it hovers near him and keeps up a continuous cry for no apparent reason, then it is held to be inhabited at the moment by a supernatural being. So also with fish, into which spirits also enter on occasion, and which betray their nature by abnormal conduct.

The same applies to the bat (*peka*) which is common in the island. Being a fruit eater it is looked on by the people as a great pest but, probably as a reflex of the same circumstances, is regarded as a creature of the gods, in particular of the clan of Tafua. Sometimes when encountered it is a manifestation of the *atua*; more often it is merely the animal itself. The statement below shows how the distinction is made on the basis of the actions of the creature when confronted with man.

'*Ka fenatu te tangata i roto te ara, sa Tafua, e tau te peka i te rakau i roto te ara, e tau e tangi, fai atu, kae sise rere, tera te atua. Kae te manu e rere te manu vare fuere.*' (Will proceed the man in middle the path, Tafua (group), is hung the bat in the tree in middle the path, is hung is crying, threaten (it), but not flies, that the spirit. But the animal flies the animal common only.')

If the bat flies away nothing is done but if it holds fast and obstinately refuses to move, even when the arm or a stick is brandished at it, then the man calls out:—

> '*Ke fuere Pu E! e tau o tangi pe ea?*
> 'You only Ancestor! are hung to cry if what?
> *Tenea sokotasi ke Pu E! se ora moku*
> That thing one you Ancestor! welfare for me
> *Sori mai i a ke.*'
> Give me from you.'

This formula is an appeal by the man to the deity, as he now perceives the animal to be, to grant him a boon—one only—that is welfare for himself. If such an experience should occur to the Ariki Tafua, chief of the clan, he pronounces the words:

> '*Ke Pu fuere e au*
> 'You Ancestor only come
> *Fakasa mai ki a kuou*
> Appear hither to me.
> *Se tangata mou e nofo i a vaerangi*
> A man for you abides in skies
> *Suki ke au o au mai se maro mou.*'
> Prick to come to bring hither an offering for you.'

This is a greeting to the *atua*, coupled with a request that a person may be found elsewhere (under foreign skies) to provide an offering for him. The exact application of the formula is somewhat obscure, but it is a conciliatory speech to the disguised spirit, expressing the wish that provision may be made for him from other sources than those of the chief.

The *peka* is not eaten by the Tikopia, and they express great distaste at the idea; 'it is disgusting'. Its characteristic odour is also regarded as unpleasant. A boy from Luaniua, who accompanied me to the island once announced his intention of cooking a bat and making a meal if it, as—he stated—is done in his own home. The Tikopia lads who were his friends and boon companions persuaded him so earnestly not to do so, however, that he refrained; the argument they employed was not that of breach of *tapu*, but that if he did so the whole land would hear of it and ridicule him so much that he would be driven to suicide in shame. The sanction behind the prohibition of eating the bat is one of derision, not of horror.

The *peka* ordinarily is treated with scant ceremony, and though not usually harmed by adults is often pelted with stones by children and occasionally brought down in triumph. Reproof from elders may follow, but only of a mild nature. A man who by intention killed a bat would be regarded as having committed an unwise action but not necessarily a sacrilegious one. Several times during my stay in the island I have known of bats killed by children without result, and myself shot a specimen series without exciting other emotions than those of curiosity.[1] The bat is a thieving animal (*te manu kaia*) and as such has little sympathy in its misfortune. But for this reason it receives on the other hand some consideration. When a man finds a bat eating fruit in his orchard or gnawing at a coconut, if he be a cautious person he does not endeavour to kill it, but merely scares it away, apostrophizing it under the name of *Pu* (Ancestor) as it flaps off, to go to other districts and obtain food. He treats it gently lest being possibly an *atua* masquerading in animal guise, it resent harsh treatment and retaliate by returning again and again to his crops.

The bat figures in a folk-tale of Tikopia which gives it priority to the presence of male humans in the land. This story, which was told me by the Ariki Tafua, does not form part of the complex mythological scheme which to the native mind provides the basis for Tikopia culture, but is one of those curious items of ancient lore which seem to exist side by side with, yet apart from the main body of belief. The story, in free translation, is as follows:

'In former times this land was a land inhabited only by females, there were no men. One woman lived here, gave birth to a female child, another woman lived here, and gave birth to a female child, and

---

[1] It is possible that this lack of interest in the bat from a religious point of view is partly due to the secession of the Ariki Tafua with whom principally the creature is connected. I have been told by Captain Burgess of the S.Y. *Sonthern Cross* that the shooting of a bat in earlier years evoked indignation from the people. Much of this, however, would be most certainly due to ignorance on their part of the white man's motive for the shooting, and consequent perturbation regarding its object and effects. (In 1952 Tikopia themselves shot bats cheerfully.)

so on. The children were those of the bats, and females only. Not a male came. And the women took husbands from the bats alone. After this state of affairs had thus long continued a man came; he came from Motlav, and his name was Swift Whistling. He came and went to live with the women, and set up house with them. Look there at his anchor which stands in the enclosure to seawards, and his stone coconut. (An observation by the narrator in corroboration of the tale.) He married a woman of Fareautaka (a *paito*, family group of Tafua clan). Thereupon she begat her children from the man. When the bats approached the woman the man killed them and took them to roast on the fire to be his food. He ate them here in this land. Then the man went to his own land, to Motlav, and stayed there, while his children dwelt in this land. That is the story of the bats.'

This tale does not link on to the other origin myths of Tikopia, as far as incident is concerned, though when analysed it is found to deal with some of the basic characters of the pantheon. Thus the names of the women whom the bats married were said by the Ariki to be 'Titi ma Kaveao'. This is one of the many joint titles by which are known a pair of female *atua*, commonly termed 'A Rua Nea' (literally, 'Two Persons') who occur in many mythical stories. The man from Motlav appears to be a character of no great significance in the Tikopia legendary scheme, since he does not figure in other tales, nor is he a local deity. With the bats, however, it is different. They are personified for the purposes of the story under the name of 'Raupere'. Another esoteric title for them was given by the Ariki Tafua as 'Tanamanu' (literally, 'His Creature') and under this guise the *peka* is invoked in his *kava* ceremony. 'Is raised in the *kava* because the creature of the women; their (dual) husband is he.' Now *atua* in Tikopia pass under many names, and these alone give no clue. But in further explanation the chief said 'That is the *atua* to whom the *uaroro* (esoteric term for "coconut") is dedicated. And if the Ariki Tafua is angry he speaks to the bat to go and cut the coconuts of the folk in the land. The people go then to their orchards, and they have been cut, that is because a formula has been uttered by the Ariki Tafua to go and work mischief in the orchards of the folk.'

It is believed by the Ariki Tafua, and by the community at large, that he has special control over the actions of the bat, and that if he is offended by some action of the populace he can, by reciting an appropriate appeal, induce the creature to go and damage their coconut crops by severing with its sharp teeth the stems of the immature nuts. As a corollary to this belief, when the people see in their orchards evidence of unusually severe depredations by bats they attribute this to the ill-will and the recital of spells on the part of the chief against them.

The peculiar relation existing between the Ariki Tafua and the *peka* is explained by the fact that the animal is regarded as the *ata* of one of his principal *atua*. This is implied by the chief in the statement given above that the coconut is dedicated to him. This is the eel-god of the shore-waters, who is invoked in the *kava* of the Ariki Tafua under the name of Fitikake. In this form he is invited to

> 'Tuck firmly under your arm your bat there
> That drink may be given him from Fruits of the Woods.'

The eel-god is here appealed to by the Ariki to prevent his animal vehicle, the bat, from going to feed on the coconut, and to promote his eating the wild fruits of the forest—as the *fetau*, the *natu* and the like—on which man is not so dependent for food.

The eel-god is himself, by mythic account, the son of the Atua i Tafua, who is supposed to have a peculiar interest in his father's ward, the coconut. Under the name of Fitikake, however, he is also summoned in black magic by the Ariki Tafua to go and destroy the coconuts of offending persons, as mentioned above. Thus the chief of Tafua has a dual relation to the *niu*; he is its protector and is responsible for its fertility, but he may also be its peculiar destroyer if occasion seems to him to warrant such action. And his position among men is paralleled by that of his deities among the *atua*. There is thus a logical completeness in their control.

Pere is an esoteric word for the common term *peka*; as such it forms part of the name 'Raupere', i.e. 'their (dual) bat' already noted. It is said by the Ariki Tafua that the women of the myth, Titi and Kaveao, also utilize the bat on earth as a medium.

'The bat is sacred to sa Tafua' is a statement commonly made by natives, meaning that the association between the animal and the members of that clan is deeper than with other people of the community—for the reason just given—and consequently that the prohibitions and ritual observances are more binding on them. This does not imply that only the people of Tafua regard the bat as unfit for food or treat it with respect in their orchards; the same customs are observed by all, but they are more incumbent on sa Tafua, and a breach by them would be regarded as more serious.

The deference of the people of all clans to the *peka* appears to indicate that this creature owes its ritual importance primarily to its economic notoriety, its powers of destruction of food, and that the link with the specific clan *atua* is of secondary interest.

Somewhat the same attitude exists in the case of the *sivi* (parroquet) and *karae* (swamp-hen). The parroquet is destructive to coconut and other tree fruits by reason of its promiscuous nibbling, which causes wastage of food even where the quantity consumed is not great. As with the bat, however, violent action is not usually adopted, being replaced by methods of suasion. A man sitting in his house and hearing the cry of a parroquet in his orchard near at hand will call out:

'Go Ancestor! to set up your sacred beak
On the crests of the hills
And leave this place here
For the preparation of a food gift for you.'

These words politely invite the bird to betake itself to the mountain heights, and allow the spot which it is raiding to stay vacant in order— so it is assured—that the crops thus left to mature may form an adequate food present for it at some future date. On hearing this, it is believed, the parroquet is under compulsion to fly off and feed in another locality.

For the *karae* a similar procedure is adopted. A person will utter the formula:

'Go Ancestor! and set up your sacred beak here
On Maunga Faea or in Soso
To eat a large taro root for yourself
And a great stem of bananas for yourself.'

Here the bird is induced to go by mention of the prospect of large crops in other places. It is interesting to note that the formulae were given me by men of Ravenga, and the invitation for the bird is issued on behalf of orchards in other localities. Such is the custom. 'People of Faea request the birds to come to Ravenga here; a man in Ravenga apostrophizes them to go to orchards of sa Faea; *e kau saere.*' (Literally 'are apostrophized walking', meaning that the bird is kept in motion by the reciprocal commands of sa Faea and sa Ravenga for it to depart for each others' cultivations.) A similar formula is used towards the bat, which is requested to go to coconut or banana trees elsewhere. Politeness is believed to be essential to ensure obedience on the part of the bird. 'The bird hears the speech that is made, goes then; it is held to be an *atua*, one speaks properly to it. But show anger towards it, and it will return, and eat completely the bananas or the taro.'

The swamp-hen is perhaps the greatest animal pest known to the natives. It is extremely voracious, and taro and banana suffer heavily from its incursions. At times, indeed, when this bird is very numerous it is difficult to obtain a ripe banana in the island. When the fruit is approaching maturity the bunch may be enclosed for protection in a sheath of coconut leaf plaited around it, but even this is not always proof against the enemy. The *karae*, taking its stand at the base of the tree, jumps up repeatedly and pecks at the bananas until the whole bunch is soon rendered useless for food to the owner. This habit of the bird is commemorated in an old song which forms one of a series of chants for a ceremonial dance performed in honour of a female child of rank. The song runs:

Tafito: '*Ia rorí! Ia rorá!*   *Safe: Karae, karae*
          Ke toea, esé!   *Taia se futi*
                                        Na ke rere, sopo!'

The words of the first part of the song are archaic, and their meaning is unknown to the natives of today. 'Not any speech among us here, speech of the *atua*,' said the Ariki Kafika, referring to their supposed supernatural origin. *Ese* (or *ehe*) was explained, however, as being a mere exclamation to lend force to the rhythm, and it is probable that the other words also represent a rhythmic combination of syllables of no special import. The second stanza can be translated, as it is in normal speech.

          'Swamp-hen, swamp-hen,
          Fells a banana
          With his running jump!'

Because of its persistent thieving habits the *karae* is very unpopular, and though recognized as the *ata* of a clan deity is nevertheless sometimes killed. One such incident is remembered because of a song. Pu Nukuariki, a man of Tafua clan, tied up a bunch of bananas in his orchard in the manner already described, to preserve it from the *karae*. When the work was finished he heard one of these birds call close at hand, and turning saw it flying towards him in the act of coming to the bananas. Angry at its audacity, with a quick movement he reversed the adze which he was carrying, and struck it down. Later he composed this song in memory of the deed.

          'Now its redness thy beak
          Now its whiteness thy rump.
          Flying here, E!
          Gliding here, E!
          Come then to thy destruction
          By the handle of the adze.'

This song is intended as a chorus to a dance of the *matavaka* (canoe bow) type, and has the common triple stanza form. The first verse refers to the two most characteristic features of the *karae*, its red beak and the white patch on the underside of its tail, which it flicks constantly as it walks. The second and third verses refer to the incident as described.

I was myself witness of the killing of one of these birds. The Ariki Kafika and I were sitting in talk in his house in Uta when from under

the eaves we noticed a swamp-hen come stalking between the huts,
Quietly the Ariki reached for a small bow and arrow which lay near.
the property of his grandson, Rakeivave. Holding the bow horizontally,
he drew back the arrow—a dry mid-rib of a sago leaf sharpened at one
end, with a small leaf vane at the other—and sighting from under the
eaves, loosed the shaft. It flew true and pierced the bird through
the body. With a wild squawk and a flapping of wings it ran from sight
and was lost, but was discovered a day or two later dead in a near-by
bush. 'Thieving thing! May its father eat filth!' said the Ariki. In this
case, as in that of Pu Nukuariki, the bird was clearly dealt with as a
mundane creature, of no supernatural attributes. Such is a common
attitude. If the chief had been performing a *kava* ceremony, however,
and the bird had appeared, then he would not have thought of injuring
it. It would have been the *atua* come to attend the sacred ritual.

The same distinction is observed with other creatures. During
one rite a rat ran along a beam and down across the floor. '*Te atua ku au*'
—'The deity has come' murmured someone, and no attempt was made
to scare or molest it. Yet though ordinarily no very active pursuit is
made of them, rats are killed when occasion offers, and a native form of
trap constructed on the spring noose system exists.[1] A European one of
the 'break-back' type which I took to the island proved immensely
popular, and being lent to Pa Fenuatara, the eldest son of the Ariki
Kafika, was borrowed by his neighbours from night to night, members
of the family sitting up to re-set the trap as it made its kill, and to keep
tally for the information of the village next morning.[2] The dead bodies
of the victims were simply flung away without regard. The trap was
also taken to Uta, and there in the sacred district was set in operation
and its effect delightedly observed by the chief and his family in his
house within a few yards of the spot where on the former occasion the
rat was greeted as an *atua*. In conversation, too, the animal is anathe-
matized not only for its theft of food and its destruction of property, but
for its habits of depositing ordure and of micturating from the rafters
at night.

As the behaviour of the Tikopia shows, there is a clear distinction
made between the animal *per se*, and the animal as the embodiment or
presentation of a supernatural being; and it is the latter only which is
the object of religious interest. Moreover, a definite basis for such
distinction—in theory at least—is afforded by the actions of the animal
itself, and the circumstances under which it appears.

The standard of judgement as to whether one is encountering an

[1] An example of this type of rat-trap, made by Pa Fenuatara, is in my Tikopia collection
formerly in the University of Sydney and now at the Australian National University at
Canberra. It resembles closely the figure and description of the Funafuti type given by C.
Hedley, *Memoirs of Australian Museum*, III, pp. 278–80.

[2] Cf. Hedley, op. cit., pp. 278–9.

animal or an *atua*, however, being empirical, is admittedly subject to error. It is understood that man may sometimes mistake the spirit for an ordinary creature, and by lack of caution involve himself in mischance. This is illustrated by an incident which happened some years ago, in which a party of men ate of a kind of crab known as the *paka forau* and died in consequence. This animal is believed to be one of the forms in which the Female Deity, Te Atua Fafine, manifests herself, but on this occasion the folk imagined that they were merely dealing with the *ata*, the physical simulation, and not the spirit. Their tragic fate, however, was evidence of their mistake. 'They called it the reflection, but indeed it was the true deity' (*'E ati te ata, nai te atua maori!'*) One of the party only, Pa Torofakatonga, refrained from eating; he dropped the morsels of food between his legs when invited to partake and so survived. In consequence of the event two dirges were composed. One runs:

> 'The stupid action of men
> Have eaten wrongly of the deity.
> One said it was only the counterfeit.
> Meet in the realm of the gods
> I shall press noses with my brothers.
> Prickling is my body
> Lie down to sleep, rise up
> Stripping off the sweat.'

This dirge was composed by Pa Torofakatonga, the survivor. As frequent in such songs some of the action of the third party is cast in the first person, as if not the composer but his dead relative were narrating the incident. The term *kita* (one) has no numerical significance, but is the impersonal usage. The final stanza refers to the feverish condition which characterized the last illness of the unfortunate men. This is described in more detail in the other dirge—composed by Pa Saraniu, a middle-aged man still living—for which there is not space here.

The idea in regard to the injuring, killing or eating of such creatures as are believed to be *ata* or *atua* is that any action of this kind which is apparently followed by no ill results has involved the animal alone; but if any misfortune should occur soon afterwards, then this is held to be proof that the *atua* was in possession at the time. This is merely a special case of the general principle that the presence of an *atua* is to be deduced from the behaviour of the animal—if eating it makes one ill, then it must have harboured a spirit. This belief in the possibility of error in attribution provides thus a means whereby accident or other untoward event can be rationalized. The eating of an animal which is thought to serve at any time as the manifestation of an *atua* is, however, an extremely rare occurrence, and is regarded as being an act of the utmost rashness by the natives as a whole. An exception to this is the giant clam, which is not, however, regarded as an *ata* of importance.

The basis of identification of the presence of a supernatural being varies somewhat with different species. Thus the black lizard which frequents the native houses and is common throughout the island is believed to be an *atua* if it presents a peculiar shining appearance.

In Tikopia view: 'The lizard is a real deity, not merely a common thing; the deity does not reside in it, but changes into it, and thenceforth it goes as a veritable deity. The ordinary animal which crawls about in the house is only a lizard, but when one appears with a glistening body as if oil had been poured over it, that is a true deity, which has entered, whatever may be the errand on which he comes: he has appeared to look on us.'

This statement, which was made by Pa Fenuatara, a most intelligent informant, seems to involve a certain confusion in first denying that the lizard is an ordinary animal and then drawing the distinction already discussed between the common creature and the god impersonating it. This is due to the fact that in his first remarks he desired to impress upon me the fact that the lizard actually served as the medium of *atua*, a point about which I had expressed some doubts, since not all creatures are so considered.

The *moko* is not harmed as a rule, nor is it in any way obnoxious to man. Sometimes when it runs over the floor and pauses to observe its surroundings it is stimulated to sudden activity by a person rustling his fingers on the dry coconut matting. This startles it and it rushes off, to the amusement of people watching. Once I observed one of these lizards roughly handled, when a son of the Ariki Kafika picked it up in jest and threw it across the house, an action which aroused no reproach from the elders present, though the *atua* which it serves to embody was of their own clan. Here obviously it was the animal and not the deity that was thought to be maltreated.

The *moko* is regarded as being the *ata* of the Atua i Raropuka.[1] The crocodile, known as *moko toro* (crawling lizard) is held to be the *ata* of the same god. This creature is rarely seen in Tikopia waters, but one is reported to have attacked a woman a number of years ago. Another, a young specimen which came to land at Tufenua in recent times, was secured by the tail with a rope, and then despatched by blows from an axe. No other cases of the occurrence of this reptile are known to the natives, but a large skink from Malaita which they observed on the *Southern Cross* while it was being transported to Auckland was termed by them a member of the same species.

As a rule the animal which is thought to serve as the *ata* of a deity is not eaten, though it may be killed on occasions. The swamp-hen

[1] See 'A Dart Match in Tikopia'. *Oceania*, Vol. I, 1930, p. 76.

for instance is never utilized for food. 'Is not eaten the *karae* in this land, not a person may eat it, because it is the *atua* which has its basis in sa Taumako.' With the pigeon the case is not quite parallel. Normally it is not eaten. Thus on a shooting expedition I was once accompanied by two men of Kafika, including the heir to the chieftainship, and a man of rank of Taumako. They were keenly interested in the sport, located pigeons and applauded each successful shot. Later they assisted in plucking and cleaning the birds. At the end of the day I offered them some of the bag, but they refused, saying 'We do not eat the pigeon, it is *tapu* to us.' Though this bird is not eaten by Taumako it may in some circumstances be used as food by persons of the other clans, though such action is rare, and would not be performed by *tama tapu* of Taumako clan, i.e. people whose mother is of that stock. One informant gave me a ruling on the question of eating the pigeon—as follows: 'If a woman of Taumako marries a man of Tafua, then she refrains from eating the *rupe* (pigeon), and her *muaki tama*, the eldest son, does also. Her younger children may eat of it. Her husband used to eat thereof, but when his wife comes and they dwell together, it is *tapu* for him then. When the eldest son marries, then his children may eat this bird; they eat then, because their own mother is different.' The *tapu* is not incumbent on the grandchildren, even on the offspring of the eldest son—unless of course, their mother also is of Taumako, in which case they too will refrain. The licence allowed by this rule is largely theoretical; in practice hardly anyone in the entire population appears to eat the pigeon, and though plentiful, it is not regarded by the Tikopia as an item in the food supply. On the other hand people even of Taumako clan are quite eager that this bird shall be shot, giving as a reason that it consumes *voia* (*Canarium*) nuts and other useful forest fruits.

The reason why the husband abstains from eating the animal which is sacred to the wife's clan is of considerable interest from the point of view of the Tikopia ideas on physiology, apart from those of religion. It is believed that the oil from the bird's flesh helps to form the seminal fluid in the man's body, and that by the process of sex intercourse this enters the body of the woman, and thus by an indirect route a portion of the prohibited animal is absorbed. The following statement indicates how definitely this concept has been formulated.

'While they two (i.e. husband and wife) continue to have intercourse the man is prohibited (from using the pigeon as food). But as he ages, he then can eat, since the body has weakened (i.e. he has become impotent) So as time goes on, and the sacred path is severed (that is, there are no more children) he then may eat. The reason is that while they two have intercourse the semen of the man still rushes into the woman, and that is the basis of the prohibition. Because when he lies with her, his body presses to that of the woman, and the oil of the bird thus comes down into her.'

The restriction of the prohibition on eating an animal associated with a clan deity to the children of the eldest born only, is paralleled by the custom observed with regard to the *tukuku* and *panoko*, two fish which are *tapu* to sa Kafika. They are not *ata* of *atua* on earth, but according to Tikopia belief have a special function to perform in the afterworld in connection with the dead of Kafika. For this reason ritual abstention is observed, but only by the eldest son and eldest daughter of each Kafika family. Moreover, when women of Kafika marry husbands of Taumako, Tafua or Fangarere, their first-born likewise do not eat of these two fish, though the later born do. My informant in this case, Pa Vainunu, a man of rank in Kafika, whose father was a former chief of the clan, does utilize the *tukuku* and *panoko* as food, since he is not the eldest child of the family. To all the younger children, *e ngafua*, it is permissible. It is noteworthy also that though a woman of Kafika who is a younger child may eat of the fish her eldest child will not do so; this is apparently due to his position as one of the principal *tama tapu* of his mother's people.

Other birds in addition to those already mentioned serve as media or simulacra for important deities. Such are the *sikotara* (kingfisher) which is the *ata* of the Atua i te Uruao, the God in the Woods, the principal deity of the Porima family. The *kareva*, the long-tailed cuckoo, which is sometimes seen in the island, is an *ata* of the same *atua*. The *sivi* (parroquet) is sacred to sa Taumako, being utilized as a material medium by the chief *atua* of that clan. The *tavake*, the bosun-bird, is called 'the creature of Tafaki and Karisi, their *ata*', as also is the *akiaki*, the beautiful white tern, with its black-capped head. Curiously enough the *unufe* (caterpillar) is also regarded as a medium of this pair of deities; 'it is regarded as their creature'. They are primarily important for the Kafika clan, but are also invoked in the *kava* of Taumako, and have a place in the ritual of the other groups as well. They are thus of religious interest to all the people in the island. In general the *ata* and the *atua* for which it is a medium is not necessarily associated with only a single clan, and in this respect the phenomena here discussed are not of the typical 'totemistic' order. The *motuku* or *keo*, the heron, is the *ata* of Nau Fiora, a female deity of Tafua clan, also important for Fangarere. The white variety of this species, the *keo kena* now probably extinct,[1] is her special medium, this association being due to the belief that the body of the deity herself is of a shining white.

A few birds are entirely free from any restriction in the matter of fitness for food. 'Some birds are permitted, is eaten the *ngongo* (noddy tern), and the *toroa* (grey duck) is eaten. Some birds are not. The

[1] The white heron is evidently a migrant visitor; several were seen in Tikopia in 1952.

miti (a species of brown shrike) is eaten by some persons; no *atua* impersonates it.'

To this 'free list' of birds may be added the *rakia* (a species of small black petrel) and the *pakalili* (martin) which are eaten by all the people, even the chiefs, when the occasion offers. It may be noted, however, that birds at no time form any important part of the Tikopia food supply, and the question of whether certain species are permissible for food or not is one which does not interest a Tikopia to any great extent. He is content to utilize the few species known to be licit at such rare times as they may be available, and to leave the matter of the edible nature of others to traditional edict. The whole subject of the attitude to be observed towards bird species is in fact not at all prominent in the social or religious life.

'ATUA' AND MARINE CREATURES

More interest is displayed in marine creatures, and the distinction between edible and non-edible species is clearly marked. The case of the *paka forau* and the *moko toro* has already been mentioned. The *fai* (stingray) and the *riringo* (also a ray, and possibly of the same type) of which there are said to be three varieties, red, black and white, are all *ata* of the Atua Fafine, the Female Deity of Kafika. 'Her body in the shore waters, the *riringo* and the *fai*.'

Most of the fish known to the Tikopia are used as food, and are not regarded as being associated with spirits or deities, but a few of them are so classed. The *sakura* and *takua*, types of swordfish, are used as *ata* by the Atua i Taumako—they are called his *tino*, his body, signifying his material manifestation—and so are sacred for the clan of that name. Special interest attaches to the *maranga*, which is apparently of the dolphin type. One variety of this is known as the *maranga sa Korokoro* since it is supposed to have special affinity with the family group of Korokoro, which belongs to the Tafua clan. If this creature is found stranded, as occasionally occurs, then an offering of green food—taro plants or breadfruit, and fresh coconuts—is set beside it by the family mentioned. This is called the *putu*, a term which is used also to denote an offering set on the grave of a person recently dead. After this ritual deference has been paid to it the dolphin is taken away and cooked. The flesh is divided among the four clans of the island according to a definite traditional rule: the head is sent to sa Fangarere, the next cut, the foremost portion of the body, is sent to sa Taumako, the adjoining portion to sa Kafika, and the tail section to sa Tafua. The portions are known as *rau*, the conventional name for 'ceremonial share' and each is the *rau* of the principal deity of the clan to which it is presented. The gift is taken in each case to the chief of the clan as representative of his people, and is eaten by him and such of his family and clansfolk as he chooses. The people of sa Korokoro group do not eat of the dolphin at all. '*E tapu*' —'It is prohibited' for them. This is due to the belief that this creature is a form of materialization of their principal *atua*.

It may be noted that here is an especially clear case in which an animal species is affiliated with a family group (lineage) but not with the whole clan of which this group is a member—the situation is one of 'family (lineage) totemism', not 'clan totemism'.

The whale is known also to the Tikopia and is termed by them the *tafora* in common speech, or in an honorific phrase, '*te Uru Pou o te Vasa*'—'the Head Post of the Ocean Spaces'. At rare intervals a whale is driven ashore, and its huge bulk attracts considerable attention. Great numbers of people of all ages and both sexes assemble, and as the men of the community go to join this crowd they each grasp a weapon and on arrival at the scene brandish it fiercely. The club is waved violently, the spear is shaken in the peculiar quivering motion which is characteristic of the Tikopia method of attack (*te tao e fakaefu*) and these gestures are directed towards the whale. Though the actions are in mimicry of fighting no actual disorder takes place. This is termed the *fakaveve* of the whale. The idea is that the creature is the material form of an *atua* which has come to land, and there is the possibility that it may be a bringer of disease, since to the Tikopia the onset of an epidemic is always associated with influences, mainly supernatural, from outside the island. The threatening gestures of the *fakaveve* are intended to frighten off any such evil-minded *atua* and so preserve the health of the land. In addition to this a *putu* of green food is carried from the orchards and placed by the carcase, as is done with the *maranga*. This is by way of offering to the *atua* so that by the dual attitude of placation and threatening he may be induced to behave favourably to the people.

The flesh of the whale, unlike that of the dolphin, is not eaten, though its bones may be utilized for barbs or shanks of bonito-hooks, pestles for preparing betel (*tuki kamu*) and more rarely, neck ornaments. A *tafora* which came ashore some years ago was buried by the people in Te Akau-roa, a long sand-spit which in those days ran out below the village of Kafika in Ravenga. The flesh of one which was stranded on a previous occasion was eaten by some Anutans who were then living on the island, but was refused by the local folk.

The name *tafora* is sometimes extended to include all very large fish of the ocean, as the swordfish, as well as dolphin, porpoise and whale, which are not recognized by the Tikopia as presenting any real structural differences.

The *ono* is a fish two or three feet in length which is found both in the brackish lake and in the sea, in which latter habitat it is known as the *paravao*. Under this name it is greatly esteemed as food. In the lake, however, it is regarded as an *ata* of Tangaroa (or as some say, Tafito) who is an important *atua* of sa Fangarere. These people therefore do not eat the fish of the lake, nor even from the sea, 'because it is the *atua* which has its basis among them'. The general custom throughout all the clans is to refrain from eating the *ono* though some folk do not observe this rule. A peculiar sacredness attaches to this fish, which is demonstrated by the following custom: 'The *ono* formerly used to eat man; this is its sacred name, *te ono*; it is not called out in the lake which stands there. But if its name is called out the fish appears, and the man is eaten and lost. If it is seen not a person will call out about it, but go past silently merely. Some people eat it.' Eating of the fish is then not regarded as a severe breach of *tapu*, but the utterance of its sacred name is prohibited under penalty of being devoured by it. Any person seeing it will grunt and direct attention to it by his gaze, but will not point at it or pronounce its name.

This prohibition of course applies only to bathers or canoemen, or people standing on the lake shore: inland its name may be mentioned with impunity. It is believed that this fish will also act as executor of black magic, and that a man who has been commended to its attentions will be attacked and killed by it as soon as he visits the lake, even though he be in a canoe or at the water's edge, since the *ono* leaps out of the water for the purpose. The fish appears to be in reality of a savage disposition, since one informant told me that a brother of his mother was killed by it while drawing a net on the shallow rock ledge which runs along the eastern side of the lake.

The octopus and the various species of eel appear to be in a different category from the creatures already discussed in that here the *atua* is more closely related to the animal itself, being in fact a personification of the species.

The octopus is regarded as the embodiment or the actual form of the Atua i Faea, a male, his personal name being Feke. Usually the deity seems to be zoomorphically rather than anthropomorphically conceived. He is credited with making excursions inland at night, and endeavouring to carry off women to gratify his passions, on which occasion he advances on the tips of his tentacles. This belief is implied in a curse uttered to women: '*Nofine te Atua i Faea!*' 'Wife of the Deity of Faea!' which consigns her to this unpleasant fate. Feke is also represented in more symbolic form by a portion of the mountain crest of the extinct volcanic crater, the tentacles consisting of the several springs of water which flow from its sides. This *atua* is also identified with the sun, the rays corresponding again to the splayed tentacles of the octopus, and the same name (*ona kavei*) being applied in each case. In addition to his own proper shape Feke also enters into or simulates certain other creatures. One of these is the *unga*, the small red hermit crab, spoken of as 'the *atua* of Nga Faea, the *ata* of Feke, his *ata* on shore'. Another is the *toki*, the giant clam, which is also regarded as an *ata* of the *atua*. It is said: 'the clam which stands there is the body of the deities, the body of the Atua i Faea, the deity goes, goes, it is open, he enters into it.' Notwithstanding this the *toki* is eaten freely by people of most kinship groups. They dive in several fathoms of water, drive a spike through the open valves of the shell, and wrench it from the rock at the hinge.

The position of the octopus in the religious scheme of the Tikopia is thus somewhat involved. The *atua* Feke is a personification of this animal species; he is able also to materialize in the form of the hermit crab and the clam, which implies considerable powers of transmutation. Moreover, he is represented also by a mountain *massif* with its springs of water, and by the sun with its beams, an identification which is based on a general factor of similarity—a central body and a number of divergent rays. Again, as a deity of the Tikopia pantheon Feke is married to Nau Fiora, goddess of Tafua clan, has children by her, and on certain ceremonial occasions of the chief of Tafua is conceived as performing the appropriate duty, on the spiritual plane, of coming to tend the oven with his bundle of firewood on his shoulder, as all good husbands do on earth. The exact degree of abstraction, the precise relation which the spiritual being Feke is imagined to bear to his material form the octopus, the sun, the clam or the mountain crest is difficult to define; it apparently varies according to the circumstances.

The position of the eel is very similar. Eel falls into two divisions—those of the lake and those of the sea. The former have no specific name beyond that which is applied to the Eel god himself—'Tuna', the term 'te Atua i te Vai', 'the Deity in the Water' being the common mode of reference. Occasionally one type is distinguished by the description '*te atua fai taringa*' 'the deity possessing ears', since it has apparently ear-like protuberances at the sides of its head. The commonest of the marine eels is the *rafua*, a sandy-grey speckled creature with a flat, cruel head. It is noted for its savagery, and several times during my stay women and children came to me to bind up lacerated fingers which had been bitten by this eel while they were foraging for small fish among the rocks on the reef. Its attack is often delivered without provocation. The *rafua* is also spoken of as 'Te Atua i te Tai', 'The Deity in the Sea', in contrast to its fellow of the lake. It is regarded as being the material embodiment of one of the most important deities of the Taumako clan. The *ngatinia*, a species of sea eel banded in brown and white, is associated in particular with the Fangarere people, since it is the *ata* of the Atua i te Ava, the Deity of the Channel, who is invoked by them. There are said to be two types of this eel, one with a red or brown head, the other with flowing 'hair'. This latter is said to be of man-eating propensities and to be of such fierceness and size that the leg of a man bitten by it would be severed. During the monsoon season of 1928 one of these creatures was reported to have appeared to three men who were fishing near the channel at Ravenga, with mouth gaping, attracted by their bait. They retreated in terror and gave the alarm. On hearing the news the Ariki Kafika pulled down a *kau*, a heavy shark hook, and suggested catching it, and hauling it to land. No action, however, was taken. The *safuti*, which is found at the seaward end of the channel ('Muri ava') in Ravenga, and is also known as the *ata* of the Atua i te Ava of sa Fangarere, is perhaps the same creature. Other types of sea eel are the *sakusakurere*, which is the *ata* of the Atua Fafine and hence is *tapu* to sa Kafika, the *kiau*, with banded or mottled body in brown or white, which is the *ata* of Te Araifo, Te Atua Fiti, and is therefore an object of ritual interest to the family group of Nga Fiti, and the *farafara*, which is the *ata* of the Atua i Tafua.

None of the species of eel is eaten under any circumstances. It is a creature for which the natives express the greatest repulsion— 'it is disgusting' they say. The eel of the lake in particular arouses this aversion. At certain times a channel which leads from the lake to the sea is opened by co-operative effort, and fish of several species are caught as they proceed down it seawards. On such occasions the eels are never interfered with. So strong is the sentiment of disgust aroused by them as they squirm their way down the narrow channel that men are known actually to turn aside their heads and vomit at the sight. Their fatness, their sliminess and their writhings are the subject of comment, always with a distinct affective reaction. This feeling of repulsion is not exhibited when other inedible creatures as birds or lizards are discussed. This definite repugnance to the eel is the more interesting since by other Polynesian peoples, as those of the Marquesas or New Zealand, this fish is eaten and highly prized. Among the Maori, as on the upper waters of the Whanganui River, it may even constitute a large element in the food supply for months at a time. From this it is evident that the Tikopia dislike of the eel cannot be taken as part of a general Polynesian attitude of recognition of a repulsive character in the creature itself. Perhaps the sentiment of aversion to it and the prohibition against eating it—a prohibition, which unlike others, is never disregarded —can be correlated with the myth as to its origin. There is not space to give the full text here, but in brief, the story is that the various species of eel in the guise of their respective *atua* were formed from the *membrum virile* of the Atua i Tafua, being cut therefrom by a female deity and flung, one portion into the salt water to become the reef eel, another likewise, to become another sea eel, and another into the lake to become the denizen of the fresh water. It is doubtful whether the recollection of this myth exercises any immediate conscious influence on a Tikopia on those occasions when he comes into contact with the eel; in his repugnance to it he is obeying a social usage engrained in his behaviour through instruction from his elders or observation of their conduct and speech from his early years. The tale in fact is likely to be a dramatization rather than a cause of the sentiment, but a relation between them is probable. Unfortunately I did not make inquiry of the people on this precise point.

The distinction between the eel and the supernatural being which is its personification, though not always clear, still seems to exist. Thus the Atua i Sao is associated with an eel of rather rare type, about two or three feet long, and banded in white or light grey. The Ariki Kafika, after seeing one on the lake shore, explained that it was an *ata* of the *atua*, that the ordinary fish are *anea vare*, common things, disliked on account of their appearance, and that it is only when the *atua* desires to appear for some purpose that he enters an eel or takes on its form. It is evident then that every eel which is seen crawling along is not necessarily the god in person. It is called '*te atua*', but is not identified with the deity. Moreover when Tuna is invoked in the *kava* of the Ariki Tafua it is as a god from the abode of gods in the heavens, not as the actual animal which inhabits the lake. To demonstrate this point satisfactorily would require the presentation of a considerable body of evidence from mythology and religious formulae for which there is not space here, but as an indication of the Tikopia attitude the above data are sufficient.

To make this survey complete, mention must be made of certain fish which are not eaten, or eaten but rarely, but which are nevertheless not associated with specific deities. Such is the *loloa*, a small fish of the lake, which is considered as unfit for food. It is not commonly termed an *atua*, but is *tenea fuere*, 'the thing only'—that is it does not merit consideration.

The *nofo* and the *pakofu*, found on the reef edge, are also spoken of in the same way, though folk may on occasions catch them with rod and line. The shark (*te mango*) is eaten by most people, and its flesh is esteemed highly. There are two opinions current on the subject of eating shark, both influenced by the fact that this fish is the enemy of man. One point of view as expressed by a Tikopia is 'The shark eats man, therefore it is good that man should eat the shark.' The other, more fastidious, adopts a negative attitude 'One man eats of the shark, another man is prohibited (*e tapu*). Because he is afraid of the shark, which eats man, therefore he objects to it,' said the Ariki Kafika. In practice it is found that nearly everyone partakes of the fish. The position was stated differently by other informants who held that of the many kinds of shark there is only one, *te atua kai tangata*, which is a confirmed man-eater and inedible. The others, which are fish-eating, are utilized for human food. The man-eating shark is a creature of the open ocean; it has a large head and fins and a small tapering body, and is described in fact as being 'head only'. It is said not to take the hook. In spite of its name it is not regarded as being associated with any clan-god. It is called *te atua* because of its man-eating habits.

The turtle (*te fonu*) is also the subject of differential behaviour on the part of the people. Some eat it, but others do not. If they should do so they will vomit, regarding it as disgusting (*fakakinokino*). It is possible that the *fonu* is regarded as the *ata* of some *atua*, though I have no information on this point (but cf. p. 362). It is of little importance in ritual life of the people and is a very infrequent visitor to the island. Occasionally a single one is taken in a net when the reef is being swept for fish, but no organized attempt at capture is made otherwise. The turtle is included in the generic name of *paka*, applied to crabs, and apparently to all hard-backed marine creatures. Distinction is made between the ordinary *fonu* and the *paka koroa* from which the shell is obtained for the manufacture of earrings (*kanga*). One of the latter, a small specimen which was caught in a net off Matautu was intended by the Ariki Tafua to be kept tethered in the reef-waters as a *manu* (pet) with the object of allowing it to grow and later yield a large shell. It was observed, however, that there was a mark on its neck, which was believed to be a *tanga toki*, an adze-cut made by an *atua*. Hence it was taken away and cooked for food by the son-in-law of the Ariki who as a *vaka atua*, or medium of the spirits, had announced the discovery.

The following table will enable the distribution of natural species and of the related supernatural beings among the various social groups to be clearly grasped.

TABLE OF 'TOTEMIC' RELATIONS IN TIKOPIA

NATURAL SPECIES—PLANTS		RELATED *Atua*	RELATED SOCIAL GROUP
Ufi	(yam)	Atua i Kafika	Kafika clan
Niu	(coconut)	Atua i Tafua	Tafua clan
Taro	(*Colocasia*)	Atua i Taumako	Taumako clan
Mei	(breadfruit)	Atua i Fangarere	Fangarere clan

BIRDS AND MAMMALS		RELATED *Atua*	RELATED SOCIAL GROUP
Akiaki	(white tern)	Tafaki and Karisi	Kafika clan
Tavake	(bosun bird)	Tafaki and Karisi	Kafika clan
Karae	(swamp-hen)	Atua i Taumako	Taumako clan
Rupe	(pigeon)	Atua i Taumako	Taumako clan
Sivi	(parroquet)	Atua i Taumako	Taumako clan
Kareva	(cuckoo, long-tailed)	Atua i te Uruao	Porima family and others of Kafika clan
Sikotara	(kingfisher)	Atua i te Uruao	Porima family and others of Kafika clan
Keo	(heron)	Nau Fiora	Tafua clan

BIRDS AND MAMMALS		RELATED *Atua*	RELATED SOCIAL GROUP
Peka	(bat)	Atua i te Tai	Tafua clan
Miti	(? shrike)	none	none
Ngongo	(noddy)	none	none
Rakia	(black petrel)	none	none
Pakalili	(martin)	none	none
Toroa	(grey duck)	none	none
Ngaringari	(rat)	General atua	none

REPTILES, ETC.			
Moko	(black lizard)	Atua i Raropuka	Raropuka family and others of Kafika clan
Moko toro	(crocodile)	Atua i Raropuka	Raropuka family and others of Kafika clan
Karamisi	(red land crab)	Atua i te Uruao	Porima, Kafika clan
Unga	(hermit crab)	Atua i Faea	Kafika, Tafua, etc., clans
Kaviki	(grey land crab)	General atua	none
Morokau	(centipede)	General atua	none

FISH, ETC.			
Sakura	(?swordfish)	Atua i Taumako	Taumako clan
Takua	(?swordfish)	Atua i Taumako	Taumako clan
Fai	(stingray)	Atua Fafine	Kafika clan
Riringo	(ray)	Atua Fafine	Kafika clan
Maranga sa Korokoro	(?dolphin)	Semoana	Korokoro family, no others of Tafua clan
Feke	(octopus)	Atua i Faea	Kafika, Tafua, etc., clans
Toki	(clam)	Atua i Faea	Kafika, Tafua, etc., clans
Ono	(*paravao*)	Atua i Fangarere	Fangarere clan
Loloa		inedible, no atua	none
Nofo		inedible, no atua	none
Pakofu		inedible, no atua	none
Tarasea		inedible, no atua	none
Mango kai tangata	(man-eating shark)	inedible, no atua	none
Tafora	(whale)	General atua	none
Tuna	(eel, lake)	Atua i te Vai	Tafua clan
Tuna	(eel, banded)	Atua i Sao	Sao family, Tafua
Atua fai taringa	(eel, lake)	Atua i te Vai	Tafua clan
Rafua	(eel, grey)	Atua i te Tai	Taumako clan
Ngatinia	(eel)	Atua i te Ava	Fangarere clan

NATURAL SPECIES—FISH, ETC.		RELATED *Atua*	RELATED SOCIAL GROUP
Safuti	(eel)	Atua i te Ava	Fangarere clan
Kiau	(eel, banded)	Te Atua Fiti	Nga Fiti family, Kafika
Farafara	(eel)	Atua i Tafua	Tafua clan
Sakusakurere	(eel)	Atua Fafine	Kafika clan

It will be noticed that most *atua* in the list have not one but several species of animal as their *ata*; no special significance attaches to the number in each case. Some of the *atua* belong to more than one special group, and in this case the animal species is treated with respect by each group concerned. Here it may be emphasized once more that the primary interest for the Tikopia is in the relation of *atua* to his own and other groups of the community, not in the partition of natural species among them.

The data given above have helped to define the relation which exists in Tikopia society between the totem species and the human group associated with it. A summary of the principal results will enable comparison to be made with other Polynesian communities.

PRINCIPAL CHARACTERISTICS OF TIKOPIA TOTEMISM

In the first place the ritual attitude towards natural species does not bulk largely in Tikopia religion, either on the part of individuals or of groups. Elaborate ceremonies are conducted to promote the fertility of the chief plant food-stuffs, but for the animals associated with spiritual beings and social groups no specific ceremonies exist, no offerings are made to them, and they receive little formal attention. Their interest in native eyes is indirect and subsidiary.

This is the result of the belief that individuals of the natural species—apart from the food-stuffs mentioned above—are simply vehicles or manifestations of gods, ancestors or other spiritual beings, and a distinction is drawn coherently by the Tikopia between an individual of the species so controlled or simulated by a supernatural being, and one which is a purely normal creature.

It is evident also from this, why the idea of the identity of the natural species or individuals of it with the social group or with any person thereof is entirely lacking. The 'totem' animal is neither a representation nor an emblem of the human group, nor is it a member of the group. Interference with the creature, or the killing or eating of it, is regarded as a hostile act, not towards group property or a fellow member, but towards the deity who may be in possession of it at the time, and who will punish the sacrilege. The material object is then differentiated clearly from the spiritual being who employs it in manifestation.

It is the *atua* who is of constant importance, who is invoked in many ceremonies; his *ata* is of interest only on random occasions. Moreover, there is no belief that the social group or any portion of it is descended from the animal with which it is thus connected. Origin may be traced through the *atua*, the supernatural being, though this concept of descent from the higher deities is not clearly formulated, and may even be denied by some informants. The common belief is that each social group traces its origin to an ancestor, endowed with supernormal qualities, but conceived as a human being, who lived and died as such. These points are emphasized here since Rivers, not having obtained any inkling of the existence of spiritual *atua* of quite distinct personality from their material vehicles, has interpreted the ritual observances, quite wrongly, as springing from these alone. He states: 'It was clear that these animals had collectively the same name as ancestors and were regarded as such, but the descent was from men who had turned into animals rather than from the animals themselves. The Kafika and Taumako believe in their descent from men who turned after death into an octopus in the one case and an eel in the other.'[1] This is inaccurate in every particular, as also are his other opinions which immediately follow. In the case of Taumako, for instance, it is held by the Tikopia themselves that they are descended from a Tongan, generally referred to as 'Pu lasi', 'Great Ancestor', who came to Tikopia in a canoe, accompanied by his *atua*, Pusi by name, whose material embodiment or simulacrum is the *rafua*, the grey reef eel, commonly called also the Atua i te Tai, the Deity in the Sea. This is a correct though brief statement of the actual native view, which distinguishes definitely the human ancestor, his god, and the eel in which the latter becomes manifest. The statement of Rivers that the ancestor changed after death into the eel, which animal becomes thus the group totem, is incorrect, and is based on a conception of the spirit world quite foreign to the Tikopia. This criticism is of some importance from a more general theoretical standpoint since Rivers bases one of the principal points of his thesis of the origin of Melanesian totemism largely on his Tikopia material. His proposition is that the Polynesian immigrants whom he holds primarily responsible for the origin of the institution, believed first in their incarnation in the form of animal or plant after death, and subsequently in their identity with plants and animals.[2] This argument, it would appear, is not sustained by an examination of the actual facts either of the totemism of Tikopia, or of Polynesia in general. The totem is not reckoned as kin with the members of the human group, they are not identified with it before or after death, nor is it that 'dominant and essential tie between the members of a social body' which according to Rivers is its basic function. Clansfolk in Tikopia do not conceive

[1] Rivers, *H.M.S.*, I, p. 304; see also ibid., II, pp. 362, 364.
[2] Rivers, *H.M.S.*, II, pp. 236–238, 338, 347, 258–363.

themselves as being linked together through common interest in a natural species; they have this common interest in it since as members of the same kinship group they have the same gods.

The contrast between vegetable food-stuffs and animal species, to which reference has been made earlier, is a most marked feature of the Tikopia system. The vegetable food-stuffs are the object of some of the most vital and sacred religious ceremonies of the people, but they are not termed *atua* and are eaten by all the people, including those of their own group. They are represented symbolically as being the body or head of the respective gods who control them, but the god is not imagined to enter into them, they are not regarded as his *ata*, and no distinction is drawn on this account between individual yams, taro, etc. The selected animal species on the other hand are inedible, or are eaten only by people of other clans, they may be termed *atua*, the gods enter into them freely, and they are spoken of as *ata*, semblances of these beings. Distinction is made between normal individuals of the species and those which at the moment are held to be manifestations of the god; but no elaborate system of rites is performed as in the case of the food-stuffs. In each case the natural species is definitely associated with one of the major social groups—conveniently called clans—though there is no belief in its identity with the group or in descent of the members from it.

It might be suggested that two distinct kinds of totemism were represented, characteristic perhaps of the different cultural or historical influences at work in the Tikopia community. A more adequate interpretation, however, and one which is of more significance from the theoretical side of the problem, may try to embrace these divergent phases of the religious life in the one broad sphere of relations, and view them as types of differential responses to the environment. They may be regarded as ritual formulations of contrary but socially appropriate reactions to sets of natural objects possessing opposite qualities from the standpoint of the native commonweal.

Yam, taro, coconut and breadfruit are the staples of life and are valued exceedingly; the sentiment for them is of a very positive approving kind—they are typified then as each representing the head or body of a principal group deity, and seasonal rites are performed to stimulate their increase. Birds, on the other hand, compete with man for the wild forest fruits, or are active in raiding his cultivations; the sentiment for them is of a negative, disapproving kind. The bat and the rat, from their character, share in this; and certain species of fish because they are inedible, or possess a savage disposition or other undesirable qualities. They then are associated with the gods, in a different way, fulfilling the functions of omens, bringers of disease, destroyers of food, executors of witchcraft and general emissaries of the abnormal and unpleasant. It is along these lines that an understanding of Tikopia totemism seems to lie.

The absence of the great body of the edible fish species from the totemic situation also appears to be comprehensible from this point of view; it may be correlated with their indefiniteness in the native social scheme before capture. They are important for food and are closely related to the religious system, but being a much more intangible entity, less differentiated at their source, are not apportioned for ritual control among the various social groups but have their allotment of ceremonies transferred and performed in connection with the sacred canoes, through which they are made available for man's needs. With food plants the social emphasis is on their growth, with fish it is on their capture. The harvest of the one is already foreseen, that of the other is uncertain till the canoe returns.

REVIEW OF POLYNESIAN EVIDENCE

The nature of Polynesian totemism in general may now be considered in the light of these results. In the central and western portion of the area as a whole the linkage of supernatural beings with social groups on the one hand and with natural species on the other is evident, though the relation seems to be with animals, and the 'plant totemism' of Tikopia is not found. To adduce the full body of evidence is not possible in this article; the position in the major island groups for which most data exist will alone be summarized here, since the collected material of Handy and Williamson is already available.

In Rotuma the community is divided into a number of *hoang* (written *hoag*) a term used either for a village group or for the extended family which inhabits it. Each *hoang* has its own deity or *atua* which is usually incarnate in the form of some animal, as the *tanifa* (hammer-headed shark), *juli* (sand-piper), or *olusi* (lizard). In addition several *hoang* may acknowledge a greater deity as head over them all, while still retaining their individual protectors. A member of the group who killed his *atua* performed funerary rites in connection with it as for a person. At times the god took possession of a human medium, and gave advice or cured sickness.[1]

In Samoa every person was at birth taken under the care of a tutelary deity, chosen from a number whose names were being recited at the time. This god, known as an *aitu fale*, god of the house, was wont to appear in a visible incarnation (*ata*) usually in an animal form, and as such was highly venerated. Injury to it, as eating of it, was thought to be followed by death, as a rule through growth of the thing so desecrated within the body of the culprit. Village gods also existed, and had their particular incarnations, heron, owl, pigeon, rail, fowl, creeper, and kingfisher

[1] J. S. Gardiner, The Natives of Rotuma. *Journal Anthropological Institute*, Vol. 27, 1897–8, pp. 466–8.

among birds, stingray, cockle, cuttlefish, sea eel, crayfish, mullet and turtle among marine animals, with lizard, white dog, bat, butterfly and centipede among land creatures. The death of one of these was regarded as a matter for mourning, but it was not held to be the death of the god, which was still alive and incarnate in all the animals of the species. The rapid disappearance of these beliefs under Christianity is perhaps an indication that they did not occupy a very vital place in the social and religious life. A number of these animal species furnished omens in war. When the animal was seen proceeding in front of the war party, for instance, it was usually regarded as a token of success; when it retired, or went behind them, then coming failure was indicated. Inanimate objects also served as media of the gods—a coconut leaf basket, a trumpet shell, the teeth of a sperm whale, the rainbow, a bundle of shark's teeth, a particular large wooden bowl, or as in one case, a skull once a year. A few gods, as Sama, La'ala'a and Moso, manifested themselves in individual men, who were recognized as their incarnations. This last appears to be somewhat different from the phenomena of spirit-possession which also are found there. The same god was sometimes incarnate in different animal species, and while in one place he might be simply a household god, in another he was worshipped as the war god of a whole village. The relation of deities and social groups is thus not always symmetrical.[1]

The gods of Tonga varied in their sphere of influence, some being held in regard by the people as a whole, others being associated with a section alone, as of a powerful chief and his relatives, while others, of still more limited range, were connected with merely the little group of households which usually formed the social unit. There was nothing to prevent a man from setting up a tutelary deity of his own if he so desired. These supernatural beings might enter into animals, as the white tern, the octopus, the gecko, the shark, or the heron, and so appear to men. They were apparently sacred to the group concerned. This phenomena is spoken of as 'totemism' by Collocott, though he does not discuss the quality of the relationship between god and sacred animal.[2]

Birds and fishes were included among the objects of worship in Tahiti, especially the heron, the kingfisher and the woodpecker, which were accustomed to frequent the sacred trees of the temple precincts. These creatures were considered sacred because it was held that a god was embodied in one when it approached the *tapu* place to eat of the food offered in sacrifice. Images were manufactured also, either to serve as representatives of the form of the god, and emblems of his character, or

[1] G. Turner, *Nineteen Years in Polynesia*, 1861, pp. 238–9, 242–3; ibid., *Samoa*, 1884, pp. 23–77; J. B. Stair, *Old Samoa*, 1897, pp. 216–21; G. Brown, *Melanesians and Polynesians*, 1910, p. 218; A. Krämer, *Samoa-Inseln*, I, 1902, p. 23.

[2] W. Mariner, *Tonga*, ii, 1827, pp. 100–101; E. V. Collocott, Notes on Tongan Religion. *Journal Polynesian Society*, Vol. xxx, 1921, pp, 159–61, 227–36; F. W. Gifford, *Tongan Society*, 1929, pp. 44, 325–6.

to act as the vehicle or instrument through which he might communicate with his people, or they with him. The animal species was spoken of as the *ata* of the god; thus the boar was the *ata* of Oro, the gull the *ata* of Tane, and Ta'aroa the Creator had the whale, the tropic bird, the parrot fish and the albatross all as his *ata*. A difficulty is felt by Handy in apprehending the precise meaning of this term *ata*, for the usage of which he has no record except in Samoa and the Society Islands; this is perhaps met by the consideration of its significance in Tikopia, as already described.[1]

The totemic system of Ontong Java, which is described by Hogbin, seems to vary from the normal Polynesian variety in that while there is no belief in descent from the natural species—as robber crab, mussel, shark or centipede—or manufactured object—as a food bowl—neither apparently is there any idea that it is the manifestation or material form of a god.[2]

In Mangaia a belief in a system of division of food-stuffs between the principal gods Rongo and Tangaroa obtained, but it does not seem to have been thought that they became incarnate or represented materially in the foods. The god Tonga-iti, however, had as his visible form the white and black spotted lizards.[3] The position in the Marquesas is somewhat similar. A number of foods were *tapu* (forbidden) to different tribes throughout the group, but these were fish, birds, or animals that were consecrated to the tribal god, and there was apparently no conception of the embodiment of the god in the sacred object.[4] The people of Hawaii had a system of departmental gods, but like the Marquesans and the Maori, possessed no institutions approaching those of totemism, in that the gods did not become manifest in animals or plants affiliated with social groups. Images of wood and stone, carved by the people themselves, appear to have symbolized the deities.[5] The religious scheme of these three culture groups on the periphery of the Polynesian area thus appears to be of a different type from that of Tonga, Samoa and other groups of the centre and west.

When the material from this latter field is reviewed as a whole certain features are seen to be of general occurrence; they are summarized below, with such theoretical considerations as they suggest.

[1] W. Ellis, *Polynesian Researches*, Vol. ii, 1829, pp. 202–3; E. S. C. Handy, *Polynesian Religion*, 1927, p. 127.
[2] *Oceania*, Vol. I, pp. 420–2, 1931.
[3] W. Gill, *Myths and Songs of the South Pacific*, 1876, pp. 10–13.
[4] Handy, *Native Culture in the Marquesas*, p. 262.
[5] D. Malo, *Hawaiian Antiquities*, 1903, pp. 112–17.

GENERAL CONSIDERATION

In these island communities the association of specific social groups, such as joint families or clans with species of animals or plants is a recognized feature of the culture. Towards individuals of the natural species an attitude of respect, sometimes amounting to reverence, is exhibited by members of the human group, and linked with this are customs which prohibit interference with the animal or plant concerned, especially in regard to the killing and eating of it. Breach of these rules entails, to the native mind, the penalty of illness, often by swelling of the viscera or other portion of the body, and not infrequently involving death. Normally action is not taken by members of the group against the offending person, the supernatural punishment being thought to be adequate in itself.

It is a feature of Polynesian totemism that the natural species concerned are generally animals, either land or marine, and that plants, though occasionally included in the list, never predominate. The reason for this preference for animals, it seems to me, lies in the fact that the behaviour of the totem is usually held to give an indication as to the actions or intentions of the god concerned.[1] Plants, because of their immobility, are not of much interest from this point of view, and the tendency is then for the more mobile species, endowed with locomotion and versatility of movement, and often with other striking characteristics in the matter of shape, colour, ferocity, or peculiar cries, to be represented in greater measure in the list of media which serve as outlet for the supernatural beings.

This leads to the consideration of what is perhaps the most significant factor in Polynesian totemism, namely that the natural species are believed to be linked with their respective social groups not by their own virtue but because they are the vehicle of manifestation of external supernatural beings—the *atua*. This term has been frequently rendered as 'god' or 'deity' in the body of this article. It is not claimed that such is the best translation under all circumstances, but it does correspond most closely to the significance of the chief *atua* in Tikopia; it is also the usage of most of the older writers of the Polynesian material summarized above. Moreover, 'supernatural being' or 'supernormal object', which is more satisfactory in general, is sometimes too indefinite to meet a particular case. Except in Ontong Java this belief in the animation of the totem by an *atua* seems to be common to the area. Even in Tonga, where according to Rivers each social group has its *atua*, an animal or plant

---

[1] For example: Mariner, op. cit., p. 101; Collocott, op. cit., p. 233; Gill, op. cit., p. 35, Turner, *Samoa*, pp. 66, 69, 72; G. Brown, op. cit., p. 248; Moerenhout, *Voyages*, i, p. 455; E. Best, *New Zealand Journal of Science and Technology*, v, 1923, p. 328; R. W. Williamson, *Social and Political Systems of Central Polynesia*, Vol. ii, pp. 251–70.

from which it traces descent, the information of Mariner and Collocott shows that it is through the entry of a god into these objects that they acquire their importance.[1] With certain animals it is true that personification of the species itself is the underlying attitude. Such is the case with the octopus, known as Feke—or variants thereof—the eel, commonly spoken of as Tuna, and the lizard, of several kinds, known variously as Moko, Mokopiri, or Pili. Here the distinction between god and animal is often difficult to see, nor is it always clearly made by the natives themselves. But for some situations it is recognized that a deity exists separate from the animal shape which is his usual habitat.[2]

The relation of the natural species to the social group may be described then as one of 'secondary' or 'derived' totemism rather than of 'primary' or 'direct' totemism. This distinction rests upon the intervention in the former case of other elements of the religious system between the natural order and the social structure. In Polynesia, as shown, the members of the social group are affiliated with the individuals of the totem species, not by the immediate linkage which obtains in Melanesia, but through a spiritual being as intermediary. The system of totemism is dependent on the belief in the gods, not separate from it.

The totemic situation must be recognized as atypical. As noted, in Polynesia there is no identity of the animal with the social group, the totem does not serve as group emblem; it does not act as an index of marriage regulations, not being associated with the rule of exogamy; a careful study of the evidence does not point to any real belief in the descent of the members of the human group from the totem.[3] And as far as the majority of animal totem species is concerned, the economic interest in them is not of a pronounced type.

In discussing the relation of the supernatural being to the natural species the term 'incarnation' has been freely used by several writers, and has been employed here in the summary of their evidence.[4] Before the validity of the expression can be accepted the relation must be more carefully studied. Analysis of the Tikopia data showed that the natives recognized two ways in which the *atua* became associated with the totem. On the one hand he entered into the body of an existing animal of the species and controlled its movements; on the other he assumed the form of such an animal, taking on an animal entity where previously there was no corresponding individual in the flesh. These two processes

---

[1] Rivers, op. cit., i, pp. 363–4; Mariner, op. cit., ii, p. 100; Collocott, loc. cit.

[2] v. Gill, op. cit., p. 10 (for the lizard); and Collocott, op. cit., p. 231 (for the octopus).

[3] The statement of Rivers in regard to Tonga (*H.M.S.*, i, p. 364) is given without evidence in support, and is probably inaccurate, as it certainly is in respect of Tikopia (v. ante; cf. also Gifford, op. cit., p. 44). The data adduced by Williamson, as he himself seems to recognize, are of the nature of stories of the marvellous, concerned with the birth of individual *monstra*, and do not suggest the descent of human groups from natural species.

[4] The theory of Rivers that the 'kava people' believed in their incarnation after death in animals receives no verification from Polynesia. (*H.M.S.*, ii, pp. 361-73.)

were distinguished by the natives fairly clearly by separate linguistic expressions; for them the terms *inhabitation* and *simulation* respectively might be used. It would seem that logically speaking, they differ from what is ordinarily known as *incarnation*. This last, it might be said, refers strictly only to the assumption of a fleshly form in actually *becoming* the object—not simply controlling its behaviour on the one hand, or posing as counterpart of it on the other. The basis of the distinction thus drawn depends on the amount of separability or autonomy which is conceived to exist when the physical body and the animating spirit are in relation. If the spirit is still conceived to exist as a separate entity, apart from the material form in which it is manifest, then this can be hardly regarded as a true incarnation. Now as far as the natives are concerned, it is undoubted that at times they make this distinction between form and content. The nearest approach to actual 'incarnation' is in the case of the personifications of Tuna and Feke, whose identity becomes easily merged in that of the individuals of their species. This term then must take its place as representing simply one type of relation between spirit and body of which inhabitation and simulation are probably more common types in the religious beliefs of the Polynesian. As a general covering term *materialization* seems the most appropriate, since, as shown later, it should include also mediumistic possession and other phenomena.

The last point to be brought forward is related to those just considered, though perhaps less easy to demonstrate in short compass. It is that the phenomena of 'totemism' in Polynesia are simply part of a general system of beliefs and customs relating to the idea that the spiritual beings characteristically manifest themselves in material shape. Polynesian totemism is in reality a department of spirit possession. The material forms in which the spirit may appear are of three classes:

     i. inanimate objects, as stones, clubs, conch shells.
    ii. natural species of animal or plant.
   iii. human beings.

The objects of the first type are regarded as representations, emblems or even mute embodiments of the gods, are held to be sacred, treated with reverence, and often decorated in special manner, with offerings made to them. These are the objects termed 'idols' or 'images' by the early missionaries.[1] The animals and plants which provide an earthly habitation for the god have been the subject of study in this article. The human beings are believed to act as the media of the gods or spirits and in this condition, apparently one of auto-hypnosis, engage in conversation with the people, utter prophecies, diagnose illness and advise as to

[1] See *Work of the Gods*, 1967, pp. 207–14.

266

treatment—practices which were widespread in olden Polynesia.[1] In each case there is normally an association between a definite kinship group, as a family or clan, and the material object, the natural species, or the human medium concerned, such association being contingent on the relation of the group with the spiritual being. Now a study of totemism is ostensibly concerned only with the affiliation of social groups with natural species; but in Polynesia the phenomena of this type should be clearly considered in conjunction with the relation of these groups to inanimate cult objects and human media as well.

The diagram below indicates the relationship in schematic form:

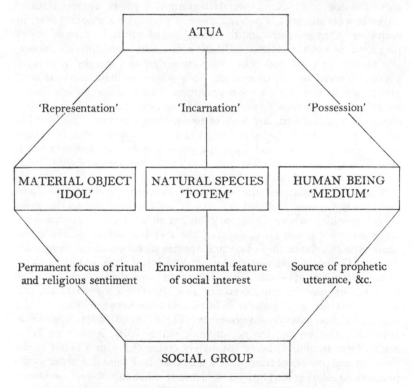

The need for the consideration of Polynesian totemism in this setting is reinforced when it is remembered that in certain of the island groups where natural species are utilized by gods or ancestors as vehicles of expression the phenomena are not held to constitute a type of totemism,

[1] For a general review of the data v. E. S. C. Handy, *Polynesian Religion*, pp. 135, 159–65; R. W. Williamson, op. cit., ii, Ch. xxvii; v. also E. Best, *Journal Polynesian Society*, vi, pp. 41 et seq., xi, pp. 53–8.

though the fundamental attitude is precisely the same as that already examined. Such is the case among the Maori, admittedly a non-totemic people, where various gods have each his *aria*, the material form in which he is seen by mortal eyes. This is not the deity himself, but simply his visible manifestation. There is no systematic linkage of natural species with social groups. On the one hand a single animal or natural feature may be regarded as the material semblance of a deity and so be the object of veneration on the part of a family group, sub-tribe or tribe, while it recognizes no particular relation with other animals of the species, or other natural features of the same type. Thus the *aria* of one deity is a particular dog, of another a special cormorant, of others, a named stream, a tree in a certain spot, a pond, a stone, a gourd, or a shooting star, in each case.[1] On the other hand the same kind of animal or type of object may serve as a vehicle of materialization for a number of different deities, and as such be respected either individually or as a species by several groups or even by the community as a whole, without distinction of group ties. In this respect the distribution of natural species in relation to deities, and to tribes (*iwi*) or tribal sections (*hapu*) of the Maori cannot be equated with any form of totemic organization. The lizard is an illustration of this, being regarded as an *aria*, visible form, of a number of gods of various social groups, especially in war, but also being held in respect and even fear not only by the followers of these gods alone, but by the Maori people as a whole.[2]

The salient points of the system of totemism in Polynesia have emerged in the course of this analysis. It has also been shown that even in communities where systematic affiliation of human groups with natural species is not an element of the social structure beliefs in the same type of relationship of natural species to supernatural beings are current. The position in all the island groups is not alike. But in speaking of the 'totemism' of certain parts of the area—and the term may well be retained—it must be considered not as a situation *sui generis*, but as a specific instance in a general field of relations between man and the objects of his natural environment. There is no sharp opposition between totemism and the non-totemic nature cults. And in its Polynesian form totemism, being intimately connected with a belief in the mobility and powers of transmutation of *atua*, is of the same order as the phenomena relating to religious emblems or other cult objects, and those associated with the possession of human media by gods and spirits.

[1] Best, *Spiritual and Mental Concepts of the Maori* (Dominion Museum Monograph, 2), 1922, pp. 16–19; ibid., *Maori Religion and Mythology* (D. M. Bulletin, 10), 1924, pp. 137–8; ibid., *Journal Polynesian Society*, xi, pp. 65, 66, 68.

[2] Best: Te Rehu o Tainui. *J.P.S.*, vi, pp. 43, 44; Omens and Superstitious Beliefs of Maori, ibid., vii, pp. 134, 135; Notes on Art of War, ibid., xi, pp. 29, 30, 38, 65, 67, 68; Occurrence of Lizard in Maori Carvings, *Journal Science and Technology*, v, pp. 321–35; *Maori Religion and Mythology*, 1924, pp. 130, 137.

CHAPTER 12

ECONOMICS AND RITUAL
IN SAGO EXTRACTION[1]

(1950)

In Tikopia sago is an important economic resource. It is also the object
of certain ritual procedures. Description of the economics and associated
ritual gives ethnographic data which can be compared with the information from other Pacific cultures. The relation between these aspects
also raises a theoretical problem that is worth analysis.

As a preface to the Tikopia data a short reference may be made to
some samples of the utilization of sago in the Western Pacific generally.

SAGO IN THE WESTERN PACIFIC

The sago palm (genus *Metroxylon*) is fairly common in the Western
Pacific islands, but its economic potentialities in leaf, fruit and starch are
not uniformly realized. Practically everywhere its leaves are used for
thatch. In some parts, notably the Solomon islands, the fruit is collected
by natives and sold commercially as 'ivory nuts'. In some areas the
starch granules of the trunk are not used for food; in some they are prepared only as slabs of pith without separation from the coarse fibres; in
others they are separated from the fibres by processes of maceration and
washing. The following references illustrate this.

In Fiji, where there are large groves of the palm, the natives were
apparently unacquainted with the use of the starch for food until Seemann and Pritchard demonstrated it to them by extracting some.[2] In the
Melanesian islands of the Eastern Solomons, apart from the sale of
ivory nuts, the leaves are used for thatch. Occasionally, as in the Lau
district of Malaita, whole sections of the solid pith are roasted and eaten
in the summer at times of food shortage. But in Sa'a and Ulawa, in the
south of the same island, sago is not eaten and generally throughout the
area no method of extraction of the starch is known.[3] In parts of the

---

[1] Reprinted from *Mankind*, Vol. IV, pp. 131–42, 1950.
[2] B. Seemann, *Mission to Viti*, 1862, p. 291.
[3] C. M. Woodford, *A Naturalist Among Headhunters*, 1890, p. 201; W. Ivens, *Melanesians
of the South-East Solomons*, 1927, p. 36. Prof. C. S. Belshaw informed me that sago is eaten
from the pith in Nggela and San Cristoval.

Western Solomons, as in the Shortland islands of Bougainville Straits, the starch is prepared by macerating, washing and sieving the pith. For this purpose long aqueducts of split areca trunk are built. The wet starch is baked into cakes but there is no preparation and storage of the flour.[1] In the Banks islands the starch is extracted and cooked in cakes, but was not, in former times at least, a common food.[2]

In many parts of New Guinea sago starch is extracted for food and the wet paste cooked, though again the flour is not dried and stored. Among the Mailu the pith is pounded out by men with stone-headed adzes and washed and kneaded by women who use as a receptacle the butt-end of the sago frond itself—the commonest technical device in the Western Pacific.[3] The people of the Purari and adjacent deltas rely to a great extent upon sago for food and extract it by scraping out the pith, beating it after pouring water over it, and sieving off the dross. This is the work of women. (Incidentally, sago grubs from a decayed trunk are an important article of diet there.)[4] The Kiwai, Trans-Fly and Marind-Anim tribes prepare the pith by very similar means; the Wiram and Keraki stamp or trample the pith in a bark bag and the Gambadi and Semariji beat it with a stick.[5] Data from many of the New Guinea tribes give a similar picture.

SAGO IN TIKOPIA

The use of the sago palm (*rakau ota*) by the Tikopia is more extensive than by most other Western Pacific communities. From the fronds they make most of their thatch.[6] The ribs of the fronds (*fa ota*) are used for rafts (*vaka fa ota*), and for a kind of single-stick (*fetaaki*). The Tikopia have also fully realized the advantages of sago starch as food. By most of the peoples of the Western Pacific who use it the starch is pressed into cakes when wet, and baked. In this condition it tends to go sour and cannot be preserved for any great length of time. The Tikopia, however, employ two methods of preparation which render it more durable. As such it can be drawn upon to supplement other foods in times of shortage.

[1] Woodford, op. cit., pp. 199–201; H. B. Guppy, *The Solomon Islands*, 1887, pp. 83, 87, 90; C. Ribbe, *Zwei Jahre unter den Kannibalen der Salamo Inseln*, 1903, pp. 34–7, 45.

[2] R. H. Codrington, *The Melanesians*, 1891, p. 319.

[3] W. J. V. Saville, *In Unknown New Guinea*, 1926, pp. 89–93; B. Malinowski, 'Natives o Mailu', *Proc. Roy. Soc. S. Australia*, XXXIX, 1915, pp. 598–600.

[4] F. E. Williams, *Natives of the Purari Delta*, 1924, pp. 10–11. For trade in sago from the Papuan Gulf, *vide* C. G. Seligmann, *Melanesians of British New Guinea*, 1910, pp. 96–110.

[5] G. Landtmann, *The Kiwai Papuans*, 1927, pp. 102 et seq.; F. E. Williams, *Papuans of the Trans-Fly*, 1936, pp. 220, 422–4.

[6] The midrib (*te ngausala*) of the sago leaf is extracted to be used as a skewer. The leaf is then bent over a stick (*te rafo*), often shaped from areca timber, and a double hole is pierced through it with a wedge-ended wooden implement (*te suki*). While the *suki* is still in position the skewer is slipped under the flap raised in the leaf. By a succession of these operations a sheet of thatch (*kau rau*) is formed.

It may also serve as provision in a compact form for overseas voyages. Hence one term for it is 'food for voyaging' (*kai te forau*).

One method of preparation is to cook slabs of the pith for several days in a large oven.[1] The slabs are used especially in times of food shortage —as 'food of the famine'. This is an economical food since the pith is eaten whole, only the coarser fibres being rejected. This, however, is regarded as a somewhat unpalatable food. Another method is to prepare the starch as flour, dry it and store it in fibre bags. The flour is used in times of scarcity, but it is also regarded as a delicacy (a food particularly for infants and old people). It is often used as an emollient to mix with other foods to give them body, flavour and softness.

The sago palm is fairly plentiful in Tikopia. It grows sporadically on the lowlands and is especially abundant along the watercourses which lead down to the sea from the hill crest and in the swampy orchards on the inner side of the old crater wall near the lake. On the lands of some families, as that of the chief of the Taumako clan, it was so plentiful in 1928–9 that immature trees were sometimes cut down to provide thatch for the repair of houses, their trunks being allowed to lie and rot as unfit for food. This was not a usual procedure and many families were not wealthy enough to treat their palms in this way. In Tikopia the palm is not planted but is allowed to propagate itself. Trees are reckoned as ancillary property to the soil on which they stand. There is no separate ownership of soil and of sago palms such as exists in part of Melanesia. The differential wealth of families in these palms leads to a system of utilization involving a payment analogous to 'rent'.

Utilization of the sago palm for starch demands some knowledge of its properties. The Tikopia judge the maturity of a palm by its flowering, they know that time must be allowed to elapse between grating and filtering to allow starch and fibre to separate, and they can also estimate the probable yield in terms of baskets of starch from a palm of given size. They have not carried their knowledge, however, to the extent of observing the difference between male and female flowers and formulating any theory of the propagation of the palm. They are also ignorant of any use that may be made of the nuts.

The extraction of the sago flour is done by a series of processes demanding considerable labour for several complete days. It is periodical, during the trade wind (cool) season only. The important factor here is the water supply, which is essential to extraction and which is more regular then. This use of water links the manufacture of sago with that of turmeric and technically they have certain common features.

The process of extraction of the starch varies in some particulars from

---

[1] Raymond Firth, *Primitive Polynesian Economy*, p. 267. Codrington mentions that sago pith cooked whole was the main provision of canoes from Tikopia which visited the Banks islands one year during his residence there. Op. cit., p. 320.

the common Western Pacific methods. The pith is removed from the trunk not with adzes or gouges but with scrapers; and the starch is extracted by kneading the material and not by beating or trampling it. Neither the hollow base of the leaf rib, nor a hollowed portion of the trunk of the palm itself is used as a working receptacle; the leaves are discarded and the trunk broken up. Large wooden troughs, made possible through the existence of big trees in the island, together with baskets of coconut leaf, are used instead. I am not able to compare the efficiency of these various technical processes. The fact that the Tikopia industry is not self-contained means certain consequences for the economic organization. The manufacture of the wooden troughs involves the services of specialist craftsmen, and the fact that they are very valuable leads to a system of borrowing and co-operation in production which affects the distribution of the product. For this reason, probably, sago-making in Tikopia is not only the work of women, or of single individuals, as it frequently is in other areas. Moreover, the breaking up of the trunk allows a group activity in the initial processes in a way which is not so easy when the trunk is reserved as a working receptacle. Primitive technical methods thus tend to be linked with specific forms of economic organization.

TECHNICAL PROCESSES OF EXTRACTION OF STARCH

The first operation, the felling of the tree, is done after the tree has been observed to have flowered. While one man chops at the base with an axe, others hold long props against the trunk. While the cutting proceeds a lad climbs the tree and lops the fronds, which are collected as they fall and carried off for use as thatch, etc. If the sago to be made is that of a chief, then he is usually present to direct the felling. He does not do any actual chopping himself. When the cut is deep enough the men with the props on the far side give a push which sends the trunk crashing.

The next process is the removal of the leaf bases (*firoi ota*) and bark from the trunk. Then follows the scraping down of the trunk. A group of men—in one case I observed a dozen—squat around the trunk at intervals and set to work. Hoops of iron which have been serrated to form blunt teeth are used for preference. But these hoops were still not common in 1928–9 and the ordinary implement was then half a coconut shell with one edge sharpened by rubbing it with a piece of coral rock. Some of these shells are serrated, some not, according to the preference and time of the person who uses them. Quite frequently the scraper breaks, and for this reason each man has by him a couple of extras. An alternative method of working the trunk is to cut it up into sections three feet or so in length, nine or ten inches square. This is done when it is convenient to do the scraping near the dwelling house, and not in the orchard. In one case I saw a long spar fitted up in a canoe-shed; it was hung about two feet from the ground on vines. The slabs were leaned against this and the men squatted on their heels before them, one to each slab. The scraping was done with a downward sweep of the shell, both hands being used with considerable pressure. From time to time the scraped material was thrown back out of the way, and the slab was reversed to keep it of even thickness. This part of the work is hard and monotonous. But it is relieved by constant talk and by joking. A man may drop out for a rest occasionally but not for long. Visitors who come may be pressed into service.

As the scrapings accumulate they are carried off in large wooden bowls and covered with leaves of the giant taro. The trunk is scraped away till only a remnant is left. The bowls of scraped pith are then allowed to stand for a day or so to allow the starch to separate from the fibres—'to be rotten that the starch may fall'.

The most important operation is the extraction of the starch. The pith scrapings are put into a coconut leaf basket of fairly close mesh, which is then inserted into another basket and set on a couple of bars of leaf rib over a large wooden trough. Water is brought in bowls and poured on to the pith, which is kneaded with the hands to free the starch granules and allow them to run through the meshes into the trough below. The kneading is done by men. Boys are usually pressed into service as water-carriers.[1] For this filtering process sea water or lake water is used, depending upon the site chosen for the work. On one occasion I saw a large canoe used as a reservoir and continually re-plenished with sea water by relays of men and children. This operation is termed *nununu* (or *nunu*) and the baskets used are termed *kete nununu*. (Linguistically and technically the process has an affinity with that of the extraction of turmeric, which is called *nuanga*.) When the trough is full of the turbid liquid (the starch held in suspension in the water) it is covered over with coconut fronds with an extra thatch of sago fronds, and allowed to stand for the starch to settle. The residue of coarse fibres and pith in the baskets is thrown away, and children go and forage among it for scraps to eat.[2]

This filtration stage of the work is taboo to outsiders. A rough fence of stakes and coconut or sago fronds is put round the scene of operations, and a frond is tied to a stake in the path some distance away to indicate that the work is in progress. Village people and travellers on the path are then supposed to keep clear. Most do, but, as I saw, if anyone with real business comes up to the barrier he is usually allowed to go through. One might suppose a rational basis for the taboo since the process of

[1] *Primitive Polynesian Economy*, Plate I.
[2] *We, The Tikopia*, 1936, Plate 10B.

filtration demands concentrated attention, which might be disturbed if free access were allowed. The restriction is in line with that imposed during canoe building and turmeric manufacture. But the taboo is not a purely rational prohibition; the sanction behind it is magico-religious. There seems to be no idea that casual visitors would steal by magical means any of the sago flour. But it is said, if people are allowed to pass through, some may be of evil mind and may cast a spell (*tautuku*) upon the work, invoking their gods that no flour may be obtained as the result of the labour. If the yield is very small it will be said 'the sago has disappeared', and this is attributed to machinations from outside. It is an example of the well-known interpretation of inefficiency or failure being due to magico-religious interference. One result of this is that the advance of the knowledge of material conditions is hampered. Inaccuracies in the estimated yield of sago flour from a palm have less chance of correction by empirical observation, and the attainment of more precise results is blocked.

When the starch has settled most of the water is poured off and the remaining liquid is transferred to wooden bowls three to four feet in length. This transference is necessary in order to free the large troughs to cope with the quantity of sago to be filtered. Usually two troughs are used alternately, filling of the one just giving sufficient time for the starch in the other to settle before it is poured off. When the starch has settled in the bowls, the water is poured off again and the starch washed with fresh water from a spring. It is then laid out on leaves to dry. At night or if rain falls it is taken in. Rain is bad, since it turns the starch black. After drying, the starch, now of the consistency of flour, is packed in bags of coconut fibre and stored away. Sometimes a variety of the food known as *fetai* is desired. For this the starch is taken wet, pressed into slabs and cooked in the oven. This gives a very hard mass which has to be beaten into pieces before it can be eaten. But it is reckoned a useful storage food.

The yield of sago flour varies of course according to the size of the tree and its quality, but is normally regarded as giving a good return for the labour expended. A small tree worked by members of the family of the Ariki Tafua yielded four bowls of flour. The tree stood in an orchard of the Ariki Tafua but permission had been given by him to his son-in-law to fell it. This man took two bowls of flour for himself and gave one to the chief's eldest son and one to his youngest son. Since the chief lived with the youngest son acknowledgement was thus made to the tree owner. The yield in this case was reckoned a good one.

ECONOMIC ORGANIZATION

The principal points involved in the economic organization are: the ownership of the raw material; the constitution of the working group; the payment to the workers for their labour; and the division of the product.

The working party is normally composed on the basis of kinship. The person undertaking the manufacture calls upon his brothers and their wives, his brothers-in-law and perhaps other relatives. Their response depends partly upon the work which they themselves have in hand, and partly upon the code of kinship behaviour. For example, while most of the sons of the Ariki Tafua were extracting sago for their brother-in-law from their father's tree, one of them, who had married a woman of the Taumako family, went to assist in sago-making for his wife's people. His affinal relationship demanded that he go as 'cook' to help in the preparation of food for their working party. As return for this labour he was given a bowl of flour by them.

Payment for labour is initially food. While the work is in progress an oven is prepared by the family of the man who has taken the initiative. The food is drawn from his orchards and cultivations and the work of the oven is done by him and his wife and the kinsfolk whom they may press into service. From time to time during the work refreshment is provided for the labourers. In one case I noted green coconuts were brought to them twice during the morning by the sago-owner. It was explained that if no coconuts had been brought then an extra oven of food would have been prepared, giving them two full meals instead of one. Major items in the cost of production of the flour are thus the expenditure of some of the owner's food and his labour and that of kin and neighbours. But while the immediate return for the labour is given, by the food they consume on the spot, a further return lies in the reciprocity from him and his family on other occasions.

But an additional recompense may also be given, based not so much on the labour by the person concerned, but on his social position. It is a portion of the sago starch. Where a younger brother will receive food only, a brother-in-law or the senior representative of an assisting family will receive some starch as well. This means a concept of labour as a social service and not simply an economic service. It means also that the activity is looked on to some extent as joint or co-operative production. The joint character of the production becomes more marked when the tree utilized is not the property of the entrepreneur. Here the general rule is that if the tree owner takes no part in the work he receives about one-quarter of the product, while if he is a participant he receives about one-half. General canons of etiquette apply to this division of the product, as also to provision of the technical apparatus used, the principal items of which are the large wooden troughs.

Throughout this productive activity every service rendered is given repayment, by subsistence or by a portion of the product, or both. Linked with this is the right to demand equivalent service with corresponding obligations of repayment at a future date. Provision is made also for the labour of organization. The person who takes the initiative in the selection of a tree, in getting permission to fell it, and in getting together and maintaining a working party is the one who has at his discretion the allotment of the product. By acknowledged right he takes a large part of it. This may be irrespective of the work which he personally may put in, though ordinarily of course he does take a considerable share in the grating and filtering. Implicitly the Tikopia recognize the function of direction in the enterprise, and admit wages of management, allied to profit.

RITUAL OF SAGO EXTRACTION

No ritual is associated with preparation of slabs of sago pith, but rites are associated with extraction of starch, probably because of the greater difficulty of the operations. Reference has already been made to the taboo surrounding the process of sago filtration and to its effects. Other ritual practices, associated particularly with the completion of the extraction process, depend upon the thesis that the sago palm is not just a tree but is a symbol, even a material embodiment, of one of the Tikopia gods. As such it is ritually associated with specific kinship groups in the community (cf. Chapter 11 above).

The rites performed are of two kinds. The first set is specific in character and is based upon the association of the kinship group of Fusi with their major deity Tarikotu,[1] who has as one of his embodiments the sago palm. Consequently the destruction and utilization of the palm by man requires some acknowledgement by the ritual elder of the Fusi group. And, since this group has precedence among those which constitute the clan of Tafua, the chief of Tafua participates also in the ritual. The other series of ceremonies is of a more general order and is based upon the fact that each of the three other chiefs invokes Tarikotu in his list of *kava* deities and therefore celebrates the making of sago as part of a wider ritual scheme of activities. The specific ritual was described to me by Pa Saukirima, elder of the house of Fusi, and he allowed me to be present during the performance.

It begins with the *putu*. This is a word used generally for the mass of green food set on the grave of a dead person to symbolize his severance from the foods which he cultivated during his lifetime. Here it is an

---

[1] The name was given by some informants as Tarikotua.

offering to the deity on the felling of the sago palm, the destruction of his 'body', as to a person dead. The elder of the Fusi group is the only person to offer the *putu* since the sago palm is 'based' upon him, as the expression goes. He goes early in the morning of the day on which the sago is filtered, and cuts a bunch of bananas which he sets under the eaves on the ritual side of his house. He then spreads out a set of bark-cloths as offerings to his deities. This act is part of the general series of performances which takes place when any ritual appeal is made to Tikopia deities. The bark-cloths are known as *maro*, which may be translated as 'ritual vestments'. As the first of these is spread the elder recites a formula:

Translation:

> 'That is your vestment, Tarikotu,
> I eat your excrement
> Your sacred body will be *putu* on this day.
> Your property will be spread out
> And your *putu* will be stood up
> Your body which has been grated by the land,
> Now too is the day on which it shall be prepared.
> Here it has been *putu*.
> Your *putu* has been stood up.
> You go and stand up the skies beautifully;
> Dry up the skies;
> Get them ready to be beautiful.

There are four principal elements in this formula: announcement of the offering; abasement before the deity; atonement for the desecration of his body; and the expression of a practical aim. The expressions of announcement and abasement need not be explained further here; they are part of the general invocation to any deity.[1] The atonement consists in the references to the *putu*, the bunch of bananas which has been stood up as a ritual acknowledgement. The change of tense in the formula is a common feature of such addresses and signifies the aggregation of activity past and future. The practical aim expressed in the last three lines is for fine weather to dry the sago flour. This deity, like many others, is held to have some control over the state of the skies.

The bark-cloth I saw spread to Tarikotu was a white one, and was followed by another white one in honour of Tufare, a sea deity of the Tafua clan. Added to this was a piece of blue European calico which the elder possessed, and which he subjoined to the bark-cloth as an honorific addition (*fakaepa*). This is a common practice. Finally came an orange bark-cloth, spread to Poumera, another of his deities. The offering of each of these cloths was accompanied by a similar formula, though the

[1] Cf. *Work of the Gods*, 1967, p. 74.

weight of interest was directed upon the initial major deity. It will be noted that the sago palm is spoken of in the formula as the 'body' of the deity. The reference to the grating of it by 'the land' means that the elder is celebrating not only his own sago manufacture, but that of the whole community, for which he stands as sponsor and mediator. For this reason when ordinary people manufacture sago they do it without these ritual performances; their ritual has been aggregated as it were in the hands of the elder.

The bark-cloths are left unfolded in the house all day. In the evening food from the oven which has been prepared for the workers is brought into the house and set out as a ritual offering. Portions are thrown from it to the deities with appropriate formulae, and the bark-cloths are then folded up and put away.

It might appear from what has been described here that the god Tarikotu is simply a personification of the sago palm and is addressed as such. This is not the case. He is believed to operate in a much wider sphere than that of sago representation.

This rite of atonement performed alone by the elder of Fusi is integrated into a wider scheme of activities by his chief, the Ariki Tafua. In 1928–9 this chief was a Christian, so he performed no ritual beyond a small food offering to his old gods. But in former days he participated with his elders in a series of ceremonies. When the sago palms were still standing, several months before they flowered, food was planted in preparation for the ritual. Then when the trees were ready, one was felled and the starch was prepared. It was cooked until it was dry. People of the Tafua clan were then invited by their chief and by the elder of Fusi to go to the cultivations and dig out the food which had been specially planted. This was carried to the temple Fusi, a house which formerly stood near the dwelling of the elder and in which the Ariki Tafua performed *kava* rites only during the elder's presence. (The elder's own temple was Farekarae, a name still borne by a kinship group which is an offshoot from Fusi.) The food *fetai* was prepared from the sago flour; it is 'the standing food' of the sago ceremonies. When all the food was ready kava was made in the morning in the temple of Fusi, and the Ariki Tafua officiated in making the offering to Tarikotu. When this was done, the party dispersed, the chief going to his temple, Tafua, and the elder of Fusi to his, Farekarae. There each performed a kava ceremony of his own to the same deity, 'announcing' the sago to him. This preliminary rite performed by the chief and his elder gave the signal for the general manufacture of sago. When the other chiefs observed that work had begun in Fusi, then they began too.

I was given this outline of the ritual by Pa Saukirima himself. He explained that the taro and other food for the ceremony has to be planted four months ahead, to be ready at the appropriate time. But sometimes the coconut was a delaying factor. If there were not sufficient dry coconuts to provide cream for the puddings then the ceremony was delayed. But meanwhile the sago palm stood in flower, to the irritation of the other people who wanted to get on with their work. This illustrates the interrelation of activities in Tikopia, the sense of responsibility that must be displayed by leading men, and the care in organization by some individuals to ensure that general productive effort can go forward.

My informant added that in olden times, in the days of his grandfather, a further rite used to be performed, in Marae, the ceremonial heart of the island. After a long time had elapsed and food had been planted, all the chiefs agreed to join and perform the kava in Marae. The food was brought and heaped together and while the chiefs and their followers sat in their appointed places, the Ariki Tafua, standing up in the centre, recited a formula to their collective gods.[1] He then presided over the distribution of the food, and the feast took place.

It has been mentioned above that ordinary makers of sago do not perform the ritual, but that the chiefs of other clans than Tafua have their ceremonies. The sago here is not so much the main object of the ritual as a point of departure for a more general acknowledgement to their gods. The rite they perform is termed *poroporo*, a term applied to first-fruits ritual for taro and breadfruit as well.

On the day that their sago is scraped and also when it is filtered, a small kava rite takes place. A couple of days afterwards some of the starch is mixed with other foods and cooked as a pudding. The ground immediately around the temple of each chief is then weeded and cleaned up, a ceremonial act which enhances the value of the ritual and is always a sign that it is an important occasion. The act of cleansing 'the sides of the house' is a kind of purificatory rite which increases the chances of attention by the gods.[2] The intent of the ritual, it is said, when performed by the chief of Kafika is to compensate for the *paku*, that is the thud made by the sago palm as it crashes down. Uta, the district in which many sago palms stand, is the scene of all the most sacred ceremonies and hence loud noises there are apt to be an offence to the deities. The ritual wipes this out. After this last kava rite no one in Kafika can fell a tree or make any similar booming noise in Uta. Silence again settles on the sacred woods. The same function is performed by the ritual of the chiefs of Taumako and Fangarere, though to a less degree.

I attended the *poroporo* rite for the sago of the Ariki Kafika. It took place at the end of February, 1929. The ground around the temple was cleaned up for some distance by men and women of the chief's family, assisted by one of his elders. The oven was prepared by four

---

[1] This ceremony is of the general type known as 'kava of Marae'. Its significance with full details has been explained in *Work of the Gods*, 1967, pp. 294 *et seq.*

[2] It is performed especially after a thunderstorm, as acknowledgement to the gods.

men and four women and when it was uncovered in the late afternoon, other men assembled for the ceremony. It was an important rite for which the chief assumed a special vestment and recited a long formula over the kava stem. This embraced not simply the deity of the sago but all his most important deities, and offerings were made to them. At the back of the chief sat one of his kinsfolk who acted as a medium for the chief's gods. This man wore no special dress or ornaments, nor was he smeared with turmeric, as is done when any important communication is to be received. But after the offerings of the kava had been made, he became possessed by one of the clan gods. He was given betel to chew, taking it in his hand and conveying it to his mouth. A cup of kava was also given to him to drink. He spoke with the chief in the thick utterance which the medium uses when he is in a state of possession. The conversation was mostly about the weather, which was bad at the time, and which the chief desired to be clear. The god, speaking through the medium's lips, gave reassuring advice saying that the weather was in charge of the gods, that they would not let it become too bad and that they would clear it up on the day after the morrow. The conversation was treated very much as a matter of course. The chief spoke soothingly to the god, agreeing with what was said in soft tones. But while the god was still in the possession of the medium, the chief cracked a joke with his elder and at the other end of the house people were talking, eating and laughing. A series of gods and ancestral spirits entered the medium, the flight of one being advertised by a trembling of the body and a convulsive jerk, and the entry of another by a quivering of muscles and a straightening of the back. Meanwhile, the medium drank cup after cup of kava. When the ceremony was over, the chief sat outside on a stone and ceremonially invested the women and children with a necklet of cordyline leaf, reciting formulae to ensure the continuance of their welfare (Plate III).

This conforms to a very general type of Tikopia ritual, and there is hardly anything in it pertaining especially to sago. Apart from the fact that it is performed when the starch has been extracted and that a small quantity of the starch is embodied in the food, there is nothing to distinguish it from other kava rites. Comparing the ritual of the elder of Fusi with that of the Ariki Tafua and the other chiefs, we see that there is a progressive diminution of reference to the sago and an incorporation of it in a wider sphere of interest. What we have to consider, then, is not a simple relation between an act of ritual and an act of work. It is a relationship of differential emphasis where the onus lies upon one man in particular to perform the ritual. The obligation upon other men grades off until ordinary people perform the work without any ritual at all. A theory of ritual in relation to economic activity must take into account this differential emphasis and its craft variation. It can be contrasted with cases where ritual and work are linked together in all instances, as in deep-sea fishing.

The ritual associated with the production of sago cannot be seen then to emerge directly out of the sago situation itself. It is dependent on a wider system of ideas and performances, partly of an economic and partly of a religious order. Some of the ritual, as that performed by the Ariki Kafika, is of a generalized order, the occasion being used for appeals to the gods for general welfare and for specific purposes other than the increase of the yield of sago. In the ritual specifically associated with the sago itself the explicit aim, it will be noted, is not to produce more sago, or to produce the given quantity more efficiently. It is to conserve the supplies and to keep the sago production in equilibrium in relation to the general economic system. It may be described as a *conservation ritual* rather than an *increase ritual*. It embodies no practices to promote growth or to facilitate planting (and there are no formulae when the fronds are cut for thatch). The ritual atmosphere which surrounds the filtration of the flour is not so much to increase the yield as to embody precautions for preserving it. It is essentially a first-fruits rite which takes the form of appeasement of the tutelary deity whose material representation has been injured. This may be contrasted with the type of ritual performed in turmeric manufacture, which does involve appeals for increase of yield; with the ritual of taro and yams which involve growth formulae; and the ritual for bananas, which consist mainly of planting formulae.

The majority of people extract sago flour because of their seasonal needs. They perform no ritual. But the performance of the ritual by the chiefs and the elder of Fusi has two functions for them. Firstly, it gives the signal to begin their own activity. Secondly, it assures them that the fertility of the sago palm, and the potential dangers of interfering with it, are being looked after on their behalf.

But the concept of fertility does not enter in the sago ritual to any great degree. It is present not as a specific theme in the ritual formulae but rather as a general background to the performance of the ritual. If this is not performed then, it is true, there is thought to be a danger of the fertility of the sago palms being damaged. But in other agricultural performances such as those for taro or yams the idea of renewal of fertility, and of cyclical reproduction of the vegetable, is much more important. This involves the concept of *mana* or *manu*, as the Tikopia more usually term it.[1] The sago ritual has a multiple function for the chiefs themselves. They acknowledge the first fruits of the sago to its deity, but

[1] See Chapters 8 and 11 in this volume.

they also make this an occasion for a general acknowledgement to all their own deities. As we have seen, they may attempt also to satisfy themselves on such immediate matters as the state of weather. The elder of Fusi, however, is in a different position. He wants sago flour for his ordinary purposes. But he must make the acknowledgement to his deity not only on his own account but also on behalf of the people as a whole. This obligation may lead him to manufacture sago each season irrespective of the quantity of flour that he may have on hand in his house. The desire for immediate economic gain is supplemented by and even controlled by the need for conformity to his social and ritual obligations.

The Tikopia premise is that a particular agricultural interest is represented by the head of a particular kinship group. Such representation is not necessarily correlated with the position of that group as the prime owner of the goods concerned. The elder of Fusi owned in 1929 many fewer sago palms than, for instance, the Ariki Taumako. But it was not the function of the latter to perform the prime ritual in connection with extraction of sago starch. A system is conceivable in which performance of ritual over a foodstuff is delegated to the person who has control over the greatest amount of it. But this would involve a type of ritual held in common knowledge or a technique of easy transmission from one person to another as comparative wealth fluctuated. A hereditary system consolidates the ritual knowledge at the possible expense of correlation between economic control and ritual performance. It presumably has social advantages in other directions. Reasons in a particular case why there should be a lack of direct association between ritual privileges and obligations, and economic control, may be obscure. In this case they rest on historical data which it is impossible to obtain. Differential growth of population in the groups concerned, and differential cutting out of sago palms may have tended to reduce the sago holdings of the Fusi group and so reverse an earlier correlation, if indeed such existed.

In any case, economic control may be irrelevant from one basic sociological point of view. Examination of the hereditary character of the sago ritual in Tikopia brings up the native ideas of unity, representation and delegation of public functions. It is a frequent phenomenon in Tikopia for a single individual, by virtue of his status, to perform a rite which is believed to be efficacious for the community as a whole, even though they do not participate in it. In such cases as this, the representative of the community may not be of the highest rank in it as far as general social purposes go. Nor may he seem to have any special title of majority economic interest to lend colour to his acknowledged rights. But such division of function allows a considerable number of individuals and constituent groups of the society to emerge at specific points in the social life, as mediators with the gods for the whole community. The Tikopia thus have given a convenient expression and scope to individual assertion and self-display. Without such outlets as these the forces of individual assertion might tend to disturb radically the privilege scheme of the rank structure. The role of individuals as mediators is obviously linked with concepts of the sacrifice and the scapegoat found in other communities, but their role is essentially passive; it is with the priest-hood that the closest comparison is to be found.

CHAPTER 13

THE PLASTICITY OF
MYTH[1]

(1960)

The general anthropological view is that myths are an integral part of religion. They may be very brief, like the Trobriand clan origin myths, or very elaborate, like the origin tales of Polynesia. They may enunciate a creed or simply illustrate it. They may outline the character of divinity or may describe only a few of the divine acts. They may justify and interpret ritual actions, and they may even purport to provide the model for rites. But whatever be the specific forms and functions of myths, in general they are reckoned to embody a system of beliefs common to the society, and to express and support a set of common basic social ideas and values. So much of the modern treatment of myth goes back to the analyses of Durkheim that we may once again adapt his statements on the Warramunga rites and say that the mythology of a group perpetuates traditions which express the way in which society represents man and the world; the myths form a moral system and a cosmology as well as a history.[2]

But while this may be so on the whole, there are some pertinent questions still to answer. Two of these concern the possibility of variation.

The first question has to do with the measure of agreement on the form of a myth that is expected among the members of a group. It is usually assumed for convenience that a 'tribe' or a 'people' have a basic set of myths, in recognizable specific form or normal version, granted that the anthropologist may have recorded a number of sub-specific forms or idiosyncratic versions of any myth. This assumption may be conceded, since the criteria for recognition of a normal or standard version have usually been carefully considered. But the problems raised by the existence of these sub-specific forms, these idiosyncratic versions, are not often examined. It is ordinarily assumed, however, nowadays, that discrepant versions of what in general can be regarded as the same myth are not simply a result of picturesque invention, but

---

[1] Reprinted from *Ethnologica*, n.s. Vol. 2, pp. 181–8, 1960.

[2] E. Durkheim, *The Elementary Forms of the Religious Life*. Trans. by J. W. Swain, 1915, p. 375.

correspond in some way to the differences of interest of the narrators. When myths of origin, for example, are in conflict, the anthropologist understands that what really is at stake is a common principle in competitive terms—that the version of each dissenting party is in effect a claim (conscious or unconscious) by a group to some kind of right or status—as to land, or to priority of title—which is acknowledged to be of basic value to the society as a whole. What each version of the myth does is to assert, apart from particular claims, the general significance of local origin, priority of arrival, control of *sacra*, or whatever may be the point of issue. The problem of 'closeness of fit' between versions of myth and group structure of the society is not usually a very refractory one. With individual versions within a single group or sub-group, the general principle is the same, but it is harder to identify the particular elements to which mythic variation should be related. Individual claims, aggressions or resentments along structural lines can occasionally be documented.[1] But at times, as we should expect, aesthetic interest in systematization, or in fantasy elaboration seems to be responsible for variation, apart from special domestic or other personal factors.

The second question has to do with the degree of fixity that is expected in a myth. Here the position is less clear. If myths represent the traditional values of the society, including the moral norms, one would expect them to maintain a firm shape, to show very little variation from one generation to another. Taking for granted that over the course of time they have been altered and garbled from their original versions, and even adopting the more extreme standpoint that they cannot be interpreted as an historical source at all but only as sociological validation of an existing structure, the projection of the present back into the past, there has still been a reluctance to treat them as possibly recent or changing items. Not, I think, that any modern social anthropologist would deny this possibility; merely that perhaps for lack of evidence, myths have been handled with a kind of timeless attitude, or have been credited with a quality of antiquity. One of the few who have recognized the problem and published some details bearing on it is Gregory Bateson,[2] who showed how in a village group of Bali a syncretist myth linking gods as siblings was introduced to provide a ritual basis for a socio-political unity. Evidence on this plasticity of myth is not easy to get, so I present here two Tikopia cases.

The first shows how a Tikopia myth dealing with some of the major gods of the pantheon, and purporting to describe the origination of one of the central sacred objects of the society, a temple, could not have

[1] I have given an example in my *History and Traditions of Tikopia*, 1961. This work also gives a general classification of Tikopia traditional material of a 'mythical' character, and a more extended analysis of its sociological implications.
[2] G. Bateson, 'An Old Temple and a New Myth', *Djawa*, Vol. XVII, 1937.

been formulated before about the beginning of the nineteenth century, whereas the period of Tikopia society to which it refers can most plausibly be put at not later than the beginning of the eighteenth century.

The myth concerns the building of Rarofiroki temple, a small thatch hut standing at the north side of the area known as Marae, the religious heart of pagan Tikopia.[1]

I was given the myth in 1929, on two occasions. The first was by my friend Pae Sao, a ritual elder of high status in Tafua clan, who was recognized as having a great deal of knowledge about Tikopia religious matters. From discussions about the Work of the Gods, and the nature of Rarofiroki temple, it emerged that the house was conceived to exist on two planes, the material and the spiritual. The actual temple in Marae had its prototype in the Heavens, where it had been built by the gods, a set of siblings known as the Brethren (Fanau). Pae Sao proceeded to tell me the tale about the building of the temple in the Heavens.

'It was built by the Brethren. As it was being built, it was lashed with coconut sinnet cord. But the Great God (senior of the siblings), standing up above, called down to his brothers to pass him up iron (nails). But they would not, they objected, and handed him up only coconut sinnet, and coconut husk and cord. They went on building the house, and when it was finished the Great God came down. He took the iron and went off to the lands of the white men, leaving behind the lands of the black men in his rear, and he brought the iron to the lands of the white men. Then he said to his brothers "You objected to giving me iron; I asked you to give me iron to secure the house. So you can stay and secure your houses with coconut sinnet and husk." Then he went to arrange the valuables in the lands of the white men, while this land had to make do with adzes of any old thing.'

As the tale proceeded it soon became clear that what I was listening to was not so much an account of the construction of this sacred temple in the spiritual realm, as an explanation of why white men and not Tikopia came to be endowed with iron tools. This was in fact an aetiological myth of common type, with the usual moral overtones. There was also, as was common with Tikopia stories of this comparative kind, a wry self-deprecatory scorn on the part of the narrator for the Tikopia technology, which had to use only relatively soft materials, and also scorn for the stupid Tikopia gods who were too obstinate to realize a good thing when they saw it. (The phrase I have rendered as 'any old thing' is more literally translated as 'foolish things', but the former expression is more idiomatic in English.) The question of how the Brethren

[1] A plan of Marae, and an account of the rites which used to take place there, are given in *Work of the Gods in Tikopia.*

happened to have iron available in the first place was of course not answered; it was just there.

At first I wondered if the narrator had not strayed from his theme, and if the text really corresponded to the announced title. But I realized from later talk with him and others that this was all there was, and that making allowance for variants, this was the matter of the spiritual temple-building. Some time later I got another version, even more exotic. This was Pa Rangifakaino, of the lineage of Tavi, of Kafika clan. According to this the temple of the Brethren was built in England, in a land of the white men. The senior brother mounted the roof and called down *in English* for nails with which to make the roof fast. But his brothers did not hear him aright, in this foreign tongue, and kept handing him up various kinds of lashing materials, which he rejected one after another. Finally they handed him up coconut sinnet cord. He drove them away in disgust, and they came to Tikopia in a canoe. Hence iron stayed with white men, and coconut sinnet cord came to Tikopia. To crown the whole story, their senior brother was 'God'!

This version of the myth, though in my pursuit of Tikopia pagan religion at the time I considered it somewhat puerile, is in some ways more interesting than the other. Pa Rangifakaino was a pagan, as of course was Pae Sao, and both appeared to believe quite sincerely in the truth of their stories (in which, incidentally, neither had any vested structural interest). But the second version was in a way more 'logical' than the first. It accounted for the presence of iron in the situation by locating the building site where iron was known to occur—in England, or at least some white man's country. And it attributed the knowledge of the properties of iron, and the wisdom to try and get it used, not to a purely Tikopia god, but to a syncretistic figure—the God of the white men who was at the same time the senior of the Tikopia Brethren.

Both versions of the myth illustrated the almost obsessional interest which—for good reason—the Tikopia had, even in 1929, for iron. But they also indicate that some part at least of this myth must be a relatively recent construct. The actual temple Rarofiroki, as a material building, was stated by the Tikopia to have been erected on the spiritual model in expiation after the expulsion of a section of the population known as Nga Ravenga,[1] at a period which can be put by genealogical evidence as possibly about A.D. 1700 Almost certainly, knowledge of iron did did not come to the Tikopia until about a century later. Whatever be one's view about these dates, one or other account is out of place on the time scale—either the real temple was first built much later, when iron was known; or the story of the abstract spiritual temple having an alternative of *iron* fastenings was an afterthought. My guess is that the

[1] *Work of the Gods*, p. 211; *History and Traditions of Tikopia*, Chapter 7.

latter happened. But in either case the plasticity of myth, its adaptive quality, is clear. There is one further point. Both of these stories can be legitimately classed as myth. They dealt with basic figures in the pantheon, they referred to one of the most important Tikopia religious *sacra*, they were told in conditions of some secrecy, they were believed to be true, and they were intended to explain a fact of very great concern to all Tikopia, namely, their lack of iron. How or by whom these versions of the myth were invented I do not know, but as to when—it cannot have been much more than a century before I made the record.

My second case concerns the genesis of myth, or rather myth-making in operation. It arises in connection with stories about a highly sacred stone, which was a symbol of the Octopus God, and which was deemed to be responsible under proper care, for fertility of the crops and especially for good fortune in fishing. This stone lay in a cycas-leaf lined bed in the orchard of Takarito, in the district of Faea, and was known accordingly as Te Atua i Takarito—the Deity of that place. In tradition, the site had been that of a long-vanished temple, and it was part of the function of the Ariki Kafika every year to complete a season's rites of the Work of the Gods by a washing of the sacred stone, a re-lining of its bed, and offerings and libations to the gods and ancestral spirits associated with the temple. In 1929 the rites of Takarito were in full operation.[1] When I returned to Tikopia in 1952 they had been abandoned. This had been done at the instance of the Ariki Kafika, probably about 1935. The events concerned with this abandonment illustrate the complexity of Tikopia religious thinking, and also some of the processes involved in the creation of myth.

With the annual ritual of Takarito was associated a ceremonial levy, in which members of the ritual party silently but publicly entered every orchard in the vicinity in turn and took a small amount of produce for offerings and a meal at the temple site. In 1929 this levy, known as *aru*, was still in operation, though the people of Faea, the district in which the symbol of the god lay, had by that time all been Christian for some years and did not support these pagan rites. In 1952 I first heard that the rites of Takarito had been given up when I was talking with a son of the Ariki Kafika about the use of orchards. He explained that he himself took food from the orchard as did his brothers too, going in place of the chief, who now had got too old to cultivate. But the *kava* ritual there had been abandoned since folk objected to the levy of the *aru*, this licensed raid on their cultivations. They were said to have scolded the chief for it, so the old man replied 'Give it up, and the *kava* there too.' When I asked the chief's son if it were good or bad for folk thus to object, he replied 'It is bad—it is good and yet bad,' meaning that they were

[1] *Work of the Gods*, Chapter X.

within their rights to protest but that they should not have proceeded against ancient custom.

A little later I was talking about the Work of the Gods with Pa Fatumaru, one of the Taumako pagan elders. I again asked the reason for the abandonment of the Takarito rites. He answered that Mission teachers had removed the stone from its resting place. His story was that some time after I had left Tikopia the 'missionaries', i.e. some local Mission teachers, had taken the sacred stone away and hidden it in the bushes. Then, he said, they waited to see the result—and it got back again in position by itself! So then they took it out to sea and threw it overboard from a canoe. Soon they observed that it was back again in position! Then they took it and used it as an oven stone in the earth oven for cooking sago. (The notion here was to degrade the symbol of the god by using it for the menial task of cooking food; perhaps they hoped also that the fierce heat would split the stone.) But the result of this manoeuvre was that through the power of the stone the food remained raw! (Laughter arose at this point from the assembled family, who were listening with me to the story.) So then the Ariki Kafika abandoned the rites.

I asked where was the stone now. The answer was 'We don't know whether it is back in position or still in the sago oven.' Then the ritual elder added that afterwards a son of the Mission priest died. He and a friend were going to voyage overseas. They went out on the reef in their canoe, and he was attacked by a shark. The god had entered into the shark and the young man was so bitten that he died. He said also that after the chief had abandoned the rites fish became scarce off Tikopia— both for men's fishing at sea and for women's fishing on the reef. This accorded with the pagan view that one of the objects of the Takarito ritual had been increase of fish.

Some weeks later I discussed this matter again with the same man. He told me that the Mission teacher who probably had interfered with the stone had been one of the younger sons of the Mission priest. I commented that nothing had happened to the offender himself. 'Oh, it struck his brother,' replied the elder's wife (herself a baptized Christian). Her husband added that the teacher actually concerned had in fact slipped and fallen one day on the hillside, had injured himself and had never been the same since. (It was true that his body did not look well nourished.) Curiously, neither of my informants mentioned the recent death of a baby son of the Mission teacher. So I inquired if this also was to be put down to the sacrilegious act? 'No; when it died the casting away of the stone had ended—this is different,' was the reply. They confirmed, however, a story I had heard in the meantime that the priest himself had been opposed to interference with the Takarito stone. According to a report he had said 'The original things of a land, they are present in all lands; do not go and interfere with them.' If this was true it may not have been due to respect but to fear, for the priest was not free from all such 'superstitions'.

Later, on several occasions, I heard from other men (including Christians and a lapsed Christian) the same story—though one gave the order of incidents in reverse. It was generally taken as a joke that the Mission teacher has had so much trouble to get rid of the stone yet all in vain. There seemed to be some difference of view as to whether the stone was now back in its bed, whether the bed was empty or whether it was occupied by another stone. However, by those most closely concerned, it was regarded as common knowledge that the stone was now back in its old place. The ritual elder told me that one of the younger Tikopia leaders, John Fararava, prominent Christian as he was but still a member of the chiefly house of Kafika, had reported that the deity was in truth there. He owned the share in the Takarito orchard, and it was reported that he had cut cycas fronds and relined the stone's bed in the ground, making a 'house' for it as in the traditional rites. A month or so later an elderly man of the same family, Fararava's father's brother, and also a Christian, told me personally that he had observed the deity there—the same one, not a different stone. It was in his mind, he said, also to cut cycas fronds and reline the bed some morning. I then asked the Ariki Kafika himself about it. He told me the story of the throwing away of the stone, that it had disappeared either in the ocean or in the oven, but that it had reappeared of itself in its home. He said that John Fararava (who was a classificatory grandson of his) saw it and came and reported to him 'Grandfather! The god has come and is there, what is to be done?' Fararava then asked if the rites of Takarito would be resumed forthwith. But the old chief had replied, 'Oh, they won't be resumed. The missionaries have persisted in making sport of it. The god has returned to dwell in his dwelling-place, but nothing more will be performed, that there is his ground.' By this he meant that the deity had come back and that was enough; the land was under his jurisdiction but no more rites would take place since the Christians had consistently attempted to interfere. He said too, that he had observed the loss of the stone the last time he went over to carry out the ritual. He saw cycas fronds in the bed, but they were empty—no deity. He searched and searched, but the stone was missing. He and his party then carried on with the rites, but they did not have any ceremonial levy as was customary. It was after this, he said, that the stone returned.

It was impossible to get an accurate idea of what finally happened in this case, and it was inadvisable for me to try and check by personal observation whether or not the stone was still there. It seemed clear that the stone had been removed from its bed by one or more Mission teachers associated with the family of the priest. It seemed likely also that the stone had since been returned—but whether by one of the delinquents fearing further disorder to his family, or by a junior member of Kafika who did not like to tell the chief that he had actually handled the sacred stone, one cannot say.

What was clear, however, was the sense of triumph rather than of dismay among the pagans—they regarded their god as having vindicated himself. The Christians did not seem to try and contradict this. On the whole, they seemed to have accepted the main incidents in the story. The abandonment of the rites of Takarito was a matter of definite decision by the Ariki Kafika. With this was associated the not unnatural objections of the Christian population of Faea as a whole to the operations of the ceremonial levy, to support a pagan ritual, and a pagan god. The reasons for his decision were as much political as religious. The handling of the stone by unauthorized outsiders was an offence; the repetition of this was an outrage and a nuisance. But the underlying cause of the abandonment was the political pressure that lay behind this action. As some people said, it was 'because Christianity has become established in Faea' or 'because the missionaries don't want the Ariki Kafika to perform the *kava* in Faea', or as the Ariki Kafika himself said 'because of the objections of the priest's family'.

As the leader with the prime responsibility for public order for the whole community he did not wish to persist in a course of action which would alienate half the Tikopia population, and make social co-operation with them very difficult.

This seemed to be a situation of crystallization of incipient myth. For in 1928–9 I had been told similar stories of the dire effects of interference with the god of Takarito.[1] When Pa Fatumaru, the ritual elder, told the stories in 1952 he also referred to the earlier cases. Over the years then, a body of putative incidents had been accumulated referring to the powers of the stone symbol of the god. These could be regarded as contemporary myths. They dealt with the powers and activities of a highly sacred object; though not in any sense secret tales they were told in some privacy as being concerned with this sacred being; they were believed to be quite true; and they supported and justified a range of beliefs and values in the Tikopia traditional scheme. The tales themselves were admittedly quite recent, and there were agreed to be divergent accounts of what happened. But save for a 'hard core' of Christian sceptics, the bulk of the Tikopia population, both Christian and pagan, seemed to be quite convinced that something of the kind described had actually occurred: initial exercise of force by human antagonists countered by super-human power of the threatened deity; ridiculous outcome of an attempt to degrade the deity's symbol; and final punishment of the sacrilegious person.

[1] *We, The Tikopia*, 1936, p. 49; *Work of the Gods of Tikopia*, p. 292.

This illustration of myth in a formative phase indicates an important aspect of its creation. It does not simply arise as a kind of intellectual or imaginative exercise. One type of myth at least arises in response to a situation of challenge, where justification or explanation of event has to be secured if status or more material benefit is not to be lost. In this case, something substantial was lost in the course of the struggle—the right to exact a levy on the cultivations in the name of the god. Yet the situation was rectified to some degree in the eyes of both Christians and pagans, it would seem, by the affirmation of the undiminished powers of the god. The myths of his return, and of his punishment of offenders against his dignity gave some satisfaction and comfort to his pagan adherents. In the upshot, these stories were a gloss on the event; the Christian zealot's attack resulted in a cessation of the rites (and ultimately in a wider context in the conversion of all pagan Tikopia to Christianity). But at least the pagans had some immaterial offset to their material loss. In this situation the creation of contemporary myth had a significant function of compensation.

CHAPTER 14

INDIVIDUAL FANTASY AND SOCIAL NORMS: SEANCES WITH SPIRIT MEDIUMS[1]

(1966)

In the traditional Tikopia ritual system spirit mediumship was an important phenomenon. In a rough classification, occasions of display of spirit mediumship can be divided into three main types: (a) public occasions, sometimes highly formal, as when a spirit medium made an impressive entry during the Work of the Gods in Marae and was treated with the greatest respect by all the participants in the ritual, including the chiefs[2]; (b) household occasions, such as the conclusion of the manufacture of a net or the diagnosis of an illness, where the medium was concerned with some family or domestic achievement or crisis, and respect was shown by those present to the medium, though the occasion was not a sacred one; (c) private seances, where a person consulted a medium on a matter of some primary interest to him, such as his wife's fertility, and where he alone or with one or two close kin formed the audience. Then the seance might be in the medium's house, and events were relatively informal. In all such cases, the entry of the spirit medium into trance was an expected feature of the proceedings. But a medium was sometimes stimulated by events into entering the trance state of his own accord without any particular urging. External shock, such as an earthquake, or internal anxiety, as when a member of the family had been lost at sea, might provide stimuli.

In most cases Tikopia spirit mediumship related to situations of uncertainty to which some kind of resolution could be given through the command or expression of opinion of the medium in trance state. This was less so with highly ritualized procedures where spirit mediumship formed merely one sector of an elaborate ritual cycle. Here the function of the performance was rather to provide confirmation of achievement and set the seal upon the spiritual recognition of what had been done than

[1] In the analysis of data on spirit mediumship I benefited greatly from discussion with Jerome Frank, Seymour Perlin and other colleagues at the Center for Advanced Studies in the Behavioral Sciences, Palo Alto, in 1959. In this present essay I have confined myself to interpretation of some aspects of my Tikopia material, and have not considered more general comparative issues as raised, e.g. by Marcelle Bouteiller, Mircea Eliade or Ari Kiev and his collaborators.

[2] See *Work of the Gods*, 1967, p. 299.

to resolve any particular uncertainty. But even here what was understood to be the entry of a particular god upon the scene helped to give assurance that the major purpose of the ritual addressed to him was likely to be fulfilled.

Relief from uncertainty obviously occurred in cases of sickness, where the role of the medium was to diagnose the illness, attribute to it a cause, indicate a prognosis and attempt some therapy. Traditionally the Tikopia knew practically nothing of what may be termed medicine. Their spirit medium procedures involved the use of prepared leaves and occasional infusions. But in so far as they had any healing virtue, these operated almost solely through psychological means. It is in this light that the persistence of spirit mediumship in Tikopia, even after a massive advance of Christianity against the pagan religion, is to be understood. To pagans, serving a spirit medium, a vessel of the spirits (*vaka atua*), was a procedure which fitted integrally into their religious system. The procedure was one of permissive rather than of automatic occurrence in the religious field, in that most religious rites could be performed without spirit mediumship. But in Tikopia belief the appearance of gods to men was regarded as part of the order of things, and for a spirit to enter a human body was therefore completely acceptable. To Christians the situation was more complex. Having accepted the 'one god', they were not entitled to worship any others. Yet those of the older generation at least acknowledged the superiority of the one God rather than believed in the falsity of the rest. Hence, many of them had a fearful attitude lest their ancient gods wreaked vengeance for their desertion. This situation was intensified by the fact that the very small amount of Western medicine available left the Tikopia for the most part without medical aid in their illnesses.

MEDIUMSHIP AT TWO PERIODS

Hence in 1952 I was not surprised to find that though Christianity had claimed a great part of the community, spirit mediumship still flourished. There were certain differences—the cult was less public, and the physical behaviour of mediums was rather more restrained. Mediums tended to sigh quietly and snort at the onset of their trances rather than shriek aloud as they did a generation earlier. In part this was due to their sensitivity to criticism by the Christians if their practices became too publicly obvious. But in essentials spirit mediumship was current in Tikopia in 1952 in the same form in which it operated a generation earlier.[1]

The prevalence of spirit mediumship in Tikopia seemed to be nearly

[1] Yet by 1966, when all the community had been Christian for about a decade, spirit mediumship was no longer practised (see pp. 356–9 below).

the same in 1952 as in 1928–9. In 1929 there were at least twenty-seven regularly practising spirit mediums, seventeen male and ten female, with possibly another five females who may have practised,[1] while in 1952 there were nineteen male mediums and seven female mediums practising. This means that roughly one in twenty to twenty-five adults was a spirit medium. What was of particular interest was that only a couple of men and a woman had continued as mediums from the period of a generation before; all the rest had died or ceased their profession on conversion to Christianity.

I knew personally a large number of these mediums and was present in all at thirty-seven seances, about half being public and the rest private.[2] I attended seances in 1928–9 with seven mediums and in 1952 with six mediums, one of these latter being a Christian medium whom I had also seen in action as a pagan a generation before. Only one of these mediums was a woman, but all my information indicates that women, with certain minor variations which I shall indicate later, practised in the same way as men. Apart from the male bias of my sample, I think I observed a fair cross-section of Tikopia mediums, since those whose seances I attended included a chief and a ritual elder as well as commoners; there were men of all four clans. Of the dozen mediums about half were pagan and half Christian.

The private seances were one of the most valuable aspects of my work on spirit mediumship. They were in line with Tikopia practice that anyone wishing to have a consultation with the spirit of a dead person could invite the appropriate medium who would then go into a trance. In such trance state the medium was usually ready to discuss freely matters pertaining to the spirit world, and I was thus able to obtain a great deal of material on the Tikopia theory of spirit existence and of spirit relationships with the world of men. In 1929 I had such private seances with only one medium, who initiated them himself. In 1952 nearly all my observations were made in private seances, mainly because public ritual occasions for spirit mediumship had become very few. These private seances were particularly interesting because, coming at a time when tensions between Christianity and spirit mediumship had become very evident, I was able to discuss these issues with men both in and out of trance who were working out these tensions in their own daily behaviour. This also helped me to realize even more clearly than before the relation between personality problems in general and the

---

[1] These five, all in Namo, were not counted in the figures I have given in an earlier publication. (*Essays on Social Organization and Values*, p. 250.)

[2] I use the term public seances for situations where the medium was acting for groups in the Tikopia community. Private seances were mainly my own personal consultations with mediums in a state of trance; not infrequently other persons were present at these.

practice of spirit mediumship. This is one aspect of the phenomena which I wish to discuss in particular here.[1]

MADNESS AND MEDIUMSHIP

As a preface to this analysis I repeat the distinction which I have drawn earlier (1964, pp. 247–8) between spirit possession, spirit mediumship and shamanism. By spirit possession I understand phenomena of abnormal personal behaviour which are interpreted by other members of the society as evidence that a spirit is controlling the person's actions and probably inhabiting his body. Spirit mediumship I take to be the use of such behaviour by members of the society as a means of communication with what they understand to be entities in the spirit world. To be capable of such use, the behaviour of the person possessed by the spirit must be intelligible or able to be interpreted; this implies that it must follow some fairly regular, predictable pattern, usually of speech. Shamanism, as I use the term, applies to those phenomena where a person, either as a spirit medium or not, is regarded as controlling spirits, exercising his mastery over them in socially recognized ways. Using the term in this sense, there is spirit possession and spirit mediumship in Tikopia but not shamanism.

I now outline the Tikopia theory of spirit relations with the human body. Every individual has when alive a spirit principle called by the Tikopia *mauri* or *ora*, which may be termed the soul. This is believed to be separated from the body at death by some rather complicated manoeuvres and may be later spoken of as *atua*, a term used generically for any external spirit. External spirits are of many kinds and degrees of rank and power. Some, such as ancestors, are clearly benevolent, but may harm people if offended. Others, such as the common wandering spirits known as *atua vare*, not identified individually, are by nature malevolent to mankind. Types of such spirits are those of the water spout at sea, who cause men to throw away their paddles and attempt to commit suicide, or those of the coconut frond, who are associated with black magic. One of these wandering spirits may take up residence in the body of a person, or may abstract his soul and make him ill. One of the important functions of a spirit medium is to expel the spirit concerned, and/or recover the abstracted soul.

Madness was believed by the Tikopia to be possession by such a

[1] I have already considered briefly some of the structural aspects of Tikopia spirit mediumship in my Huxley Lecture (*Essays on Social Organization and Values*, 1964, pp. 247–56). I have also published a brief account of the operations of a Tikopia spirit medium in regard to a sick patient in 'Acculturation in Relation to Concepts of Health and Disease' in *Medicine and Anthropology*, ed. Iago Galdston, New York, 1959, pp. 133–7. The relation between spirit mediumship and the formal structure of the Tikopia pagan religion will be examined in *Rank and Religion in Tipokia* (still to be published).

spirit, but by one with whom by its nature no social relationship existed and therefore with whom effective consistent communication was impossible. There were in 1928–9 several people in Tikopia who, from time to time, manifested wild, crazy behaviour. One man who had had a fight about an orchard ran shrieking down into the lake and was finally overpowered by half a dozen men and dragged ashore. He had periods of madness lasting from six to ten days, and these were said to occur only in the trade-wind season. A young unmarried woman remained for months in a strange state. In a high wind she lit small fires in a space between houses, to the great danger of their thatch. One evening she took some large coconuts that her mother had been treasuring for water bottles, broke them open and distributed the flesh as food to young people; being chased by her mother with a knife she took refuge with kinsfolk on the other side of the island, let her hair grow long like a man and became unkempt.[1] Another woman, married, in fits of madness used to cast aside her skirt and go naked; after the death of her husband she became pregnant 'by other men' and finally committed suicide by swimming out to sea. Such conditions were characterized according to intensity as mindlessness (*seke atamai*; meaning euphemistically also a scatterbrained person) or craziness (*varea*; the related term *vare* being commonly used for silly, stupid, irresponsible behaviour)

The Tikopia recognize that madness may be linked with family relationships—'it works in each generation, it does not miss'. I was given examples, including that of a family where a man's sister, brother and grandson had all committed suicide through this cause and another sister and his daughter had also had periodic attacks of madness. It was said that such families were ashamed of their affliction and therefore it was not publicly discussed.

All such conditions are regarded as due to spirit possession. I was told of one mad person that the wild look in her eye was that of the spirit possessing her. Treatment for madness might consist in summoning a spirit medium who, in trance state, would bid the invading spirit to depart. The spirit might agree, whereon the afflicted person would become sane again. If the spirit objected, no more would be done unless the crazy person had to be restrained from doing damage, when he might be bound or a further attempt made to expel the spirit, as by burning the patient with the end of a glowing stick or twist of bark cloth.

When, however, a person behaved strangely but seemed capable of fairly coherent action and conversation, then he was characterized as a

---

[1] Once she entered a circle of dignitaries talking with the Bishop of Melanesia and respectfully presented to him one of my cooking saucepans which she had abstracted and filled with sand. The Bishop, disconcerted, was uncertain whether this was a native Tikopia custom or not.

vessel or vehicle of the spirits (*vaka atua*) and used as a means of communication with them. The line between madness and spirit mediumship was by no means a rigid one. Few spirit mediums would be described by the Tikopia as mad. Many seemed at first sight quite normal individuals. But discussion with them usually revealed some history of disturbed psychological experience, sometimes accompanied by some degree of cataleptic state; I describe some of these symptoms later. One man who did have periodic fits of craziness (he who rushed shrieking into the lake) was the spirit medium for the principal god of Kafika. As such, even when mad he would on the appropriate ritual occasions enter into the trance state and behave in an organized manner. His psychic controls were evidently strong enough so that the social call of duty restored him to some equilibrium, from which he relapsed again when the rite was over. Communication and control were essential elements in the spirit medium situation.

Spirit mediumship in Tikopia was not regarded as being necessarily hereditary. Though it was believed that madness might run in families, there was no Tikopia conception that the son of a medium should himself become a medium. There was, however, a Tikopia structural principle involved which facilitated family succession. This was in terms not of the physical or psychological propensity of a human being but of the volitional activity of spirits. It was thought that a particular spirit or group of spirits required expression in lineage terms and would seek a medium out from among the lineage members. In our terms, this not infrequently resulted in a hereditary transmission of the role. Pa Rarosingano, one of the most forceful and well-known mediums in 1952, said he had as predecessors in the profession his father, his father's father, his great-grandfather and two still more remote male ancestors. Sometimes mediumship seems to have been exercised not by immediate forebears but by collaterals. Pa Nukufuti and his sister Nau Sao, who were both mediums, had been preceded by their father's brother and two of his sisters, their father's mother and a more remote ancestor. Mediumistic propensity often seemed to skip a generation or so. Neither the father nor the mother nor the father's father of Pa Motuata had been mediums—but his father's father's father had been one.

In this assumption of role it would seem that some tendency to suggestibility was combined with a realization of family or lineage expectations. So Pa Nukufuti explained 'I here will continue to dwell and then when I die to whomsoever of my sons the spirits will come he then will practice as a medium just as I am following my ancestors. In a family into which the spirits press there is a constant succession (literally the mediumship 'follows walking'). My father's bachelor brother followed my grandmother from Rarokofe who used to be a spirit medium.' I asked him which of his sons would take on his mediumship

—did he know? He replied that he had no indication, that it was not certain, that it followed the wish of the spirits, that the spirits themselves made the choice. 'Spirit mediums do not disappear, they are not lost. They are there in the wish of the spirits and whoever will be the man that they will enter, they enter him.' Clearly here the Tikopia ascribe a primacy to personal psychological factors but present these in terms of a theory of autonomous spirit action.

EVIDENCES OF SPIRIT MEDIUMSHIP

How does spirit mediumship begin? I myself was not able to see the initial stage of any person becoming a medium. But many descriptions were given me by Tikopia in their own terms. It is useful to look at the matter from two points of view in identification of the phenomenon —that of people among whom the medium begins to operate, the social experience of onset; and that of the medium himself, the personal experience of onset.

I asked Pa Fenuatara in 1929 how did the members of a household or lineage recognize a spirit medium? He explained that when the spirits first come to a man he is unaware of it, and other people also do not recognize the reason for his strange behaviour. The man sits and does not answer when spoken to when the spirits first 'tread upon him'. Bystanders become alarmed and imagine that he is going mad or that he is drunk with *kava* (both betel and *kava* in large quantities produce a disorganization of the faculties akin to drunkenness). 'We go and press his body and wonder what it may be. When we go and work over him, the spirit goes away and the man becomes clear (the same expression as used for the weather clearing up) and sits up. As he abides, it comes again at another time and as it returns he speaks. As we go to massage him he thrusts us away. People go and speak to him. "Who is the spirit who comes to work here? Utter your name as to who you may be. Spirit who comes, come properly then to enter your vessel." Then if he speaks, he speaks; but if not, not. Thereupon he goes and returns again at another time. When he returns the relatives observe the man's body shows gooseflesh. Then he comes to speak to the relatives. Then he goes. Another time he comes, is given betel and is addressed by the relatives: "Now you who have come, go you and come again tomorrow." The next day the relatives go to their cultivations and return with food and green coconuts. They prepare the food and stand it in the house, together with betel. They say to the spirit "Your betel there; come and chew your betel." Thereupon he jumps in. Oil is lifted down and he is cleansed. He chews his betel, then the food and the valuables are announced to him. Thereupon he goes.' It must be noted that once the mediumship of a person has been established he acts as the vehicle for only certain specified spirits. (That is, his personality phases are restricted and each given identification.) People can commonly tell what spirits enter any particular medium (and often who enters first), and conversely what person serves as medium for any particular god or spirit.

The ceremony with food, bark-cloth and betel is termed *furunga atua*, 'cleansing the spirits'. From the Tikopia point of view it may be regarded as the formal means of establishing a definite social linkage with the spirit or spirits manifesting themselves in the medium; to the anthropologist it is obviously a dedication of the medium to the assumption of a particular personality and to the social purposes which hereafter this must serve. In this account the establishment of a person as a medium is clearly a matter of gradual definition of his role by his kinsfolk. Initially the psychic abnormality which he reveals does not receive definite identification. Left to itself it might recur merely in some kind of trance form. But by their questioning and by the channel of procedure into which they force him, the kinsfolk of a person convert him into a *speaking* medium. In this way they are undoubtedly aided by the fact that the man is already cognizant of the procedure followed by other mediums, which must exert an effect upon him in his trance state. As one man said 'In this land people are accustomed to spirits coming to men.' Existing mediums too may help in the identification of the symptoms. Apart from this formal induction and use of existing models there is no specific training for Tikopia spirit mediums.

The use of food and bark-cloth is common procedure in relations with spirits; the smearing of oil on the body is a rite of unction which takes place in a number of situations where contact is to be established between persons and spirits. (Part of the Tikopia theory of the use of oil is in the effect which its scent produces on spirits.) With reference to this cleansing ceremony Pa Fenuatara said 'When a spirit has come to be cleansed, when he goes away to the realm of spirits the oil is smeared upon him and he has pouched his betel. Other spirits who have not come among men press about him and say: "Give us oil for ourselves." "Give me betel for myself." "Give me a valuable for myself." They ask him "Whence are your own things there?" Thereupon the spirit says "I went among men; I was oiled by men." Thereupon the spirits call out "Alas! You indeed have gone to chew betel and be oiled by your own men. Do your own doing. We indeed stay here. We are not asked for by our own men."' The Tikopia theory is that spirits desire these pleasures and are largely dependent upon men for them. They are envious of those of their number who can secure such attentions through their mediums. This desire 'to go among men' is relevant also to the theory of the medium being possessed in turn by a chain of spirits, all jostling round him to 'jump into his body'.

The Tikopia recognize that some people are much more susceptible to mediumistic phenomena than are others. This susceptibility is conceptualized metaphorically in terms of a person being 'a path' along which a spirit can come to men. Some people can provide a clear path, others offer only a dark or cluttered path. The latter are not so attractive to the spirits and so do not become mediums regularly, or may resist mediumship completely. One man said to me, 'We here (i.e. mediums) have become light in the path of the spirits. The path of the spirits has become light. A spirit prepares his path to be light, that it may be clear.' The term (*teatea*) translated as 'light', refers primarily to whiteness or paleness of colour, but it can also refer to brightness, as of the sky. The term (*marama*) translated as 'clear', means ordinarily daylight, as opposed to darkness. Alternatively or in conjunction, therefore, the two terms indicate that a person who is a spirit medium is regarded as being free from obstruction, open to the passage of spirits or, changing the metaphor, having good conductivity.

When a spirit comes into a person he may have to struggle through because, in Tikopia terms, the person does not present a clear path or, as we should say, is not a good medium. The struggles of the spirit, it is thought, are expressed by the writhing and other convulsive movements of the medium. Hence, the more placid the medium, the less resistance he will offer to spirit passage. But with some people the spirit never succeeds in getting through. 'He comes and works away, works away, but he does not descend upon the man—that is where the path to men is dark.' I asked what happens when the spirit sees that his way is clear, but the man himself objects to serving as a medium? The reply was that the spirit just comes all the same. At first he may come jerkily causing the man to convulsive movements, but later he will come quietly because he has become used to being among men. He 'just comes'.

There is then a logic in the Tikopia interpretation in that they make an equation between the character of bodily behaviour and ease of possession by the spirit. What they do in effect is to translate notions of differences in personal psychic conflict, suggestibility and susceptibility to trance into terms of relation between an external spirit entity and the bodily characteristics of the medium.

So far I have given a generalized view of the first onset of spirit mediumship. Now I turn to some descriptions of their own experiences by mediums themselves.

PERSONAL EXPERIENCES OF ONSET

A ritual elder whom I had known as a medium in 1928 and again in 1952, Pa Nukurotoi, told me that he first became possessed as a spirit medium when he was a lad. His grandfather, Pu Ratia (who brought the name Nukurotoi from the world of spirits and from whom it was inherited by the present holder) descended on his head and went over his body—came as if it were a wind. The medium had not been previously ill (as is a common experience); he was quite well. 'Time passed and the spirit came again, and chewed betel among men, that is, I chewed betel. My ancestor came, but when Christianity came to this land he went to live in Nukutureki, among the dwellings of the gods. Thereupon came Pu Veterei. I had become baptized, but he still came, but he came alone, only one spirit. Thereupon the Ariki Taumako (a pagan) plucked areca nut and invited Pu Veterei to enter. Then came fish in the time of famine and the land ate.'

I asked him why he thought the spirits came to him. He said 'They tell me that it is clear in my body. The path to men is clear'—he was a good subject. I asked him how did his kinsfolk know that it was a spirit who possessed him? He said that the spirit announced it himself. I asked him if his marriage had made any difference to his mediumistic performances, and he said no, that the spirits came to him equally both before and after marriage. (As indicated later, sexual maturity seems essential to mediumship but performance of sex functions seems irrelevant.) His description of the onset indicated no unusual features in his history nor suggested that his family felt his position unusual. Nor could I find any indication of pressure upon him from his family to be a spirit medium. It will be noted that the advent of the new religion and the medium's conversion to it did not have the effect of ending his mediumship. But it did alter his personality phase in that one spirit, his own ancestor, retired from the scene and another more distantly related kinsman took over. Evidently the medium had suffered some mild disarrangement of his attitude, but not enough to end his susceptibility to dissociation.

In some contrast to this was the experience of Pa Motuata. I had not known that Pa Motuata was a spirit medium, although he was an old friend of mine. I was told early in 1952 by someone else that he used to be a spirit medium, but gave it up when he became a Christian because of the opposition of the priest and of his own family, and that the spirits now no longer entered him. He himself had never spoken to me about this side of his activities. But not long afterwards he stopped me as I was returning from a visit to another spirit medium, to say he wanted to talk to me in my house with no one else there. When he came it was to tell me with a laugh, though a little shamefacedly, that he was a spirit medium and that he had hidden this from me. He asked if I had heard. I told him that I had—and I suspect that it was because he knew this that he now spoke of it. He said that he had started his mediumship after I had left the island, which was why I had not thought of him earlier. He felt the first onset long ago, when the former Ariki Taumako was alive (i.e. probably in the 1930s.) He said 'A man who is going to become a spirit medium dwells and dwells and is called "the path of the spirits". It is like a man who has drunk *kava*, white man's style (he meant alcohol); the person goes crazy. The beginning of a spirit medium is that the man feels that his body has gone dead, that he has lost control of it. With some men the beginning of the spirits comes at a dance. A man is dancing away in a competitive manner, and as he dances he gets gooseflesh, gooseflesh comes to his body. When an expert is dancing and people see that his dance bat has begun to quiver, that is the spirit who has come, the spirit who has wanted to dance, and so the man becomes a vessel of the spirits.' He said that there are two kinds of dances in which this occurs, the *mori* and the *raki*. (These are both posture dances of formal style; significantly, the mediumistic seizure does not seem to take place during the *matavaka*, a dance of violent bodily action in which the dancer sways regularly from side to side with increasing motion.) Pa Motuata said that the spirit did not come upon him at once, but gave premonitory signs. He felt as he was dancing that he had lost control of himself. 'My dancing had become crazy. I was not dancing correctly. My postures had become crazy. Thereupon people spoke to one another that it is a spirit who is dancing.' He said, 'I did not wish to be a spirit medium, but *he* strove to enter among men.' He explained that plenty of people don't want to be mediums, but the spirit sees that the path is clear to men and he jumps into the person. 'He' in this case was a spirit of the coconut fronds from Sikaiana (Stewart Island, an atoll far to the north). His name was Mataimarae, and he first came in Pukenga, a former Ariki Tafua. The association with coconut fronds, as mentioned earlier, suggests to the Tikopia black magic. Another spirit who possessed Pa Motuata was his agnatic kinsman, the elder brother of the former Ariki Taumako. Other spirits who came to him were a classificatory brother of his in Kafika, and occasionally the spirit of his father's brother, the renowned *maru*, Pae Avakofe. From time to time the descendants of this man invited him to go so that they might hold converse with their ancestor. This spirit was a great chewer of betel[1] and, in accordance with this status, the betel wad had to be huge, made from eighteen areca kernels instead of the normal one or two! This wad was disgorged by the medium after the seance or it would make him ill; it was divided up among the men present for chewing. (According to Tikopia practice, no woman would dare to take betel from a male spirit.) Pa Motuata, although for reasons of policy as a Christian convert he kept quiet about his performances, was quite clear in his belief in, and quite elaborate in his knowledge of, spirit possession. He simply assumed its truth, though personally he did not consciously wish to be a medium.

---

[1] This spirit, it was alleged, had wished to come to Pa Nukurotoi but, since Pa Nukurotoi had no teeth, rejected him!

The onset of mediumship in another medium, Pa Rarosingano, had been more complex. He was a man of vigorous personality, rather loud-voiced, inclined to shout and force our conversation by abrupt changes of topic. His right leg was somewhat withered below the knee, so that he limped very awkwardly—one might infer that his forceful personality was to some extent a compensation for his physical deficiency. He was open in exposition, not ashamed or furtive in speaking of his profession, though he was a Christian in the Christian district of Faea. He said that he did not go to church, although the rest of his family were practising Christians. He emphasized that the reason for his abstinence lay, not in his own wish, but because he was 'chased away' by the missionaries. In reply to my question he said that his spirits did not object to the chapel services; they held them to be good. He practised regularly as a spirit healer, and I saw him at work on one of his cases which he asked me to attend with him.[1]

Pa Rarosingano said he first became possessed during a funeral, and it was a most violent affair. 'I was sleeping in the night. I had not yet gone to the funeral when the spirit came on that day. He came among men in the house which stands here, Farefikai. I had a dream in the night as I slept, and I looked upon a man who came in with his hair bound up ready for delousing. Thereupon I woke with a start, and I said to my father, "Father, a spirit has entered with his hair bound up for delousing. He was girt with a girdle of mature coconut fronds." (These were the symbols of the Atua i Kafika.) My father replied "Who? It was not somebody from among your uncles?" (My father was a nephew of Sa Tafua.) I said "No, that one was a giant, terrifying." My father asked, "As you slept, did you sleep well or evilly?" (Meaning did you have an impression that he was good or bad?) "Not especially evil. He didn't look at any other place. He looked simply at me." He said "They are staring at me." My father thought that the apparition had come to afflict me, that I should be harmed by the spirits; but, no?' I asked my informant did he know whether the apparition was going to enter? He said he didn't know, he had not thought of it. He didn't know that he was a spirit vessel. The next day he didn't go out. He felt that his body was completely limp, without energy. Then he slept. He was awakened by his mother, to eat. Then came news of the funeral, the dead person being a close kinsman. He prepared to go to the funeral, but he was scolded by his parents, who wished him to eat and 'bind his belly'. He explained to me that the way of spirits to men is clear only when the belly is not 'bound with food', i.e. his parents, if they suspected that he was likely to become possessed, wanted to take precautions against this. But neither they nor he knew that a trance was impending. 'I felt as if I was full, yet I had not eaten. I went. We sang three dirges, but I

[1] For details see reference in footnote, p. 296.

304

felt that my body had taken on gooseflesh completely. I felt that the spirit had jumped among men. Thereupon as he jumped among men (my informant emphasized very strongly the word *sopo*, jump) people rushed to grasp me. They grasped me, but I rose up above. I stood with my head in the crown of the house. But as for my arms, men grasped my arms, and women too. One woman grasped my waistcloth, while other women embraced my body. But I lifted them all up. There was not a one who could hold my body. The people were lifted up while I arose at the end of the house there, opened it up and threw it completely outside. Then I went outside. People came and pressed my body; they pressed, pressed, pressed my body. It cleared; the spirit had gone. Then I came home and slept in my house.'

The spirit came again next day when the funeral oven was being kindled, and the medium struck people in the house. Then again people pressed his body and the spirit went. The next day he went to bathe, and he felt the spirit ready to jump among men. He hurried up from the beach and just got inside the door when the spirit came upon him. He stood up and yelled. Then he sat down and locked his hands together. Oil was brought and his father crawled to him and entreated him (i.e. the spirit) to come gently, that things had changed in the land (since the spirit had lived as a man) and that he should not show fight to people. So he was quieted.

In explanation the medium told me that the spirit who initially came to him was named Tukarefu and had fought in battle, that he had been a son of a former chief of Tafua and a woman of Namumanga. In the spirit world he was a friend of Noakena, the dead son of Pa Rangifuri.[1] who also came to the medium later. The medium told me that Noakena had said to his friend Tukarefu that it was not right to go yelling among men, as the work of the Gospel now stood in the land. Noakena said to him, 'You keep quiet. Do not go among men because the sacred work now stands, so don't enter among men.' Thereupon Tukarefu abode and did not go again to men. I asked if he did not object to being so blocked. My informant said, why? The reason why he came among men was only that he was invited by his friend Noakena. Tukarefu came among men only for about five or six months, and after he ceased then Noakena took possession.

This case was very interesting. A violent phase of onset was succeeded by a quiet phase of persisting mediumship; but the violence and the succeeding phase of quietude were interpreted in terms of social and religious norms and not in personal and psychological terms. It was to the existence of Christianity, with its rules of non-violence, and to the Tikopia ideology of bonds of friendship between spirits that the succession of psycho-physical phases was attributed.

[1] See *Elements of Social Organization*, 1951, pp. 61–2.

There is thus an interesting relationship between the personality and fantasy development of the medium and the general system of social control. Even although spirit mediumship was frowned upon by the Christian teachers, this did not prevent Pa Rarosingano from having his trances. Moreover, the initial onset was of a very violent character in which aggressions of various kinds obtained expression, among them perhaps aggression against his father, who crawled to his son, pressed nose to his knee and addressed him with respect in the spirit phase. On the other hand, once the medium had established his new personality and released the forces that had built up inside him, he was ready to recognize the moral force of Christianity and to conform up to a point with its canons. Yet he phrased this conformity in terms of his own personal spirit universe, not in terms of any conscious yielding of ground.

SPIRIT MEDIUMSHIP, PERSONALITY AND SOCIAL POSITION

We can now review briefly the question of what kind of person fitted the Tikopia pattern of mediumship. Obviously it had to be someone who was moderately suggestible, who could enter a trance state or assume a multiple personality with reasonable ease when the occasion demanded. Most Tikopia who became spirit mediums seemed to have had at some time in their history an event of psycho-physical disorder which then, as it developed, was interpreted by others as spirit possession. I emphasize again the importance of communication and of control as features of mediumship. In most mediumistic performances there seemed to be some kind of balance between involuntary behaviour and the exercise of personal control. Much of a medium's speech tended to be thick, blurred, clogged and clearly some mediums at times had difficulty in bringing to the surface things which they wanted to say. Sometimes it seemed to be difficult for a medium to maintain coherence in what he said; he would shift without warning from one subject to another, as he tried to deal with the several topics he was attempting to hold in his mind. Again, when more than one spirit was said to have entered the medium in sequence, an effect of struggle was apt to be given and the medium appeared to feel distressed. Sometimes he appeared to be under pressure to allow still another aspect of his personality to come to the fore. Moreover, the departure of one spirit or the entry of another seemed to occur often abruptly without the medium's volition. The medium could undoubtedly induce a trance by auto-hypnotic behaviour—putting himself in the appropriate position, locking his hands, tautening his muscles, etc. But once the trance had begun its course this seemed in varying degree to be beyond his conscious control, though most of the events within it followed a fairly set pattern. The concept of a 'familiar' who watched over the interests of his human bodily vehicle, jumping into the seance to break the chain of spirits, seems to have been a recognition of one aspect of the control forces of the personality. Moreover, it would appear that to some extent the medium himself was capable of ending his trance. The expression 'I am about to descend' spoken by the spirit presentation was sometimes deliberative, indicating fore-knowledge well in advance of the physical change, but sometimes, it seemed involuntary, hurriedly forced out of the medium by the realization that his assumed personality was slipping from him. Different mediums appeared to have different strengths of control, different combinations of expressive and controlling mechanisms.

It is common to regard such spirit mediums as being special personality types in their society, deviant, neurotic, perhaps seeking expression through trance channels for personal and social disadvantages from which they suffered in ordinary life. I think that for Tikopia such a characterization of mediums as a class would be incorrect. There seemed to be some individuals to whom these labels would certainly apply. But there also seemed to be others without such obvious neurotic or psychotic characteristics; were it not for their capacity of shifting personality by means of the trance state they would be regarded as quite 'normal' individuals. Such people seem to have been only mildly suggestible and to have been persuaded into developing their suggestibility to a point at which they could serve as mediums on fairly regular occasions. From this point of view, then, a Tikopia spirit medium was not deviant, but rather a conformer to social dictates. Someone who is pressured into 'abnormality' by the requirements of his society can be regarded as 'abnormal' in only a rather special sense of the term.

This is illustrated by the few cases made known to me of men or women who refused spirit mediumship because they were unwilling to endure its burdens and unpleasantness. By any Tikopia medium the physical phenomena of spirit mediumship were generally regarded as wearisome. Unconsciously mediums may have enjoyed their role, and it would seem from their fantasy account of spirit adventures that some of them undoubtedly did so. But the purely physical manifestations did not seem to be at all pleasant. Many complained about the dragging effects, the tiredness, the drunkenness or sickness from betel chewing, and similar troubles. Some people simply refused when asked to take on the obligations which mediumship entailed, and appeared to suffer no ill effects by this refusal. They behaved in fact like ordinary men who refused to do a rather tiresome job of work. They had some predisposition to suggestibility, but in refusing to allow it to come to full expression they maintained themselves as ordinary members of society. But, traditionally, refusal to be a medium on one specific occasion was said to have cost the man his life. As the Tikopia put it, the god wished to come upon him, and when he would not behave as a medium in the most sacred rites of Marae, the god drove him mad so that he put off to sea and was lost. Here the violent expressive forces of the personality did seem to be of 'abnormal' character, so that when not given their prescribed, conventional social release they drove the man to self-destruction.[1]

Susceptibility to trance seemed in some cases to be a matter of rather delicate adjustment between different facets of the personality. I was told that some women took action to avoid becoming spirit mediums. 'When a woman feels that a spirit is about to jump upon her she grasps anything stinking and smears it over her head and her body, that she may be stinking, that she may become disgusting to the spirit, so that he does not enter.' For this purpose lime, or the evil-smelling liquid produced by fermenting salt water in coconuts was used. This was an interesting link between smell and dissociation. Spirits were supposed to like the aromatic scents of crushed fragrant leaves or of turmeric, so that the use of odours of opposite types could strengthen a notion of opposition in the mind of a suggestible person. Moreover, the violent action in rubbing the head and body, with frictionating of the skin, may well have been not conducive to suggestibility. Yet in some cases the disturbing elements of the personality seemed to have been too powerful to have been repressed. Pa Ngatotiu told me that when his mother first became a vehicle of a spirit she objected. But the spirit of his grandfather wanted to come to men. 'She said that he should go and dwell among the spirits and not enter among men, but he bored away to come to men. So the oven was prepared and he was called to come and be cleansed. So he came and his oil was smeared, smeared upon his breast, his valuables were offered, his betel was presented and then he descended.'

Spirit mediumship in Tikopia was then a subtle blend of personal and social characteristics. The physical trance state involving some shift of consciousness, fantasy elaboration and assumption of other than ordinary personality characteristics was regarded by the Tikopia as based upon a reality of spirit form, and as having a definite job to do. Hence persons with traits of suggestibility were sometimes stimulated by their own interest and sometimes by members of the household or lineage to cultivate this suggestible tendency and utilize it for social purposes. Phases of their personality revealed in trance state could be identified as spirit entities, sometimes assuming the form of persons now dead but known in life, sometimes the form of remote ancestors or spirits who had never been men. Such displacement of personality allowed of consideration of public and private issues in a different idiom

[1] See *Work of the Gods*, 1967, p. 301.

and from a different standpoint than that of everyday life. Moreover, the postulate of spirit utterance assigned authority to the statements of mediums. So issues could be resolved and decisions taken which the conflicting claims of everyday life might have inhibited. Public opinion and personal opinion tended to coincide to a high degree in utterances of these suggestible persons in trance state. What was especially significant was that the institution of spirit mediumship provided a kind of alternative channel for decision-taking than the socio-political channel of chieftainship. The activities and views of spirit mediums filled in the interstices of the framework provided by a system of chiefs. But spirit mediums were always there as a possible countervailing force who could express public opinion with authority in cases where the decisions of chiefs were consistently lacking or too overbearing. Spirit mediums thus had their place as part of the system of checks and balances in the traditional Tikopia social system.

Spirit medium performances on public occasions associated with inter-clan, clan or lineage events were of periodic occurrence. More irregular was mediumship for private consultation. 'Private' is to be understood in the Tikopia sense, that is, where a person seeks discussion with another, but is usually accompanied by a brother, a son or a trusted neighbour in support. Such consultations with a spirit medium might occur when a person wanted to inquire about a theft, when he wanted information about his illness or his wife's uterine affairs, or when for some reason of sentiment he might wish to talk to the spirit of a person whom he had known well in life. Such private seances, unless the matter under consultation was secret, tended to resolve into household con-claves, since other kin, neighbours and friends might drop in, being curious to know what was going on.

I participated in a number of such seances. But apart from these I had private consultations which were really secret, i.e. they took place between myself and a spirit medium alone. This was partly because the medium did not wish to have publicly known just what kind of infor-mation he was giving me—in particular when he told me the names of gods—and partly because I wished to have the opportunity to question him in the trance state about his feelings and attitudes. I found these seances very productive.

One of the most helpful mediums whom I knew in 1928–9 was Pa Tekaumata. In ordinary life he was a humorous, joking man, able to wheedle easily and of considerable charm. One of his legs was somewhat shrunken, which made him hobble—the result of a seizure when he was a young man, when he lay as if asleep with his leg in the fire until he was pulled out by his wife, cursing. He was of Ngatotiu lineage and Taumako clan, but his wife was the daughter of the Ariki Tafua, and he acted as a medium for the Tafua household on occasions. But mainly he engaged in general practice for the curing of the sick anywhere in the community. The suggestion of our private seances came from him; with the object as he put it of enabling me to talk with spirits and receive information 'straight from the spirit's mouth', so to say. Like all Tikopia, he was eager for European tools and, as was common, he invited me to a meal in order to press his claim. I went, and we all partook of food. The medium then entered the trance state. This was heralded by a quivering of his body and by a rapid sibilation. He emitted his breath through his lips, which quickly opened and closed, making a *spip, spip, spip* sound (as I recorded it—like the sound of steam escaping intermittently from a small valve). He gave me what seemed to be a rather pitiful smile—weakly, as of a person about to faint. After a few seconds his major symptoms ceased. There was left only a curious twitching movement of the right breast, apparently non-voluntary, which continued throughout the seance, and which I observed in him subsequently in trance state but never in his normal state.[1] Then the medium began to speak in his spirit phase—his voice was thicker and lower-pitched than usual. 'You desire conversation?' 'Yes.' 'You want to know about us, the spirits?' 'Yes, that is my wish.' 'It is good!' A pipe was then prepared by members of his household and given him. I provided the tobacco, it being explained to me that this particular spirit always smoked. A piece of bark-cloth was then folded in the usual style of offering, and laid by the medium's side with an announcement to the spirit; the medium then took it on his lap. He spoke again, calling me by name. 'Fosi!—that is his name, is it not?' he asked, turning to his wife and brother-in-law who were present; they answered in the affirmative. (This was the name by which the Tikopia knew me.) Then the medium plunged directly into a mass of technical information about the names of gods and spirits, their residences, their titles, etc. After a while I asked him, 'You, who are you?' he replied 'Toivai', and explained that he was a spirit child created when his ancestor Pa Tekaumera had been overcome by a female spirit. 'Where have you come from?' I asked him. 'Rangievaeva' he said (one of the heavens). 'Do you, the spirits, walk as do men or do you fly as birds do?' To this he replied about spirit

---

[1] He knew of this reaction and once in discussing it, when in his normal state, pulled at his breasts with his hands to illustrate it—apparently it was an involuntary reflex. On another occasion on emerging from trance he grasped his right breast and kneaded it saying that it ached and was numb; it had been the place where the spirit had descended upon him.

flight and gave further information on the ways of spirits. He spoke coherently, but his discussion was broken at intervals by an abrupt transition to a list of names, titles, etc., of spirits. As I recorded at the time, it looked as if the medium had in mind beforehand a subject for conversation which was present as an *idée fixe* in his trance state—hence his abrupt reversions to it. He knew, of course, that I was anxious to obtain as much information as I could about the Tikopia religious system, and he apparently had prepared himself to furnish what he could in the trance state.

This seance was ended by darkness which prevented me writing further. The spirit expressed regret and added that if I wished he would come again, this time in my own house. Uncertain of protocol I asked him, 'Is it good that you should enter in my house?' He replied 'It is good. I will enter into my vessel and we will come to your house and talk further in the ways of spirits, that the conversation may be complete.' I answered, 'Yes, that is my desire. Come to my house. Great is my wish to know of the ways of you spirits. I have learned of these things from men, but never before have I conversed with a spirit.' Abruptly the medium said 'I am going to descend,' and with a quiver of his body and a repetition of the hissing sound, he returned to his normal state. He took the bark-cloth offering from his lap, muttering 'I eat your excrement' and laid it down.

Three days later he came to my house at night unannounced. 'I am a spirit,' he said, as he stood in the doorway, and it appeared when he entered that he was in trance state. Round his neck was a knotted frond of young coconut, and at back of his belt a branchlet of *ngasu* shrub, both ritual emblems, to secure welfare, and befog the eyes of evil spirits.

On various occasions I discussed with him his physical condition during and after trance. The first time he said that he did not feel tired. When his 'father', i.e. his spirit control "Foival' entered him he did not feel tired, but when other spirits 'jumped' on to him he felt tired when they went. Sometimes he felt numbness in parts of his body afterwards. Once in coming out of trance he stretched out the leg on which he had been sitting and massaged it for some time, with a wry face. He said that he had 'pins and needles' in it; that the spirit had pressed it down. Asked if he had heard our conversation he replied that he heard only indistinctly. (I learned later that after I had gone the first time he asked his wife 'What was the conversation which Fosi had with my father?', and his wife replied 'They talked about the ways of spirits.') On another occasion he said, apparently quite sincerely, that when spirits came to him he heard the talk of the first one, but that when later spirits arrived he became confused like a crazy person—that is, he could not distinguish clearly what was said. When he was in trance on one occasion he said 'I who am sitting here am a spirit; he here does not hear the speech, his body has become confused.' In trance he consistently used 'I' for himself as spirit, 'he' for himself as man, and 'we' whenever he spoke of both together, or of spirits generally.

I had in all nine private seances with Pa Tekaumata. I received from him a great deal of interesting information, both about the Tikopia religious system in general and about his own particular spirit presentations, five of which he displayed to me.

One of these presentations was made under the name of Manutuiteata —Bird Standing in the Shadow. I give here a section of his description of this 'spirit' which indicates the type of fantasy construct often indulged in by spirit mediums in trance. He began by saying that he was not the soul of an ordinary man who had died, but a foetal spirit.

'I indeed did not die, there was miscarriage. Then I was picked up by Nau Taufiti (a female deity) and carried to Tarafare (a spirit home). There I was cleansed in the water. An umbrella palm leaf was set at my back as in the style of men and a fern frond was set on my head— the plume of Te Araifo (a god) was given me there to stick in my hair. Then Mekiteua came bearing oil, and Tangiteala, who gave me bow and arrows. (These are all gods of Vanikoro and the Santa Cruz area, linked in Tikopia with the lineage of Marinoa, from which the mother of the medium came.)

'In the summer night I descend to the ocean to shoot sharks. Then come men in their canoe; they catch the shark. When they come ashore they say "See, here it has been wounded by the arrows of a spirit!" Then I come and fly to my vessel here (the human medium). A man comes in, an elder, and makes my bark-cloth offering. I take the offering and my areca nut. They bring it and I chew betel. When I have finished my mother's brother Pa Fetauta (head of Marinoa lineage) goes and fills a pipe that I may smoke. Finished, they bring a cup of kava, which is first poured for Te Araifo. (Other libations are then poured to other gods.) Then they take up the ornaments of the Atua Fiti (Te Araifo) and place them at my sides, and then they bring me coconut oil. They bring it and I drink, drink until it is finished. I give back the cup, take up the ornaments, and I set them at my back. Then I rise and fly away. I go to Maunganefu (abode of the gods in Santa Cruz).

'I who am informing you, I am the person who gives potency (*manu*) to the kava of Pa Fetauta. What? Am I a spirit who has sinned? Have I killed men? I am a spirit who has come for conversation with you!'

The medium still in his trance role of the spirit Manutuiteata, discussed with me his role in carrying off the spirit of a man near to death. 'I come to the sick man; he is lying prone but he is not dead. I take his hand and call out "He and I will go." Then the relatives look towards me; the dying man gasps; he is on the point of death, his life has been struck down by me. So it was with the father of the present Ariki Taumako. All the gods were summoned (to cure him) but it was of no use; the gods worked, but no, no, his body disintegrated. Finally a messenger goes to Pa Tekaumata (the medium in trance is speaking of himself as human being as another person) who enters the house. Then Pa Taumako who dwells here (the present chief, son of the dying man) said "Let Manutuiteata enter among men." Thereupon I jumped hither (i.e. entered his medium). They pick up areca nut and place it at my side. I chew betel while the valuables of bark-cloth which have been spread out are piled up. I chew betel until it is finished, then I go and pick up the pile of bark-cloth. I depart. First I go to Sakura (Atua i Taumako, principal god of the dying chief) and tell him "The chief should be brought away." He says to me "Let him stay for a while." (The medium then narrates how he approaches other gods who all also object and tell him to defer for a short time the death of the chief, i.e. the carrying off of his soul.) Then I come to the world of men. I come to speak to Pa Taumako and I say "Your gods object." I sleep. In the morning I speak to the people who are assembled. "Go and prepare food. When the sun goes down I will come and we will go together, I and the chief." Then the relatives call to me "I eat your excrement." But I say I shall go to Pu Tafua Lasi (a powerful ancestor, long dead). I shall return hither, but afterwards we will go. Then I go to see Pu Tafua Lasi and he says to me "What are you fussing about? Why don't you bring him hither?" I return; the oven has been uncovered, the areca nut has been set there. Then I sit and chew betel. I chew betel until it is finished and then I call out "Eat your food quickly; he and I are going." Thereupon they call to me that they are satisfied. I grasp his hand, we go, while the relatives look on. His body has jerked. Then the relatives rush to him and wail "Oh alas! my chief!" Then we, he and I, go, while they get out the guns of the white men's style, ancient guns, and they fire a salvo. When this is over, they make a procession to perform the obsequies—the token of the chief who has died; they beat the roofs of the houses.'

This excerpt, typical of many such statements by mediums, illustrates several themes which often occur. The medium, in trance, identifies himself with a spirit of power, describes himself as supported by and conversing with other powerful spirits of the pantheon known to all Tikopia, decorated with their symbols, with ritual offerings made to him. He is served humbly by men who in ordinary life are his superiors and gives himself credit for providing the virtue of their religious rites and the material tokens of their success. In fantasy and in actual discussion he takes on the responsibility of arranging the death and soul-carrying of the chief of his clan. Yet with all this the medium's fantasy construct uses conventional Tikopia concepts and follows ordinary Tikopia norms of etiquette and morality.

These private seances were held in special conditions, relative to the ordinary Tikopia mediumistic performances. They began at the medium's suggestion and his motivation was probably a compound of desire to give me information and boast of his own powers and status, with an ultimate wish for tobacco and other goods, including a knife. The conditions of extended dialogue between us made for much more 'free formulation' than was likely in any ordinary mediumistic performance. No set patterns of reply were expected from him as in many mediumistic rituals. Consequently, the medium was much freer to let his mind range over the whole field. This allowed some comparison of his personal imagery with the framework generally assigned by others to the Tikopia supernatural world. Again, much of the material Pa Tekaumata gave me was in the form of specific information about spirits in a discursive, conversational way, whereas in an ordinary seance there was much less talk about the character and doings of spirits and more of their relation to day-to-day affairs. These private seances helped to demonstrate to me the flexibility of seance conditions in Tikopia, and the degree of individual variability.[1] They also indicate how a medium in his trance state builds up an elaborate imaginative construction in which he assigns to himself a role of power. It is a reasonable inference that such fantasy constructions allow the medium to express his desire for self assertion which his social standing and the institutional framework of the community deny to him in ordinary affairs, but which can thus be expressed harmlessly in a manner which does not conflict with existing social privileges.

MY TALKS WITH THE DEAD

Whereas in 1928–9 other spirit mediums came often to see me and talked about their affairs, none but Pa Tekaumata actually came in a state of trance. But in 1952 most mediums with whom I talked entered the trance state at some point or other specifically for further conversations with me. It occurred to me that perhaps the heightened tensions between Christians and pagans on the subject of mediumship gave these mediums an added sensibility in talking about their profession, and in this way increased their tendency to trance entry.

I have discussed earlier the onset of mediumship in Pa Nukurotoi. By 1952 he had become baptized, but I discovered that he occasionally still practised as a spirit medium. After various ordinary conversations,

[1] Seances were not the only occasion on which I saw a person in a state of trance or proximity thereto—for example, Pa Rangifuri, affected by a ritual recital, was threatened with an attack. (*Work of the Gods*, 1967, p. 298.)

I was invited to go to his house and talk with the spirit. I went, and gave him a short knife, with which he was very pleased. He put on a new red calico waistcloth and adjusted it very carefully. As he sat on the mat his hands locked together and began to tremble. He gave a kind of sighing sound—*whish*—and a snort, and this was repeated twice. His hands trembled more violently, his shoulders moved up and down alternately, with writhings. I saw the muscles moving on his sides and thorax. Then he spoke (in a trance), 'Are things well with you?' 'They are well.' 'This is my day on which I have come. I have come with fish. I have just come today.' I asked his name. He replied, 'My name is Veterei, and my name among the spirits is Tafakifenua (roughly equivalent to "treading down the lands").' He then described himself as the friend of the captain of the Mission vessel, the *Southern Cross*. (This was correct; I knew from the former master of the vessel, Captain H. Burgess, that Pa Veterei had been a friend of his.) I said that I had heard of him, but that we had not met when I was in Tikopia before. He replied 'I was then absent. I was dead.' He said that he lived in Ngarumea with his namesake and grandfather (or great-great-grandfather of the same name) Pu Veterei. He said that he went travelling around among the islands and among the dwellings of spirits. His son said to the medium 'Tell him (i.e. me) that you do good work.' He did not answer directly but murmured 'I am not smoking', whereupon I gave him a stick of tobacco. Prompted by his son he said 'Thank you' in English, and then asked 'Is that white man's talk?' I asked him if he knew English. He said he had forgotten it all when he died. (This illustrates the consistency of the medium's presentation. Pa Veterei had known some English, but Pa Nukurotoi knew none, hence, he had to account for the discrepancy.) He said that he came only with fish and not for healing. He said that the land was hungry—it was a time of great food shortage. I asked him weren't the spirits sorry for the land? He replied that they had not got fish under their control, only he had. I asked him who was responsible for the recent hurricane? He said 'The God of the Church, prompted by the chiefs.' He said, 'Because the chiefs do not speak correctly. One chief speaks properly but another speaks witchcraft. Hence the hurricane struck.' He accused the Ariki Kafika of this, and defended his view by saying that he himself, Pa Veterei, sprang from Kafika on his mother's side, and that he picked up the gossip about these things in Taufare-i-Kafika, the Kafika spirit home. In this kind of spirits' club he had heard that the Ariki had appealed to them for help in destroying people. Then he described the Atua i Kafika, a principal pagan deity, as having four eyes, two in front and two behind. (At this point the medium turned to a small child who was interfering and said, 'Go, go away.') His body was black or red, depending upon the occasion; his hair was not long. He said that the Atua i Kafika went in the sky making lightning. Then the medium *qua* spirit appealed to me, 'Can I go now? Are we finished?' I asked first if he supported or opposed Christianity. He said 'The Church which stands in this land, I confirm its works. The one God who is strong in the skies is the God of the Church.' Then he said suddenly, 'I am going, friend.' He tautened his hands, there was a shuddering of his shoulders and a series of snorting sounds, *whish, whish, whish* . . ., while his shoulders moved up and down. Then he made a kind of lifting and easing movement with his shoulders and relaxed. He smoothed down his arms, removed his red calico, took the water bottle and drank deeply.

I asked him how he felt. He said 'My shoulders have been trodden upon. They ache, but after a while they will be all right. When the spirit comes, he does not stay long. He came for our talk and usually, when he has smoked his pipe, he goes. The spirit comes into the arms, shoulders, diaphragm and head of the medium, but it is only the arms and shoulders which are sore, because he descends upon them.' (Some mediums said that on the first descent of the spirit there was a feeling of the right shoulder being very heavy, of an enormous weight on it, and of pressure on the head similar to a headache. Likewise, according to them the spirit departed from the right shoulder and from the head.) I asked him if he heard the talk we had been having. He replied 'Oh, I heard because he spoke from here'—and he felt his throat. 'Do you get a singing in the ears like waves?' I asked—a common description by other mediums. He said 'Yes, the wind of the spirits.' The medium continued by saying, 'The spirit is very sorry that you are going. (I was leaving the island soon.) Great is his affection. Great is his affection to the whole land. Great is his affection—he brings in fish for food. All the dwellings of the spirits obey him completely. He goes and tells them that there should be fish for food.' He added that the spirit of Pa Veterei had come the night before and wanted me to visit him to hear that the fish were coming today. But (prudently) his son did not summon me at once, thinking it better to leave it until daylight.

This seance, like most others, fitted into certain patterns. On the one hand, the medium had evidently felt a desire to talk to me, expressed at another level by his going into the trance state and asking for me to be summoned. The association of the trance with the coming of fish was either a long shot or a shrewd prognostication (since a shoal of fish did actually appear that morning); but it gave the medium an opportunity of boasting of his power. The medium had his own trance routine. As with most mediums the trance was relatively short—lasting about the length of time it took to smoke a pipe which, in Tikopia, is small-bowled. The medium was obviously rather disturbed at my prolongation of the seance, and finally his earlier conditioning proved too much for him and he abruptly terminated our interview on the spirit plane.

As mentioned earlier, one of the uses of Tikopia spirit mediumship is to allow people to hold conversations with the purported spirits of dead kin and friends. Such an experience is interesting and somewhat disconcerting to an outsider since the personality change in the medium is apt to be sufficient to give the impression that one really is talking to someone else. One such experience, not without its moving side, was that in which I had a seance with the widow of my old friend Pae Sao during which as a medium she presented him in spirit form. I went to see her at her house in Uta. After some preliminary talk we came to the question of mediumship, and she admitted that she was a practising medium, although she had denied this to me earlier. She said she had been startled and shy, otherwise she would have let her familiar spirit appear to discuss the matter with me. While I was writing, I heard something like a hiccough repeated.[1] I looked up to see her regarding me intently with a fixed smile. She said 'You have come', then at once in the presentation of her familiar spirit, her 'son', she plunged into a recital of how she first began as a spirit medium. After a recital of the various spirits who came to her in her first series of seances, she began to speak to me of a variety of matters concerning the spirit world. Here her talk at length became rather disjointed and she began to press the claims of the lineage of Sao in very much the same terms as her husband used to do, arguing that the prime god of Sao was the origin of things in Tikopia and the source of the gods. Like him too she stressed the ignorance of Tikopia in general about this. Later I said I would like to talk to the father of her familiar, that is Pae Sao himself—knowing that his spirit was supposed to appear in her. Her familiar asked 'Shall I descend?' I said 'Yes', and the medium then passed out of her familiar phase.[2] She composed herself, then after a brief period of concentration and looking vacant, gave something between a hiccough and a gulp, there was a contraction of her chest muscles and a settling down of her body. A moment of silence followed, then a second hiccough, then again contraction and settling down. The process seemed to consist essentially in a tensing of the muscles lasting for five seconds or so, and then a relaxation. (The movements were very similar, except for the sound,

[1] Traditionally, female mediums adopted a different technique of trance entry than did men. In conformity with their ordinary sitting position the feet were stretched out in front, one foot crossed over the other, hands clasped and resting on knees. Unlike men, they did not rattle their hands on the floor mats, nor did they shriek but gaped in an expression described by the Tikopia themselves as being like a yawn. In recent years the techniques of men and women in trance seem to have approximated more closely.

[2] There are resemblances between phenomena of Tikopia spirit mediumship and descriptions of multiple personality (e.g. C. H. Thigpen and H. M. Checkley, *The Three Faces of Eve*, London, 1957; cf. also Evelyn Lancaster and James Polling, *Strangers in my Body*, London, 1958). One resemblance is in the way in which spirit (personality) B can be reached only through spirit (personality) A, which must be the form first assumed by the individual.

with those by which her brother also entered the trance state.) Then the medium was ready for speech in the Pae Sao phase.

In the first part of the seance Nau Sao had addressed me as father since her familar spirit was a titular son to her and Pae Sao; later, in the Pae Sao phase, she addressed me as brother. She greeted me 'Oh! my brother! it is good that you have come back to this land.' We looked at each other hard for a moment. Then I did what was expected of me, went forward and we pressed noses in greeting, as I used to do with my old friend when alive. (I noted, however, that the widow did not touch me with her hand, a customary female reticence.) Then she began a recital in a rather deeper, firmer voice than before, with no great change of personality but a rather more assured bearing. Speaking as Pae Sao, she told a rapid story to the effect that he had not died simply because of sickness. He had gone to see the Ariki Taumako who had been ill, and they were talking about aeroplanes which had been seen overhead. Said the chief to him 'I shall not get well.' Said Pae Sao 'Then I will come with you. If you go there is no man of rank who will look after me. People can throw stones at the side of my house' (a figurative way of expressing his lack of protection). The chief said 'Oh, do not talk like that, stay and look after our son' (meaning the chief's son and heir). Pae Sao reiterated his statement that he was a stranger in a dwelling of another clan with no man of rank other than the chief to protect him.[1] He returned home. That night the chief felt a chill and three days later Pae Sao felt a chill too. He was carried to two ritual elders in turn and then taken home, but despite all efforts he did not get better. On several occasions his wife's familar spirit was summoned through her trance state to come and give prognosis. On the last occasion the spirit said 'This is your night, father, your eyes shall sleep this night.' The spirit was right. Pae Sao died the same day as the Ariki Taumako, while folk were wailing for the chief. The funeral rites were then divided and the body was taken to Uta. The Ariki Tafua heard the news and came over—'But by the time he had arrived I was buried; he sat and wailed at the side of the grave.' All this was described in fast, vivid style. I was then told how after five days, when the ritual was completed, his soul and that of the chief went together to their ancestors. The Ariki Taumako then said to Pae Sao, 'Let's go shooting about the skies', so they went rushing through the heavens. Then Pae Sao divided his abode in heaven to give a dwelling to the Ariki Taumako, who reciprocated from his dwelling under the sea. Pae Sao then inquired whether his son and successor had treated me properly; I assured him that this was so. After some more general talk I said I must return home and the Pae Sao phase ended. One of the women sitting by said it was good to see the two of us talking like that. I said that I had hoped to see Pae Sao

[1] *Social Change in Tikopia*, pp. 221–3; *History and Traditions of Tikopia*, pp. 112–13.

alive and talk to him in the world of men, but failing that it was good to have talked with him in the world of spirits.

In the Pae Sao phase his widow stressed how he had waited for me to return to Tikopia—hence the compulsive recital of the reasons why he had died and not been here on my return. In the Pae Sao phase she repeated several of his characteristic expressions and reference was made to a Canarium almond which had been meant to provide nuts for me—which I had greatly liked—but which a storm had partly broken down. But despite various reminiscences of Pae Sao, I would not regard it as a close mimesis. This woman was possessed in trance state by at least three spirits, all male—of an ancestor, a husband and a son generation. I did not get the impression that this was an assertion of masculinity but rather the selection of roles, sex indifferent, which gave some prospect of power and influence and attracted some attention.

MY TALKS WITH SPIRIT CHILDREN

An interesting series of private seances arose in connection with a Tikopia belief that my illness in 1929 had been the result of action by a malevolent spirit. My house was not far from a pool believed to be frequented by a powerful female spirit known as Pufine-i-Vaisiku. She was believed to overcome men and generate children from them in the spirit world, with the result that they fell ill. Some time after I had returned to Tikopia in 1952 I was asked about my former illness and my 'sons' in the spirit world. Surprised, I made further enquiry and learnt that this was a widely believed view. Later a neighbour, Pa Ngatotiu, asked me if I wanted to talk to his deceased father, i.e. a spirit, and learn the names of my children in the spirit world. He said it was agreed that I had been 'overcome' (*toa*; *tafina*) in 1929.

Later I went to his house and we had a private seance. This began almost without sign. The man, who was a ritual elder as well as a medium, sat silent and began to chew betel. He had sent his nephew out of the house saying that the two of us were going to talk. He put a thick wad of betel in his mouth, then gave a couple of snorts or gulps and made a long slow brushing movement to clear the lime from his hands. As he did so a slow smile spread across his face. He said 'You wanted to speak to me?' He was now representing his dead father, whose name he said was Stretched Out On the Reef (Takoto-i-te-Akau); this was his name in the spirit world. As our conversation went on from time to time he knotted his hands in front of him and tensed a shoulder; a muscle in his left cheek twitched spasmodically. His speech was much as usual but rather deeper and more slurred. His eyes were rather wide open and had a wild, staring look as if he were slightly drunk. (He explained to me that the eyes are the eyes of the man, that the spirit used the physical body of the medium, his eyes and his tongue, but that the voice is different, it is the voice of the spirit.) After a few preliminaries I asked him if he and my old friend Pae Sao had died together. He said no, that he had died first, that this god Semoana had wished him as 'a seating mat', hence had come and carried him off. He then asked me if I wished to know the names of my 'sons'. He said they were working and helping their mother Pufine-i-Vaisiku. Their names were Rakei-Suru-Mero (the younger) and Saro-i-te-Vai (the elder). He said they were bachelors, young and bearded and, like all the children of spirits, had grown very quickly. They did not speak English (the medium himself did not). The spirit explained that the speech which we Europeans used was not known among the (Tikopia) spirits. He said that my 'sons' were well disposed towards me, that when I went in the vicinity of the pool to ease myself I should call on their names and they would protect me. The spirit pointed out also that Pufine-i-Vaisiku had expended much energy on rectifying the minds of my children (she was 'dead' from her work) and hence she wished the gift of a bark-cloth skirt as offering and recompense. I agreed to present a fathom of white calico to her on the day on which the temple of Pa Ngatotiu would be reconsecrated, since she was worshipped there. The seance ended with two loud gasps from the medium and a lifting and then relaxing of his body. He resumed his normal state and sank back. On my questioning him he said that his body was not limp, that the spirits came on to his shoulders, indifferently on the right or the left, but did not go on his head. They spread over the body but did not lodge in his belly. If one did so that would be bad.

About ten days later I had another seance with this man, who said that his dead father would come first and then, if I wished, one of 'my sons' would come. The trance began with the same movements as before, and the spirit spoke saying that he had come first to enquire whether I wished to speak with my 'son' who, as a spirit child, was very shy indeed. The spirit said that he would chew betel but he preferred to reserve the few areca nuts which were available for my 'son', his friend, since 'betel is absent among men' (owing to famine). So I went and fetched tobacco for him to smoke. After another warning about the sensitivity of my son he said 'I am about to descend.' An expulsion of breath announced the departure of the spirit. The medium chewed areca nut in silence, then gave a gasping sound twice repeated like a constricted cough. This was the entry of my 'son', Rakei-Suru-Mero (Adorned with Red Calico). He said 'You asked after the two of us.' I replied 'Yes. When I came here I didn't know of you and so I have asked after you.' He warned me that the place where our house stood was evil. Many familar spirits were around, the attendants of Pufine-i-Vaisiku. They overcame men. He said that he and his brother had had their minds rectified (worked over) by Pufine, and that he had affection for me. He said he came at night (invisibly of course) and looked on me while I was asleep. He said that he had expressed to his friend, the dead father of Pa Ngatotiu, his wish to see me and that he and his brother attended the kava rites of Pa Ngatotiu.

All this, uttered in a gentle, timid voice, was a preface for a request for a cloth offering (*maro*) for him and his brother, a request hard to refuse in the circumstances. But I did refuse on the plea that my cloth was exhausted and I did not know beforehand that he and his brother were here. He said that I had given out cloth to plenty of ordinary people. After some discussion we compromised on my offer of some fish hooks, and I reminded him of my promise of an adze to Pa Ngatotiu.

A fortnight later I had a further seance with my 'son' who entered the medium with a couple of gasping grunts and a heave of the chest. My 'son' asked me when I was leaving the island and said that when I died I was to come back to Tikopia and my dwelling would be prepared by my 'sons'. He then received my present of three large and four small fish hooks—asking me if there were not any other size available as well! He said that when I was ill on my former visit my two 'sons' were not responsible. (A spirit child is often credited with the illness of its mortal parent.) I asked why didn't he and his brother look after me when I fell ill this time—from influenza? He said it was a sickness from abroad; he saw it rising like smoke, that spirits themselves fell ill of it, they coughed and coughed. 'Did they die?' I asked. 'No', he replied, 'they became ill and then got well.'

This was a relation conducted on two levels. At the level of spirit description, the medium in trance state and I conducted our conversation as if he really were a third party, in this case my putative spirit 'son'. On the realistic plane the situation was explicable in terms of five elements in combination: my physical illness in 1929; the Tikopia belief that such illness was due to spirit causes; their belief in the sexuality and procreative power of spirits; the tendency to suggestibility of the medium in 1952; and his interest in sharing in the distribution of my goods. The medium, in ordinary life a helpful neighbour who had given me much ritual information, was himself receiving an adze as a present. But doubtless semi-consciously he felt that he might share in other goods as well. The situation was 'softened up' by him telling me in the guise of his dead father of the interest of my 'sons' in me, and the way in which their spirit mother had prepared them to look upon me with favour. The stress upon the sensitivity of my 'sons', that if spoken to harshly they would go away and weep, clearly was meant to draw off my anger if I should want to protest too much about the suggested gifts. On the other hand, this must not be meant to imply that the medium was practising any conscious tactic to obtain more gifts. He did not begin this story of my 'sons'; I learnt it from others and he was brought in only later. Moreover, the offering which I made to Pufine did not go into circulation as an ordinary calico garment, but was displayed ritually and then put away as a perpetual offering to her. The increase of wealth to the medium was thus primarily in the spiritual sphere and the requests for wealth were conformable with the system of religious ideas rather than with the system of ordinary utilization of consumer goods. The asking for offerings by the spirits, i.e. by the medium in trance state, was then not just a trick to get more calico for men to wear. The psychology of the medium was of a prestige-recognition kind rather than of a material-acquisition kind. By his assumption of different phases of personality—'spirits'—and by having these recognized individually by me and others, the medium thus gained a kind of enlargement of personality. Moreover, there was also the element of completion of ritual patterns of ideas in that a spirit of any importance has ritual offerings made to it. With this was linked the notion of completion of social pattern in that fathers make gifts to their 'sons'.

REWARDS OF SPIRIT MEDIUMSHIP

I can now proceed to a more analytic interpretation of these phenomena in social and in psychological terms.

In traditional Tikopia situations the rewards of mediumship were small. When a medium passed into a trance state it was normal to offer him bark-cloth, food and betel material. On standard ritual occasions neither the food nor the valuables were retained by the medium; they were returned into household stock or into ritual custody after announcement to the spirit. The medium commonly received betel to chew and sometimes kava or coconut milk to drink. Some spirits expressed a preference for smoking tobacco. But the amounts so consumed were usually much the same as could be obtained by an ordinary member of the household and could not be regarded as any substantial incentive to enter the trance state. Occasionally the amounts of betel consumed were very large—as when several spirits in succession entered the medium; the result was that when the seance was over the medium might feel so ill that he had to vomit. When a medium performed a therapeutic role and tended a sick person he did receive a contribution for his professional services. This consisted of a basket of food with perhaps a pair of sprouting coconuts or a piece of bark-cloth; in modern times he almost certainly received some tobacco. Those mediums in greatest demand received a significant income from their services. But this was never so large as to relieve the medium from ordinary agriculture or other work. I think that the prospect of a gift of tobacco and of a more valuable article, such as a length of calico or a knife, undoubtedly was part of the inducement to spirit mediums in stimulating them to engage in private discussions with me in trance state. But these benefits were of the same general order as were obtained by many other persons in the Tikopia community with whom I was involved in improving my understanding of Tikopia ritual and belief. Entering the trance state was only one way in which people could take advantage of access to my wealth, and all these informants were mediums of some standing when I arrived.

Spirit mediumship as an avenue to status and prestige raises more complex questions. As I have pointed out elsewhere,[1] the Tikopia system of spirit mediumship partly supported the institutional religious structure and partly provided a parallel route of access to what were conceived to be traditional gods and spirits. Spirit mediums then could play a role both inside and outside the formal religious system and to the degree that they operated outside it they could be thought to seek prestige and status thereby. To be a spirit medium offered a way of obtaining a position in the social structure which a person could not reach by hereditary means. Now it is true that a spirit medium who was in frequent demand to visit the sick and had acquired a reputation for his therapeutic powers did acquire personal prestige. And the spirit medium who, as a vessel of a principal god, entered Marae in the panoply of scarlet turmeric pigment and leaf decoration, struck awe into those who saw him. But the Tikopia distinguished fairly clearly between the power of the spirit, and the personality of the medium; it was the former and not the latter that tended to be credited with social prestige. Again and again in a public or domestic rite I have seen a medium in trance state as the centre of attention being treated with great respect, his every word listened to with care. But before and after it he was simply a man, even a junior member of the household, and treated as such with no respect whatsoever. Some of them (bachelors, poor shiftless commoners, old widows) definitely carried much less prestige than many other folk who were never mediums.

In so far as one would argue that there must be some gains out of being a spirit medium in Tikopia society, it would seem that the gains were to be sought less in the everyday social condition of the medium and more in the trance state itself. The attitudes here comprise several different components. One is the sense of social obligation. Normally every major lineage needed to have a medium of its own to present the entry of the major gods and spirits of the lineage at specific rituals. With this in view senior members of the lineage would often encourage a member who showed signs of trance or allied behaviour to enter into this state in order, as they thought, that they might hold communication with the god or ancestor concerned. There was then distinct

[1] *Essays on Social Organization and Values*, 1964, pp. 252–6.

public pressure on persons who showed themselves suggestible to assume a mediumistic role. Another component would seem to be the opportunity offered by the trance state of displaying aggression to members of one's social group. In the trance state it was the medium who set the tone of the conversation. He could be brusque, commanding, chiding, and he would be answered softly and with deference. It is a plausible hypothesis that there were satisfactions to be gained, especially by junior members of a group, in assuming such a role even temporarily.

But display of aggression by the medium was not invariable and his opinions in trance state were sometimes even challenged.[1] What he did in most circumstances was to resolve a situation of some anxiety and ambiguity. On the formal ritual occasion the entry of a medium into trance state, even without his pronouncement, served to validate the rite, to reaffirm the benevolent interest of the god or ancestor concerned. When someone had been lost at sea or was ill, statements of the medium were such as to decrease uncertainty and indicate a practical course of action. It is my hypothesis that this resolution of uncertainty and the decision-making role were among the most important features of Tikopia —and indeed much other—spirit mediumship. The opportunity which this role gave for assumption of control of a social situation, even though temporarily, was in my view one of the inducements for entry to the mediumistic state.

What would seem to be an exemplification of this, if in a somewhat obscure way, was the desire of certain people to become spirit mediums. Most people subject to trance seem to have been taken by surprise by their condition and not to have sought it. But a few people appear to have sought a medium's role. It was explained to me by one of them that the basis of this desire lay in the wish to be able to cure members of their household and lineage who might become ill. But the assumption of such a role had its social risks. If recovery of patients did not on the whole tend to follow the spirit medium's ministrations, then he might be regarded as inadequate and lose prestige. In 1952 I asked a medium who of those in Ravenga was the most effective in curing the sick. He did not commit himself very far, but gave me names of two men who were very effective. As regards those who were rejected by the people because they lost their patients, he said there were none at present, but did cite a man recently dead who he said had 'bewitching lips'. When he uttered his formulae some of his patients got well but others died, so he was left to practise in his own household alone.

It is significant to examine the social category of people who became spirit mediums in Tikopia. As mentioned earlier, mediums were to be found among men of all social grades. But children did not become mediums—if one asked why one was told simply 'because they were

[1] *Essays on Social Organization and Values*, 1964, pp. 72–4.

not grown up; only adults become spirit mediums'. It was said too that girls never became spirit mediums before menstruation. On the other hand, both women and men became spirit mediums, but women did not go into trance state during their monthly periods, which appeared to vary between two and five days. According to the Tikopia view, the spirit waited until the time when the belly of the woman was in proper condition, was empty. If a female medium was summoned to attend a sick person when she was menstruating, she refused with the explanation that she was in a condition unpleasing to the spirit. When, however, a woman had passed the climacteric she could continue as a spirit medium without this handicap. In other words, to act as a medium and assume the requisite personality change, individuals had to be physically mature. And while they had to observe no taboos on sex intercourse, the regular demands of the female cycle were held to impede trance effectiveness.

Now what was especially interesting was that while, with very few exceptions,[1] female spirits were believed not to enter male mediums, male spirits could enter female mediums freely. Such a male spirit was thought not actually to enter the body of the woman, in particular to reach her vital organs, but simply to go and stand on her shoulder. This sex asymmetry in mediumship was consonant with the fact that whereas men had ample ritual roles available to them in the Tikopia religious system, women had not. Consequently, it is a reasonable interpretation that the assumption of male roles in the trance state gave women an opportunity for self-assertion—or at least the illusion of self-assertion—which men did not require, and which the assumption of female roles would not for the most part have given them. In other words, women became men, but men became sons of chiefs and other men of power, hardly ever women.

TRANCE BEHAVIOUR AS IDIOM OF EXPRESSION

The phenomena of spirit mediumship may be regarded as a kind of idiom for the expression of ideas and emotions about social status, and about personal and social crises. Issues of both public and of private concern could be expressed through its agency. When a person had been lost at sea, for instance, after a period word often came through a spirit medium in a trance that the person had died, either at sea or on a foreign shore. This news was uttered when the spirit medium became possessed either by the spirit of the dead person or by some other spirit who narrated the alleged circumstances. Now what was really being expressed here was a kind of consensus of public opinion. As the months had passed without news it came to be generally believed that the person

---

[1] Pufine ma in Porima and Makupu in Sao, very powerful, were believed to be the only female spirits to enter male mediums.

who had been lost must have died—even though his closest relatives would not admit this. What the spirit medium in trance did was to resolve this situation, declare the death and thus clear the way for a public celebration of the funeral. Spirit mediumship was not the sole mechanism for such resolution; a dream by one of those closely concerned might provide an equivalent catalyst[1]; but trance pronouncement seemed most common.

More private personal issues could also be resolved by the same means. I give three instances of different types. The first was the illness of Pa Ngatotiu (see above p. 319). 'I became ill, my belly was sore and I had acrid urine. It was awful. I tried and tried, but no, I felt I was dying. Then my father (who was dead) came to me among men and the illness was severed and disappeared.' I asked Pa Ngatotiu whether when he was ill he dreamed of his father (he said no); and had he called upon him (he said yes). 'I used to call upon my father to come and look at me that I might get well.' But he explained he just called upon him, he did not spread offerings and he did not expect his father to come into his body. But, he added, 'the spirit wished to come to men', and so used his son as a medium. Pa Ngatotiu said that his father came to him out of affection; seeing that his son might die he came of his own volition. He did not come at once, he took two days during which the invalid's body twitched in his shoulders. On the third day the spirit spoke through the invalid's mouth to the assembled relatives. When this happened they prepared an oven and when the food was cooked filled a basket with it and added bark-cloth as an offering to the spirit. 'These were his things, to go with him to the realm of the gods. They were offered, oil was reached down and smeared on the chest because having gone to the realm of the gods he had descended again among men, and so his valuables were prepared that they might go with him to the gods.'

The second case is that of a man, Pa Sukuporu, who was a spirit medium but who became a Christian. He used to be possessed by the god Tangaroa, the tutelary of his lineage. But when he became baptized the god departed from him. On his taking this decision for baptism he summoned his kinsfolk and an oven was prepared. This was to be the celebration for parting from his god. He entered into the trance state and the spirits spoke. At first they objected to his decision but finally agreed that they would go and dwell in their own place and not return to him. However, they still really objected to his having deserted them and they made him ill in a sickness from which he was cured by the Mission teachers. Even then one of his gods, the eel god, afflicted his womenfolk by producing miscarriages, and his daughter was seized by the spirits and became ill. Finally he gave orders for another house to be

[1] For such a case see my *Elements of Social Organization*, 1951, pp. 61–73.

built nearby for the women to sleep in so that they could be free of the spirits' attention. The eel god, who came to Tikopia with his ancestor, is still under the house, but nowadays is benign.

The third case was the most dramatic of all. In 1929 a son of the Ariki Tafua fell ill and the chief became very disturbed about this. He had been baptized as a Christian, but this had not meant that he had abandoned all belief in the reality of his traditional gods and spirits. He regarded the illness of his son as due to the action of some malicious spirits, and seeing his son get weaker and imagining that he would die he attempted suicide by hanging (p. 138). This was a despairing act given the rationalization of shaming his traditional gods for not looking after his family. When his suicide attempt had been prevented (and it was never quite clear how far the chief had hoped it would be prevented) he addressed his gods, reproaching them for wanting to take the life of a young man while he himself, an old man, still remained. According to Tikopia belief, in response to this reproach the gods allowed his son to recover, but made the chief himself ill. From this illness he was in turn in Tikopia eyes saved by the effort of his peers, the Ariki Kafika and Ariki Taumako, both pagan chiefs, who visited him and laid hands on him. In the course of the rites which accompanied these proceedings the Ariki Tafua, who was a spirit medium, twice entered the trance state, and in spirit form gave utterance to reassuring statements. But the day before he became ill he had also had a trance and in spirit form spoke to the assembled company, saying 'Who is the man who told the chief that he should hang himself?' The spirit appeared to be very angry. His eldest son and another senior man crawled across the floor of the house to him, and pressed their noses one to each of his knees in token of obeisance. Then they and all the others present in the house assured the spirit that he was mistaken, that it had been the idea of the chief himself alone that he should commit suicide, that no one else had advised him to do so. At last the spirit appeared to be appeased and the trance ended.

In attempting an interpretation of these events, I think one must necessarily use some psychological as well as sociological concepts. My use of them is tentative, and is not in order to conduct a psychological analysis, but to provide some basic assumptions which will render the sociological analysis clearer and more meaningful.

Each of these three cases appeared to involve some conflict and was concerned with physical illness at some stage. In the first case the person himself became physically ill and in his distress invoked the spirit of his dead father, that is, called upon an authority principle which he regarded as external to himself. Consciously he was not expecting more than external aid—he said so himself. But the effect upon his own psyche in conjunction with his anxiety was so powerful that unwittingly he

327

underwent some transformation of personality, in effect using his own suggestibility as a force of therapeutic value. Whether his illness had psychosomatic components or whether a physical cycle had been in progress and his body had accomplished its own healing it is not possible to say. But it does seem probable that resolution of the man's illness was assisted by his own psychic transformation into another personality which assumed authoritative powers suggesting restoration to health, and had curative effect.

In the second case the man's conversion to Christianity had clearly left him with regrets, doubts and fears relating to his continuing belief in the reality of his traditional gods. The conflict was exemplified in his parting seance (not an unusual Tikopia custom) in which in his trance state the resistant and anxious elements of his mind were able to come to the surface and express themselves freely. They took the form of spirit objections to the man's desertion of his traditional faith. Restatement of his conviction of the rightness of his decision emerged in final spirit statements that they agreed to depart from him and come to him no more. But this reassurance evidently did not carry complete conviction. An ensuing illness was interpreted as due to the traditional influences and only the intervention of the Christian teachers, to whom he had transferred his authority notions, produced a cure.

The third case was an instance in which conflict in a chief's mind between his conversion to Christianity and his continuing belief in the power of his traditional gods was focused on the illness of his son. His attempted suicide was both an acknowledgement of the validity of his traditional beliefs and a protest against them. I was not present at this incident, but I had arrived in the house soon after the chief's attempted suicide and, without knowing the cause, noted the grave, disturbed air of those present and the old man's fiercely gloomy attitude. In his ordinary state he and others spoke of his attempt at suicide as his own conscious measure to compel the gods to save his son. But it seemed clear that the situation had been one of mental struggle, and that he had been 'in two minds' about making this attempt to kill himself. When his inhibitions were removed in the trance state then his reaction was to deny personal responsibility and to suggest that the reasons for his actions lay with others, not with himself. This issue of responsibility was then publicly debated and clarified, so that he accepted it—possibly as a tribute to his status. What the entry into the trance state did was then to allow the old chief, by objectifying himself as a separate entity, to bring to the surface his own reservations about this act. In the debate, when in trance state, he could separate himself to some degree from his ordinary personality and resolve a question which had been troubling him. His major conflict was still unresolved, and only after the pagan chiefs, representing the authority of the system to which he formerly adhered, came and laid hands upon him did he feel free in trance state to express his reassurance.

What emerges in all these cases is that Tikopia spirit mediumship provided a kind of idiom for expression of personal anxieties and conflicts. It is uncertain whether one can speak of dissociation of personality in each case or not, but the trance state by allowing temporary suspension of some aspects of ordinary consciousness, gave an opportunity for some of the submerged elements of the personality to be made articulate, externalized and brought to public attention. In the trance experience some apparent resolution of the difficulty was usually achieved, even if only in a formal way. Empirically the person having the trance experience appeared to benefit physically from this.

In studying such trance phenomena one can hardly avoid making reference to the mental life of the persons concerned. But this mental life is clearly linked intimately with their social life. The problems, anxieties and conflicts in which these subjects were involved were made manifest in and created by social situations. Major social issues and major principles and norms of social structure were the pivots of the personal problems. Recognition of authority and responsibility in the kinship role of father and in the political role of chief, conflict of interest between the traditional system of the pagan religion and the advancing system of Christianity were among the cardinal elements in the three cases cited. The idiom in which these personal phenomena of anxiety, conflict, illness and recovery was couched, was one in which the physical and psychological syndrome of trance was described in terms of social constructs, including notions of spirit powers and spirit action. What is so striking about the Tikopia situation is that such personal trance phenomena, expressed in the idiom of spirit mediumship, had been incorporated by the society into its system of therapy. The trance phenomena were so construed that the process of finding the solution to personal problems had been converted to social use and made to serve the needs of others. Moreover, the Tikopia, by giving persons subject to psychological disturbances a social job to do, enabled them to use the therapy they purported to apply to others to find their own self expression.

CHAPTER 15

THE FATE OF THE SOUL[1]

(1955)

We are assembled here to do honour to James George Frazer. More than any other man of his time he was responsible for the general development of public interest in anthropology in this country. Yet he is not merely the laymen's anthropologist. Not only the breadth of his learning and the grace of his writing, but also his perception of basic motives in human thought and endeavour have given him an enduring place in anthropological science.

Frazer collected and examined a great mass of evidence on concepts of the fate of the soul—primarily in Oceania—in lectures delivered between 1911 and 1922, and published in his three-volume work, *The Belief in Immortality and the Worship of the Dead*. This massive work is full of fascinating data. The coverage is encyclopaedic, and the occasional generalization—as, for instance, about the Maori belief in immortality as a sanction for private property and for the status of chiefs—anticipates much modern treatment of social relations. But Frazer was primarily an ethnographer interested in the accumulation and classification of social facts. Personally a most reticent man, he was averse to much theoretical construction—or to what he recognized as such. Hence to the modern social anthropologist, who is avid of theory, revels in abstractions, and is highly sensitized to the influence of personality upon material, Frazer offers no clear lead. One can read him with profit—but one must supply one's own framework.

My framework in this lecture is for the most part that common to all social anthropologists. But in dealing with such a delicate subject as ideas of the soul, about which there is such diversity of view, my approach must be to some extent a personal one.

Goethe, in 1834, expressed the keynote of many human ideas on this subject when he said that he had a firm conviction that the human spirit is a being that cannot be destroyed. Just a century ago, in a general review of the natural history of Man, James Cowles Prichard, who may be described as a proto-anthropologist, said more cumbrously 'there is nothing more remarkable in the habitudes of mankind, and in their manner of existence in various parts of the world, than a reference,

[1] This Frazer Lecture, delivered in Cambridge on March 7, 1955, was published in 1955 by the Syndics of the Cambridge University Press. A modified presentation of this theme was also given as a public lecture in the Department of Anthropology, University of Chicago, in May 1955.

which is everywhere more or less distinctly perceptible, to a state of existence to which they feel themselves to be destined after the termination of their visible career.'[1]

Prichard was concerned here as elsewhere with evidence to demonstrate the common origin of mankind. But granting an almost universal interest in life after death, it is the variation rather than the uniformity in such beliefs which seems so striking. E. C. Dewick (in a book on primitive Christian eschatology some forty years ago) has pointed out that primitive peoples, as contrasted with civilized, are concerned with individual eschatology rather than cosmic eschatology. It is the fate of souls in their own society, not the fate of the world which interests them. Even within this sphere there is much further variety, as Tylor, Boas, and Frazer himself have helped to show. In all this there are several points of special interest that I want to make.

The first is that in most primitive communities it is continuity rather than immortality that is assumed. In some societies, like the Manus, there is provision for termination of the soul. In most, it is believed to endure, but there is no positive notion of eternity as such.

Secondly, as a rule the fate of the soul is not associated with any concept of rewards or punishments after death. The doctrine of retribution on a moral basis after death is generally lacking. In this there is a strong contrast to the beliefs of followers of most of the major religions. Most primitive peoples are like the Tongans, of whom Frazer has pointed out that they do not appeal to another life to redress the balance of justice which had been disturbed in this one. Their pagan faith does not rest its ultimate sanction for conduct on what Frazer has called 'the slippery ground of posthumous rewards and punishments'.[2] It is a common view that moral sanctions are discoverable in ideas about the future of the soul only in so far as they repose on the belief in such retribution. I regard this view as incorrect, and later shall show why.

The third point is that, like many people who belong to the more sophisticated religious systems, members of most of the primitive communities have no great *concern* about the fate of their own souls. Their ideas may be formulated in terms of a general problem of knowledge. Each individual does not worry in advance about the personal problem of his future life. This does not mean that such people have a poverty of religious ideas in general. In those societies which, like the Nupe of Northern Nigeria, have few developed concepts of the persistence and fate of the soul there are nevertheless elaborate ideas about the existence and actions of spirit beings or powers of other orders, and elaborate practices for constraining or propitiating them to promote the ends of man.[3]

---

[1] *History of Man*, 4th ed. rev. by E. Norris, Vol. II, 1855, p. 661.
[2] Op. cit., Vol. II, 1922, p. 147.
[3] S. F. Nadel, *Nupe Religion*, London, 1954, pp. 34–5.

The fourth point is that primitive beliefs about the fate of the soul are usually not polarized, as they are in the great religions. The field is more open. Not uncommonly, there is wide variation of belief, or at least of statement, about the possible fate of the soul, even in a single community. Radcliffe-Brown has pointed out that in every Andamanese tribe there are alternative and inconsistent beliefs as to the place where spirits go—up to the skies, beneath the earth, out to the east where the sun and moon rise, or into the jungle and the sea of their own country.[1]

One thing, he says, is clear—that the Andamanese ideas on this subject are 'floating' and lacking precision; they have no fixity or uniformity of belief. One might speculate about the reasons for such lack of precision. I suggest three possibilities. One is that different destinations of the soul are structurally determined, being associated with different group alignments. Another is that obscurity in itself in such a matter has a social function, allowing dispute and differences of interpretation according to existing committal of interest. The third possibility is that this doctrinal sphere is one in which 'a free vote' so to speak is possible; that a crystallization of dogmatic terms is not relevant because it offers no particular social advantage.

These alternatives cannot be tested on the Andamanese material. But I mention them here because they foreshadow some of the lines of my own analysis.

A fifth point is that most primitive eschatology is dynamic, with plenty of social interaction. Unlike the Western view, in which the departed soul is effectively depersonalized in favour of group dependence upon the Divine, the primitive gives departed souls a field of concrete social activities. First, they interact with one another, and secondly, with the world they have left behind. In the West, we have reduced the volitional field of the departed soul. We have given the soul after death a direction but no magnitude. We have removed from our dead and our ancestors the ability to make choices, to participate effectively in the society of the living. As Le Van Dinh has pointed out in comparing Western beliefs with the cult of the dead among his own Annamite folk, we in the Occident 'liquidate the past' as far as our dead are concerned. In the light of our emphasis on the importance of the individual this might seem surprising, were it not for the inference that it is the individual freedom of the living that demands the annihilation of the exercise of decisions by the dead. But of course the difference is one of procedure rather than of principle, since in the primitive system, one may argue, the dead are merely the living in another guise. In particular, in an ancestor-cult, they are a means of expression of social obligations, and an important element in the process of decision-taking, by an indirect route.

[1] A. R. Radcliffe-Brown, *The Andaman Islanders*, 1922, pp. 168–70.

From this you see that my problem is not that of the ethnography of the soul—of exploring concepts of the fate of the soul descriptively to see the range of ideas of which man is capable in conceiving this subject. It is concerned with these beliefs in terms of their social functions—the way in which they have been expressed and their correlates in social action. I am interested, too, in relating such expressions to the structure and organization of a society where a change of religious system is taking place.

Let us examine further some primitive notions of the soul or human spirit.[1] By soul in this context I mean a symbolic extension of the human personality, invisible, believed to be responsible for supra-physical activity and for the most part to be capable of survival after physical death. Lack of primitive interest of any intense kind in the fate of the soul after death does not mean a corresponding lack of interest in what Frazer has called 'the perils of the soul' during life. Most primitive peoples have quite elaborate theories about the souls of the living and their liability to attack. They may even believe in the existence of multiple souls—several such personal entities of different types all attached to a single human individual and each sensitive in different ways to environmental influences. Again, the distinction is commonly made between the soul of a living person and his soul after death. At the death of the body the soul undergoes a radical transformation, or there is a substitution of personality in which one type of soul takes over, as it were, from another the spiritual continuity of the man. Such different types of soul have usually different names, giving rise to semantic problems for the anthropologist.[2]

For primitive peoples even more perhaps than for civilized, there is a sharp recognition that death is what Gustav Fechner has called 'the great climacteric disease' which the spirit of man as well as his body has to go through. But what is the implication of this recognition and emphasis? Is it that once the body of man has passed beyond our care, concern for his personality reaches out beyond the grave to promote his future well-being? In some cases this may be so. Attention is focused on an invisible object, the personality of the departed. He is held to endure

[1] I am tempted in view of the vagueness of terms in this field to adopt the following distinctions: *soul* for an immaterial entity which represents the survival personality of the human being both before and after the death of the body; *spirit* for an immaterial entity which may include the category of soul but also other categories in which the human connection is minimal or imprecise in emphasis; *ghost* for the survival personality of the human being after death, in apparitional or manifestational form. But though such distinctions would be useful they would seem too artificial in comparison with current usage.

[2] C. von Fürer-Haimendorf has pointed out the confusion resulting from the common failure of Western observers to make this distinction between types of soul when writing about Indian tribal beliefs. He also gives an interesting example of the way in which one Indian tribal people, on abandoning their own dialect for Telugu, have fallen into the same semantic confusion ('The After Life in Indian Tribal Belief', *J.R.A.I.*, Vol. LXXXIII, 1953, pp. 37–49).

in some immaterial form and to be cared for by the appropriate actions of those he has left behind, such as funeral rites and offerings. Is it again that the emphasis upon continuity of the soul after death is one form of protection of the personality; an assertion that man's will to survive has reality and not merely yearning? This wish-fulfilment type of explanation has a wide currency far beyond the primitive field. I take at random (from *L'École des Vacances*, a novel by André Bay, a translator of Lewis Carroll and of Swift into French) such *obiter dicta* as 'every kind of faith is a protection against death' or that 'the ideas of the continuity of the soul are part of the barrage that life invents against death'. These have an important element of truth. But I hazard an hypothesis here. It is rather as a framework for activity in *this* world and for positive experience in *life* that concepts about the continuity and fate of the soul are developed rather than as protection against death. In the ritual behaviour where crude fear of the dead seems to be the salient theme, the concern for freedom of action of the *living* is most marked. But apart from this highly negative reaction there are more positive and more subtle aspects. In many primitive religious systems, it is true, the soul of a dead person is regarded at times with fear and horror. But this is only part of the reaction. On other occasions it is looked upon with respect, even affection, and is held to be in frequent welcome contact with the living.

It is difficult to accept literally Linton's statement that in some societies death is regarded simply as a transfer comparable to that from child to adult, and that—as with the Tanala—the dead remain an integral part of the clan, merely surrendering one set of rights and duties and assuming another.[1] Even in the traditional ancestor-cults of the Annamites and the Chinese, the dead are 'members' of the social group in a very different way from the living. But there is an important point made in this statement in its emphasis on the way in which the concept of the behaviour of the souls of the dead is used as an instrument of social control of living human behaviour.

In placing the weight of interpretation of primitive eschatology on its social functions, I do not intend to deny other highly significant elements. In the ideas of the fate of the soul, intellectual and rational components are easily perceived. The early history of Christianity in Western Europe has demonstrated how important is the theoretical problem of where does the soul go after the death of the body, and why does it go to the destination appointed. Here are two vital questions. On what principles is the fate of the soul determined? Who are the agents who activate or operate these principles? Such questions have their parallel in the less sophisticated form in primitive religious systems although they tend to be implicit, not explicit. But, however they are

[1] Ralph Linton, *The Study of Man*, New York, 1936, pp. 121-2.

framed or implied, they do represent an attempt to handle a difficult and puzzling problem in terms of reasoned relations and not merely in terms of emotional solutions. In this respect the approach of Edward Tylor has tended to be under-valued. It is easy in the light of the work of the psychologists over the last century to point to Tylor's failure to recognize the importance of emotional construction in primitive religious phenomena. But while the religious premises may be basically emotional the associated argument may be mainly rational. At times indeed it may be intellectualistic, even metaphysical. What one must acknowledge in any primitive series of concepts about the fate of the soul is that there is some logical relation seen and explainable between the condition in which the soul of the dead finds itself or manifests itself at any given time, and some particular social circumstance. What is usually lacking in the primitive field is the retribution-theme of drawing this social circumstance from the past behaviour of the living person whose soul is now active after his death. What is, on the other hand, very manifest in the primitive field is that the social circumstance is drawn from the behaviour of other living persons here and now.

In much of the primitive material about the fate of the soul there are also aesthetic elements. In many primitive religious systems, institutionalized spirit mediumship brings back to the living in word or in deed the presence of the dead. Often, the words attributed to the soul of the dead are in descriptive or narrative form, with much use of imagery. They may tell of how the living man met his death and his soul released has come to notify his kin. Or they may tell of adventures dramatic, ludicrous, erotic or simply mundane, of the soul among other spirits in the after world. As with the visions of medieval Christianity, the narrative sequence of plot and incident and the stimulus of the imagery of colour and harmony undoubtedly give outlet for aesthetic creation and for aesthetic satisfaction.

Such intellectual and aesthetic elements are subtly intermixed. The anthropologist often collects material about the fate of the soul in descriptions of a generalized kind through set interviews with informants. The stories therefore are often robbed of their social context and full meaning. This meaning is more clearly demonstrated in an oral recital of experiences by some subject who tells the story of a vision or a dream about the afterworld or describes some ordeal of ghostly visitation which he has undergone. Here the eschatological evidence may be more closely linked with a personal satisfaction of a meaningful kind. The author of visions or other accounts of the after life and the fate of souls may be seeking confirmation for personal decisions, standpoints, relationships. He may be expressing in a roundabout way the dilemmas or solutions of some personal problems.

In the primitive world such accounts take the place of the literature to which we in the West owe far more than we realize of our notions of the Hereafter. In such literary recital the element of direct subjective experience varies greatly. On the one hand there are men writing down what they themselves have felt they experienced of visions of the fate of souls—or, like St Catherine of Genoa, describing Purgatory by personal analogy. On the other hand there are the obvious literary devices of a Virgil, of a Dante, or of the composer of the Buddhist Lotus Sutra, which reveal to us the scenes of heaven, hell and their ancillaries. Yet now that, to quote Tylor, 'the dead have been ousted by geography from any earthly district, and the regions of heaven and hell have been spiritualized out of definite locality into vague expressions of future happiness and misery',[1] the role of such literature as information is much less important. (This is all the more so now that modern astronomy on the one hand and space-fiction on the other have pushed the limits of the accessible or conceivable universe still farther back.)

Now that Sartre has replaced Dante as our eschatological authority, each statement above the Hereafter becomes more than just a piece of descriptive material about another world. It expresses even more strongly a personal attitude about action in this world.

A word more about Hell in our immediate context. Primitive peoples have in their pagan religion no idea of Hell. Nor have they usually any doctrine of the Last Judgement as satisfying the demands of perfect justice. Only recently through Christianity have such notions come to them. Now the importance of the idea of Hell as a direct moral sanction has often been emphasized. What has been less clearly noted is that sociologically, the idea of Hell is a very useful defining element for a religious system. Unequivocally, it separates those who belong to the religious body from those who do not, by carrying the boundary fence into the Hereafter and preserving the moral differentiation. As Franz Cumont has shown for the Orphics of the Greco-Latin world, Dewick for the primitive Christians, and quite recently, Maquet for the Banyaruwanda Ryangombe sect, the pains of Hell were the distinguishing fate for those unpurified by initiation into the special cult.[2] Hell then was the ritual defining factor for the system. Belief in Hell is in modern times possibly less of a negative personal moral sanction than of a positive social reinforcement—part of the ideological structure supporting the integrity of the Churches who maintain it and the uniqueness of their members.

[1] E. Tylor, *Primitive Culture*, Vol. II, p. 101.
[2] Franz Cumont, *After Life in Roman Paganism*, New Haven, 1922, pp. 170 et seq.; E. C. Dewick, *Primitive Christian Eschatology*, Cambridge, 1912; J. J. Maquet, 'The Kingdom of Ruanda', in *African Worlds, Studies in the Cosmological Ideas and Social Values of African Peoples*, International African Institute, 1954, pp. 171, 183–4. According to S. Angus (*Mystery Religions and Christianity*, 1925, p. 152) only the 'lower and popular' Orphism stressed Hell in order to exact fees from the initiates.

I give this example as a pointer to the situation in primitive religious systems.

Let me now take an example for more detailed analysis and outline the main ideas about the fate of the soul after death in an Oceanic community, Tikopia—an island in Frazer's field. First there are the traditional ideas of pagan Tikopia. (The ideas of Christian Tikopia I shall mention later.)

The Tikopia have no theory of multiple souls. They believe that in life a person has a single vital principle or soul, as we may call it, variously termed *mauri* or *ora*.[1] This may go away from the body during dreams[2] and have other experiences. Some time after death there is a change of terminology with change of function; the soul now comes to be referred to as *atua* not *ora*. This implies its emergence as an entity in its own right, no longer in direct association with its body.

Its relation to the body is interesting and needs a brief linguistic discussion. The Tikopia soul is what Tylor called an ethereal image of the body. The proof of this is that the soul is always expected to be recognized by its friends and kin by its appearance. But the Tikopia here play a kind of three-card trick, which is not uncommon in eschatology. They distinguish the body, called *tino* when alive and *penu* (*husk* or *shell*) when dead, from the soul, called *mauri* or *ora*—the immaterial essence, the ethereal image. But they also have a third entity in between, a kind of symbolic body—perhaps 'etheric body'—which is regarded as physical or not according to circumstances. This is the *ata*, the semblance. Now ordinarily the *ata* is the shadow, or the reflection. But in certain circumstances a wandering ghost can get into the dead body of a person and walk abroad in his shell. Yet here comes the problem. On the one hand, the Tikopia will say it is the corpse that is animated; on the other, they will say that the corpse is still in the grave, and that it is only in the semblance of the dead man, his *ata*, that the foreign ghost appears. Of course this question: When is a body not a body? involving a subtle transition from the physical to the symbolic sphere, is a problem not confined to the primitive. As the sophisticated arguments of theologians from Athenagoras to Karl Barth, about the exact nature of the bodily resurrection, have shown, there is grave difficulty here.

The Tikopia soul at death, though it leaves the body, does not

[1] Most Tikopia I consulted asserted that the *mauri* and the *ora* were the same thing, that is, they referred to a single entity. A few said they were different, but were not able to give any clear criterion of differentiation. Certainly the two terms seem to be used interchangeably in practice.

This usage is different from that of the traditional Maori, who have three terms for human vital principles: *mauri*, *wairua*, and *hau* (apart from *ora*, meaning life), and do seem to have differentiated between them to some extent. (See Elsdon Best, 'Spiritual and Mental Concepts of the Maori', *Dominion Museum Monograph*, No. 2, Wellington 1922; Raymond Firth, *Primitive Economics of the New Zealand Maori*, pp. 268–71.)

[2] See Chapter 7 of this volume.

immediately set out on a journey to the afterworld, but remains in the vicinity until after the burial, or later, until conducted away by the ancestral spirits of its mother's patrilineal kin group. In some versions the soul must pass a barrier or test—walk over a slippery stone which turns under its feet and projects it down to annihilation if certain conditions have not been complied with. But in most accounts, the soul passes without hindrance to its first destination.[1] This is a pool in the afterworld, guarded by two grim spirits, with a curious function. The newly arrived soul is lowered into the pool by its mother's gods or ancestral spirits. The two guardian spirits then devour, or rather chew up the soul, mumbling its substance between their gums so that its essence, described as 'blood', runs down into the pool. This blood is then collected by a Female Deity in a gourd, in which it begins to assume once again human form, growing arms, legs, head, etc., and finally taking on full human shape, but of spirit character. This process of maceration is not regarded as victimization. No Tikopia expresses any abhorrence of it. It is looked upon as a necessary procedure in the conversion of crude souls with the taint of mortality still upon them into refined spirits capable of taking part in the life of the afterworld. In the early stage, indeed, before this grim refinement, the soul is known as the 'living man' (*tangata ora*) by other spirits. Now it is the *tama furu*—the 'cleansed child', an *atua*. Then comes another curious procedure, in typical Tikopia idiom. The re-created spirit of itself is a weak thing, of no particular capacity. It is therefore fitted out with special powers. These are known as its 'swiftness' (*vave*) and enable it to travel with speed through the skies. But they also enable it to perform superhuman deeds. In particular this 'swiftness' is exemplified by, and in a sense identified with, thunder. Thunder is a phenomenon clearly outside the human field; in Tikopia view it is made by spirits. The ability to make it in common with other weather phenomena, is a mark of the more powerful spirits. The equation of *speed* with *power* is itself an interesting one. But here again, the spirits of the mother's patrilineal kin group play their role; it is they who endow the newly re-created soul with his 'swiftness'. They do it by the concrete act of sticking at the back of the soul's waist-cloth a tuft or spray of leaves in the form of a dance ornament. This does not just symbolize the 'swiftness'; to the Tikopia it bears or is the swiftness. So we have the equation in different contexts, or at different levels of abstraction of: *spray of leaves=spirit swiftness=spirit power=thunder*. Into this elaborate system of thought comes yet another element of a structural kind. The various major kin groups have each a particular type of plant or shrub which they and they

---

[1] According to the Ariki Taumako in 1952—son of my informant of 1929—the slippery stone (*fatu sekeseke*) is encountered at a later stage. But this would not easily fit into the sequence.

alone are properly entitled to use in this spirit investment. Hence the re-created soul goes off decorated with the particular emblem of his mother's group, a fact which is significant in various kinds of linkage and identification in many other ritual and secular contexts.

Thus equipped, the soul goes off, making various visits of observation and courtesy to his ancestral and other spirits. But sooner or later he settles in a dwelling-place (*noforanga*). There are very many of these: I have the names of at least two dozen, each under the control of a lineage god or other spirit of rank, and there are many more spoken about without being named. Some are in the ocean, some in the mountains or elsewhere in distant lands, but many are in the skies. Those in the skies are known as *Rangi*, Heavens, a term affiliated with that for sky, *vaerangi*, and are said to be similar to the clouds floating above. These Rangi have a complex and not entirely consistent structural order. Firstly, as a most general statement, there are often said to be ten of them in horizontal layers, and numbered from top to bottom, in their names as 'First Heaven', 'Second Heaven', and so on. In the topmost heavens live the senior gods and most important ancestors, with lesser gods and spirits in the lower strata. (The lowest heaven, number ten, is also known as the Heaven of the Turnstones, because this migrant wading bird, like a small curlew, is believed to wait up there during the winter season until its time comes to descend and be seen again.) Rather ill-fused with this schematic numbered arrangement (which, incidentally, is very reminiscent of that in other parts of Polynesia) is another, rather less systematized, but more elaborate. There is a directional allocation. The Tikopia of course traditionally had no compass points, but they divided the circle of their horizon up into something very like it, in the form of wind-points—the directions from which the major winds come. Each of these major wind-points, of which there are four, is the home of a major deity of the Tikopia, who is a prime clan and lineage god. He controls the wind and weather from that particular direction. (The prime god of Kafika controls the west, of Tafua the north-west, of Taumako the south, and of Fangarere the south-east.) Each of these quarters, as we may call them, is in spirit terms made up of a number of Rangi, Heavens. Names are given to these heavens, according to their various characteristics. They are arranged in layers, but in fact when these names are counted, in any quarter there may be more or less than ten. (One reason for this I will explain in a moment.) In the topmost division lives the deity who is known as the Post or Stay of the Heavens, the controller, who presides over his whole set of heavens. Below him live the 'small gods' as they are sometimes called, and the souls of ordinary men. These heavens can be identified with the tenfold scheme mentioned earlier, but in practice no one seems to bother to do so unless asked by the anthropologist.

Some of these heavens are peculiar. One, belonging to a particular lineage, is a Heaven of the Halt, or the Lame; spirits who limp have that as their home. Another is the Heaven of Cannibals, spirits who eat flesh and who have only one nostril, one ear, one leg, one arm, etc., apiece. Other heavens are sloping, others still unstable. I have an account of heavenly doings, telling how a spirit may be standing on a sloping unstable heaven, to the irritation of the owner-spirit. He is annoyed; he wants the other to leave. So he gives his heaven a tilt, and slides the other spirit off, making him take flight to another heaven. He goes off, flying like a bird, because of the 'swiftness' of the dance-ornament at his back. Unmarried women have their own heaven, as do married women, married men, and bachelors. But the rules of abodes in the hereafter are elastic; as in Tikopia, there are fixed dwellings determined by social affiliation and by status in sex and marriage, with additional provisions for physical defects. But choice among these dwellings and visiting from one to another is free. The lame spirits and the rest, like the gods, go strolling about as they wish. In the heavens there is eating and drinking, and some spirits go and work in the cultivations. But the great occupation is dancing. In many ways it is a pagan South Seas version of the Elysian fields—or of Marc Connelly's *Green Pastures*.

But what does it all amount to? What does it mean? To some degree it is just sheer fantasy. The notion of a heaven for the lame, or one-eyed, or of a spirit playing a malicious joke upon another by tilting up his heaven and sliding him off, or many of the erotic adventures described for some souls, have no deep social roots. They are embroideries, more or less socially accepted, on the main themes.

But we accept the view that Tikopia eschatology is not just fantasy. To what does it correspond? In psychological terms there are various aggressions symbolized in the images of spirits chewing up the souls of the dead so that the blood flows, or wish-fulfilments in spirits flying with speed. But in social terms there are other points to be made.

Firstly, it is of the character of religious belief that it must bear some relation to the state of society in which it is held. These statements about the destination and the fate of souls, are restatements of social structure, at a symbolic level. The hierarchy of gods and spirits in the heavens parallels the principles of rank on earth. The names of the heavens relate to significant social differences. Not only this, the souls of the dead retain their earthly status when they arrive in the afterworld. The system of clan dwellings, the special position of chiefs and ritual leaders, the particular assignment of married and unmarried, all broadly follow Tikopia alignment.

Here comes a second point—that the reproduction of this social structure is not just an imaginative simulacrum of the world below; that one important function is its expression of the *continuity* of the structure. It is reassurance that not merely the personality, but also the society, goes on. When the society is not threatened by external forces this aspect is not so significant. But if it is so threatened, then the emphasis of the eschatology upon continuity may become critical.

But the fate of the soul is not a simple reflection of the structural positions of the living. Firstly, not all human elements of the structure are catered for. In the Tikopia world of souls there are no guardians of public order corresponding to the executive officials (*maru*)—the 'policeman', they call them—on earth. Again, there may be a compensation mechanism. It is true that primitive eschatology knows little of the *ubi sunt* principle—'where are the kings and emperors, the great ones of the earth . . . ? They are now as common men . . .' Unlike the overt egalitarianism of most of the great religions, those of the small-scale societies usually place the soul in the situation ascribed to the individual in life. But occasionally some souls do rise in the hierarchy higher than their human status would seem to have entitled them. However, this is rare.

But the fate of the soul offers material for manipulation. The spirit-mediums and other charismatic leaders are able to use the material dealing with the fate of the soul to bolster up their own authenticity and confirm their powers. In the course of their recitals of doings in the spirit world they use a great deal of creative imagination. They give adventures to the soul. They enlarge the geography and social structure of the spirit world. They introduce the names of heavens, some new to the listeners. This is the reason why the number of heavens, and who live in them, is not always identical and clear. The spirit-mediums can do this because the souls of the dead are regarded as active. In Western belief souls of the dead are not in action—except to a limited extent as in the cult of Saints. They remain at a distance—wherever that may be. In Tikopia it is not so; they are in social movement.

But support to position of spirit-mediums and other ritual leaders does not in itself throw much light on the firmness of belief the Tikopia have in this general picture of the fate of the soul, and the intense interest they have in detailed accounts. As a general proposition I have said that this belief and interest seem to be less oriented towards their own ultimate individual fate, than towards current concerns. What is the relationship? In essence it is that the pronouncements of spirit-mediums, ritual elders, chiefs, and the frequent other references made to the afterworld and the fate of the soul relate directly to practical and personal issues of weather, food supply, sickness, accident, the fate of kinsfolk abroad, and many other daily affairs.

Here comes a further hypothesis, that in all this the implicit moral bearing is very important. For instance, the Tikopia stress the theme of the soul being carried by the gods and ancestor spirits of its kin to its spirit home. Not to be carried is a terrible thing. The soul must wait until some other spirit takes pity upon it and bears it away. This is a powerful restatement in symbolic language of the moral role of kin.

The moral aspect appears in the relation between funeral ritual and ideas of the fate of the soul.

Some form of rite for 'speeding the soul' is very common in primitive religious systems. It is often said that the reason for this is to stop the soul from afflicting the living by remaining in the vicinity of the corpse and being tempted to interfere with the affairs of the survivors. This interpretation often seems to be correct. But there are more complications and rather different reasons in some cases.

Many of the funeral rites seem to be essentially associated with ideas of completeness of sequence in human affairs. That relations with the person who has died physically may be properly terminated socially, needs formal recognition. This termination of social relations is acknowledged, as it were, by being notched in memory by a specific rite. In the last resort this notion may perhaps be reduced to aesthetic criteria.[1]

The analogy here is quite close with the ordinary ceremonies of farewell. But when there have been strong emotional attachments to the dead person the rites of speeding the soul then represent, not so much a formal emotional severance as a formal emotional shift from the *vital personality* associated with the body to what may be called the *survival personality* associated with the spirit.

But there may be other forms too, indirectly concerned with the fate of the soul. As part of the funeral rites the Tikopia have a custom called 'pressing down the grave mat'. This is partly a technical operation of firming the sandy soil after the burial and partly a ceremonial operation of covering the grave mat—plaited from coconut fronds—with aromatic leaves. This helps to protect the body of the dead person, now empty of its soul, from wandering spirits. If this is not done a wandering ghost may enter the corpse and walk abroad in it in the semblance of the dead person. Apart from the protective physical barrier of the aromatic leaves there is a spirit barrier. The spirits of the family of the mother of the dead person are expected to sit by the grave side and keep watch, chasing away any alien wandering spirit that approaches.

One of my friends in Tikopia, a spirit medium, described to me in 1929 a dream he had had after he returned home from several nights' watch by the grave of a dead kinswoman. He said, 'I had a dream last night. I was asleep in my house and two men came in with two women —spirits of the grave mat which I had pressed down. They came and said to me "You, there, abandoned the mat and came home, why did

[1] See also Raymond Firth, *Elements of Social Organization*, 1951, pp. 63–4.

THE FATE OF THE SOUL

you not stay and ask for coconuts to be broken and to be put on the mat for us to drink? Here we have come to tell you to return where we were; we have abandoned the mat, we are hungry." Thereupon I spoke to them, "What is to be done? The earlier nights (i.e. the first phrases of the rite) are finished." Then they called to me, "Why did you not stay to add on the later nights to complete the affair?" Then a little child came running and called to me, "Father, Father, come and let us go to the mat of my mother, the mat has been deserted by the guardian spirits, the corpse of my father's sister will be entered, come and have a look at it, Father" (he was our son from among the spirits), and I woke up. This was my dream.'

The expression of this dream shows some anxiety and guilt for his not having stayed longer by the grave side, although in fact he had completed his normal duty. There may have been some element of accusation for the omission of libations of coconut milk because the people concerned were Christians. But I do not think so since my friend behaved in all matters as an ordinary spirit worshipper and such coconuts were offered on other occasions to spirits as appropriate. In other words, this was not a culture-conflict dream of the kind which I later collected in 1952. What is does show is the Tikopia conception that there is some relation between proper completion of the sequence of funeral rites and the appearance of a semblance of the dead person to the living immediately afterwards. This point is relevant for our later discussion, in regard to ghosting by souls of the dead and not only by alien spirits.

In terms of kinship also the perpetuation of very marked family affection is thought to endure among the spirits of the dead. A sick person will say to his mother, his brother or his son, 'I shall be buried by you under your sleeping mat, I shall lie below while you live above, at the place where my head lies to sleep. I shall go among the spirits, and look down at you sleeping on my mat.' There are many such informal ways in which the nostalgic sentiments of Tikopia spirits for their kin is shown through statements about the fate of souls. Apart from this, the formal procedures of conveying the spirit to the afterworld, cleansing it from its taint of mortality, equipping it with its spirit power and assigning it to its permanent home, all are expressed in kinship terms. Particular weight is laid on the role of the ancestor spirits and gods of the mother's patrilineal kin group. It is they who are crucial in the proper care for the new soul, just as they are crucial in care of the person throughout life.

Tikopia statements and actions concerned with the fate of the soul involve then to a very large degree statements and actions about the rightness of social relations in their own society. Accounts of the journey of the soul to the afterworld and of its treatment in the afterworld are *inter alia,* affirmations and extensions of the operation of basic moral principles of Tikopia social structure.

In saying all this I do not mean to imply that in traditional Tikopia eschatology there is anything of the specific didactic kind which one meets for example in accounts of medieval visions of the Christian afterworld. When the thirteenth-century Essex peasant Thurcill had his vision of the brilliantly lit Cathedral with the foetid smoke of Hell swirling up outside its walls, he was told by his guide (St Julian) that the coughing of unhappy souls in this smoke was caused by the tithes they had unjustly retained. The brilliant light in the Cathedral, on the other hand, was due to the tithes that the just had rendered. When Thurcill unfortunately happened to cough twice from a whiff of the smoke, his saintly guide suggested that he must have been remiss in paying his tithes. Thurcill admitted this, pleading poverty, to which the saint replied that the giving of tithes increases the fertility of the soil, so that it would have been more profitable for him to have paid up. Such didactic details in the visions were used in local medieval sermons, we are told.[1] But little of this plain speaking occurs in pagan Tikopia accounts. The story of the test barrier of the slippery stone has sometimes been given with a moral connotation—those who have not done their duty by the kava rites miss their footing and are precipitated down no-one knows whither. But this story and its implications have no wide currency.[2] What is much more common however is for spirits of the dead to appear in dreams to the living, or in the trances of spirit mediums, and complain that they have not had proper attention paid to them. Here the tone *is* definitely one of moral application to the survivors, and this is recognized by the living Tikopia who are spurred on by the belief that if they do not do what is asked the spirit will afflict them with illness or death.

As Tylor has pointed out, the retribution theory is far from universal among mankind. Unlike the sophisticated religions, primitive religions make few distinctions between good and bad in the afterworld. What is weak in the pagan Tikopia eschatology is an overt moral judgement of a *generalized* kind, differentiating the fate of the soul by reference to the moral condition of the person in life. What they do give fairly fully is indirect or tacit moral approval to conditions in *this* world by their mere way of stating conditions, structural alignments, activities, in the *next.*

---

[1] A. B. Van Os, *Religious Visions: The development of the eschatological elements in mediaeval religious literature,* Amsterdam, 1932, pp. 3, 75, etc.

[2] In 1929 the Ariki Taumako told me this. He also told me that people who have lived properly and not killed or committed theft go to their heaven without trouble. Those who have slain men or stolen do not. But he said that this information was generally not known, nor did he have any clear idea what happened to such evil-doers. I noted at the time that this was not a current ethical concept, and regard it as a personal gloss due probably to the unconscious effect of Mission teaching, and the desire to represent pagan knowledge as at bottom no less ethical. There was no evidence in other contexts that the chief paid attention to such a belief.

In brief, one may say that statements about the fate of the soul are in many respects symbolic affirmations of moral judgement about human action in society. In primitive religions these statements are moral expressions as much as moral sanctions. But looking at them from this point of view raises a question of the extent to which behaviour in human society is likely to correspond to the approved line of treatment of the soul. In many cases human behaviour is likely to be unaffected by the moral view expressed through statements on the afterworld. A woman who dies in childbed and whose soul therefore goes to a different spirit home, cannot be influenced in her situation in advance by the knowledge that some souls have this fate. It is doubtful if a warrior, whose soul will go to an undesirable spirit home if he is killed in battle, is likely to be stimulated to much greater warlike energies thereby. A status of an ascribed kind such as that of chief cannot be normally changed, despite the fate that awaits the soul of the office-holder. Even where as in the major religions the rewards and punishments allocated to the soul vary according to the behaviour of the person among the living, the evidence as to just how effective these notions are as sanctions is ambiguous and contradictory. It seems as if the ideology of the fate of the soul operates rather as an inert or latent factor called into operation by some special *other* experience or controlled by some countervailing principle—such as that the expediency of the action saves the soul from a bad fate, or that some final and all-embracing act absolves one from the moral quality of previous actions.

A further test of some of these proposals is given by the behaviour or people who, having previously been pagan, have now joined a major religion. Examples of this are many Tikopia, some of whom were Christian when I first met them in 1928–9 and some who became converted from paganism to Christianity in the intervening time before I visited them again in 1952.

The tenets of the Christian about the fate of the soul are formally those promulgated by the Melanesian Mission. I asked the Motlav priest, who had been in charge of the Tikopia Christians for many years, what he taught about the souls of the dead. He said that when God created Adam he blew into him the breath of life. This is the soul. When man dies his body gives jerking spasms and the breath leaves. As the soul it returns straight to God who gave it. This is in the case of people who have behaved properly. Those who misbehave have their souls go straight to Hell. I asked about the ideas of the pagan Tikopia. He said, 'They do not know. They think the dwellings of spirits are in the world of men.' I asked him then, what about the spirits who walked abroad as ghosts, why was it they had not gone straight to God? He said, 'Oh no, they don't walk.' Then I reminded him of an experience he had told me twenty-three years before, of an apparition of his dead father-in-law which he had seen in open day on the path. He said, 'Oh, you remember it?' and he went over it again in clear exact detail, almost identical with what he had told me a generation before. He said that this was the only time that he himself had seen such a spirit. But he gave me examples of other people who had seen ghosts, the spirits of dead people, recently. The priest then said to me, 'We say that the soul goes straight to Heaven, but then we see people standing there. We don't know if it is their soul or not, it is not certain'—and he turned to me and asked, 'What do you think?' I said too, 'It is uncertain.'

The views of the more sophisticated Tikopia Christians follow those of their priest. For example, one man who had himself been a Mission teacher discussed the Christian attitude to suicide. Each man's soul belongs to God and each man should await the time of his death, 'following the will of the Lord'. Hence the man who commits suicide does not go to Paradise, he goes to Satan. The reason for this is that the Bible says it is wrong for a man to take his own life. If a person should commit suicide then it is for the priest to make the proper prayers at the altar of the church so that the soul of the man may go to the proper place. The family of the person cannot themselves perform this service or intercede with God in any way—only the priest can do this. Normally the family of a suicide does not make any special inquiry about his fate. But if they do worry about the situation they may go to the priest and ask him for special prayers, and they substantiate their request by presenting to the priest a pandanus mat. But, it was added, 'once a man is in the ground people do not worry about him or think too much of him unless he starts to "walk".'[1]

This question of the 'walking' of the soul of the dead as a ghost is a crucial one in modern Tikopia eschatology. In the Western world we have a long history of ghost belief, and traces of this still remain in some popular notions and in humorous references. But it is no longer fashionable nor necessary in Western Europe or the United States, for instance, to see ghosts. In Tikopia it is an accepted experience and there were several cases during my visits. Psychologists have shown how greatly perception and memory may be conditioned by social circumstances. So it is not surprising that the Tikopia see their apparitions as Tikopia, as persons known to them, and in the forms of dead kin. Some are attributed to alien spirits who impersonate the dead, others to the actual souls of the dead revisiting for various reasons the human scene.

[1] These observations were collected by J. Spillius from Pa Raroifi. In 1929 the same man, then known as Pa Motuangi, gave me the traditional account of the fate of the soul. He said nothing about going to Paradise but told me that on death he would go first to the heaven of his mother's brother to be decorated and equipped with speed, then he would go to either Maunganefu, the cloud-capped mountain of Vanikoro, or to Tarafare in the ocean, both spirit homes of his own kin group. In the intervening generation he had evidently adopted the conventional Christian view.

This formerly was regarded as a matter to be treated with caution, likely to make people afraid. But on the whole there was little structural interpretation or moral emphasis attached to it. Now it has become a matter of heightened interest, and with some moral overtones.

I wish to examine the history of a couple of cases which were almost notorious in 1952.

The first was that of a young man, unmarried and a pagan, who fell from a high cliff while climbing to net birds nesting on the rock face. His spirit appeared on various occasions, causing talk and some fright. But the attitude of Tikopia to such apparitions is often very matter-of-fact. The lad was regarded as having lost his life through foolhardy tempting of his skill, and judgement on this comes out in the spirit encounters. A friend of mine told me how the lad appeared in spirit form to one of his kinsfolk who was awake in his house at night. He called out 'Brother' and the living man recognized the voice of the dead. He replied in a curse, 'Here you are coming and calling out to me—I excrete in your gullet.' Then the ghost went away. 'What was the ghost's idea?' I asked. 'His affection, it might have been', was the reply. Another of his kinsfolk had a similar experience when the ghost opened the door of his house. He called out something that, freely translated, was, 'You fool, what have you come peering in here for? It was your own stupid fault that you went and fell off the cliff.' Rebuffed again, the ghost then went on to the cookhouse of his father's dwelling, and finding his father absent he apparently began to wail and was heard crying by people. He is said to have pulled aside the doors of several houses. It was not known if the father had seen his son after death or not. My informant had not seen him, but he told me that another man had seen him by day in an orchard up the mountain, and ran from him. He explained that only recently had the soul of the dead man been caught by the guardian spirits. He pointed out that a person who dies on a bed of sickness is all right; the spirits take his soul to the realm of the spirits and then they return it later to listen to the funeral rites and the wailing. But when a person is killed by a fall from a cliff, his body crashes down and his soul rises and floats about like a petal alighting on tree branches and wailing at its fate, but not perceived and secured by its spirit guardians. This is what happened to the dead young man, who had been heard wailing in various orchards near where he fell.[1]

---

[1] When a person falls and lives his soul is collected by spreading out bark cloth near the spot and beating the bushes round with sticks until a petal or an insect alights on the cloth. This is then wrapped up, brought back and opened on the body of the man, to allow the soul to re-enter its habitation. Cf. J. G. Frazer, *Belief in Immortality*, Vol. II, p. 206; Margaret Mead, *Social Organization of Manua*, Honolulu, 1930, p. 101.

Note that in Tikopia this ceremony is never performed when a body is lost at sea or a person killed by accident on shore; it is only done in the case of injury. If it is not performed the person goes into delirium, because his soul has not been re-united with the body.

But why should such a spirit walk? Partly, it may be, in Tikopia belief, the result of his own choice. When a young man dies, 'he is angry with his friends'. He knows that other young men and maidens are still going about among the living. So he is annoyed and 'walks' to object and disturb them. Or he wishes to make contact with his kin, from whom he has been so suddenly wrenched. One explanation given (to J. Spillius) was that the soul newly parted from its body by death is confused, does not know where it is, does not know that it can no longer communicate with them in the normal way, and so approaches them. On the other hand, older people, it is said, are content to be dead.

But to some degree the walking of ghosts is regarded not as a matter of choice, but as a reflection of the present divided structure of Tikopia religion.

The dead boy in the first case was a pagan. To Christian Tikopia the 'walking' of his ghost was a sign of the inadequacy of his faith. Now the stereotyped Christian view is that souls of Christians who have been given proper burial do not 'walk' (i.e. appear to the living immediately after death), because they go to Heaven. But even the Christian priest admitted that there are cases to explain. One of these is the second example I wish to discuss.

The name of the young man concerned was Samuel. Soon after death he was seen not only by Mission teachers, but also by other people. One of the teachers, for instance, had seen the recently buried lad standing by the seaward side of his father's house, clapping his hands and making the sound 'Wo, wo, wo . . .' as if dancing. The teacher said to him, 'You don't frighten me; I am on my way to our father the priest' and feeling protected by his ritual mission, went on quietly. When he arrived at the priest's house he said nothing. A little later a son of the priest, also on his way home, saw the ghost too, was afraid, and ran. When he got to the priest's house he told what he had seen, where-upon the other man told his story too. Innocently one day I asked the dead man's father about the stories that his son was 'walking'. He replied hotly, 'It is just untrue; people are lying; he was buried in the Faith.' He added that the story was one put out by people of another district and that no one in their district had seen him. When I said that in fact it *was* by someone of their district, he replied, 'Well, no one in our village has seen him, no one in this village, the one which buried him.' He added again, 'It's lies.' But he had heard rumours of these stories, obviously, and he changed the subject quickly. His difficulty was that the dead are common property; other people cannot be stopped from seeing their ghosts. Whereas the family of the deceased, knowing that he has been buried with proper rites, may strenuously deny that he is 'walking', others see him and report. The implication is disturbing to them. It suggests an insecure status, perhaps moral condemnation.

When I first talked about these matters in 1952, the Christians I saw told me that only pagan souls walked. Later this opinion was controverted by both Christians and pagans. An old friend of mine who had become a Christian recently, when I asked him if it was true, said, 'They've been lying to you—those that are walking there are baptized people, they have been rejected by the gods.'

When I asked a Christian lad who had been baptized as a child what caused the spirits of the dead to 'walk' he answered, 'A person who is correct with the spirits does not walk, but a person who is not correct with the spirits returns among men to walk about. So it has been from of old. The person who is correct is not discovered among men (i.e. his apparition is not seen). He who walks has not been carried by the spirits.' When I asked, 'Are those who are given Christian burial also liable to be seen as apparitions?' he said, 'A person who is buried with prayer can walk, there are many of those buried with prayer who have walked.' Then he added, 'Because this land rejoices—it rejoices in the work (i.e. Christianity)—the people oppose the things of the chiefs.'

My old friend Pa Fenuatara and the Ariki Taumako also denied strongly that only unbaptized spirits walk. Pa Fenuatara was very definite: 'People of the gospel who die, it is terrible; they stand midway in the sphere of men and of spirits. The reason is that they have opposed the gods and are rejected by them. Hence they are left to wander until the judgement day. Some Christian souls sleep peacefully—the reason is that they have given adherence to the gods. Baptized folk who have acknowledged that the gods are true are cleansed, but the man who denies the gods is rejected by them and not cleansed.' In other words, in Tikopia belief Christian spirits walk because of the present spiritual situation. It will be remembered that the souls of pagan Tikopia are carried off, cleansed by their maternal kin's spirits and then go to their ancestral gods. But under the new dispensation ancestral gods are antipathetic to the Christian God. Hence it is believed he will not allow the souls of the baptized to pursue their traditional pagan course. So there is danger that they will be rejected by their ancestral gods and neglected by their maternal kin spirits. So left they wander about on the borders between the human world and the spirit world. And in this condition of uneasiness they are wont to come as apparitions, until in the end they are carried off out of pity.[1] To Christians this is a matter of regret, to pagans a matter of some pleasure and scorn. This is the plight of Christians as seen by pagans, and it is one of the few sanctions

---

[1] Some people, Christian rather than pagan, apparently try to avert this fate by making a treaty with a spirit medium. Traffic with such mediums is, strictly speaking, not approved of by the Church, but many Christian Tikopia resort to them. Pa Motuata told me, 'Nowadays whoever may behave well to spirit mediums, give them tobacco, and the makings of betel (the food of the spirits is tobacco and betel), then the spirit will speak to him thus, "You, when the time comes for you to die, I shall await you"—to carry off the soul.'

that the pagans can still use. But it is shared by Tikopia Christians in that they themselves are still confused about the immediate fate of the soul. They have no consistent theory about it. Moreover, they have no purgatory which could take care in part of their complicated loyalties.

Note that the fate suffered in pagan eyes by the souls of Christians who have denied the gods is assimilated to that of pagan Tikopia who have not supported the kava ceremonies. An implicit morality has become converted to an explicit morality. In former generations when Tikopia was completely pagan, it must have been rare for any man to have consistently absented himself from the kava ceremonies of his chief. Hence there must have been only minimum grounds for interpretation of the walking ghosts in such terms. But in modern times when a person can refrain from attending the kava without necessarily being a Christian, the net effect is the same and the punishment in after life is therefore equated.

So much for the immediate facts of Tikopia belief; what is our further interpretation?

The appearance of ghosts in Tikopia is a facet of the interpretation of physical experience. Certain untoward happenings occur; as a person is passing along a path at night a cool breeze from nowhere suddenly blows upon his body, or to his nostrils comes a strong smell—of turmeric or of putrescence.[1] Or else he is startled by a sudden sound. These things need explanation and they find it within the general framework of Tikopia belief in the mobility of spirits, including those of the dead. The sight of a ghost needs more complex explanation. But the Tikopia seem prone to interpret in human shape visual experiences of some uncertainty, and most of such statements about seeing ghosts refer to dusk or other conditions of poor visibility. There is no reason to doubt their sincerity; there is much other evidence for crediting them with a lively imagination.

There is plenty of scepticism—one young man said to me, 'A spirit who walks will appear to one person but not to another person—and so the person who did not see him will deny it. When he appears to a person he does not just appear, he chases him. It is not certain the reason why he comes to chase a man.' About one particularly pervasive ghost there was much affirmation and denial, but as one man said to me, 'If a person goes about a great deal and does not see it, he denies that it has come. For instance, I denied because I had not seen it. This is the

---

[1] The curious odour, the stink, which the soul of the newly buried bears with him, is termed *namuelo*. This is not to be confused with the ordinary physical products of decomposition. It is the soul that smells because of the recent death of its body. It is the taint of mortality from which it is later cleansed. 'An ancient spirit when we look at it we are not certain whose it might be, but a new spirit, from a death of recent days, when we look at it we know at once because it has died that day and still has its stench.'

custom of the land—who has not seen it denies but the people who have seen it say so.'

So denial of any specific appearance is regarded as reasonable; it is the obvious reaction of people who have not seen the apparition in question —it is denial not about *ghosts in general* but about *particular* cases.

The question of identification is interesting. How is it that it is known that the apparition is indeed that of the dead person? There are various signs for this. Usually someone who has seen it will describe it in reference to the clothing and ornaments with which the body is known to have been buried (sometimes a person who has been abroad at the time of the funeral will, on his return, see the apparition, which he cannot identify, and describes it in such terms as the relatives immediately recognize).

But granted that the Tikopia believe what they think they see, let us look at the social correlates for the experiences described.

The first concerns the attitude of the survivors to the death of a member of their group. There is first the direct emotional interest of members of the family in someone whom they have lost. In this respect the Tikopia practice concretely the more abstract formulation of Gustav Fechner, restated by A. E. Crawley—that when they think of a person who is dead, his image is not a mere inward semblance, it is the very self of the dead consciously coming into the personality of the living.[1]

But the manifestation of the dead may not be a simple response to yearning for a loved one. It may involve resentment at the rejection by a loved one has who gone away in death. This is the theme which is borne out by Tikopia linguistic expressions at death, accusing the dead person of having abandoned the living. But this in itself is not a simple reaction. It may embody elements of horror, of neglect, and even of the waste of a life carefully nurtured by members of the deceased's family. Aspects of all of this emerge in the reaction of people to an encounter with a ghost. Sometimes they run away, sometimes they curse, sometimes they object to the ghost's meddling, sometimes they accuse him of selfishness. The seeing of a ghost can be both the cause and the product of emotional disturbance.

But this emotional disturbance is not simply an individual matter; it is dependent upon the position of the person in his family and kinship circle. As Morris Opler has shown for the Apache and Clyde Kluckhohn for Navaho, ghosts may be understood as projections of the largely inconsequential hate and distrust that the living have felt towards dead members of the intimate family circle.[2]

[1] *On Life after Death*, from the German of Gustav Theodor Fechner by Dr Hugo Wernekke, 1937 ed., Chicago and London, 1914, pp. 102, 103; A. E. Crawley, *The Idea of the Soul*, 1909, p. 212.

[2] C. K. M. Kluckhohn, 'Conceptions of Faith among the South Western Indians', *Divinity School Bulletin*, Harvard University, 1948, pp. 5–19.

But these explanations alone may not be adequate. In Tikopia the appearance of ghosts is in part an indication of structural strains in the society. Pagan ghosts seen by pagans indicate a temporary breakdown of the system of care for the soul. Pagan ghosts seen by Christians represent an index of the inadequacy of pagan eschatology to secure the peace of the soul. Christian ghosts seen by pagans indicate the results of abandonment of the traditional faith for a new one. Christian ghosts seen by Christians indicate the incompatibility between the two faiths and an uncertainty as yet unresolved as regards their absolute correctness.

This is of course an over-simplification for any single case. But the interest caused by the stories of ghosts seen in Tikopia was not merely due to bits of exciting gossip, nor to the personal interest of those who encountered them and of members of the ghost's family. It also had an undertone of challenge and demonstration linked with the antagonism between the rival faiths. By contrast with this was the view of both Christians and pagans about the fate of the souls of chiefs. It was agreed by everyone with whom I spoke that the souls of chiefs did not walk; they went through the traditional procedure straight to their ultimate spirit home.[1] This unity of the Tikopia about the fate of the souls of chiefs, Christian or pagan, is in line with the full political and social support which they give at the present time to their chiefs, irrespective of religious affiliation. Chiefs, no matter what be their faith, have a religious status and a value as social symbols sufficient to ensure their proper treatment. They are not as ordinary men, they do not return to walk as ordinary ghosts. In Tikopia, conversion to Christianity means change of belief in the fate of the soul from a complex eschatology of status to a simple eschatology of non-status—but a special allowance is made for chiefs. This re-emphasizes that in such a system statements about the fate of the soul are in many respects symbolic affirmations of moral judgement about the social order and the position of persons in that order.[2]

I have not tried here to present a general theory of primitive eschatology. But I hope to have shown by analysis of the material from one primitive society the possibility of certain social correlates.

My argument may be summarized as follows. The framework of ideas about the fate of the soul is in many respects a framework of ideas about the state of society. But this need not be completely so (e.g. even for an isolated primitive society, and still more when that society is affected by a religious ideology of an external, more sophisticated group, an

---

[1] They might later decide to roam about. (See p. 318).

[2] Compare the study by Le Van Dinh (*Le Culte des Morts en droit Annamite*, Paris, 1933) which demonstrates how the legislation of the ancestor cult of Annam promoted family continuity.

egalitarian principle is apt to come into play as an offset against the traditional differentiated status structure). Again in many primitive societies the eschatological beliefs appear to be variable, differing views being put forward by different people. This variation may be simple vagueness, an outcome of lack of interest. But the offering of alternatives is socially valuable, or at least socially significant. It may be associated with social position, and be a structural variation. A strongly marked ancestor cult of lineage type may offer one correlate. Or it may have specific moral associations. However, in such a variant eschatological system, difference of the fate of the soul on a theory of a moral retribution is secondary; destination of the soul in terms of social group home is primary. To operate both together fully would lead to inconsistency if there is only a unitary soul concept. (The Chinese, for example, keep their clan and lineage interests, and also maintain their moral emphasis on the fate of the soul by operating spirit homes in terms of ancestral temples and spirit kingdoms—but with a multiple soul concept.)

With change in the major religious system comes also an eschatological change, a simplification of the spirit home alignment, and the introduction of a specific moral criterion as a basis for differentiation.

But lack of a specific moral criterion in many primitive eschatological systems does not mean lack of all general moral interest. Statements about the fate of the souls are not simple projections of human personality into the future. They do not arise from a simple longing for immortality or even continuity. They are also expressions of contemporary human problems. They give views on what is thought to be right or wrong about the state of things and on the behaviour of people and groups. They are judgements on social action of a more diffuse kind than the specific theory of individual moral retribution. They give opportunity for manipulation of affairs and for the expression of social lineage and cleavage. Their metaphysical implications offer a field for some of the most refined, wide-sweeping and noble speculations about the destiny of man and the bases for his right conduct. But eschatology is also an instrument in human organization.

To conclude in the words of Dewick, and in the spirit of Frazer, in primitive eschatology '. . . simple ideas akin to those of primitive man probably underlie much of our own more developed language. . . . There appears to have been no break in the continuity of thought, and the great problems of life have remained the same.'[1]

[1] E. C. Dewick, op. cit. p. 10.

CHAPTER 16

A COMMENTARY

(1966)

My first visit to Tikopia in 1928–9 focused my attention on the pagan religious system, but also raised the question of its relation to Christianity and the modifications it had already undergone in the attempt to meet the new challenge. In 1952 I was able to study this situation further. The essays in this volume deal primarily with traditional forms of ritual and belief, though some—on privilege ceremonies, on spirit mediumship, on the myths of Takarito and on concepts of the fate of the soul—also illustrate processes of change and adaptation to new conditions. In 1966, ten years after the pagan chiefs had abandoned their traditional rites and the whole Tikopia population had become united in Christian worship, I was able to revisit Tikopia again. This brief commentary outlines the modern position of some of the rites and beliefs described in the earlier chapters.

As regards the general framework for this analysis, the sketch of Tikopia social structure and culture drawn up nearly forty years ago (Chapter 1) is still valid. The village, district and clan alignments operate as before. In the economic sphere the agricultural map of the island presents much the same shape, orchard boundaries and lineage tenure are of the same order, and the division of labour in food production and other daily pursuits is very much as described in the initial account. What has changed radically is the general labour situation. Tikopia now has a considerable labour export and colonies of Tikopia, including whole families as well as unmarried men, have been established in various other parts of the Solomons. Working for wages for a period is now a significant part of the life of all Tikopia adult males. The results have been a massive accretion of Western consumer goods to the island, and a familiarity with money economy which was quite alien to Tikopia of two generations ago.

But to a significant degree the Tikopia social structure has retained its traditional form and vitality. What the Tikopia at home and abroad now tend to refer to as the 'custom' (using the English word)—the intricate relationships involved in the lineage and kinship system, in the exchanges of initiation, marriage and funerals as well as in the rules of etiquette and hospitality—still obtain in very much the traditional style. Markedly the institution of chieftainship still plays a central part in public affairs. The detailed description of these aspects given in my previous works[1] is still operative.

But while the basic structural principles of Tikopia society still operate in the secular field, the complete conversion of the people to Christianity and the greatly increased contact of many Tikopia with the outside world have led to abandonment of many practices which had formerly a pagan religious content. Many beliefs have also been modified in the direction of more sophisticated or at least more Christian interpretations.

CEREMONIES OF YOUNG PEOPLE

Of the ideas and practices treated in this volume, many of the ceremonies for children (Chapter 2) and most of the rites of special privilege for kinship groups (Chapter 3) have now been abandoned. The primary criterion for abandonment has been whether or not the ritual employed formulae of worship of the traditional gods and ancestors, or of address to analogous unseen powers. Hence the Fire Ceremony for a firstborn babe with its formula of magical command, and the *pea*, with its association with the pagan Female Deity, have now ceased to be performed. (By 1966 the *pea* had been seen only by men of the most senior generation.) Rites of signalization, such as smearing of turmeric on mother and newborn babe, or the elaborate ceremonies of male initiation which involve no reference to spirit powers, are still carried out and regarded as obligatory, in all cases. Even in the proprietary song recitals, some elements of social privilege remain, stripped of their former religious associations. To my surprise I learned that the traditional chants of the Sao family (Chapter 3), including songs to Rangi Tokerau and to Makupu, had been performed quite recently. The term *Ruku* seemed now to be unfamiliar, but under the head of 'dances of Sa Sao' the songs were known.

The principal ceremony of young manhood, the 'tying' of bond friendship, with the attendant obligations, was of a purely social character, with no ritual formulae or religious associations; it still obtained in Tikopia in 1966. Men continued to exchange initially property such as bowls, coconut sinnet and calico, and money did not seem yet to have entered this particular ceremonial sphere. The bond friendship was further knitted by periodic exchanges of food. On the day on which I landed, one of the social events was a present of food given by a young bachelor in return for a gift by his bond friend. It appeared that normally such exchanges nowadays took place twice a year, in December and April, that is round about the Christian seasons of Christmas and

[1] *We, The Tikopia: A Sociological Analysis of Kinship in Primitive Polynesia*, 1936, 1957; *Primitive Polynesian Economy*, 1939, 1966; *Social Change in Tikopia*, 1959.

Easter. Young women also were said to have bond-friends of their own sex. Their initiating gifts were of property appropriate to females —tobacco, betel materials, calico. This custom seemed new (cf. p. 108).

In 1966, as before, young men and women formed recognized associations with members of the opposite sex, also referred to as 'friends'—a term which seemed largely to have replaced the former sweetheart ('perfume'—p. 81). 'Canoe friend' was a term also used. But the heterosexual tie was a much less formal link. Though shown by occasional gifts of calico, tobacco, betel materials, scent and other things desired by youth, the presents were largely one way, from man to girl. They were thought to involve her in individual attentions to the man, such as providing him with regular dance garlands, if not with more substantial favours. No food exchanges took place, that is, the relationship was not ceremonialized.

Ceremonies of marriage and of funerals, involving elaborate preparation and exchanges of food, took place in 1966 in the same major form as before. (Plates V–VIII.)

SOME SOCIAL ASPECTS OF PERSONALITY PROBLEMS

A most spectacular change, involving complete cessation of ritual practices, was the ending of spirit mediumship. In 1928–9 and in 1952 spirit mediums flourished, in the Christian sector of the community as in the pagan sector (Chapter 14). By 1966 no one was practising the cult. Everyone to whom I spoke agreed that spirit mediumship had ceased completely and I could find not the slightest evidence of any private or secret practices of this order. The current attitude was epitomized in the statement that formerly the gods were many, and now they were only one, the God of the Gospel—hence presumably, all appeals to spirits could go through the Church. Of the score or so of spirit medium practitioners in 1952, about three-quarters had died, most in the severe epidemic of 1955–6. But those remaining had definitely given up mediumship. The reason given was specifically the interdict of the Melanesian Mission priest, himself a Tikopia familiar with the manifestations of the cult. The mediums were 'blocked by the Gospel'; 'the Gospel is strong'. In support of their decision former mediums and other people said that after conversion to Christianity had become complete the priest said it was not right that spirits should continue to come to men. So he forbade the practice. He baptized one woman medium, ordering the spirits to refrain from coming to her any more; since then she had 'simply sat' as the Tikopia put it, without trance behaviour. Another medium, a man who used to enter mild trance states, gave a farewell feast to his spirits and ceased to practise. This abrupt cessation led to no apparent disturbing results, not even dreams of an unpleasant nature. Another woman, however, still continued to go into trance despite the priest's ban. Soon after, she died. The priest himself denied that there was any causal relationship; though he agreed that she had disregarded his instructions. 'Some people blame me. But God knows, I did not do it.' But here is an instance of a theme in Tikopia belief which appears in various other contexts—the power of the spoken word to affect the physical as well as the mental state of the person designated.

Seeing that the cessation of trance behaviour appeared complete, I was intrigued by two major questions. How did the person who formerly used to go into trance, and so presumably find outlet for certain dissonant forces of his personality, now cope with the strains that seemed formerly to exist? And how did the sick in particular, for whom the spirit mediums went into trance, now receive the diagnostic and reassuring treatment which they used to obtain?

To the latter question the answer seemed to be twofold. Increased medical facilities, including the presence of a dresser and much greater availability of modern drugs, gave more accurate diagnosis and often more speedy cure. And when a person was ill, prayers were now said for him in church, asking for the illness to be taken away. Belief in the efficacy of prayer, as laid down in the Book of Common Prayer used by the Melanesian Mission, was very strong among the modern Tikopia, and presumably now filled much the same function as did former belief in the powers of the spirit medium.

The first question is more difficult to answer. But essentially it would seem that the controls of faith in the Church and in the power of the priest had been sufficiently strong to inhibit those manifestations of the personality which formerly appeared to demand expression. The case of Pa Rarosingano is particularly illuminating here. This man was noted earlier for the violence of his trance manifestations (see p. 305) and it was plausible to think that he might still have to go into trance, despite his own wishes and the ban placed upon these phenomena. Yet my discussion with him and others established beyond doubt that this was not the case. The popular belief seemed to be that the priest had gone to him and called on him to cease his mediumistic activities and turn again to the Church (he had been baptized years before), otherwise he would die. He himself described the situation somewhat differently when I interviewed him. He said that he no longer practised as a spirit medium; he no longer wished to do so, and he had not been asked to practise. 'The land has changed; all the people have gone to follow the work of the one God.' As dramatic evidence that he no longer followed the cult, he spat out a stream of betel juice on to the former ritual side of the house —once sacred to his gods and ancestors—and called my attention to this profane act. He gave as the primary reason for his cessation an injunction of the Ariki Tafua. About 1955, Father Ellison, the Melanesian priest, went with the Ariki Tafua through the district and buried the oil bottles dedicated to the spirits and used by spirit mediums in their healing rites. This was after the great epidemic, when the land had recovered. The Ariki Tafua came to Pa Rarosingano's house, where an oven was prepared. Breadfruit was cooked, and the oil bottle and ceremonial bark-cloth offering to the spirit laid out. The medium, his wife and children and the chief then partook of a farewell meal, the medium having gone into trance state. He was allegedly possessed by his familiar spirit, the 'son of Tafua', Noakena, the chief's own dead brother.[1] The Ariki then told his brother's spirit to cease coming to men and to go and stay in limbo. Then he put his hand on the medium's head and 'blocked the path of the spirit', at the same time making the sign of the Cross on the medium's forehead. The spirit did not resent this prohibition, because it was his brother (and a chief) who came to order him to desist. The spirit was reported to have said, 'You are right, brother. You have told me to go into limbo, and this is fine. But had you come just to make me go while continuing to perform your own kava, it would have been very bad.'

I asked Pa Rarosingano if after he had ceased to practise he had any particular dreams. He said yes, a few days after, as he was sleeping with his head towards the ritual side of the house, the 'son of Tafua' appeared to him and asked 'Are you in good health? In the time since I have gone into limbo, are you well, friend?' The erstwhile medium replied 'Yes, remember the time when your brother came.' Then the spirit went away, presumably satisfied.

There are several interesting points here. Firstly, it is obvious that the medium still clearly believed in the existence of spirits, and regarded his freedom from trance as due to their exclusion from the world of men, not to their unreality. Secondly, in his view their exclusion was due to more powerful forces constraining them, not to a demonstration of their falsity. Thirdly, the withdrawal of the spirits was conducted in terms of the canons of Tikopia etiquette and norms of respect to a chief. Thus the medium was able to validate his rejection of the trance state in volitional terms. He phrased his own withdrawal in terms of spirit withdrawal, and was able to satisfy his ego by a formal yielding to the dictates of polite behaviour—having a chief come to call on him, speak to him as an equal, and lay hands on him in blessing. Moreover, what would seem to be his misgivings at giving up his mediumship were dissipated by his dream, in which his alter ego, in spirit form, obtained and gave reassurance that the course he was following was correct.

This reinforces the demonstration given in Chapter 14 of how different phases of the medium's personality have been interpreted by the Tikopia in figurative terms of independent spirit action. But what was parti-

[1] See p. 305; *Elements of Social Organization*, 1951, pp. 61-3.

cularly interesting was the modern attitude of the Tikopia, that spirit mediumship ceased because there was no longer any demand for it. The Church ban on the practice of spirit mediumship effectively inhibited people from asking mediums to come and cure their sick. With the parallel advent of more adequate medical facilities people came to call for the medical dresser rather than the spirit medium. To my question why there was no practice of the cult the reply was given: 'That is its basis—men used to call upon the spirit to come, and so the spirit came.' It seemed to me that there was a shift of interpretation since 1929 and even since 1952. Then, it is true, the relatives of a person might try and persuade him to become a medium in the interests of healing their sick. But the emphasis was largely on the existence of forces intimately related to his own personality (spirits) struggling for expression through his body. Now the theory had altered to some degree, and suggestion from the community was implicated much more strongly. In this way the theory of spirit mediumship had accommodated itself to the control situation. The problem of how an internal personal solution could be found to the imposition of an external sanction was thus neatly sidestepped by denying in effect that any problem existed in personal terms at all.

What was of great interest here was a modernization of the theory of illness at the same time. In traditional Tikopia belief, most illnesses, especially the graver ones, were the work of spirits. Now the view had changed radically. 'Formerly when the land became ill, it was greatly because of spirits. Now it is not so, because the land has become different. Sickness is from the vessels that come from the sea, just as in the Solomons. Is this correct, friend?' The inference from this assumption was of course that since illness was now the product of external influences, not of spirits, it was remedies of an external order, not of a traditional spiritual order, that were required. Here then is another instance of a modification of belief to conform to a more pragmatic interpretation of a situation powerfully affected by external forces.

Two other problems were also dealt with at the same time. One was the question of forces in the personality too strong to be completely inhibited by any external sanction and incapable of being organized by the personality itself. The Tikopia theory of madness continued to be in terms of the notion of spirit possession. But it was possession in a socially non-viable way; the belief that unnamed wandering spirits were responsible did not conflict with the view that the named kin-related spirits had retired in dignified fashion to their dwelling places. The second problem concerned what may be rather loosely indicated as the psycho-somatic aspects of the illness. Previously these appeared to be catered for fairly effectively by the spirit medium performances; what then could take their place? The Tikopia answer here was clear—the power of prayer. The 'laying on of hands' of the Christian priest, and prayers said in church for the sick, seemed in 1966 so far to have met this need, at least in public estimation.

I turn now to another set of personality problems with an obvious social component, those of suicide and suicide attempts. In the brief time available to me in 1966 I could make no detailed enquiries about these. But such evidence as I obtained indicated that by this time there had been a dramatic fall in the suicide rate. There seemed to be two main reasons for this. The first was that the provision of ample employment abroad and considerably enlarged shipping facilities removed much of the need for men, especially young men, to take a canoe and put their fate to the test in the open ocean. A young man deeply shamed or angry with his relatives, and meditating desertion, could bide his time and slip abroad, out of their reach. The other factor was the increased influence of the Church, with the complete conversion to Christianity of all the pagans, and the coming of a Tikopia priest who understood the local customs. Once the three pagan chiefs had joined the Church their reinforcement of the Christian view that a person had no right to take his own life or risk it unnecessarily had much greater impact. These two factors were explicitly given by the Tikopia themselves as the reason for the drop in suicide.

It was held that the idea of suicidal behaviour still occurred—a man might have no thought of living, be angry and think only of death. But going off to sea by canoe was now blocked by the chiefs. They regarded it as not good that a man should go to die, and in fact no recent cases had occurred. No cases of suicide by hanging were cited either.

Yet sometimes, despite the inhibiting factors, the tensions in a person did seem to lead him to an obsessional suicidal act. A woman I had known in 1952 swam off to sea some years later; because, it was said, she had a quarrel with her family. In another case a man told his wife that he was going fishing, but in reality, so it was interpreted, was intending to go to his death—not in a canoe but by swimming. The usual searching fleet went out to find him; but was unsuccessful.

The story told in the latter case illustrates one important aspect of Tikopia belief—the reality conveyed in dreams. It also reveals the complexity of Tikopia attitudes towards the suicidal act. When the searching fleet was out, it was said that a shark was observed going up and down along the side of one of the canoes. Not unnaturally the crew interpreted this as a sign that sharks were in the vicinity and that the lost man had been eaten, so turned for shore. Later, however, the canoe owner had a dream in which the dead man appeared to him and made known his fate. The shark had not been there as his slayer; it was a protector and was intending to show the crew that the man was still alive, and to lead the canoe to him. But seeing that the crew

refused to follow, the shark turned back and did eat the man. In the
dream, the dead man bewailed his fate in a song:

> Turn to me your stern
> Turn to me your stern
> But the fish went in the path
> Of the ocean.

> My swimming, my long swimming
> In the ocean wastes
> My body nuzzled by the grey birds (albatross?)

This story confirms the view expressed earlier (Chapter 5) that for
Tikopia the suicidal act may be a risk venture, in which the would-be
suicide at some point wishes for rescue, but may have weighted the
chances too heavily against himself to survive. Even if in this case the
fact may have not been so, the dream illustrates the Tikopia concept of
suicide mentality.

The story also illustrates one important continuing aspect of Tikopia
belief—that dreams express an external reality and not a reality purely
internal to the dreamer. This external reality still commonly includes
what may be termed spirit entities. (A full commentary on modern
Tikopia dream beliefs must be reserved for separate publication.)

NATURE, MAN AND SPIRIT

I now turn to the sphere of more clearly formulated beliefs concerned
with the relation of man to natural objects. As I showed earlier (Chapter
11), these beliefs could be described as a complex variant of totemism.

In the sphere of Tikopia 'totemism' there was still in 1966 a division
between species or individuals which were regarded as simply natural
birds, fish, etc., and those which were *atua* or inhabited by *atua*. In 1966,
as previously, the small martin and two species of petrel, all of which
nested in cliffs on the island, were treated as natural birds, and were
netted from time to time and eaten. Duck on the lake also were not
classed as *atua*, they were 'food'. But most Tikopia did not eat duck,
though this was a matter of taste and habit, not ritual aversion. (My
informant had himself eaten duck.) Some clan affiliations still held.
Pigeons, formerly regarded as presentations of *atua*, were in 1966 in an
ambiguous condition. My informant, of Taumako clan, would not
commit himself. 'They are not spirit presentations, perhaps?' He said
that formerly some Tikopia not of Taumako clan might eat pigeon, but
that Sa Taumako never did. In modern times some of Sa Taumako had
eaten pigeon; he himself had tried it as an experiment, in the time of
epidemic and food shortage, but it made him vomit! Herons, however,

which were formerly regarded as presentations of a female spirit, were still not eaten in 1966.

The position with regard to birds in general seemed to have been that they were no longer believed to be inhabited by spirits, but that traditional custom still inhibited most people from using them as food. Much the same seemed to be the case with the large fruit bat. The idea of this as food was regarded as disgusting by the Tikopia, much as European peoples regard the eating of dog or cat. (A Bellonese visiting Tikopia was teased by children because he and his countrymen ate these bats.)

Fish were in a different category. Unlike birds, which could never offer a very substantial contribution to Tikopia diet, fish offered a bulk resource and were drawn upon very freely—even with kinds such as the shark, individuals of which were identified at times as being inhabited by *atua*. This was the case in 1966 as before.

Belief in the capacity of spirits to enter the body of sharks and other sea creatures continued. An example here was the turtle. A man of Fangarere living abroad described to me in all seriousness how the Atua i Raropuka had his title in the sea as Te Mokotai and how his 'body' was the turtle. 'The turtle is our god from of old.' People of other clans were afraid of the turtle, but a man of Fangarere in danger at sea could be saved by a turtle who clasped him to its breast, having jumped up on the deck of his canoe for the purpose.

A very special negative attitude obtained in 1966 as before towards eels, which were still an object of marked aversion. They were classified as *atua* and regarded as deadly if eaten, though no one still ever appeared to have put this to the test. 'People call the eel an *atua*—if a person eats it he dies.' 'Why?' 'Because of course it is an *atua*, an *atua* from of olden times. If a man eats of it, his belly swells. Birds are all right, but that which you speak of (the eel) no! The kava of the chiefs used to be performed to it, that is the origin. I have heard' (continued my informant) 'that Nga Ravenga[1] used to eat of it but it was something Nga Ariki could not eat—the body of people of the chiefs.'

Here it appeared that the build-in attitude of disgust at the eel—associated in myth with the phallus(p. 254)—was so strong as to result in the persistence of a belief which had not survived in the case of less symbolically suggestive species. The fact that the Tikopia knew that the Maori ate eels in no way altered their opinion that eels were lethal to eat. 'I don't lie to you,' said my informant very seriously.

TAPU AND MANA

Other concepts which had survived the complete sweep of Christianity

[1] *History and Traditions of Tikopia*, p. 128.

were those of *tapu* and of *mana*. In English the historically cognate concept of taboo implies prohibition. The prohibitory aspect of *tapu* was apparent in several usages in 1966. The wife of a chief's son was pregnant, and so it was taboo for him to take part in the domestic preparation of coconut oil; the chief had to do the household work unaided while his son just lay in the house. The son commented: 'It is proclaimed in this land from of old; if the oil is being prepared, it will disappear—it is held to be *tapu*, it has been made *tapu*.' The young man added, 'I don't say if it be true or not.' But he did not oppose the idea, holding that if coconuts were plentiful and the oil yield by chance turned out to be poor he would be blamed. So though he seemed rather sceptical he followed the traditional rule. Similarly he could not go and help in the preparation of sago; here too it was commonly held that the success of the operation would be imperilled if the taboo were disregarded. (I found that this notion obtained among young men abroad as well as in Tikopia.)

Coconut frond signs of *tapu* of crops were visible in places. The common use of such signs seemed to be an indication of reservation of a resource—a bark-cloth tree, a ripening bunch of bananas, or areca nut —a 'Keep Off' notice.[1] But as before another use of such signs was as formal protest against unauthorized use of property, especially theft. Though 'locking the stable door after the horse had been stolen', it apparently served to relieve the author's feelings and especially to give a public advertisement that the owner was not prepared to take further depredations lying down—a warning to prospective thieves.

Another connotation of *tapu*, not normally implied in the English word taboo, is positive. Such a quality of *tapu* was accorded by Tikopia to men of rank and generally to people of superior status. It implied behaviour of the kind termed *fakaepa*, respect, with which prohibition and avoidance were associated. In 1966 as before it was *tapu* for a son to utter his father's personal name; the name of the father was *tapu* to the son. Filial respect implied name avoidance, otherwise the son would be thought to be 'making sport of' his father. Many times I was told in 1966, as before, that a chief was *tapu*. 'We respect him, he is *tapu*; he is superior.' This equation of *tapu* with high status was not applied only to Tikopia. They themselves drew the analogy between their chiefs and the High Commissioner of the Western Pacific, who, they said, was also *tapu*. To clarify the issue I demurred, saying that surely Government officials were not *tapu*—what about the District Commissioner, who was also of high status, and I did not think he was described as *tapu*? 'Oh,' my informants replied, 'The District Com-

[1] A more modern equivalent was a notice (in Tikopia) printed and hung on a papaya tree: DO NOT TOUCH THE PAPAYA I DO NOT WANT ANYONE TO TOUCH IT SPLIT YOUR HEAD—with the initials of the owner.

missioner too is *tapu*; we say his countenance is *tapu*; we don't go and approach his countenance; we stand afar.'[1] Generically, a Tikopia view was that anything which was 'big' was *tapu*; that is, anything of great social importance. 'The Church we say is *tapu*, because it is great.' Similarly the priest was regarded as *tapu* because of his sacerdotal role. 'He is the man who does the work of the Church; he gives the Holy Communion; therefore we say he is *tapu*. His *mana* is produced by the Holy Spirit because he works for Him, for God. Is this correct?' The equation of *tapu* with social importance, not only ritual importance, was made by the Tikopia themselves. 'Anything *tapu* is anything weighty, heavy.' So, they said the *tapu* of chiefs and the *tapu* of Holy Communion was of the same order.

In summary, one may say that in 1966 the Tikopia still held the concept of *tapu*, that it carried the notion of avoidance of contact, and that for persons and institutions it tended to be an attribute of respect, especially to persons and things of high status. What of the quality of dangerousness, sometimes made a prime criterion of taboo? This theory appears to have only very limited validity. On the electric power generators at Honiara was the Melanesian notice TAMBU. When I commented on this a Tikopia said graphically, 'It has been made *tapu*; death is there in it.' But it was significant that the 'death' resided in the electric power, not in the taboo, and was not automatic. The taboo had been imposed because contact with the mechanism meant death; the death did not arise simply from breach of the taboo. Moreover, the supernatural sanctions formerly attaching to some of these Tikopia taboo signs seemed to be completely lacking, now that Christianity had come. 'Nowadays there is no evil (using the English word in a Tikopia sentence). We have worshipped the Holy Spirit, and their (pagan) spirits were different.' In brief, the modern Tikopia concept of *tapu* referred to respect behaviour towards things of importance, not necessarily of danger.

In this respect-connotation *tapu* was associated to some extent with *mana* (Chapter 8). When in 1966 I asked a couple of men whether chiefs had *mana* nowadays they said, 'No, because they have become different; they have been baptized.' But they said that the Church was *mana*, and exemplified this in traditional style. Its priests ask for rain and it is given; they ask for sunshine and it is vouchsafed. As before, the terms *mana* and *manu* were specifically stated to be equivalent. Some modern Tikopia however, even when not literate in English, rendered the term *mana* by the English word 'power'. For example, we were talking of snakes biting people, and of the effects of their poison. One man commented, mingling Tikopia with English: 'Their *mana*, their

---

[1] They said the same quality of taboo also applied to me, as a chief. (I was frequently addressed as Te Ariki, especially by older men.)

power', meaning by this the effective element in their venom.

With people this power was demonstrated by the fact that utterance was followed by event, hence the tendency to attribute event to utterance. On a rainy walk through Uta I had made a joke about being responsible for the weather, as I had brought showers to Uta many years before (p. 147). Later, as I was photographing clouds on the beach, a man came up and said that my Tikopia companion on the former occasion had told him that I was *manu*, I was *mana*, because I brought rain to crops. I said he must have been joking but my informant said no. 'The man who speaks correctly is correct.' *Mana* here was equated with accuracy of statement, with particular reference to prediction. The statements were *correct* in advance *because* they could be implemented—the speaker had the *power* to do this—such was the idea.

Such power in 1966, as formerly, was accredited particularly to chiefs: 'From of old, if the chief speaks for the ocean to be calm, it is calm; if he speaks for the rain to come, it comes. This is the sign. Thereupon people say that the chief is/has *mana*.'[1] This was still believed to occur despite the fact that the chiefs had given up the ancient gods. 'The chief is *mana* because he is the chief. He is not *mana* as a common man, but as soon as he is made chief—because his dwelling place is sacred.' In other words he had *mana* by virtue of his office, not of his qualities as a person. Even the men who denied that in the context of the ancient gods a chief had *mana* any longer, said specifically in another context that he possessed it. 'If a chief speaks evil of a man he will get sick or die. Death is in him, in the chief. Is he then *mana*? He is.' Another man, son of a chief, and relatively sophisticated, with an English education, said that formerly people died if they offended chiefs but now their bodies became distorted. He instanced two women who stole areca nut from the orchard of his grandfather the chief (formerly Pa Rangifuri, my old friend). The chief struck the tree trunk with his knife, and said that who so stole the areca should look at the curving branch and their backs would become crooked in sympathy; this happened according to his word.

In former times certain artefacts or quasi-human objects were credited with being *manu* and were treated with considerable respect. In 1966, I enquired about the ritual adze of Pa Nukutapu which was formerly one of these (p. 222). He told me that this principal adze of his no longer had any ritual connected with it. He simply took it down and used it in canoe-building, calling on no gods to give it efficiency. But he said the adze was still *manu*; if it struck wood which had been weakened by borer the wood would become sound—this

---

[1] Before we left Tikopia the weather had been very rough. I was told that from affection to me the Ariki Taumako had prayed for the sea to be calm, and that this would be efficaceous—the chief was *manu*. (In fact the sea did become calm for a time.)

happened nowadays! He said that he didn't call upon the god, as formerly—but the idea was there. 'I don't say this because I want to boast.
But though I don't utter words, the thought is there.'

SECULARIZATION OF A GOD SYMBOL

An object with both human and supernatural associations, and formerly credited with miraculous powers, was the stone known as the
Atua i Takarito (Chapter 13). In 1966 I was able to get details of its
recent history, especially since the conversion of the Ariki Kafika in
whose religious sphere it lay. I first was given a gloss on the story as
I had it earlier. I was told by a son of the Melanesian Mission priest
that the son of a former Mission teacher had thrown the stone away and
hidden it. Later he was pierced in the back by a garfish, went to Vanikoro, became ill and died. The implication was that this was because of
the power of the stone. My informant boasted that he had himself put
his foot on the stone but felt no pain thereafter. He was not afraid, he
said, because of the Gospel. He described the stone as having eyes, nose
and mouth (a *fuateka*). Formerly it was *tapu* but now not at all; formerly it was regarded as having *manu* and if put in the channel would go
back to Takarito of its own accord, but it no longer had this power. He
denied the stories of its return, etc., given to me formerly by pagans. He
said that his brother took the stone and buried it. It seemed to be generally agreed that the stone now wasn't *tapu*, it hadn't *mana*, since the
one Gospel had been accepted by all the people.

A little later I heard from a boy that the brother had indeed hidden the
stone, but he could not remember the place where he had put it. This
tale of a forgotten burial place sounded improbable, but was confirmed
by the brother himself. In a private session he gave his account of his
dealings with the stone. He said he removed it because people went and
excreted and urinated upon it, arguing that it was something of the unbaptized folk. He told his father the priest, who instructed him, 'You,
my son, take care of it until the Bishop comes; then if he wishes he can
take it.' He accordingly had put it in the Church, at the back of the altar;
he had not hidden it. There it was seen by a teacher, who neither respected it nor was afraid of it. He took it and threw it in the sea, saying
it was not right that such an evil thing should stand in the temple of
the Lord—he called it Satan.

The priest's son denied that the stone had returned of itself; formerly
it had *mana*, but not now. It had been thrown into the sea at high tide
and women going out net fishing at night saw it at low tide. They reported to him that the stone was in the sea, and that the teacher had
been seen with it by children in the evening. He went then with the
women, shouldered the stone, which was heavy but portable, and re-

turned it. Then he went and upbraided the teacher, who did not repeat the act. Later, hearing that Tikopia were selling adzes and other ancient things to visitors, he offered the stone to a labour recruiter, who said he was willing to pay £10 for it, but then returned it saying that he wished its history as well. (Perhaps he was repenting of his bargain when he saw what appeared to be only a stone of natural form.) When he tried to sell it, he told the Ariki Kafika. The chief replied that he himself having been baptized he would not look back—he did not want the stone. The priest's son commented to me that if he had been successful in selling the stone he would have given the money to the Ariki Kafika, to whom it belonged.

When the church was about to be rebuilt the priest's son buried the stone just outside his house. He protested to me this was five years ago and he could not find it, and had indeed spent two Sundays since our arrival looking for it (hoping to sell it to us?). My colleague and I came to the conclusion that his story of having mislaid the burial spot outside his house was probably true.

He stated that objections had been raised to the stone by the Christians of Faea because in a time of food shortage the exactions of the ritual levy had become heavy and the people had resented the drain upon their supplies. He said that he was not afraid of the stone; he did not make a god of it. He described it as reddish-brown in colour, about 15 inches in height, with no facial attributes (as commonly stated) but a hole of about 1 inch diameter going right through it. This hole was not made by man, but the stone was born that way from its mother. I asked if this tale of the birth of the stone was true, and he replied, 'The old people say so, that it is correct.' Asked if he agreed with them he replied 'I don't know, the Bible says all that is created, from heaven down to here below, springs from God.'

What was of particular interest in this conclusion to the tale of the god of Takarito was the indication it gave of the process of stabilization and secularization taking place in attitudes regarding the symbols of pagan religion. No longer was the stone regarded as a sacred object, nor was it looked upon as an object of dangerous evil powers; it was shorn of its former strength. It still carried the interest of people because of its one-time ritual context, but those who had once revered it now looked upon it with curiosity, if still in a somewhat defensive spirit. The stone seemed to have sunk within a lifetime from a sacred symbol into an historical relic.

FATE OF THE SOUL

I have shown that the changes in Tikopia ritual in recent years have been accompanied in most cases by some changes in belief. This appears to have been especially so in regard to beliefs in the soul and its fate (Chapter 15). In 1966 it was evident that the religious unification of the Tikopia had removed much of the basis of controversy which formerly marked discussion of the fate of the soul. There was still difference of view as to what happened to souls after death, and in some cases uncertainty as to the precise order of spiritual procedure. But with the removal of the pagan-Christian differentiation in practice, the theoretical or postulated issues of soul treatment had receded into the background.

Belief in the soul as an essential part of personality, a spiritual counterpart of the body, was still general, and firm. I could discover no evidence of agnosticism or scepticism on this point, even among the young sophisticates. At death, the breath of a man, his *manava*, stops, his heart ceases to beat and his soul, his *ora*, leaves the body at once. This much is agreed. But as to exactly what happens to the *ora* at this point ideas seemed to differ, and to be often vague. The soul goes to Heaven, in accordance with Christian doctrine—this was the general notion, subject to some qualification of a personal kind, as mentioned later. But when I asked did the soul go to Heaven at once after the person's death, the answers became imprecise. The general view seemed to be that it waited awhile—three nights or maybe four—and then rose to Heaven. But on the question of where the soul was in the meantime no very clear-cut reply was given.

The dilemma here was twofold and related partly to traditional ritual and partly to traditional belief. The problem in regard to ritual was one of relevance. If the soul goes to Heaven at once, the rites performed for several days have reference only to a corpse. Any satisfactions involved can only be those of the surviving kin; the spirit of the dead person cannot be aware of what is being done. There was a temptation then to delay the flight of the soul to Heaven to allow it to observe and appreciate the rites performed. In 1966, the problem in regard to belief was not as before, that of deciding between alternative solutions to the fate of the soul—Heaven and an ancestral home. It was that of deciding whether a traditional Tikopia cleansing process could be interposed on the passage to Heaven.

According to traditional belief the soul was in the region of the body for the duration of the funeral rites, and at their conclusion the maternal ancestors came and bore it off for cleansing. This neat concept was specifically denied by a Christian teacher of long standing. He said this was no longer believed; that it was held to be simply untrue because it was contrary to Christian doctrine and people had seen that the Christian doctrine was correct. But other people were much less definite. A man who in 1952 had still been a heathen said that formerly the maternal ancestors came and put the soul in the grave mat, in the grave valuables, to listen to what the relatives should say, and to await the ceremonies of exchange, and the formulae of farewell. Then it was carried off by the ancestors to be cleansed. Nowadays, he said, the same idea still held, but anything that took place was the work of the Lord.

Another view was given me by a man of long-standing Christian background, who was a leader among expatriate Tikopia. He had composed a song commemorating a traditional belief, referring to the macerating of the soul by the gods in the cleansing pool and the subsequent re-generation of the soul by a giant fish from the blood. He explained: 'This was our "custom" (using the English word) from of old. When a man dies, he will go to the realm of spirits, goes to the place where the giant fish dwells, to be eaten by it. It drinks the blood of the man.' According to him this fish operates from the head of the pool while another fish at the rear of the pool chews up the dead body to allow the blood to flow. This conceptualization of the re-generation process differed a little in detail from versions recorded by me in earlier years, but was essentially of the same order. The point here, however, is that even after a lifetime of Christianity this man still said, 'I don't know if it be true or not.' He regarded the whole process as one designed to improve the status of the soul of the dead person in the spirit world. But a difference of conceptualization was represented between generations. The composer was middle-aged. The song was sung to me by four young men, who gave it quite a different and mundane interpretation. They thought it referred to the carrying of messages to Tikopia! When, puzzled, I later asked the composer, he said, 'They don't know', and told me the correct theme.

The opinion which seemed to fit Christian concepts most closely was that the souls of people who had been proper in their doings go straight to Heaven (whether directly, or after an interval of funeral rites). Other souls, whose doings in the mortal body have not been proper, stay in the grave, in the ground, until the Last Day, when the trumpet shall sound and they shall come forth. But belief in ghosts walking was still current in 1966. As earlier, some people said that these stories of ghosts were untrue but most seemed to give credit to them. Some said that the reason why ghosts of the dead walked was unknown, others gave a moral interpretation. Should a soul be seen to walk as a ghost, this meant that its doings on earth had not been good, so people were able to look upon it. 'Anyone whom we do not see after death has gone to Heaven; his deeds have been good.' This is where the traditional belief had been retained by some people in 1966, though with another interpretation.[1] For some people, perhaps near to paganism, while the souls of the good went to Heaven, those of other less moral people were taken by the ancestors to be cleansed and to wait in the ancestral

[1] The story of the ghost of the Mission teacher's son (Chapter 15) was repeated again in 1966, though not in terms of lack of burial with prayer.

homes until the Last Day. Who were these people who didn't go to Heaven? Those who had sinned, gone with women, stolen, etc. But cautiously, 'Since we don't know the minds of men, we don't know who go to Heaven and who do not.'

By 1966, therefore, with all Tikopia now Christian, the former Christian-pagan dichotomy of fate of the soul no longer applied. But with many people the outline of traditional belief still persisted, though the categorization had altered from pagans to ill-doers.

A summary of the Tikopia situation may be of more general relevance in the understanding of religious change in small-scale, isolated peasant communities. Religious pressure in Tikopia was backed by economic and political pressure so that change in religious belief and practice was reinforced by new social commitments. The results of proselytization and conversion from paganism to Christianity were complex. There was a large-scale abandonment of religious observance but not of social (ceremonial) observance. There was a new theological system but not a complete abandonment of traditional ideas about gods and other ancestors. Tikopia belief patterns still show a mosaic of traditional and modern elements. What is commonly termed belief in spiritual powers has two aspects—intellectual and emotional conviction that they exist and credence in the attributes that are postulated for them. What has happened in Tikopia in recent times is that belief in the existence of the traditional spirit entities still survives, but belief in some of their former attributes, in particular their power, has been lost. From this it results that belief in the efficacy of what were formerly regarded as their symbols has altered; these objects are no longer regarded as valid in any but a material, technical way. The acceptance of the new theology necessarily entailed a radical change in the ritual system of the people, and this in turn involved changes in their associated beliefs. But while the adoption of new ritual has been complete throughout the society, the adoption of new beliefs has been very uneven. The considerable degree of variation even in such a small population is note-worthy, and indicates a point of significance in the investigation of other religious systems in change.

INDEX

Abortion, 32, 33, 138
Adoption, 32, 33
Aesthetics, 118, 162, 285, 335, 342
Ancestor (cult), 159, 176, 185, 189, 190, 193, 194, 200, 227, 233, 258, 259, 280, 296, 308, 332, 338, 339, 342, 349, 353, 363, 369, 370
Allport, G. W., 141n, 146
Angus, S., 336n
Animism. 171–2
Anuta, 29–30, 67, 121, 196n, 251
Aru (levy), 82, 85, 86, 94, 96, 288, 290, 291
Ata (semblance), 236–60, 263, 337
Athenagoras, 337
Atua, 25–8, 68, 164 *et seq.*, 209, 227, 228, 230, 232–68, 296, 298, 300, 330, 361–2 (*v.* also God, Spirit)
Authority, 161, 193, 327 (*v.* also Chief, Family: parent-child)

Barth, K., 337
Bateson, G., 285
Bay, A., 234
Belshaw, C. S. 269n
Benedict, R., 176
Berndt, R. M., 159n
Best, E., 264n, 268n, 337n
Birth, 39–46
Blood-brotherhood, 108, 115
Boas, F., 331
Bohannan, P., 116
Bond friendship, 108–15, 130, 305, 355–6
Brown, G., 226, 262n, 264n
Bruner, J. S., 141n

Capell, A., 176
Cargo cult, 126, 157–61
Carstairs, G. M., 116
Ceremony (ceremonial), 12–13, 31, 79–80, 61, 73–8; privilege, 79–107, 354, 355
Chapple, E. D., 74
Chief, 22, 27, 83, 86, 87, 98, 113, 114, 129, 133, 135, 137, 143, 148, 150, 159, 165, 166, 171, 176, 197, 199, 219, 224, 250, 305, 330, 341, 345, 349, 352, 354; authority, 23–5, 136, 138, 161, 309, 358, 363; and social control, 120, 153, 154, 156, 360; and economics, 18, 81, 95, 271, 272, 274, 275, 282; female, 63, 64, 65, 86, 87, 93, 100, 199n; illness, 139, 313, 318, 337, 328; *mana*, 179–90, 193–4, 365;

and ritual, 26, 38, 41, 42, 47, 72, 198, 200, 209, 210, 211, 212, 217, 220, 222, 223, 227–32, 253, 276, 278, 279, 280, 293, 295; voyaging, 127, 128
Checkley, H. M., 317n
Childhood, 32, 34, 111, 324; rites, 23, 31–78, 355
Christians, 95, 152, 157, 354–5; belief, 87, 88, 93, 94, 106, 208, 209, 211, 214, 240n, 262, 363; fate of soul, 123, 331, 334, 335, 343, 345–52, 368–70; and pagan ritual, 73, 80, 98, 99, 100, 101, 107, 109, 210, 278; and spirit mediumship, 294–5, 302–6, 314, 316, 326–9, 356–60; and suicide, 124, 130, 360; and Takarito, 288–92, 366–7 (*v.* also Melanesian Mission)
Clan, 81, 86, 96, 110, 111, 115, 135, 170, 227, 318, 340, 354; and natural species, 26, 27, 228–32, 234, 249, 250, 356–9 264; in ritual, 64, 276; temple, 82, 84 (*v.* also Chief)
Codrington, R. H., 175, 177, 178, 270n, 271n
Collocott, E. V., 262, 264n, 265
Communication, *v.* Rumour
Connelly, M., 340
Coon, C. S., 74
Covenant, 108, 109, 110, 115
Crawley, A. E., 351
Cult, 158, 160 (*v.* also Cargo cult)
Culture-hero, 25, 28, 40, 215
Cumont, F., 336

Dance, 63–4, 65, 68, 83, 84, 87, 88, 99, 101, 109, 143, 186, 196, 303
Death, 110, 113, 119, 120, 126, 143, 155, 156, 166, 167, 168, 198, 221, 259, 264, 313, 316, 330, 331, 33, 334, 335, 350–1, 357, 365 (*v.* also Funeral, Suicide)
Demography, *v.* Population
Descent, 22, 161, 198, 227, 259
Dewick, E. C., 331, 336, 353
Dreams, 34, 146–7, 162–73, 224, 237, 342, 344, 356, 358, 360–1
Driberg, J. H., 175
Duff, R., 218
Dumont, L., 336
Durkheim, E., 116, 117, 118, 119, 130, 131, 171, 175, 177, 284
Durrad, W. J., 15

371